The Rule of Love

The Rule of Love

The Power of Presence for Reforming Health Institutions and Global Health Leadership

THANA C. DE CAMPOS-RUDINSKY

OXFORD
UNIVERSITY PRESS

Oxford University Press is a department of the University of Oxford.
It furthers the University's objective of excellence in research, scholarship,
and education by publishing worldwide. Oxford is a registered trade mark of
Oxford University Press in the UK and in certain other countries.

Published in the United States of America by Oxford University Press
198 Madison Avenue, New York, NY 10016, United States of America.

© Oxford University Press 2026

All rights reserved. No part of this publication may be reproduced, stored in a retrieval system, transmitted, used for text and data mining, or used for training artificial intelligence, in any form or by any means, without the prior permission in writing of Oxford University Press, or as expressly permitted by law, by license or under terms agreed with the appropriate reprographics rights organization. Inquiries concerning reproduction outside the scope of the above should be sent to the Rights Department, Oxford University Press, at the address above.

You must not circulate this work in any other form
and you must impose this same condition on any acquirer.

CIP data is on file at the Library of Congress

ISBN 9780197762370

DOI: 10.1093/9780197762400.001.0001

Printed by Integrated Books International, United States of America

The manufacturer's authorized representative in the EU for product safety is
Oxford University Press España S.A. of Parque Empresarial San Fernando de Henares,
Avenida de Castilla, 2 – 28830 Madrid (www.oup.es/en or product.safety@oup.com).
OUP España S.A. also acts as importer into Spain of products made by the manufacturer.

To Jordan
Totus Tuus

Contents

Acknowledgments   ix

Introduction   1

PART I. A TYPOLOGY OF LOVE—A CONCEPTUAL ANALYSIS OF AGAPE IN THE CONTEXT OF HEALTHCARE AND GLOBAL HEALTH

1. On Mercy   19
2. On Compassion   54
3. On Beneficence   89

Concluding Remarks—On Agape   123

PART II. A PRINCIPLED TRIPARTITE FRAMEWORK—A NORMATIVE EXAMINATION OF AGAPIC LOVE IN THE CONTEXT OF GLOBAL HEALTH GOVERNANCE

4. On Solidarity and Communion   139
5. On Subsidiarity and Community   175
6. On Stewardship and Communication   215

Concluding Remarks—On Agape and Governance   249

Conclusion   252

Bibliography   257
Index   279

Acknowledgments

It takes both a family and a village to do pretty much anything in life, including writing a book. *The Rule of Love* was conceived in 2018 and gestated through the 2020 pandemic, when Jordan and I got married, and through the loss of our first son Iain in 2021, the loss of our second child Marion in early 2022, the birth of our daughter Isabel in 2022, and the birth of our son Samuel in 2024. Most of the ideas presented in this book were developed through my (difficult) conversations with Jordan, and my reflections on challenges and joys of marriage and family life. The presence and accompaniment of my village have been crucial throughout. This village, both local and global, has deepen my understanding of what agape requires and does not require.

I am especially grateful to some members of my village, who helped me in a variety of ways, from discussing ideas related to this book as I was thinking about them to reviewing parts of the manuscript and providing feedback as I wrote and rewrote the chapters, all the way to simply being present by offering a listening ear; walking with me through the storms; and offering wisdom, strength, and consolation in difficult seasons when no easy solution was available. *The Rule of Love* would not exist without: Lauren Woodside Alegre, Iain Matthew, Caterina Milo, Matthew T. Lee, Alisha Montes, Carolina Yoko Furusho, Peter Howard, Angela Wu Howard, Dawn Zehr, Laura Bramon Hassan, Federico Ponzoni, Maite Etchegaray, Christina Lamb, Brian Bird, Ana Benítez Carracedo, Johanna Fröhlich, Pier Paolo Pigozzi, Mariana Canales, Sofia Bernier, Toby Lees, Lena Rose, Sarah Bosha, Daniel Wainstock, Maria Carolina P. Pinheiro, Norfran Rodriguez, Donnie Collins, Nilia Wood, Peter Wood, Fernando Contreras, Paulina Vergara Ramos, Paulina Taboada, Claudio Vera, Mariel Deak, Carola Zurob, Francisco Urbina, Marguerite Gautriaud de Urbina, Ignacia Saavedra, Christopher Tollefsen, John Keown, Trudo Lemmens, Ewa Rejman, Jonathan Herring, Alessandra Waldorf, Mark Retter, Maria Carol Pinheiro, Carina Yumi Furusho, Camila Perruso, Cristián Borgoño, Rodrigo López B., Pavlos Eleftheriadis, Anne Gelling, Scott FitzGibbon, Josephine Smith, Milena Olsovska, Alberto García Gómez, Daniel Philpott, Paolo Carroza, Veronica Rodriguez-Blanco, and John Tasioulas, who coined the term *The Rule of Love* during a meal in Chile back in 2018.

I also owe thanks to: the *Olga Woytjla Community*, especially Iain Henriquez, Pamela Cajales, Trinidad Henriquez, and Catalina Henriquez; the *Von Hügel Institute*, especially Lidia Ripamonti and Vittorio Montemaggi; the *Independent*

Resource Group for Global Health Justice (IRG-GHJ), especially Caesar Atuire and Sridhar Venkatapuram; the *Global Health Law Consortium*, especially Roojin Habibi, Sharifah Sekalala, Steven Hoffman, and Pedro Villarreal; the *Princeton Institute for International and Regional Studies* and the *Fung Fellowship Program*, especially Nicole Bergman, Sandy Bermann, and the 2020 cohort (Awol Kassim Allo, Jiazhi Fengjiang, Jernej Habjan, Fabrice Langrognet, and Mallika Leuzinger) for helping me understand the intrinsic nature of the local within the global; the OUP production team, especially Lucy Randall; the Facultad de Derecho UC, especially Carlos Frontaura and Gabriel Bocksang; the *Instituto de Éticas Aplicadas UC*, especially Alfonso Donoso, Camila Barahona, and Juan Larraín; and the *Escuela de Gobierno UC*, especially Eduardo Valenzuela, Osvaldo Larrañaga, and Andrea Repetto for showing me the kind of community that good leadership can nurture, and Caridad Merino and Marianela Barraza for our conversations on being a caregiver to others while caring for ourselves, too.

To my family—Anne, Steve, Lauren, Jacob, Dani, Shelby, Osvaldo, my cousins, Caio, Paulo, Raphael, our nana Julieta, and my godparents Ogarita and Paulo—I offer my heartfelt thanks. My eternal gratitude goes to my parents, Antonio, for his unwavering commitment to serve with generous love; Tomie, for her firm discipline that makes our shared journey of love steadfast and sustainable; and to my brother Kin, who, through his wise attentiveness, reminds me that I am seen and loved in my idiosyncrasies. The three of them taught me that to love is to show up consistently and to give ourselves through our silent presence without being overpowering. And finally, a word of gratitude to Jordan, the main Other in front of me, who challenges me to love him in his unique otherness. Through our shared journey of presence, woven into the messiness of real life, my life with Jordan has become the ongoing fieldwork for *The Rule of Love*. It is in this space that the raw data for these chapters have been observed, collected, and tested. As a continuing shared journey, *The Rule of Love* remains a work in progress.

Introduction

> "Love begins where justice ends."
> St. Alberto Hurtado SJ, Santiago/Chile

The power and authority of love as a moral value have long been undermined. Partly this is attributable to the indeterminacy of the idea of love.[1] Of its numerous possible meanings, the idea of love as romantic feeling or a fleeting, "wishy-washy" emotion with no moral weight is usually the first to come to mind. But what I mean by love here is rather different: a virtue and a practical reason that carries significant moral authority. This book seeks to reclaim[2] the moral force of love and to leave readers with the conviction that love carries a stronger moral weight than one might have originally assumed. The book advances the following thesis: although love and global affairs do not typically appear together, they should, and if put together, love would change the dynamic of global affairs in general and the design of global health institutions in particular. In what follows, I will explain (i) why I defend this thesis, (ii) the knowledge gap that this book fills, (iii) the contribution it makes to the literature of ethics and global affairs, (iv) its key findings, (v) how the chapters unfold, and (vi) the takeaway message of this book.

Section 1. Why Love, Global Affairs, and Global Health Governance Belong Together

It is difficult to imagine that global affairs and global health governance (GHG)—with their distant, bureaucratic, and impersonal structures—could make room for the parlance of love. For one thing, it is not even clear what GHG means. Agreed, GHG is an obscure concept. GHG has been defined as a complex amalgam of stakeholders,[3] including the WHO and other international

---

[1] On the polysemous nature of the word love, see, e.g., Lee, "Love as a Foundational Principle," p. 10.
[2] My project is not just a nostalgic longing for the past when love had moral weight. Instead, my project is fundamentally a 'work of retrieval' that recovers something important that has been lost along the way. For a similar enterprise yet focused on the patient–clinician relationship, see: Tate and Clair, "Love Your Patient as Yourself." On "work of retrieval," see: Taylor, *The Ethics of Authenticity*, p. 72.
[3] See: Harman, *Global Health Governance*.

organizations, countries (including their ministries of health and public health officials), international non-governmental organizations (such as Médecins Sans Frontières and the Red Cross), private donors (such as the Bill and Melinda Gates Foundation and the Global Fund), pharmaceutical companies, as well as universities and medical researchers, local hospitals, hospital administrators, healthcare professionals, and even the media.[4] This long and eclectic list of actors, however, tends to obscure rather than clarify what GHG actually is.

GHG is an overly broad and underspecified concept. To clarify it somewhat, I start by distinguishing three interconnected levels of decision-making authority within GHG: the global (or macro), the local (or meso), and the micro levels. Each level encompasses not only institutional dynamics but also interpersonal relations—for example, between a patient and a doctor, or between a local recipient of developmental aid and a provider.

With these caveats in mind, I specify GHG mainly as the set of transborder laws and policies among diverse institutional actors that regulate global public health matters, such as public health emergencies of international concern,[5] like pandemics. These laws and policies require international coordination because global public health issues cross political borders and directly impact the lives of people, their families, friends, and caregivers. Yet, despite affecting us all, GHG remains a remote, cold, faceless, red-tape apparatus of care—one in which the language of love is conspicuously absent. This impersonality may partly explain why love is so often overlooked in discussions of GHG.

While the moral value of love has been neglected, the moral value of justice (or global and social justice, to be more precise) has profoundly influenced the evolution of GHG's laws and policies, especially through a human rights-based approach. The scarcity of healthcare resources, high costs of medical treatments, and the pervasive inequality in healthcare systems within and across countries have made access to adequate medical goods and services the cornerstone of healthcare justice. As a human right, health has been established as a claim-right to be demanded against social structures of injustice and poverty that perpetrate

---

[4] For a thorough description of all global health stakeholders, see: Youde, *Global Health Governance in International Society*, pp. 75–94; Clinton and Sridhar, *Governing Global Health*, pp. 48–82.

[5] A public health emergency of international concern (PHEIC) is defined as "an extraordinary event which is determined to constitute a public health risk to other States through the international spread of disease and to potentially require a coordinated international response." This is the definition offered by the 2005 International Health Regulations, a binding international legal agreement overseen by the WHO, involving 196 countries. The purpose and scope of the IHR (2005) are to "prevent, protect against, control, and provide a public health response to the international spread of disease in ways that are commensurate with and restricted to public health risks, and which avoid unnecessary interference with international traffic and trade." A PHEIC is declared by the WHO Director-General, aided by the members of an IHR Emergency Committee (including international experts in relevant fields). See: WHO, *2005 International Health Regulations*.

avoidable illnesses. The progressive realization of the right to health worldwide over the decades has been celebrated and marks a necessary ongoing change to address avoidable health injustices. Nonetheless, I see at least two significant limitations with the justice and right-to-health framework's reliance on individual claim-rights.

The first limitation comes from the prominence given to individual independence, which the idea of claim-rights inescapably carries. The modern emphasis on individual autonomy narrows justice to a set of entitlements divorced from relational context. This has reinforced the modern view of healthcare as a commercial transaction, where the patient becomes a mere client, and the recipients of developmental aid a mere number and passive object of charity. Do not get me wrong: there is no doubt that the agency and freedom of both patients and beneficiaries of aid must be respected, and that medical paternalism and global health coloniality must be addressed, as defended throughout the chapters of the book. However, the overemphasis on autonomy and individualism that characterizes modern medicine and the contemporary scheme of developmental aid fails to understand the reality that when a person is ill and vulnerable, they inevitably experience a diminished capacity for autonomy and a heightened dependence on love and caring relationships. An individualistic reading of justice that focuses primarily or exclusively on access to material goods and services—as essential as these are to meet the basic health needs of patients—falls short when confronting suffering, illness, and vulnerability.[6]

My book, *The Rule of Love: The Power of Presence for Reforming Health Institutions and Global Health Leadership* offers an alternative to this modern conundrum essentially by (re)introducing the moral value of love into the moral discourse of healthcare justice. True, the moral weight of love has been limited largely because our current frameworks of justice and rights presume the weakness of love as a grounding practical reason.[7] But in showing love's moral robustness, and in challenging this individualistic conception of justice, *The Rule of Love* also restores the original, relational, communal understanding of justice (i.e., justice as a relational idea between rights-holders and duty-bearers),[8] which the modern overemphasis on autonomy and individual rights has distorted. Love, properly understood, neither overpowers the agency of the cared for (this is what medical paternalism and global health coloniality do), nor acquiesces

---

[6] Two examples here are Paul Farmer and Rose Busingye. Both were committed to bringing medicine to those they served in Peru and Uganda, respectively. However, they soon discovered that their patients were not taking their medications, so sunk were they in a lack of love and self-worth. For a discussion of Farmer's work, see Chapter 3 as well as Griffin and Weiss Block, *In the Company of the Poor*; Weiss Block OP, Lysaught, and Martins, "A Prophet to the Peoples," Ch. 9–11. On Rose Businge's life, see: Perillo, *Your Names Are Written in Heaven*.

[7] See, e.g., Buchanan, "Preparing for the Next Pandemic," pp. 283–305.

[8] See, e.g., de Campos, *The Global Health Crisis*.

without critical judgment to whatever the patient or (a corrupt) local government receiving aid demands simply to comply with a presumably unfettered autonomy of the receiver of care (see Chapters 2 and 5).

The second limitation of the justice and right-to-health framework lies in its presumption that severe illnesses are inherently unjust. No doubt poverty-related diseases—for example, Chagas disease, human African trypanosomiasis, and leishmaniasis—that disproportionately afflict the poorest in remote populations stem from structural injustices and must be addressed with urgency. But there are also grave illnesses that do not easily qualify as unjust—cases resulting from brute luck (for instance, an inherited cancer caused by a gene mutation present at conception] or personal choices (e.g., cirrhosis of the liver due to long-term alcohol abuse). Do individuals and institutions have no ethical duty to care for those suffering from misfortune or imprudence? Global health justice theorists have been debating this question indefinitely. Their answers vary according to their conceptions of justice and rights and, by extension, to their thresholds for a just duty of care and corresponding claimable health rights.

The Rule of Love offers a solution to this long-standing problem essentially by starting from a different premise: by establishing that a stringent duty to love and care for those in great medical need exists regardless of the justice or injustice of their suffering.[9] I am not simply avoiding the vexed question of the injustice of suffering. I have addressed the injustice of certain illnesses at length in my previous monograph, *The Global Health Crisis—Ethical Responsibilities* (Cambridge, 2017). There, I offered an account of what is just and unjust in the global context of healthcare, and concluded that several diseases, though severe, do not ground justice-based duties and claimable health rights. This does not mean, however, that one can abandon those suffering from these grave (though not unjust) illnesses, and still be morally excused from caring for them in one way or another. Although these illnesses may not qualify as unjust, there remains a stringent ethical duty to care for all those who are ill and suffering. This compelling duty, however, is grounded in a different moral value.

Section 2. The Knowledge Gap on Love

The overlooked moral value of love provides the missing justification for the ethical responsibility to care for those with no claimable individual rights, suffering with the kinds of medical conditions that, though grave, may not necessarily

---

[9] I define suffering as "a disruption of flourishing that arises when love or justice is violated or absent — and that calls for a communal response" in de Campos-Rudinsky "Flourishing Through Suffering." On medical suffering, see also, e.g., Tate and Pearlman, "What We Mean When We Talk About Suffering"; Tate "Objective Suffering."

be unjust. This is the specific knowledge gap that *The Rule of Love* fills. Indeed "love begins," as St Alberto Hurtado of Chile says, "where justice ends": this book organically starts from where my previous monograph ends. Just as love complements justice,[10] this book builds on my previous reflections on the institutional injustices that exist in GHG.

Love complements but does not replace justice. The term 'Rule of Love' is intentionally reminiscent of the term 'Rule of Law'. As political and legal theorists recognize, the concept Rule of Law captures the truth that the government of a community, as well as the creation and administration of its rules and institutions, must be guided by reasonable standards of action. The Rule of Law is a remedy against the great malaise of arbitrary action. A community that abides by the Rule of Law is thus more able to secure and realize basic requirements of justice. In this book, I argue that love—in addition to justice—must govern institutional dynamics and interpersonal relations (e.g., between patients and caregivers, or between local recipients of developmental aid and providers). By way of analogy, then, I propose that if institutions and relations are to flourish and achieve their full potential, they must abide by the principles of love.[11]

For the sake of clarity—given the many meanings the word "love" can carry[12]—I use the term *agape* to foreground its often neglected moral significance. Love is essential for human flourishing. We are all called to love others in our communities: our families, local associations, our nation, neighboring countries, and the global community. Agape is commonly defined as a universal love for all humanity. But I want to offer a refinement. Agape is not a vague good-will toward all; it is a universal yet personal responsibility—a call for both individuals and institutions to respond attentively and concretely to those who are suffering from serious illnesses that cross political borders. In this sense, *agape* is a form of practical reason—a reason to act for the good of each and every Other before me, regardless of origin, status, or proximity.

Now, to discern what is truly good for another, one must engage in attentive[13] deliberation—the very heart of agape. Though love may begin as a feeling or perception, it matures through reason. At its foundation, agape is moral reasoning that leads to a deliberate choice: the offering of one's attentive presence as a gift of self. In practice, this gift takes the form of concrete, responsive care, tailored to the person before me. Through the habitual act of choosing presence for the sake of the Other, I cultivate virtue—and learn how to love. Agape, then, functions

---

[10] Supporting that agape demands justice, see, e.g., Jackson, *The Priority of Love*; Wolterstorff, "Love, Justice, and the Law." See also Simone Weil, who defends that "we have invented the distinction between love and justice." Weil, *Waiting for God*, p. 139.

[11] I owe thanks to Fernando Contreras for making this analogy clear.

[12] Lee, "Love as a Foundational Principle," p. 10.

[13] On the centrality of attentiveness for the definition of love, see: Murdoch on the "just and loving gaze" in Murdoch, *The Sovereignty of Good*, p. 34. See also Chapter 3.

both as a practical reason that guides ethical deliberation and as a moral disposition: a virtue that commits me to truly see and understand those entrusted to my care.[14] And in seeking the good alongside the Other, love becomes a shared journey—a community of mutual care grounded not in transaction, but in attentiveness, responsiveness, and shared responsibility.

In *The Rule of Love*, agape is an umbrella term that encapsulates three distinct, more specific types of love, namely mercy (which I define in Chapter 1), compassion (which I examine in Chapter 2), and beneficence (which I analyze in Chapter 3). Together, these three chapters present a typology of love, offering a conceptual analysis of agape (see the Concluding Remarks of Part I of the book). From my typology of agape emerge three practical principles of love: namely, solidarity (which I define in Chapter 4), subsidiarity (which I examine in Chapter 5), and stewardship (which I analyze in Chapter 6). As *practical* principles, they provide reasons for action in effecting agapic love. Together, they form a Principled Tripartite Framework of GHG, presented as a normative analysis of agapic love applied to three perennial global health problems in Part II of the book (more below). My proposed framework offers an *agapic* vision for the future of health institutions and global health leadership. In challenging institutions and individuals to fulfill their co-responsibility to care for the most vulnerable not only in their illnesses but also beyond instances of medical suffering, my principled tripartite framework inevitably goes beyond GHG and has broader implications for the dynamics of global affairs more generally.

Section 3. Contribution to the Literature

The Rule of Love primarily contributes to the fields of ethics and global affairs. However, as a book that reimagines global health through the moral lens of agape, its interdisciplinary reach is unavoidable. I bring contemporary medical anthropologists, organizational psychologists, epidemiologists, physicians, and legal scholars into conversation with philosophers, theologians, and literary thinkers—including Thomas Aquinas, Dr. Martin Luther King Jr., Emmanuel Lévinas, Iris Murdoch, and bell hooks. This dialogue between diverse traditions yields a rich conceptual account of agapic love (Part I), which, in turn, grounds a normative framework for reforming GHG (Part II).

---

[14] I thank Fernando Contreras, Mariana Canales, and Francisco Urbina for helping me further clarify my definition of agape.

Section 4. Main Findings

The moral force of love, when love is properly understood, leads individuals to change and institutions to be reformed. Agape, as I conceptualize it, is in this sense a revolutionary concept. Agape revolutionizes in at least two ways: by offering three challenges to traditional institutional design and by offering three lessons of leadership. These are the main findings of my book and the main consequences of the Rule of Love. While these challenges and lessons are presented in the context of GHG, they are also applicable to global affairs and beyond.

4.1. Three Challenges

Agape challenges traditional institutional design by presenting three main moral requirements, discussed throughout Part I of the book:

4.1.1. To De-prioritize Productivity and Efficiency

Agape first challenges institutions to de-emphasize productivity and efficiency. As discussed in Chapter 2, this does not mean that productivity and efficiency are not important: they are indeed the conventional hallmarks of a functioning healthcare system. However, agape requires that individual and institutional deliberations ground primarily the responsibility to lead and care effectively, before grounding the duty to manage cost-effectively (I differentiate good leadership and management in Chapter 6). Agape can only be nurtured in spaces where encounter is not rushed, because agape requires being fully present, totally attentive to the person in front of me, in an act of contemplation (see Chapter 3). An excessive preoccupation with doing tasks in a productive and efficient manner robs people of their contemplative presence with another (see Chapter 2).[15] So, agape challenges institutions to create and maintain spaces where people can be fully present with each other, in communion and forming community.

4.1.2. To Emphasize Active Participation and Meaningful Inclusion

Meaningful inclusion (defined in Chapter 1) and active participation (defined in Chapter 2) of care recipients are only possible if institutions shift away from a relentless pursuit of productivity. This second challenge requires, however, a reasonable degree of self-sacrifice from leaders and carers who need to deny their urge to find a solution as quickly as possible, and permit themselves to

---

[15] On the transactional character of modern medicine and how this relates to clinician's lack of attentiveness to the patient, see: Tate and Clair "Love Your Patient as Yourself."

"waste time" in order to empathetically listen to, humbly learn from, and deeply see those under their leadership and care, before hastily assuming things and paternalistically making decisions based on those assumptions, as discussed in Chapter 2. This "waste of time" need not be contrary to cost-effectiveness and should be neither idle nor financially reckless. Active participation and meaningful inclusion, allowing for institutional self-reflection and empathetic appreciation of different voices from all levels of governance, are paramount for an agape-based leadership (see Chapters 1 and 5).

4.1.3. To Respect the Agency of the Other Through Shared Decision-making Authority

The third challenge depends on the second, in that for shared authority (defined in Chapter 3) in decision-making to exist, active participation and meaningful inclusion need to be real and in place. Participation cannot be a mere perfunctory exercise of bedside manners where going through the motions of listening is mistaken for genuine engagement (see Chapter 2); likewise, inclusion cannot be a mere checkbox exercise of empty diversity, equity, and inclusion institutional rhetoric (see Chapter 1). These are not only mechanical and empty but also alienating—undermining, rather than enabling, truly participatory, and inclusive processes. Shared authority, to be real, needs to tolerate some degree of inefficiency and slowness that characterize a process of true co-deliberation and co-creation of a shared vision for life (and for a new governance structure) moving forward (see Chapter 3).

These three challenges posed by agape to traditional institutional designs are essential ingredients to reform global health institutions toward decolonization—a central theme in GHG introduced in Chapter 1 and further examined in Chapter 5. They illustrate what equal respectful consideration and loving attention to Global South partners should look like, as Chapters 4 through 6 demonstrate. For shared authority (defined in Chapter 3) to be a reality in GHG, the active participation of typically silenced voices of local communities from the Global South and their meaningful inclusion at the GHG negotiation tables are crucial. The empathetic (not rushed) listening of these voices would necessitate a reasonable degree of epistemic humility from Global North stakeholders, requiring them to counter their impulses to presume knowledge, and to jump into action and immediate solution through global health interventions. While such tendencies have the appearance of greater productivity and efficiency, this is not an expression of good, loving leadership but an expression of paternalism and coloniality. Effective leadership, reframed in the light of agape—as Part II suggests—calls for less control over processes and outcomes and more of a posture of mutual learning.[16]

---

[16] Martins, "Bioética e saúde global a partir de baixo," p. 113; Martins, "A escuta Como Método e os Pobres/Oprimidos como Sujeitos."

4.2. Three Leadership Lessons

Besides challenging traditional institutional designs, agape revolutionizes by offering leadership lessons. These lessons are presented throughout Part II of the book, through the discussion of three complex, perennial issues in global health (namely, the scarcity of healthcare resources, the reform of the WHO, and the distrust in global and public health authorities), where each illustrates the application of a different principle of love (namely, solidarity, subsidiarity, and stewardship).

4.2.1. Agape and Partiality Toward and Prioritization of Certain Individuals and Communities

Agape, in being both universal and personal, challenges the concept of equality as equal treatment or equal concern for all members of the community. Agape indeed requires co-responsibilities to care for those suffering from illnesses that cross political borders. These co-responsibilities that agapic love requires are universal (meaning, applicable and accessible to all), yet personal (tailored to the unique needs of the person before me). They are shared, yet differentiated (not homogeneous). That is, love does not require leaders to treat everyone in the same standardized way or to be concerned with individuals in an identical manner. Love allows—and in some cases even requires—a reasonable degree of partiality, prioritizing certain individuals and communities based on their distinct needs, vulnerabilities, and closeness of ties. This is the leadership lesson offered by an agapic interpretation of solidarity (see Chapter 4), which I identify as the first practical principle of love.

4.2.2. Agape and Delegation of Authority to Care for One Another

Agape, by necessitating non-abandonment, challenges the traditional view of authority as the centralized control of power, resources, and decision-making, deemed necessary for caring for those under one's leadership. Love allows—and in some cases even requires—a reasonable degree of delegation of authority to care for another, which respects the agency and fosters the integral human development[17] of the cared for. This is the leadership lesson offered by an agapic interpretation of subsidiarity (see Chapter 5), which I identify as the second practical principle of love.

---

[17] In recognizing that human flourishing is not solely about economic growth or material possessions, integral human development proposes a holistic approach that aims to promote the well-being of every person and the whole person, encompassing all aspects of life, including social, economic, political, cultural, personal, and spiritual dimensions. See, e.g., Sedmak, *Enacting Integral Human Development*. See also: Debeulin and Sedmak (eds), *Integral Human Development*.

4.2.3. Agape and the Need for Honest Communication Tempered with Discretion

Finally, agape challenges the traditional notion of the leader as an infallible expert authority whose decision-making has no shortcomings. Love requires leaders to communicate truthfully—that is, with honesty tempered with discretion—in disclosing their expertise as well as limitations in knowledge with a reasonable degree of vulnerability, an important ingredient to build leaders' trustworthiness. This is the leadership lesson offered by an agapic interpretation of stewardship (see Chapter 6), which I identify as the third practical principle of love.

These leadership lessons that agape offers are essential for reforming global health institutions toward decolonization. The lesson of solidarity counters the imposition of one-size-fits-all prescriptions on Global South partners. The lesson of subsidiarity, by delegating decision-making authority and responsibility directly to local communities, empowers them by restoring their agency. Finally, the lesson of stewardship, by emphasizing empathetic listening as part of truthful communication, ensures responsive accountability and fosters shared authority in determining the best way forward for all.

Section 5. An Overview of the Book

The Rule of Love is the integration of Part I's conceptual analysis and Part II's normative examination of agape. While Part I's typology of love aims to define agapic love and its distinctive expressions, Part II's principled tripartite framework of GHG further explains agape's normative requirements as applied to global affairs. The book thus does three things: it defines the moral value of love; it grounds our co-responsibility to care for the most vulnerable; and it challenges the current architecture of health institutions across the world. I show how the moral value of love complements the moral value of justice in further justifying the allocation of ethical responsibilities of care to reduce suffering caused by diseases that spread across political borders, and in so doing, I challenge the interpersonal dynamics and institutional arrangements of healthcare, at global and local levels alike.

Part I (Chapters 1–3): A Typology of Love—A Conceptual Analysis of Love in the Context of Healthcare and Global Health

In Part I, I examine three types of love that are the most relevant to global health and healthcare: *mercy* (or love of enemy), *compassion* (or love of neighbor, near and far), and *beneficence* (or love of the Other before me, regardless of whether they are an enemy, friend, stranger, neighbor, family member, or beloved). Although these terms are often used interchangeably with one another and with the term love, my typology clarifies what is distinct about each type while also highlighting their commonalities. I devote a chapter to each of these three forms of love. Then, in the Concluding Remarks of Part I, I introduce the broader, umbrella term—agape—and present my working definition:

> Agape is a directive for both individual and institutional deliberations that grounds a universal yet personal responsibility to care for those suffering from serious illnesses that transcend political borders. To care for *all* who suffer, one must journey with each sufferer *personally*. Ultimately, as a shared journey of presence, agape nurtures a community of mutual care—this co-responsibility requires the firm commitment to accompany the sufferer by offering the reasonably self-sacrificial gift of one's presence.

From this definition, I derive three practical principles that I examine in Part II of the book: the principles of *solidarity*, *subsidiarity*, and *stewardship*. What follows is a brief overview of each chapter's contents.

Chapter 1, defining mercy as forgiveness (or love of enemy), argues that we should conceive of mercy as a decisional process that depends not only on the vulnerability of the receiver of mercy (who depends on forgiveness to be set free from his culpability) but also and more fundamentally on the vulnerability of the giver (who bestows forgiveness and opens herself up to potential ridicule for her generosity toward the undeserving). The theme of trust is relevant here, and I examine it further in Chapter 6.

This mutual vulnerability that mercy requires from victim and perpetrator should be understood as a reciprocal gift-of-self: not only does it benefit the offender in assuaging the guilt of his wrongdoing, but it also empowers the victim by restoring her agency. This is the distinctive, most fundamental feature of mercy: the victim restores her agency by deciding to make herself vulnerably present to her enemy through the gift of her forgiveness. When the process of mercy is fully complete, the victim and the perpetrator are in each other's peaceful, vulnerable presence, and there is a reciprocal gift-of-self. While mercy may or may not entail reconciliation (restoration of companionship), it heals a broken relationship and repairs the fabric of the community.

Both mercy and compassion, discussed in Chapter 2, are best appreciated as processes that produce a gift of self, given in response to suffering. The distinctive feature of compassion, however, is the choice to share in the sufferer's wound by accompanying him. In other words, compassion means to make oneself present with the sufferer. More specifically, Chapter 2 argues that we should conceive of compassion as a three-stage process that results in presence. The first stage of compassion is affective; I call it sympathy. The second stage is an intellectual process that I call empathy. The third stage is effective: it leads to a conduct of care, and I call this final stage compassionate care. Chapter 2's central idea of compassion as a process that results in presence introduces themes taken up in succeeding chapters: the tension between being with the sufferer and doing things with or for them (Chapter 3), the ideas of equality of dignity and equity of care (Chapter 4), and notions of proper self-care (for self-constitution) and reasonable boundaries that allow for sustained generosity (Chapter 5).

In Chapter 3, I set out my argument that we should conceive of benevolence (i.e., willing the good of another) as a step toward beneficence (i.e., a conduct—whether action or inaction—that benefits the Other). Put differently, benevolence is an intentional intellectual step toward the effective step of beneficence. Like the move from empathy to compassionate care that characterizes compassion, this move from benevolence to beneficence also produces a conduct of care, grounded on genuine love. Chapter 3 argues that the core feature of beneficence is being present with and contemplating, rather than doing things for or with the Other.

These different types of love—mercy, compassion, and beneficence—apply to both interpersonal relationships and institutional dynamics. Interpersonally, they share the common feature of producing a gift of self, meaning here being fully present with another in adequately caring for and about[18] him. While performing tasks for and with a sufferer is often a necessary, simply doing things is not sufficient; genuine care requires presence, which is the most essential element when addressing medical suffering.

Within institutional dynamics, these types of love also shape GHG. Mercy plays a crucial role in the relationships between givers and receivers of developmental aid, especially in contexts of epistemic injustice.[19] By restoring the agency of victims of such injustice, mercy serves as a direct response to coloniality.[20] Compassion as presence in interpersonal interactions within healthcare and GHG institutions also challenges existing institutional design and shows how love can reform them. Moreover, the central idea of love as a shared journey of presence develops the concept of shared authority in decision-making, which was introduced in Chapter 1, developed in Chapter 3, and further examined in Chapters 5 and 6.

---

[18] On the distinction between care for and care about, see: Herring, *Law and the Relational Self*, p. 51; Tronto, *Moral Boundaries*, pp. 127–34.

[19] For definition, see, e.g., Chung, "Structural Health Vulnerability," p. 205.

[20] For definition, see: Atuire, "Some Barriers to Knowledge from the Global South," p. 335.

Part II (Chapters 4–6): A Principled Tripartite Framework—A Normative Examination of Agapic Love in the Context of GHG

In establishing the idea of *agape* as a journey of shared presence, Part I introduced some normative considerations challenging the design of existing healthcare institutions at the local and global levels. Part II shows more fully how agapic love would reform these institutions. It presents an agapic vision, predicated on the practical principles of solidarity, subsidiarity, and stewardship, that will foster communion (Chapter 4) and community (Chapter 5) through communication (Chapter 6). This vision furnishes us with a Principled Tripartite Framework for GHG.

Chapter 4 offers a new way of understanding communion in community and of responding to the current backlash against multilateralism by substantiating the need for more complementarity and cooperation among global health stakeholders. It discusses the first practical principle of love, solidarity, using the controversy surrounding the global allocation of scarce COVID-19 vaccines as a test case. I develop a revised theory of moderate cosmopolitanism, grounded in my agapic interpretation of the principle of solidarity tempered by subsidiarity (further discussed in Chapter 5). Solidarity among peoples entails global responsibilities of mutual care among nations, but not, I argue, equality of treatment and resources, nor of care and concern. Instead, it necessitates equity: shared yet differentiated duties to care for those in need, according to their needs and our relationships to the most vulnerable. My conception of solidarity is predicated on the idea of equality of dignity (introduced in Chapter 2)—equal respectful consideration and loving regard among persons and nations.

Chapter 5, using the WHO as a case study, explores the second practical principle of agapic love, subsidiarity. Agapic love calls for subsidiarity, since love necessitates both non-abandonment and respect for the agency of those in need of aid. It therefore requires shared authority (as discussed in Chapter 3), characterized by the active participation of patients (defined in Chapter 2) and the meaningful inclusion of aid-receiving local communities in decisions on treatments and priorities (defined in Chapter 1). Hence, I challenge the widespread view that centralization is the best route for the WHO to enhance its capacity for leadership and care for those in need.

My robust decentralization approach, predicated on the principle of subsidiarity, allows for the integral human development of those who are cared for and offers a different understanding of good leadership in GHG, one which fosters solidarity, interdependence, and mutual self-giving (as discussed in Chapters 1–3). The WHO ought, therefore, to humbly recognize its strengths and its limitations (as discussed in Chapter 2), and restrict its mandate accordingly. Specifically, it should focus on coordinating communication among other global health stakeholders in situations of public health emergencies of international concern, because that is what it is uniquely placed and equipped to do well.

The third practical principle of agapic love, discussed in Chapter 6, is the principle of stewardship and its requirement for truthful communication as an essential element of trust. My case study here is the existing distrust of health authorities, who should act as stewards of global and public health. These authorities include, for example, (i) at the global level, the director of the WHO; (ii) at the national level, ministers of health and public health officials; and (iii) at the local level, directors of local hospitals, clinicians, medical researchers, and so on.

In challenging the conventional wisdom that leaders should present themselves as decisive, infallible authorities, Chapter 6 proposes the stewardship model of good communication, grounded in a philosophical interpretation of truthfulness, disclosed with a reasonable degree of vulnerability. Agapic love does not, I argue, require that leaders be infallible experts; instead, leaders should communicate with honesty tempered by discretion. Communicating the truth with love enhances trust and social cohesion (themes introduced in Chapter 1), and therefore greater communion within community (themes introduced in Chapters 4 and 5, respectively).

Section 6. Takeaway Message of the Book

The book's conceptual and normative examinations offer a way of broadening the reach of ethics in global affairs in at least three ways: by crossing traditional disciplinary boundaries, by moving beyond frameworks grounded solely in justice and rights, and by proposing love as a foundational lens not only for thinking and doing global governance but also for thinking and doing ethics more generally: love is, I conclude, the foundation of all ethics.

This book is written for scholars of ethics and global affairs, especially those with a focus on global health ethics. It also speaks to practitioners in healthcare, human rights, and public policy. Above all, however, the book is written for those who may be suspicious of the moral seriousness of love, yet who are open to engaging diverse voices across disciplines—voices that suggest otherwise.

My hope that you will leave this book with a deeper understanding of love, not merely as an emotion but primarily as a virtue and practical reason—one with far greater moral weight than often assumed. The central takeaway is to take seriously the moral value of agape, so that you may reconsider not only your understanding of love and authority but also your practical approach to caring and leadership.

Be not naive: love is hard. To choose love after being wounded—by life, by others, even by ourselves—requires the virtue of courage. To love is, indeed, to be brave. And because we are fallible, we love imperfectly. One may choose to love with the most sincere and resolute heart and still falter. For to love is also to be patient.[21] Yet the core message of this book is that the normativity of love—though demanding—is neither impossible nor an optional flourish. Love is not a utopian dream, nor a luxury that strained, resource-constrained healthcare systems cannot afford. No. Love is vital. And its demands are reasonable: there is a practical reasonableness in the duty to love. Love asks for our full effort —a free and total gift of self—but it must remain guided by reason. To be attentively present to the Other is arduous work. It does require self-sacrifice, but never to the point of unraveling one's self-constitution through burnout. Such self-annihilation is not love, but its distortion. Sure, love is generous. And yet, love does not depend on grand gestures or eloquent declaring. More often, it is revealed in the quiet dignity of presence, in a single thoughtful act that allows the Other to feel truly seen in their wound. To love is simply to be human—and to recognize the same humanity in the Other before us.

---

[21] I owe thanks to Fernando Contreras for pushing me to make this point clearer.

PART I

A TYPOLOGY OF LOVE— A CONCEPTUAL ANALYSIS OF AGAPE IN THE CONTEXT OF HEALTHCARE AND GLOBAL HEALTH

> King Edward IV: No, by my troth I did not mean such love.
> Lady Grey: Why, then, you mean not as I thought you did.
> King Edward IV and Lady Grey, in Shakespeare,
> *Henry VI*, III, ii, 66–67

Love has taken on so many meanings today that it has nearly lost its significance.[1] As a moral value, love has also lost its authority, perhaps because of its emptiness as a signifier. In Part I, my hope is to restore love's moral force by clarifying what it means and what it does not. This part offers a conceptual analysis of love, focusing on three types that most often shape the interpersonal and institutional dynamics within healthcare and global health: mercy (Chapter 1), compassion (Chapter 2), and beneficence (Chapter 3). These terms are often used interchangeably with one another and with the term "love." My aim is to distinguish what is unique about each type while identifying what they share in common. This is the purpose of the typology presented in Part I.

A typology orders and classifies previously unrelated concepts by clustering them into meaningful categories and clarifying their distinct features. While all typologies have limitations and blind spots, they also provide new insights by advancing fresh ways of organizing knowledge. The typology I offer and the conceptual examination it contains do not claim to be totally novel, as they rely a great deal on a long and living tradition of conceptualizing love not merely as a

---

[1] Lee, "Love as a Foundational Principle for Humanistic Management," p. 10.

feeling but fundamentally as an act of the will. My typology revisits traditional concepts of mercy, compassion, and beneficence while incorporating recent developments. It juxtaposes classical and contemporary definitions and applies these debates to the practical realities of healthcare institutions at both local and global levels. My contribution lies in organizing and linking the concepts of mercy, compassion, and beneficence in a new way, creating a dialogue between intellectual traditions that often remain isolated. Ultimately, I highlight their complementarity under the umbrella term *agape*, which is presented in the concluding remarks of Part I.

The upshot of Part I is the creation of a shared vocabulary around mercy, compassion, and beneficence as types of agapic love, enabling more meaningful discussions in clinical health, public health, and global health contexts. This vocabulary is valuable for those who are familiar and unfamiliar with these fields, as it provides much-needed clarity to terms that are often loosely used and poorly understood. Their lax interpretation, stemming from an assumption of a shared commonsense understanding, has led to more confusion than constructive dialogue. By examining these terms more closely, Part I offers a conceptual analysis of love and establishes normative premises for each type, which will be further explored in Part II.

1
On Mercy

> The quality of mercy is not strained. It droppeth as the gentle rain from heaven upon the place beneath. It is twice blest. It blesseth him that gives and him that takes. It is mightiest in the mightiest. It becomes the sceptered monarch better than his crown. His scepter shows the force of temporal power, the attribute to awe and majesty wherein doth sit the dread and fear of kings; But mercy is above this sceptered sway. It is enthroned in the hearts of kings; It is an attribute to God Himself; And earthly power doth then show likest God's. When mercy seasons justice. Therefore, Jew, though justice be thy plea, consider this: That in the course of justice none of us should see salvation. We do pray for mercy, and that same prayer doth teach us all to render the deeds of mercy. I have spoken thus much to mitigate the justice of thy plea, which if thou follow, this strict court of Venice must needs give sentence 'gainst the merchant there.
>
> Portia, in Shakespeare's *The Merchant of Venice*, Act IV, Scene i, lines 190–212

Introduction

There is a general consensus that mercy is an act of the will,[1] broadly understood in theology and philosophy as the decision to respond to another's suffering.[2] This broad definition often equates mercy with compassion, and the two are frequently used interchangeably by theologians and philosophers. However, I will differentiate these terms by adopting a more specific definition of mercy as forgiveness, commonly employed in law and policy literatures, particularly within the context of criminal justice. More recently, this narrower understanding of mercy as forgiveness has been recognized as critical in healthcare and public

---

[1] Campagna, "The Miracle of Mercy," pp. 1096–1118; Perry, "Mercy," pp. 60–89; Murphy, "Mercy and Legal Justice," pp. 1–14; Parrish and Tuckness, *The Decline of Mercy*, Ch. 9; Twambley, "Mercy and Forgiveness," pp. 84, 87.

[2] See, e.g., *ST* ii-ii Q30, a3; MacIntyre, *Dependent Rational Animals*, pp. 123–25.

health contexts.[3] Using this perspective, I will conceptually examine three key characteristics of mercy, highlighting its distinctive features and relevance to GHG.

This focused definition of mercy is vividly illustrated in Portia's soliloquy from Shakespeare's *The Merchant of Venice*. In the play, Portia attempts to persuade Shylock, a Jewish moneylender, to forgive Antonio, the merchant, for his debts. Mercy, in this narrower sense, involves the decisional process by which an authority figure—like Shylock—chooses leniency to alleviate a wrongdoer's suffering caused by punishment. Disguised as a male jurist, Portia appeals to key qualities of mercy in a Venetian courtroom, aiming to awaken Shylock's merciful dispositions to forgive and spare Antonio's life. I will focus on three characteristics central to mercy—discretion, gratuitous generosity, and the reciprocal gift-of-self.

The first quality of mercy relates to Portia's declaration that it is "not strained," highlighting its discretionary nature.[4] By discretion, I mean that while authorities are under no legal obligation to grant mercy, they are free to do so. In philosophy, this is often referred to as an "imperfect duty"[5]: mercy-givers are not legally bound to be merciful—there is no legal entitlement to forgiveness—but they remain unconstrained by law in their choice to grant or withhold pardon. This discretion is exercised toward the mercy-receiver, typically someone less powerful, facing punishment, and who stands to benefit from the pardon.[6]

The second quality stems from Portia's assertion that mercy is "above this sceptered sway," emphasizing that mercy transcends justice (symbolized by the "sceptered sway"). As something "freely given"[7] to an undeserving perpetrator, mercy is often conceptualized as a "gift."[8] I call this second quality *gratuitous generosity*. By this, I mean that mercy is an unearned gift extended by a powerful authority (such as Shylock), who freely chooses to act generously toward an offender (like Antonio), someone who is powerless and vulnerable to that authority.

The third quality is captured in Portia's statement that "mercy is twice blest." While Portia acknowledges the asymmetry of power and vulnerability between the giver and receiver of mercy, she also notes that mercy is a blessing (a gift) for both. Although her precise meaning is ambiguous, I interpret this quality

---

[3] See, e.g., VanderWeele, "Is Forgiveness a Public Health Issue," pp. 189–90; Bulger, *The Quest for Mercy*, pp. 362–73.

[4] Murphy, "Mercy and Legal Justice," pp. 2–3; Perry, "Mercy," pp. 73–74.

[5] Perfect duties correlate to rights that can be claimed. Imperfect duties have no correlative rights. O'Neill, *Faces of Hunger*, p. 101; O'Neill, *Constructions of Reasons*, pp. 191, 224.

[6] Tuckness and Parrish, *The Decline of Mercy in Public Life*; Campagna, "The Miracle of Mercy," 1096–1118; Perry, "Mercy," pp. 60–89.

[7] Twambley, "Mercy and Forgiveness," pp. 84, 87.

[8] Campagna, "The Miracle of Mercy," pp. 1096–1118; Murphy, "Mercy and Legal Justice," pp. 2–3; Perry, "Mercy," pp. 60–89.

as a *reciprocal gift-of-self*. By this, I suggest that mercy requires mutual vulnerability: the mercy-giver and the mercy-receiver must each open themselves to the presence and humanity of the other.

The idea of mercy as forgiveness is often conceived, as Portia demonstrates, as a discretionary act performed by a person or institution (such as Shylock in the Venetian courtroom) with the authority to forgive someone in a vulnerable position. However, this is not always the case. In many instances, the victim of an injustice—the one deciding whether to forgive their offender—is in a relatively less powerful position than their perpetrator. This dynamic is particularly evident in the context of healthcare and global health, where the mercy-giver and victim of an injustice (the patient or recipient of aid) are generally in a more vulnerable position than the mercy-receiver and wrongdoer (medical authorities or global health institutions).

In this chapter, I argue that mercy should be understood as a decisional process that relies not only on the vulnerability of the mercy-receiver, who depends on forgiveness to be freed from culpability, but also—more fundamentally—on the vulnerability of the mercy-giver, who extends forgiveness despite the risk of ridicule for their generosity toward an undeserving offender. This mutual vulnerability is central to mercy and can be understood as a *reciprocal gift of self*, expressed through the giving and receiving of forgiveness. Mercy benefits both parties: it frees the offender from accusations while empowering the victim by restoring their agency. The process of mercy begins with the granting of forgiveness but reaches completion only when that forgiveness is received and accepted. In this exchange, both the accused and accuser are present to one another in peace and vulnerability. Through this mutual gift, mercy restores unity within the community, initiating the healing of the broken relationship. While this healing does not guarantee full reconciliation—defined as the restoration of companionship and the ability to work together—it is an essential first step.

Section 1 of this chapter introduces my conceptual account of mercy in the context of healthcare and global health, drawing on the three qualities of mercy identified by Portia. In Section 2, I address key objections to my account. Finally, in Section 3, I apply my conceptual framework to the relationships between givers and receivers of developmental aid in global health institutions, with a focus on epistemic injustice.[9] Here, I demonstrate how mercy, by restoring the agency of those subjected to such injustice, serves as an appropriate response to coloniality,[10] which often diminishes the agency of aid recipients. The idea that love is a decisional process of making oneself vulnerably present as a gift to another, with the aim of restoring unity in the community, is introduced in

---

[9] For definition, see: Chung, "Structural Health Vulnerability," p. 205.
[10] For definition, see: Atuire, "Some Barriers to Knowledge from the Global South," p. 335.

this chapter and will be further explored in subsequent chapters. Chapter 1 also introduces the theme of trust, which will be examined in greater depth in Chapter 6.

Section 1. A Conceptual Analysis of Mercy

1.1. Mercy as Forgiveness within the Context of Healthcare and Global Health

It may not be obvious why one needs to talk about mercy as forgiveness in the context of healthcare and global health. The answer to this question in one word is: brokenness. The reality of fractured relationships within healthcare practice and the institutional dynamics of global health justifies the need for mercy. A real-world example is helpful for the purpose of clarification and contextualization here.

Physician and researcher Christopher L. King and his team at Case Western Reserve University were conducting community-based research in Papua New Guinea's East Sepik Province to stop the spread of lymphatic filariasis.[11] The research project involved the administration of a single-dose drug treatment with approval from the National Department of Public Health. While mass drug administration such as this has benefited millions of people in both high- and low-income settings, unintended harmful side-effects can happen, just as in any other medical intervention.[12] A week into the project, resistance from local communities emerged. The team learned that a woman had miscarried shortly after taking the drug, and her family and community blamed the medication for the loss.

Though the connection between the drug and the miscarriage was inconclusive, the team recognized the need to honor the community's grief. Dr. King instructed his team to put effort in carefully observing the local customs, intently learning about their reality, to then be able to discern more thoughtfully what to do to meet their need. In a word, Dr. King urged his team to practice *attentiveness*, a central element of love and care (more on this below). They learned that the community believed miscarriages were caused by bad spirits, not medical intervention. Dr. King and his team realized that what the local community needed was mainly sincere repentance: by apologizing, Dr. King's team would be taking responsibility and acknowledging that the miscarriage *could* have

---

[11] This real-world example is recounted in Addiss and Amon, "Apology and Unintended Harm in Global Health," pp. 19–32.
[12] Ibid.

been the result of the drug, and therefore not of witchcraft, and this explanation would provide the relief the community needed in their experience of grief. As Dr. King recounts:

> We sat down with the family. We explained why we were doing this research, that it was a mistake on our part if we gave her the drug without asking about her last period. We asked if they would accept our apology. Sitting down with them provided an opportunity for us to accept some responsibility for the mistake and to let them know that we would do our best to ensure that we wouldn't give the drug to pregnant women in the future. Our taking the time to visit them, listen, offer apology, and explain things calmed their anxieties. When we went back again to resume the research, the community welcomed us and participated in it.[13]

This example shows how repentance and apology, followed by mercy and forgiveness, can lead to reconciliation: there was a complete restoration of the partnership between Dr. King's research team and the local community. However, in global health, the large scale of programs inevitably diffuses the responsibility for unintended harms across a widespread global network of state and non-state actors.[14] This makes it unclear who should apologize and on whose behalf.[15] This ambiguity makes reconciliation challenging, though not impossible.

Mercy, as a type of love, is deeply personal. It is relational, in that it is requested through repentance and given through forgiveness. This means that the process of asking for and bestowing mercy occurs most effectively at the interpersonal level. This was the case both in the first example of Shylock and Antonio and in the second example of Dr. King and the pregnant woman. Mercy, however, also has a crucial institutional component: the court of Venice in the first case, and the Case Western Reserve University in conjunction with the National Department of Public Health in Papua New Guinea, which were directly supporting Dr. King's research, in the second case. They can offer an institutional or collective mercy, grounded on the idea of shared or group agency.[16] The idea of institutional mercy—or more precisely of requesting repentance and giving forgiveness at the institutional level—may seem merely *pro forma*, insincere, and callous, especially if the faces of the victims and the faces of the offenders remain hidden under this institutional veil and are never put in

---

[13] Center for Compassion and Global Health, "The Value of Apology."
[14] Addiss and Amon, "Apology and Unintended Harm in Global Health," p. 25.
[15] Ibid.
[16] Perry, "Mercy," pp. 60–89; see also: List and Pettit, *Group Agency*, pp. 39–40.

each other's real, vulnerable presence.[17] However, while an exchange of mercy at the institutional level may not necessarily involve a face-to-face encounter, it still requires choosing to be vulnerably present to the other, and that has a key societal impact: the (public) bestowal of institutional mercy shows the kind of people, the kind of institutions, and ultimately the kind of communities that we are and want to become by the choices we make in caring for one another and in forgiving one another for our fallibilities.

Requesting and giving mercy offer an opportunity for a broken relationship to start again and build a better way of forging interactions and designing institutions that are more attentive to the needs of those who they serve. One cannot create an institutional framework for meaningful inclusiveness, belonging, and true service that is focused on shaming and blaming: a culture of accusation is incompatible with a culture of diversity, equity, and inclusion that goes beyond empty rhetoric, and is so crucial in healthcare and global health settings. The process of mercy, in the requesting and giving forgiveness, heals the brokenness of the relationship between Global North and South, offering the possibility of reconciliation, where their companionship in working together for a shared end may be fully restored. Reconciliation and full restoration of companionship between specific global actors are not a necessary outcome of mercy—it may not be always advisable to resume working as a team and sharing life together again. The loving thing to do is always to forgive your enemy while not necessarily reconciling with them. Regardless of the further step of reconciliation and restoration of companionship, the process of mercy heals the brokenness and restores the unitive fabric of the international community, strengthening international cooperation and multilateralism in general, even though there may not be direct cooperation, fruit of reconciliation, between the former enemies. This healing only depends on the wrongdoer's and the victim's choice to be in each other's peaceful, vulnerable *presence*. This reciprocal gift restores the unity of broken communities (again, one may attain peaceful co-existence and unity with another without being their companion and working together in direct cooperation with them). In short, there is a need for mercy in healthcare and global health institutions because there is brokenness, perpetuating wrongdoings. The requesting and extending of mercy are the opportunity to set the stage for the hope of something new, as Section 3 will demonstrate.

---

[17] There is no consensus on the concepts of institutional mercy and institutional forgiveness. For Angela M. Smith, these two can be synonymous (Smith, "*Institutional Apologies and Forgiveness,*" Ch. 7); for Charles Griswold, these two are fundamentally different (Griswold, *Forgiveness: A Philosophical Exploration*, Ch. 4).

1.2. What Mercy Is Not

Before providing a picture of what GHG could look like if it were to be grounded on mercy, I should clarify some terminology, explaining first what mercy is not and then proceed to define what mercy is and what its three qualities (discretion, gratuitous generosity, and reciprocal gift of self) entail. This clarification is particularly important to address certain conceptual confusions about mercy that often lead to the false understanding that forgiveness is unreasonable and a practically impossible ideal.

First, mercy in bestowing forgiveness does not mean condoning bad behavior, forgetting the harm, or pretending that no injustice occurred.[18] Mercy does not hide the truth about the injustice of a wrongdoing. That is to say, mercy does not mean foregoing justice: one can be merciful in forgiving a wrongdoer without excusing the wrongful conduct and while still pursuing justice to repair the harm.[19] As Dr. Martin Luther King Jr. puts it: "forgiveness does not mean ignoring what has been done or putting a false label on an evil act."[20] This would be contrary to the truth, and in order to forgive something, one needs to name it as the evil it is. If the decision to act mercifully is to be rooted in true facts rather than in lies, mercy cannot contradict the truth that an injustice is indeed an injustice.[21] There should be therefore no inconsistency between mercy, justice, and truth. Mercy acknowledges that an injustice happened and honors the punishment that is just: in offering leniency, the merciful does not contradict justice (and the just punishment it prescribes) but chooses to go beyond just retribution through forbearance for the purpose of reducing the suffering that such punishment causes.[22]

Second, mercy in bestowing forgiveness does not (necessarily) mean reconciliation.[23] Reconciliation can mean different things in different contexts: from restorative justice practices in politics and international relations that complement human rights, rule of law, and democracy, to mental health programs that seek healing of trauma, justice, and peace.[24] By reconciliation here I simply mean

---

[18] VanderWeele, "Is Forgiveness a Public Health Issue?" pp. 189–90; Worthington, *Forgiveness and Reconciliation*; Enright and Fitzgibbons, *Helping Clients Forgive*; Holmgren, "Forgiveness and the Intrinsic Value of Persons," pp. 341–52.
[19] On the consistence between forgiveness and punishment, see: Philpott, "An Ethic of Political Reconciliation," pp. 389–407.
[20] King, *A Gift of Love—Sermons from Strength to Love and Other Preachings*, p. 45.
[21] Philip, *Interior Freedom*, p. 65.
[22] On forbearance and forgiveness, see: Minow, *When Should Law Forgive*.
[23] VanderWeele, "Is Forgiveness a Public Health Issue?" pp. 189–90; Stump, "Love, by All Accounts," pp. 25–43; Stump, "The Sunflower: Guilt, Forgiveness, and Reconciliation," Ch. 8.
[24] See, e.g., Philpott "An Ethic of Political Reconciliation," pp. 389–407; Potter (ed.), *Trauma, Truth and Reconciliation*; Lederach, J. and Lederach, A. J., *When Blood and Bones Cry Out*.

full restitution of companionship.²⁵ This sort of reconciliation that I am talking about depends both on the victim and on the perpetrator—as well as on a careful evaluation of their current state of mind and circumstances. Mercy, as a type of love, is unconditional, depending most fundamentally on the agent's choice to forgive. Sure, full process of mercy also requires the acceptance of such forgiveness through repentance, but the giving of forgiveness is still the primary and distinct feature of mercy, and it happens independently of the receiving end. Reconciliation, however, is conditional on several things. First, it is conditional on specific actions by the offender (e.g., repentance coupled with a sincere expression of apology, acts of reparation, and penance) for the removal of their guilt.²⁶ Reconciliation also depends on the healthy state of mind of those involved and adequate circumstances. This means not only that reconciliation might be morally unavailable if the wrongdoer cannot or does not do what is needed to remove their guilt, but also that it might be morally impermissible in cases where the restitution of companionship would be imprudent (e.g., abusive and oppressive relationships).²⁷ Refusing to reconcile with such wrongdoer does not need to contravene any moral obligations. In fact, it would be the most loving (reasonable) thing to do. The full process of mercy (in the giving and receiving of forgiveness) repairs a broken relationship and restores the unity in community by bringing accuser and accused in each other's peaceful, vulnerable presence. For reconciliation to then happen, both parts have to take further specific steps to restore their companionship, continue to build trust and work together for a new vision of partnership.

Third, mercy in bestowing forgiveness is not merely an emotional response that arises out of the feeling of pity toward the perpetrator's misery (see Chapter 2 on the definition of pity). Instead, it is an act of the will that results from an intellectual, discretionary process. Mercy is primarily a decision to give the gift of forgiveness—a gratuitous and generous gift—to one's offender. In this discretionary act of bestowing forgiveness, one chooses to stop willing the ill of the wrongdoer, and to replace it with willing the good (the benefit) of the wrongdoer. Mercy, in this sense, is an internal dynamic process of replacing ill-will with good-will.²⁸ But this is often also followed by the reduction of negative thoughts, emotions, and behaviors (like anger, resentment, and vengeance) toward the

---

²⁵ For a different perspective, see: Philpott "An Ethic of Political Reconciliation," pp. 389–407. For Daniel Philpott, forgiveness entails reconciliation, which he defines more narrowly as "a concept of justice" centered on restoring "right relationships within a community." By focusing on the restoration of *right* relationships, his account emphasizes that reconciliation need not involve restoring companionship, particularly in cases of abuse or oppression.
²⁶ Stump, "Love, by All Accounts," pp. 25–43; Stump, "The Sunflower," Ch. 8.
²⁷ Ibid.
²⁸ Perry, "Mercy," pp. 62, 87; VanderWeele, "Is Forgiveness a Public Health Issue?" pp. 189–90; Worthington, *Forgiveness and Reconciliation*; Enright and Fitzgibbons, *Helping Clients Forgive*; Toussaint, Worthington, and Williams, eds. *Forgiveness and Health.*

offender and their replacement with more positive thoughts, emotions, and behaviors.[29] There is here a crucial conceptual distinction that needs to be laid out in more detail: the difference (and the link) between decisional and emotional forgiveness, as elements of the discretionary process of mercy.

1.3. Three Typical Characteristics of Mercy

1.3.1. Mercy as Discretion: Navigating Decisional and Emotional Forgiveness

The internal dynamic process whereby the mercy-giver bestows forgiveness has two different though often interlinked mechanisms, one that has to do with the will and another that has to do with the emotions. The former has been called "decisional forgiveness," the latter has been called "emotional forgiveness."[30] The former is considered fundamental, not only because it often precedes but also because it triggers the latter to follow.[31] Without overlooking the existence and contribution of emotions in the internal dynamic process of bestowing forgiveness, here I focus on the discretionary, decisional foundations of mercy.

To understand the discretionary nature of forgiveness and the role emotions play in it, it is worth examining the concept of discretion. Legal theorist H. L. A. Hart defines discretion as the intellectual virtue of practical wisdom or prudence, allowing one to discern what is appropriate in various situations.[32] It involves judgment and discernment, not simply the ability to choose. For Hart, discretionary power is not synonymous with the ability to choose: while choice is necessary for discretion, it alone is not sufficient. Discretion is not about whimsical decisions or acting based on arbitrary emotions. Instead, it is a deliberate act of will, informed by knowledge and reason. Hart argues that emotional choices are undesirable, especially in legal or policy contexts, because they can be arbitrary. However, discretion is not simply about rational calculation either. In clear-cut cases where principles apply straightforwardly, there is no real room for discretion, Hart argues, because the answer is already determined. Discretion

---

[29] For the several physical, emotional, and spiritual health benefits linked to forgiveness, see, e.g., VanderWeele, "Is Forgiveness a Public Health Issue," pp. 189–90; Bulger, *The Quest for Mercy*, pp. 362–73; Toussaint, Worthington, and Williams, eds. *Forgiveness and Health*.

[30] Decisional forgiveness is the intention to treat the offender as a person of value, and emotional forgiveness is the replacement of negative emotions with positive, other-centered emotions. See: VanderWeele, "Is Forgiveness a Public Health Issue?" pp. 189–90; Worthington, *Forgiveness and Reconciliation*.

[31] Ibid.

[32] Hart, "Discretion," p. 656.

comes into play in more complex cases, like the choice to forgive or not, where both options—based on love or justice—can be reasonably justified.

Hart's conception of discretion might lead one here to conclude that the internal dynamic process that the mercy-giver goes through, guided by prudence and practical reasoning, is linear and that the process is finished after it generates the discretionary act of bestowing forgiveness. This is however not the reality of our humanity, which makes the process of bestowing forgiveness much more complex and the moral value of mercy much more demanding. While it is true that the internal dynamic process of bestowing forgiveness is led primarily by the will and not by feelings (in other words, decisional forgiveness often precedes and triggers emotional forgiveness to follow),[33] this does not mean that a one-time choice to forgive suffices to permanently produce the goods (the benefits) of forgiveness. As a dynamic, rather than a linear process, bestowing forgiveness often requires an ongoing choice for mercy toward the offender, as negative feelings return. Mercy and forgiveness thus take time and effort. The negative emotions of anger, resentment, and vengeance typically come and go in waves, often arbitrarily. The repeated resurgence of these negative emotions requires repeated self-denial in choosing to overpower these negative emotions and to forgive again and again—"seventy times seven."[34] As Dr. Martin Luther King Jr. puts it: "Forgiveness is not an occasional act, it is a constant attitude."[35]

Mercy in bestowing forgiveness is not, therefore, in the words of Dr. King, "soft, anemic, and sentimental."[36] Instead, it is a strength that requires self-mastery and self-possession. It necessitates a sacrifice of the self in not giving into feelings, negating the instincts to be angry, to act resentfully, and to pursue vengeance.[37] While acknowledging a just punishment, mercy requires going beyond (not against) justice by forbearing one's rights (such as the right to receive the payment of a debt, illustrated in Shakespeare's *The Merchant of Venice*).[38] Since mercy requires a constant strength of the will in restraining oneself and in choosing, instead, the good of an undeserving offender, the discretionary act of mercifully forgiving can be best appreciated within the rationale of gift[39]—a generous and gratuitous blessing or benefit to the wrongdoer.

---

[33] VanderWeele, "Is Forgiveness a Public Health Issue?" pp. 189–90; Worthington, *Forgiveness and Reconciliation*.
[34] Matthew 18:21–22.
[35] King, "Draft of Chapter IV 'Love in Action.'"
[36] King, "The Strength to Love," p. 513.
[37] In *De Clementia*, Roman Stoic philosopher emphasizes this self-sacrificial quality of mercy. Addressing Emperor Nero, he advises that good leadership requires self-control over anger, resentment, and temptation to dominate. Seneca frames mercy as an (imperfect) duty requiring leaders to control impulses, and choose mercy for the good of those they govern. Thus, mercy becomes essential to good leadership. See: Seneca, *De Clementia*, pp. 214–15. See also: Perry, "Mercy," p. 87.
[38] See, e.g., on forbearance and forgiveness, Minow, *When Should Law Forgive*.
[39] Campagna, "The Miracle of Mercy," 1096–1118; Murphy, "Mercy and Legal Justice," pp. 2–3; Perry, "Mercy," pp. 60–89; Twambley, "Mercy and Forgiveness," pp. 84, 87.

1.3.2. Mercy as Gratuitous Generosity: The Rationale of Gift

A gift, by nature, is gratuitous—it is given freely and unconditionally, without expectation of return.[40] This disinterested,[41] uncalculated[42] act of giving excludes manipulative forms like bribery or commercial transactions. This means that mercy to be an authentic gift of forgiveness must be freely and unconditionally given, independent of the wrongdoer's repentance or request. Mercy is a gift because it goes beyond merit; it is given to an undeserving wrongdoer, even without genuine repentance or a vulnerable plea for forgiveness.

To understand mercy's gratuitous generosity, one needs to distinguish it from false generosity. Generosity is often seen as an Aristotelian virtue: excessive generosity leads to overgiving, while deficient generosity leads to undergiving. The virtuous middle ground aims to meet the receiver's needs without unreasonably exceeding the giver's limits. Now, what truly distinguishes virtuous from corrupted generosity is not the amount given but the intention behind it.[43]

Excessive generosity may stem from imprudence, manipulation, or a desire to control others. A giver who overgives to gratify his impulses, benefit personally, please others, or control them, does so mainly with self-interested motives. Similarly, deficient generosity, often driven by stinginess, is also self-centered, focusing on calculating exactly how much to give to secure personal gain.[44] Both extremes, driven by selfish desires for wealth, power, or honor, fail to truly benefit the other.

In contrast, virtuous generosity involves a prudent giver who sacrifices in a reasonable manner, maintaining healthy boundaries that ensure sustainable giving. It requires discretion, grounded in prudence and exercised through practical reasoning,[45] with the primary goal of benefiting the other without expecting anything in return. When considering mercy as a gift, it is essential therefore to examine whether my forgiveness is motivated by the good of the other or driven primarily by self-interest.

To further understand the motivations why one might bestow forgiveness, it is also helpful to consider the opposing dynamics of giving, as outlined by French philosopher Paul Ricœur. He juxtaposes "the logic of superabundance" with "the logic of equivalence."[46] The former is exemplified by the virtuous, prudent

---

[40] Murphy, "Mercy and Legal Justice," p. 3; Twambley, "Mercy and Forgiveness," pp. 84, 87; Baviera, English, and Guillen, "The 'Logic of Gift,'" pp. 159–80.
[41] Frankfurt, *Reasons to Love*.
[42] MacIntyre, *Dependent Rational Animals*, p. 121.
[43] I thank Lauren Woodside Alegre for making this point clear.
[44] For this reason, organizational psychologist Adam Grant calls the stingy giver a "taker." See: Grant, *Give and Take*.
[45] MacIntyre makes a similar point when he highlights the need for the virtues of prudence and temperance when defining a generosity that is just. See: MacIntyre, "Dependent Rational Animals," p. 126.
[46] Paul Ricœur, "Love and Justice," p. 34.

giver; the latter by the stingy giver, or "taker."[47] The logic of equivalence is seen in market transactions, where giving is based on a calculation of equivalents—one gives to acquire something of comparable utility.[48] This exchange is not generous or gratuitous but self-interested and calculated. In such a transaction, giving is about maximizing gains and minimizing costs,[49] fostering a competitive dynamic where relationships are reduced to winners and losers in a context of scarcity. In contrast, the logic of superabundance is about giving without expectation of return, rooted in gratuitous generosity. This logic is incompatible with the self-interested, calculated nature of equivalence that cannot foster a culture of authentic gifts. Within the logic of equivalence, the giving of one's self as a gift—primarily for the benefit of the other (as is required for mercy)—is impossible.

The giving of oneself as a gift—primarily for the benefit of the other—is only truly possible within the logic of superabundance, where giving is not about gaining something in return. As Ricœur explains, one gives because one has first received.[50] In other words, within the logic of superabundance, one "pays it forward" rather than "paying it back."[51] This kind of giving is motivated by gratitude for past generosity, creating a multidirectional web of "uncalculated giving and graceful receiving,"[52] as philosopher Alasdair MacIntyre describes it. This fosters a virtuous cycle of gratuitous generosity and a culture of gift-giving.[53]

Now, if giving oneself as a gift for the benefit of another is only possible within the logic of superabundance, then mercy, as a gift of forgiveness, can only truly exist within this logic. Applying the "pay-it-forward" logic to mercy, the answer to why one bestows forgiveness becomes clear: one gives mercy because one has first received it. Following Ricœur's reasoning, we forgive because we have been forgiven. One may want to contend here that not everybody has experienced mercy and received forgiveness. Perhaps. But if one is minimally self-aware, one can also appreciate that we are all equally vulnerable to error and fallibility. It is therefore highly improbable that a person has never wounded another who then had to forgive them for the hurt caused. Although I may not have wounded another as gravely as my offender (there are different degrees of vulnerabilities and woundedness), we are still all undeserving wrongdoers: equally susceptible to mistakes and failings for which we have received some degree of forgiveness. We

---

[47] Grant, *Give and Take*.
[48] Benedict XVI, *Caritas in Veritate*, para. 39.
[49] MacIntyre, "Dependent Rational Animals," p. 126; Baviera, English, and Guillen, "The 'Logic of Gift,'" pp. 159–80.
[50] Paul Ricœur, "Love and Justice," p. 34.
[51] The Cambridge Dictionary defines the idiom "pay-it-forward" as: "to do something kind and useful for someone because someone else has done something kind and useful for you."
See also Emmons, "Pay It Forward."
[52] MacIntyre, *Dependent Rational Animals*, p. 121.
[53] Baviera, English, and Guillen, "The 'Logic of Gift,'" pp. 159–80.

all have the choice between "paying-it-forward" with mercy or "paying-it-back" with punishment for a wound that was unjustly inflicted on us. The latter may be just, but only the former can engender a virtuous cycle of gratuitous generosity and a sustainable culture of gift.

1.3.3. Mercy as a Reciprocal Gift-of-Self

The distinctive and most fundamental feature of mercy is the giving of the gift of forgiveness: the mercy-giver vulnerably gives themselves (through their forgiveness) to the undeserving wrongdoer, who may not have repented or asked for forgiveness. In choosing to forgive what was unforgivable,[54] and in choosing to give the gift of forgiveness to an unworthy evildoer, the sufferers regain their moral strength, overcome their victimhood, and restore their agency. They join themselves in the gift of forgiveness, and they offer their vulnerable presence to their enemy. It is precisely in this vulnerable posture that they move internally from victim to victor who stands empowered by their moral resilience. The full process of mercy starts with this internal, dynamic, and discretionary process that the mercy-giver goes through, guided by their prudence and practical reasoning. But to be complete, the process of mercy depends on another, independent internal dynamic process of discretion that the mercy-receiver has to go through to be able to acknowledge their wrong and sorrowfully repent from wounding another. Only then can they receive the gift of forgiveness and, in gratitude, reciprocate with true, vulnerable repentance—a gift of themselves to the one they wounded.

The process of mercy is thus complete with a reciprocal gift of self: forgiveness is vulnerably given, gracefully received, and vulnerably reciprocated with repentance. It is here, when the accused and the accuser are in each other's peaceful, vulnerable presence, that the harmony and unity in their community are restored. There is healing of their wounded relationship and a reweaving of their broken communal fabric. They may or may not move forward to reconcile and reestablish their companionship and build the trust needed to be able to work together toward their common good. Nonetheless, the full process of mercy has here run its course: the broken relationship between the parties has been replaced by loving peace because the gift of forgiveness was vulnerably given, gracefully received, and vulnerably reciprocated with the gift of repentance. Only then the ripple effects of the logic of superabundance, creating a multidirectional web of "uncalculated giving and graceful receiving,"[55] can be established.

---

[54] I thank the Derridean scholar Fr. Federico Ponzoni for making this point clearer.
[55] MacIntyre, *Dependent Rational Animals*, p. 121.

32   THE RULE OF LOVE

For the cycle of giving and receiving mercy to be complete, the question arises: does the mercy-receiver have a duty to reciprocate with gratitude and reciprocate with the gift of repentance? The Stoic philosopher Seneca addresses the communal implications of mercy. In *De Clementia*, he discusses the leader's duty to be self-sacrificial and merciful, while in *De Beneficiis*, he focuses on the duty of gratitude when receiving gifts. Seneca explores how excessive or deficient gratitude, such as fake gratitude (repaying too soon or too much) or ingratitude, can harm social cohesion.[56] He argues that failing to fulfill the duty of gratitude brings serious harm to the community. As he writes in *De Beneficiis*: "Among the many and diverse errors of those who live their lives recklessly and without due reflection, almost nothing that I can mention, excellent Liberalis, is more disgraceful and hurtful to society than the fact that we do not know how either to give or to receive benefits."

Seneca's discussion of gifts (including mercy) and gratitude is primarily concerned with those favors and benefits that Roman public officials gave and received, but his account of gifts and gratitude is also pertinent to other, more general relationships—including interpersonal relationships (e.g., doctor-patient relationship) and institutional relationships (e.g., giver and receiver of global health aid).

In a nutshell, Seneca's account emphasizes the communal value of the "imperfect duty"[57] that we all have to extend a gift and be grateful for a gift—including the gift of forgiveness. The receiver of a gratuitous and generous gift (such as the gift of forgiveness) has a moral duty to reciprocate with gratitude and respond with repentance. In this sense, while the giver of mercy has no legal right to claim the gift of repentance in gratitude for one's forgiveness, there is a moral requirement and therefore a duty for the receiver of mercy to be grateful, which is expressed as repentance. These imperfect duties create the rules by which a web of giving and receiving can form and provide an explanation to skeptics of the logic of superabundance that I have shown is necessary for the full process of mercy to be established and replicated. These duties also have their place in healthcare and in GHG, and without them, as Seneca's account indicates, serious harm can come to the community of healthcare institutions, providers, and patients. For example, from the case of Dr. King's research team, if Dr. King had been unwilling to admit potential fault, and accept the forgiveness of the community, or if the community had been unwilling to gratefully accept the apology and extend mercy to the research team, then the vaccination program would not

---

[56] Seneca, *De Beneficiis*, iv; Aquinas, *ST* ii-ii Q 106, a4.
[57] Perfect duties correlate to rights that can be claimed. Imperfect duties have no correlative rights and cannot be legally claimed, though they are morally required. O'Neill, *Faces of Hunger*, p. 101; O'Neill, *Constructions of Reasons*, pp. 191, 224.

have been able to continue, and the community would have been left unprotected from that particular disease.

The key point that I want to add, however, and to which I will come back in Section 3, is that such imperfect duty to be grateful (just like the imperfect duty to be merciful in forgiving one's enemies) not only helps to deepen and forge interpersonal relationships of generosity, but it also calls for the design and reform of institutions that can help foster an institutional culture of graceful receiving. When institutions embrace mercy and gratitude there is a movement or journey from a culture of animosity, divisiveness, and suspicion to a culture of restored peace, unity, and greater trust. In the face of significant distrust in GHG, this is just the shift in culture that is needed to re-weave the communal fabric of global health systems. In Section 3, I apply my account of mercy to reimagining GHG dynamics and institutions.

Section 2. Responses to Objections to My Conceptual Account of Mercy

I have thus far defended an account of mercy that is conceived as a discretionary process that depends not only on the vulnerability of the receiver of mercy (who depends on forgiveness to be set free from their culpability) but also and more fundamentally on the vulnerability of the giver (who bestows forgiveness and opens themselves to be ridiculed for their generosity toward their undeserving perpetrator). This mutual vulnerability that mercy requires of both victim and wrongdoer should, I contend, be understood as a reciprocal gift-of-self: the accused and the accuser are in each other's peaceful, vulnerable presence and, as an upshot, their wounds and the unitive fabric of their community are healed. In what follows, I will respond to three objections that can be raised against my account of mercy, and in responding to them I will further specify my conceptual account of mercy.

2.1. Objection Regarding Suppression of Negative Emotions

In Section 1, I have defended the view that, as a discretionary act, the internal dynamic process of mercy that the mercy-giver goes through in bestowing their forgiveness is led primarily by their will and not by their feelings: decisional forgiveness often precedes and tends to trigger emotional forgiveness to follow.[58]

---

[58] VanderWeele, "Is Forgiveness a Public Health Issue?" pp. 189–90; Worthington, *Forgiveness and Reconciliation*.

The mercy-receiver goes through a similar internal dynamic process in processing what happened, acknowledging the consequences of their actions, and deciding to give the gift repentance to the one they wounded. As dynamic, rather than linear processes, a one-time choice to forgive or repent does not suffice to permanently produce the goods (the benefits) of mercy—let alone to ensure the lastingness of the emotions that accompany the decision to forgive and repent. As a dynamic process, bestowing forgiveness often requires an ongoing choice for mercy toward the offender, as negative feelings return. While this tends to be more recurrent for the mercy-giver who was wounded, the mercy-receiver is not immune to the return of resentment and other negative feelings toward the mercy-giver. Mercy thus takes time and effort: it requires a self-mastery and self-possession that allows the moral agent to freely choose the sacrifice of the self in forbearance by choosing not to be ruled by one's feeling and controlling their instincts to be angry, to act resentfully, and to pursue vengeance.

One may object here to my account of mercy predicated on self-restraint and claim that, while rumination of hatred toward someone is not beneficial, the suppression of hatred, as my proposed self-sacrificial account of mercy would seem to demand, is also harmful for the mental health of the forgiving agent. Is it morally reasonable to demand such an overpowering and shutting down of one's emotions?

Surely, to merely suppress—meaning to bottle up—negative feelings, like anger, resentment, and vengeance (or the repression of any other feelings generally speaking) is detrimental to one's health and well-being. To merely suppress feelings is to ignore them, either by minimizing the impact of its cause or by pretending that their cause never existed. However, there is nothing in my account of mercy that suggests that negative feelings should be shut down. Mercy in bestowing and accepting forgiveness does not entail emotional suppression: it does not ignore the evil, harm, and injustice that happened. Instead, it entails taking full account of the wrong done, including why and how it hurts.[59] As an internal dynamic processes of giving and accepting forgiveness, mercy requires a constant examination of one's feelings toward an enemy and the constant choice of forgiveness, especially when negative (re)emerging thoughts, emotions, and behaviors are detected. In confronting and internally processing one's negative feelings toward an enemy, one is, in actuality, doing the opposite of suppressing undesirable emotions: instead one is freeing oneself from the resentment that jails us in negative ruminations.

There are two prominent intervention models of forgiveness that practically help one to confront and internally process the negative feelings toward an enemy, helping one to choose mercy (and therefore freedom). The first,

---

[59] See, e.g., Headland, *Loved as I Am*.

Enright's Process Model, breaks the process of mercy and forgiveness into four phases, namely: (i) uncovering negative feelings about the offense, (ii) deciding to pursue forgiveness for a specific instance, (iii) working toward understanding the offending person, and (iv) discovering unanticipated positive outcomes and empathy for the forgiven person.[60] The second, Worthington's REACH model, breaks the process of mercy and forgiveness into five phases, where each letter of "REACH" represents one such phase: (i) Recall the hurt, (ii) Empathize with the one who hurt you, (iii) Altruistically give the gift of forgiveness, (iv) Commit to the forgiveness you experienced, and (v) Hold on to the decision to forgive when in doubt.[61] These two models are predicated on the understanding that forgiveness takes time and effort, and that mercy is a process that necessitates a continual choice to love one's enemy and oneself (in being patient with one's returning negative thoughts, emotions, and behaviors). These two forgiveness interventions lead to mercy by gradually easing recurring negative thoughts, emotions, and behaviors and progressively replacing them with a clearer sight of the offender's humanity—albeit flawed. While there are evidence-based benefits for the use of these intervention models, care must obviously be taken, in contexts where these models could facilitate the dynamics of prolonged abuse or intimate partner violence.[62] As discussed in Section 1, extending mercy does not mean condoning, excusing, or enabling bad behavior, nor is it to be confused with reconciliation and fully restored companionship.[63]

2.2. Objection Regarding Imbalance of Power

Section 1 has established that, as a discretionary act, the internal dynamic processes of mercy replace ill-will toward an enemy with good-will.[64] I defined forgiveness as an unmerited gift, generously and gratuitously given by a person or an institution (like Shylock at the law court of Venice) with the moral agency and capacity to forgive an offender. In Shakespeare's *The Merchant of Venice*, Shylock is a powerful authority: he is in the position to choose to either punish or forgive his offender Antonio, while Antonio, being at Shylock's mercy, is vulnerable to Shylock's authority. Shakespeare's classic example of mercy seems to show an imbalance of power and vulnerability within the dynamic of mercy giving.

---

[60] Enright and Fitzgibbons, *Helping Clients Forgive*.
[61] Worthington, *Forgiveness and Reconciliation*.
[62] VanderWeele, "Is Forgiveness a Public Health Issue?" pp. 189–90.
[63] Stump, "Love, by All Accounts," pp. 25–43; Stump, "The Sunflower," Ch. 8.
[64] Perry, "Mercy," pp. 62, 87; VanderWeele, "Is Forgiveness a Public Health Issue?" pp. 189–90; Worthington, *Forgiveness and Reconciliation*; Enright and Fitzgibbons, *Helping Clients Forgive*; Toussaint, Worthington, and Williams, eds. *Forgiveness and Health*.

For philosopher Martha Nussbaum, this account of mercy as "the free gift of an all-powerful ruler to those way down below"[65] is objectionable. Its top-down, hierarchical structure produces a patronizing power dynamic between the giver and receiver of mercy. She argues that this account of mercy, in being influenced by Christian doctrine, "is modeled on the mercy of an omnipotent and fault-free God, and its starting point is a huge gulf: between God and mortals, perfection and guilt."[66] Anthropologist Didier Fassin makes a similar point about the belittling power dynamic that can come out of the idea of gift, particularly in the context of humanitarian aid. Like Nussbaum, Fassin stresses the inequality between the giver and the receiver of gift, which, as he observes, "explains the shame felt by the poor, beneficiaries of aid, all those who receive these gifts... and [accounting] for the resentment and even hostility sometimes expressed by the disadvantaged and the dominated towards those who think of themselves as their benefactors."[67]

For Nussbaum, the crux of the problem with this Christian, condescending account of mercy is the hardness of heart of the powerful (the giver of mercy). In their inability to be humble and empathetic, the powerful authority is blind to the common humanity that they share with the offender, receiver of forgiveness.[68] In their blindness, the authority is unable to acknowledge, as Nussbaum emphasizes, their equal vulnerability to error and fallibility—and also, I would add, their equal need for mercy and forgiveness. As Nussbaum puts it:

> The monarch can bestow mercy not because of a recognition of common humanity, but because of a secure knowledge of permanent difference and hierarchy. Nor does monarchical mercy require any effort of sympathy or imagination: for all are alike low, base, and sinful, so imagining the heart of another will show us no particular reasons for mitigation and would thus be a waste of time. It is notorious that Portia makes absolutely no effort to imagine what a Jew in Venice might feel, what experiences of stigma and hatred might have led to his obdurate insistence on his bond.[69]

This objection about the power dynamics that can ensue between the giver and the receiver of mercy is a critical one. As acknowledged in the Introduction, it is not always true that the victim of an injustice, who will decide whether or not to forgive their offender, is in a position of power in relation to their perpetrator. And this is clear in the context of healthcare and global health, where the

---

[65] Nussbaum, "If You Could See This Heart," p. 232.
[66] Ibid.
[67] Fassin, *Humanitarian Reason*, p. 3.
[68] Nussbaum, "If You Could See This Heart," p. 234.
[69] Nussbaum, "If You Could See This Heart," p. 232.

mercy-giver and victim of an injustice (i.e., the patient or the receiver of global health aid) are generally speaking in a relatively more vulnerable position than the mercy-receiver and wrongdoer (i.e., the medical authority or global health institution). Think here again of Dr. King and his research team (mercy-receivers) and the pregnant women and her community in Papua New Guinea (mercy-givers). Nevertheless, Nussbaum's and Fassin's objection should be considered relevant also in the contexts of healthcare practice and global health development aid, since cases of paternalistic, abusive care that reduces people's agency have marred both the relationship between the patient and the healthcare professional, and the relationship between the giver and the receiver of global health aid. Traditionally hierarchical relationships such as these, when left unchecked, provide the conditions for predatory behavior. Nussbaum's concerns with a tyrannical and hard-hearted mercy that exacerbates power imbalance leading to oppression should therefore be taken seriously. Yet, her reading of Christian mercy is disputable.

In his book *On Mercy*, Art historian Malcolm Bull emphasizes that the Christian account of mercy "has always been posited on the "recognition of common humanity" in the incarnation."[70] What Bull means is this: the Christian account of mercy not only recognizes but is also grounded on the common humanity between the authority (God, the giver of mercy) and human beings (the receivers of mercy) through Christ. It is through the incarnation that God shows His empathy for the sufferings of humans, as He chooses to humble Himself and become fully human (yet maintaining His full divinity) in Jesus. It is in Christ crucified that the humanity and vulnerability of God are made radically visible. Jesus was unjustly crucified. Although he was innocent, Pilate (the Roman governor and official who presided over the trial of Jesus) sentences Christ to death on the cross. Reacting with meekness (rather than anger, resentment, or vengeance), Christ forgives all those who unjustly crucified him—after they had betrayed, ridiculed, harshly treated, imprisoned, spit upon, scourged, and humiliated him.

Here it might be worth including a parenthetical explanation of the Christian definition of meekness, since it is often wrongly interpreted as a call to be a weak and blindly submissive person. Meekness in the biblical sense does not mean being a doormat, foolishly following anyone's lead; nor does it mean being a passionless coward. It means, in actuality, the opposite of weakness: the Christian definition of meekness means strength under control, as illustrated by the way Jesus reacts towards all those who unjustly crucified him.[71] Meekness is, in the Christian sense, a virtue, discretionarily exercised with more or less

---

[70] Bull, *On Mercy*, p. 166, fn. 12.
[71] See, e.g., Matthew 5:5 and 11:29 or 2 Corinthians 10:1.

assertiveness, and where one's strength lies in forbearing purely emotional impulsive reactions such as hatred.[72]

While anger, resentment, or vengeance would be an expected or even justified answer to the betrayal, ridicule, harsh treatment, imprisonment, spitting, scourging, and humiliation, which preceded Jesus' unjust crucifixion, Christ responds with meekness and mercy. The suffering of Christ is extreme and so are the vulnerability and humanity of God in Christ. This is the reason why the Christian understanding of mercy is best portrayed by the cross, and not by any symbol of power and authority. The cross reminds Christians of the greatest suffering and the greatest act of mercy and forgiveness ever known: the ultimate gift of self, where one gives their life to save their undeserving friends (and enemies)

The Christian idea of mercy as a gift of self therefore challenges Nussbaum's interpretation of a vertical and callous mercy. In requiring mutual vulnerability, the Christian idea of mercy as gift of self is horizontal and calls both the victim and the wrongdoer for an openness of heart, in self-sacrificially letting their guards down and turning towards each other, face-to-face.[73] I am not saying that the idea of mercy as a horizontal relationship is an exclusively Christian one, or that it is incompatible with other religious and cultural traditions. In fact, mercy as forgiveness is professed across traditions (from Buddhism,[74] to Confucianism,[75] to Hinduism,[76] to Baha'i,[77] to Islam,[78] to Judaism[79]) as a prerequisite for peaceful unity in community.

To say that mercy requires horizontality means that the wrongdoer has to become vulnerable in facing the consequences of their actions and taking responsibility for them by asking for forgiveness. Their vulnerability lies both in

---

[72] See: Ephesians 4:2–3, "With all humility and meekness, with patience, forbearing one another in love; Endeavoring to keep the unity of the Spirit in the bond of peace."

[73] Mercy therefore is horizontal, rather than vertical, contrary to Nussbaum's argument. Its very purpose is to correct the inequality created by the normal and just application of the law. By transcending justice, mercy corrects such (just) imbalance through mutual vulnerability. Mercy is, in this sense, a legal exception, justified by the good of the offender and the common good. See, e.g., Campagna, "The Miracle of Mercy," pp. 4, 23; Perry, "Mercy," p. 60.

[74] "All major religious traditions carry basically the same message, that is love, compassion and forgiveness ... the important thing is they should be part of our daily lives."—*The Dalai Lama*.

[75] "If one sets strict standards for oneself and makes allowances for others when making demands on them, one will stay clear of ill will."—*The Analects (15:15), Confucian text*.

[76] "Forgiveness is virtue; forgiveness is sacrifice, forgiveness is the Vedas, forgiveness is the Shruti [revealed scripture]. He that knoweth this is capable of forgiving everything."—*Mahabharata, Hindu text*.

[77] "Verily, the breezes of forgiveness have been wafted from the direction of your Lord, the God of Mercy; whoso turneth thereunto shall be cleansed of his sins, and of all pain and sickness. Happy the man that hath turned towards them, and woe betide him that hath turned aside."—*Bahá'u'lláh, Baha'i prophet*.

[78] "Those who have been graced with bounty and plenty should not swear that they will [no longer] give to kinsmen, the poor, those who emigrated in God's way: let them pardon and forgive. Do you not wish that God should forgive you? God is most forgiving and merciful."—*The Qur'an (224:22)*.

[79] Newman, "The Quality of Mercy," pp. 155–72.

depending on someone's forgiveness to be set free from their culpability and in exposing themselves to the risk of having their request for forgiveness and acceptance of repentance denied. In turn, the giver of mercy also has to become vulnerable in facing their wounds and taking the responsibility to tend to them by bestowing unmerited forgiveness.[80] The risk here is to be mocked for being too naïve, overly generous and imprudent, or to be betrayed again by the perpetrator or someone else. All of these risks for both sides, however, are outside of their control. Yet, it is only when one chooses to be exposed to these risks and to embrace uncertainty that vulnerability can happen. Risk and uncertainty are the very conditions for vulnerability. And it is in this mutual vulnerability—this mutual openness of heart—that the moral agency and the human dignity of both victim and wrongdoer are strengthened: the gift of forgiveness respects the agency (and responsibility) of the offender, while retaining the victim's self-respect and restoring their agency as a resilient victor; the gift of repentance honors the wounds of the victim, while keeping the offender's self-respect as an agent mature enough to acknowledge in humility and vulnerability their fallibilities.

We should therefore conceive of mercy as a decisional process that depends not only on the vulnerability of the receiver of mercy but also on the vulnerability of the giver. The mutual vulnerability that is required for the full version of mercy I have argued for challenges Nussbaum's and Fassin's claims of a necessary power imbalance between the giver and the receiver of the gift of forgiveness. This mutual vulnerability that my concept of mercy requires is a reciprocal gift-of-self.

A yet another remarkable outcome of this reciprocal dynamic, however, is that it is precisely in the vulnerable giving of oneself that one receives, in turn, yet another gratuitous, generous gift: the gift of freedom. As two independent, internal, dynamic, non-linear processes within the mercy-giver and the mercy receiver's discretionary powers, mercy can be therefore pictured also as a journey to freedom, both for the offender and for the victim. As a reciprocal gift-of-self, mercy frees and benefits both the receiver and the giver of forgiveness. It should be clearer how mercy would benefit the receiver of forgiveness in that they, as the wrongdoer, would be free from debts, blame, and culpability. It may still not be clear, however, how and from what mercy would free the giver of forgiveness.

The great temptation for the victim is to cling to fury and indignation against their enemy, keeping themselves "enclosed in a world of calculation and self-interest,"[81] with persistent negative thoughts, emotions, and behaviors towards

---

[80] There are several physical, emotional, and spiritual health benefits linked to forgiveness. See fn. 32.
[81] Philip, *Interior Freedom*, p. 69.

those they hate. Lack of forgiveness keeps the victim imprisoned in anger, resentment, and vengeance. The problem with this imprisonment is that it absorbs a large part of one's attention, leaving little room for love (or more specifically for attentive thoughts, emotions, and behaviors that love requires and that one should be focusing on instead to live a good and fulfilling life).[82] As a consequence of being trapped in these ruminations, one also gradually begins to define oneself primarily as a victim—a product of the wounds that the enemy caused upon them. Mercy, therefore, frees the victim from such identity confinement and weak sense of self-worth. Although one has wounds—and wounds should be acknowledged and honored—one is not merely the sum of one's wounds. In brief, the mutual vulnerability required by mercy should be understood as a reciprocal gift-of-self: it not only benefits the offender in freeing them from the victim's accusations but also empowers the victim by restoring their agency in their moral capacity to choose forgiveness and to redefine themselves as a victor.[83]

Now, it is by inviting the accused and the accuser to turn toward each other and to be in each other's vulnerable, face-to-face, open-heart-to-open-heart presence that mercy restores their inner freedom and outward peace. Their interior freedom allows for the restoration of a peaceful unity in community, which does not necessarily mean reconciliation and fully restored companionship. One may attain peace with another without being their companion. To be one's companion is to work together with the person toward a shared end and common vision for the future that upholds their common good (see Chapter 3 on the idea of shared authority and shared ends as components of beneficence). Companionship therefore requires a degree of trust that may not yet be attained solely by the merciful exchange of forgiveness and repentance. Nonetheless, acts of mercy and forgiveness, however small, re-weave the frail, ruptured unitive fabric of community. What allows for the re-weaving of unity is what I would consider perhaps the chief yet hardest moral lesson of mercy, namely that I, the wounded, am more similar to the one who wounded me than I would like.

Woundedness is a universal experience (while a deeply personal one). We are all wounded and we all wound others—though in different ways and degrees. It is through the decisional and vulnerable process of mercy that we become more self-aware of our own divided self, contradictions, and hypocrisies. In other words, it is through the experience of mercy (both giving and receiving forgiveness) that we more deeply acknowledge our common humanity and our

---

[82] Ibid., p. 66.
[83] See, e.g., Frankl, *Man's Searching for Meaning*.
    The reframing or mindset shift from victim to victor has been attributed to psychiatrist and Holocaust survivor Viktor Frankl. For him, individuals, as moral agents, can either remain victims of their circumstances or adopt the mindset of a victor.

equal vulnerability to error and fallibility. Mercy therefore frees us from our own self-righteousness, removing us from our own pedestal.[84] This realistic humility (i.e., the true knowledge of self, of one's strengths and one's weaknesses) in letting go of pride and a sense of superiority is particularly vital for those in leadership roles, who are called to lead those entrusted to their care. Realistic (not false) humility is indeed the mark of good leadership (as we will further discuss in Chapter 5, the principle of subsidiarity guides the delegation of functions through humility and self-knowledge to empower and honor the freedom of those under one's leadership).

Thus mercy (both giving and receiving forgiveness), rather than being dependent on a great power imbalance, is, I contend, a great equalizer between the victim and the wrongdoer: both are released into the power of freedom through humility and vulnerability. These two dynamic process of mercy are independent and are not a mere bi-directional trade transaction. True, the external expression of repentance through an apology can help in the process of forgiving and is a surely a necessary (though not always a sufficient) condition for the further process of reconciliation. However, the internal processes of mercy do not depend on such external expressions. Put another way, where the process of reconciliation necessitates a bi-directional reciprocity (giving a sincerely repentant apology coupled with other specific actions necessary to completely remove my guilt in exchange for your forgiveness and our reconciliation), the full process of mercy is better appreciated as a multidirectional reciprocity (i.e., a web of "uncalculated giving and graceful receiving"[85] that supports, as discussed in the previous section, a virtuous cycle of gratuitous generosity and a sustainable culture of gift.[86] This process is multidirectional in the sense that those from whom one receives are often not the same people as those to whom one gave.[87] This multidirectional reciprocity within the logic of superabundance helps to generate further bonds of trust and commitment between givers and receivers of mercy, and these bonds further unite them all in stronger community.[88]

2.3. Objection Regarding the Duty to Reciprocate the Gratuitous Generosity of a Gift with Gratitude

Section 1 has established that the gratuitous generosity of mercy is expressed through the unconditionality of the gift of forgiveness: the mercy-giver should

---

[84] Thompson, *Forgiveness.*
[85] MacIntyre, *Dependent Rational Animals,* p. 121
[86] Baviera, English, and Guillen, "The "Logic of Gift," pp. 159–80.
[87] MacIntyre, *Dependent Rational Animals,* p. 126.
[88] Ibid., p.121.

in this sense expect nothing equivalent in return. Such gratuitous generosity grounds this multidirectional reciprocity, that is, this web of "uncalculated giving and graceful receiving."[89] Now, although the giver of the gift of mercy is not entitled (has no right) to receive anything back, many, including myself and Seneca, have argued, nevertheless, for an (imperfect)[90] duty to reciprocate a gift with gratitude.[91] Here one may want to take issue with my conceptual analysis of the gift of mercy, since, on the one hand, it is as a generous, gratuitous gift, but on the other hand, it grounds the recipient's duty to reciprocate with gratitude. This duty of gratitude would seem, my objectors would argue, to rob the essential quality of gratuitous generosity from the gift of mercy. Given (i) the debt that originates from the giver's expectation to receive something in return, as French philosopher Jacques Derrida emphasizes,[92] and (ii) the moral obligation to repay, embedded in gift-giving practices, as French sociologist and anthropologist Marcel Mauss points out.[93] There seems to be no gratuitous generosity after all, if the giver has an expectation to receive something in return and the receiver has a moral obligation to repay the gift received. Also, this dynamic would suggest, yet again, an imbalance or asymmetry of power between the giver and receiver of the gift, as French anthropologist Didier Fassin underlines,[94] reinforcing objection 2 above on the vertical, top–down quality of mercy.

The French trio Mauss, Derrida, and Fassin seem to be framing their conception of gift and gratitude within the conventional view of bi-directional reciprocity. Their reasoning reflects what yet another French theorist, Paul Ricœur, has called "the logic of equivalence,"[95] where one gives in a calculated manner, in order to gain something with a comparable utility in return.[96] As discussed in Section 1, within this logic of equivalence, the act of giving is ultimately a self-interested (rather than disinterested), calculated (rather than uncalculated) transaction, but equivalence is not the only available framework to conceptualize the rationale of gift and gratitude. An alternative way is what Ricœur himself called "the logic of superabundance", which I have used to guide the conceptual analysis of mercy put forth in Section 1. The main difference between these two frameworks is that, within the logic of superabundance, one does not give in order to gain something; rather, one gives chiefly because one has first received; to "pay-it-forward," so to speak. Sure, the generous giver may expect

---

[89] Ibid.
[90] Perfect duties correlate to rights that can be claimed. Imperfect duties have no correlative rights. O'Neill, "Faces of Hunger," p. 101; O'Neill, *Constructions of Reasons*, pp. 191, 224.
[91] The themes of gift and gratitude have been explored extensively by theorists as diverse as Seneca, Marcel Mauss, Jacques Derrida, and Jean-Luc Marion.
[92] Derrida, *Donner le temps*.
[93] Mauss, *Essai sur le don*, pp. 30–186.
[94] Fassin, *Humanitarian*, p. 3.
[95] Paul Ricœur, "Love and Justice," p. 34.
[96] Benedict XVI, Caritas in Veritate, para. 39.

that their gift be received gracefully. But this expectation of graceful receiving is not their primary reason for giving generously (they are generally detached or even indifferent about whether any act of thanksgiving will follow). The generous giver's primary motivation does not lie in the expectation of receiving commensurable, proportionate gratitude in return for their generosity. Instead, it lies in giving generously in gratitude for the generosity that they themselves had previously received from others in their life. It is this logic of superabundance that generates a multidirectional web of "uncalculated giving and graceful receiving."[97] Importantly, within the logic of equivalence, gratitude is reduced to a mere commodity of exchange, but within the logic of superabundance, gratitude is an invitation to acknowledge our dependence on others[98] and to deepen our relationships (interpersonal and institutional relationships alike, as I will explain next).

Here one may want to revive the question about those who have never experienced generosity and live in misery, having never felt the joys of gift receiving. True, if one has never experienced the logic of superabundance, it is highly probable that one will live by the logic of equivalence: one might extend some level of forgiveness but it is likely self-interested and calculated. Still, one is always capable, through their moral agency, of choosing to extend mercy that is truly motivated by gratuitous generosity. At a minimal, one might be sufficiently self-aware of one's own fallibilities, being therefore more capable of empathetically understanding[99] their wrongdoer and therefore of choosing to extend them forgiveness (because in spite of having never received any forgiveness themselves before, they would have wanted it).[100]

One might want to insist, however, that the logic of equivalence is too pervasive, leaving no room for the gratuitous generosity of mercy. True, the utilitarian logic of market transactions and calculations is widespread, including in clinical settings, healthcare policies, and in the context of global health institutions. While I do not believe that the logic of equivalence, though common, is necessarily the norm everywhere, even if it were, the logic of equivalence would still not render gratitude completely trivial. Even if one sees gratitude as a mere ceremonial obligation to reciprocate a benefit received in a proper manner according to custom, such performative[101] gratitude can still, I think, help forge

---

[97] MacIntyre, *Dependent Rational Animals*, p. 121.
[98] MacIntyre, *Dependent Rational Animals*, p. 127.
[99] On the concept of empathy, as the second step of compassion, see Ch. 2.
[100] I thank Lauren Woodside Alegre for making this point clear.
[101] On the concept of performativity that emphasizes the political aspect of performance and exercise of power, see, e.g., the work of philosophers Judith Butler ("Performative Acts and Gender Constitutions") and Jacques Derrida ("Performative Powerlessness," pp. 466–67). On how the law and legal discourses are inherently performative and its normativity, rationality, and universality are a mere façade, see: Allow, *Law and Resistance*, Ch. 3.

interpersonal relationships of generosity, and encourage, albeit in limited ways, an institutional culture of grace. The key point that I want to make is that even if gratitude is not wholly gratuitous or authentic because it is just perfunctory, it still has a place in helping to deepen and shape interpersonal relationships based on generosity and grace, and in so doing it fosters a culture of graceful receiving that calls institutions to design spaces and policies that nurture the logic of superabundance, albeit imperfectly.[102]

The logic of superabundance on which the full process of giving and receiving mercy is grounded is a powerful tool for reimagining GHG and reforming its institutions. The importance of forgiveness and gratitude for GHG lies in the fact that mercy gives global health stakeholders the chance to have a fresh start and move forward with a renewed sense of belonging to a common project of service to the common good. A robust theory of mercy produces the hope that the current state of international affairs need not continue to perpetuate animosity, divisiveness, and suspicion. Instead, global health stakeholders can choose to restore peace, unity, and trust, and present to the next generation a new way of doing things in global health. As mentioned in Section 1, through mercy, a cultural shift can be initiated toward restored peace, unity, and greater trust. These are the products of mercy that can also help us reimagine a GHG based on love, GHG not centered on blaming and shaming, but instead focused on building a culture of belonging and true service to the common good, where there is cooperation without domination in respecting the agency and freedom of all members of the global health community. This is a feasible goal, as Section 3 will show by applying my account of mercy to the interactional and institutional dynamics of global health. (The theme of an international cooperation that respects the agency and freedom of local communities will also be further discussed in Chapters 4 and 5).

Section 3. Application to GHG: Mercy-based Decoloniality

I have thus far argued for a theoretical account of mercy, responded to its main objections, and I now proceed to apply such account to the relationships that unfold within global health institutions. My examination focuses on the relationships between givers and receivers of global health developmental aid, particularly in a context of epistemic injustice, a wrong that has plagued global health institutions since their inception. The example of epistemic injustice explains the need for mercy in global health by clearly illustrating the

---

[102] I thank Lauren Woodside Alegre for making this point clear.

interpersonal and institutional circumstances that lead to wrongdoing and brokenness in the relations between Global South and North.

3.1. Coloniality and Epistemic Injustice in Global Health

Anthropologists João Biehl and Adriana Petrina and legal scholar Matiangai Sirleaf discuss the colonial origins of global health and its ongoing implications.[103] They argue that global health has its roots in colonial practices, where Western powers imposed their biomedical models and systems on colonized regions, often disregarding local knowledge and practices. This history has shaped contemporary global health practices and policies, perpetuating power imbalances and epistemic injustice.

Epistemic injustice occurs when the knowledge and perspectives of local, marginalized communities are disregarded in processes involving global health institutions.[104] Epistemic injustice is rooted in the dominance of Western knowledge systems in global health. This dominance marginalizes other ways of knowing and understanding health, healthcare, and public health, often ignoring the local context and lived experiences of communities. The colonial roots of epistemic injustice in global health stem from this power imbalance in knowledge production, use, and circulation, where dominant actors, often from high-income countries and their academic institutions, exert control over what is considered legitimate knowledge, while the voices and knowledge of marginalized communities are sidelined.[105]

This colonial history of global health explains the present call to decolonize global health institutions. To recognize and incorporate Global South epistemologies, including indigenous and local knowledge systems, philosopher Caesar Alimsinya Atuire emphasizes the need to center on the recognition of diverse forms of knowledge and local agency.[106] Atuire defines the specific moral wrong of colonialism as the subtraction of the agency of communities and peoples, where their agency is removed in the service of the interests of colonizers.[107] While the colonial era is over, coloniality nevertheless persists. Coloniality, for Atuire, is the *modus operandi* that perpetuates the injustices of colonialism—even in the absence of evident colonizers. Coloniality therefore perpetuates the

---

[103] See, e.g., Biehl and Petryna, "A Critical Global Health," pp. 1–20; Biehl, "Theorizing Global Health," p. 128; Sirleaf, "White Health."
[104] Chung, "Structural Health Vulnerability," p. 205.
[105] Bhakuni and Abimbola, "Epistemic Injustice in Academic Global Health," pp. 465–70.
[106] Atuire, "Some Barriers to Knowledge," p. 335.
[107] Ibid.

power imbalance between center and periphery, which has been coupled with a lingering sense of superiority and inferiority.

Furthermore, Atuire critically analyses the global health developmental aid system, centered on the mere provision of multiple capacity-building initiates that are not *attentive* to actual local needs. In other words, these initiatives are implemented without a critical and careful consideration of local communities' needs and capacities (see also Chapter 5 on this matter). As Atuire puts it, these initiatives imbed coloniality and epistemic injustice "by acritically transferring Global Northern knowledge systems and epistemologies to the Global South."[108] As a consequence, capacity-building initiatives typically reinforce the colonial narrative that the periphery needs assistance to develop, and that the Global North knows best how to solve the peripheries' lack of progress. Within this narrative, Global North institutions bringing capacity-building initiatives to the peripheries are typically portrayed as heroes who can efficiently save the margins from their poverty.

But this narrative of the "altruistic heroes" of the Global North has been challenged. It has been revealed that the existing global health developmental aid system is chiefly driven by the agenda of donors, normally located in the Global North (see also Chapter 5 on this discussion).[109] It has been argued that these donors are committed primarily to advancing their agendas, rather than understanding, responding to, and meeting the actual needs of the people in the Global South who they should be serving and assisting.[110] It has been also shown that donors, including research funders who have a central position in the process of global health knowledge production, often dismiss Global South's expertise or undermine local agencies, questioning their academic credibility and marginalizing their interpretation simply because their methods and epistemic focus are different from those classically used and favored by Global North institutions.[111] For example, the Global North scientific perspective characteristically focuses on filling a knowledge gap in the global literature (where global literature means scientific papers published in English, and acknowledged as published in top journals ranked by Global North institutions according to their standards and methods).[112] But the Global South scientific perspective usually focuses instead on examining and making sense of a situation and thinking about how to change social institutions.[113] The emphasis is not in finding a

---

[108] Ibid.
[109] Ruger, "Global Health Governance," pp. 653–61; Gostin and Mok, "Innovative Solutions," pp. 451–58. Koum Besson, "How to Identify Epistemic."
[110] Ibid.
[111] Abimbola. "The Uses of Knowledge in Global Health"; Koum Besson, "How to Identify Epistemic."
[112] Ibid.
[113] Ibid.

lacuna within an anglophone debate and dialoging with a few English-speaking interlocutors in the Global North about a knowledge gap. Global South's focus and methods are different and consequently dismissed.[114] Not only are their distinct forms of knowledge ignored, but in doing so their agency is also removed.[115]

3.2. Mercy-based Decoloniality as an Alternative

If epistemic injustice subtracts the self-determining agency of individuals and local communities, by questioning the credibility of their local knowledge and devaluing their experiences, there is a need to decolonize global health knowledge systems. What I want to suggest is that the moral value of mercy (*in tandem* and not in opposition to justice) offers a direct response to coloniality in general and to epistemic injustice in particular, primarily by restoring the agency of the victims of epistemic injustice, and empowering them to move forward in brave forgiveness.

Again, mercy does not mean condoning bad behavior, forgetting the harm, or pretending that no injustice occurred by,[116] "ignoring what has been done or putting a false label on an evil act", as Dr. Martin Luther King puts it.[117] As an act of the will, mercy empowers the victim of an injustice: in choosing forgiveness and bestowing it upon their perpetrator, the merciful agent frees not only the offender but also themselves from a weak sense of agency and self-worth that inevitably accompanies the identity of victim. Forgiveness respects the agency (and responsibility) of the offender and retains the victim's self-respect. One outcome of forgiveness is a merciful agent, with a restored and empowered agency—empowered by the agent's renewed sense of self-worth as a resilient person or institution, able to make the difficult choice to love their enemy.

Sure, the restoration of the agency of the victims of epistemic injustice, though crucial, is not itself sufficient to sustain a whole decoloniality approach to global health knowledge production. The decolonization of global health knowledge systems necessitates at least two main changes: (i) that diverse knowledge sources, including indigenous and local knowledge, would be valued and recognized, and (ii) that decision-making for global health policies and practices would be shared, meaning being inclusive by giving greater weight to the voice of local communities as equal partners in shaping global health interventions.[118]

---

[114] Ibid.
[115] Atuire, "Some Barriers to Knowledge," p. 335.
[116] VanderWeele. "Is Forgiveness a Public Health Issue?" pp. 189–90; Worthington, *Forgiveness and Reconciliation*; Enright and Fitzgibbons, *Helping Clients Forgive*; Holmgren, "Forgiveness," pp. 341–52.
[117] King, *A Gift of Love—Sermons from Strength to Love and Other Preachings*, p. 45.
[118] Atuire, "Some Barriers to Knowledge," p. 335.

While extending forgiveness alone may not automatically lead to these changes, the full process of mercy (forgiving, recognizing wrong-doing, and accepting forgiveness) is the necessary groundwork to a sustainable decolonial approach to global health knowledge systems.

The full recognition of the unique value of local knowledge and local voices depends on two conditions. First, it depends on the repentance of the perpetrators of epistemic injustice, who would then acknowledge their harmful error and more attentively listen to Global South's contributions at the negotiation table. Second, it depends on the Global South's restored willingness to contribute to the discernment processes about global health interventions. This restored willingness to contribute depends on the trust that their knowledge and voice will now be considered credible and will not be ignored again. No doubt this trust vulnerably exposes Global South actors. And it is precisely because of this vulnerability that the recognition of the unique value of local knowledge and local voices also depends on Global South's restored agency, which empowers their confidence in their contribution. For this greater trust to be reached, the complete cycle of mercy must occur through a process of giving and accepting mercy. Mercy offers a dynamic process of repentance and forgiveness that can ensue an institutional framework for meaningful inclusiveness, belonging, and true service. Mercy replaces the preexisting framework of accusation, shaming, and blaming, which is incompatible with a culture of genuine diversity, equity, and inclusion that goes beyond empty rhetoric, and that is so crucial in healthcare and global health settings.

There are certainly different ways to achieve the goal of decoloniality, but the foundational importance of a mercy-based decoloniality remains, especially when it comes to mercy's implications for the victim of epistemic injustice. Victims are always faced with a decision to move forward either with anger and resentment, or with forgiveness and resilience. In the former, victims are also choosing to continue to define themselves as victims; their identity is defined in relation to the perpetrator who has offended and wounded them. In the latter, victims are deciding to not define themselves primarily as victims. While the injustice they suffered may never be forgotten, and while wounds must be acknowledged, honored, and respected, the identity of the merciful is defined by their (brave) choice to forgive, coupled with their restored agency in making such choice, and their resilience emerging out of this vulnerable process.

In choosing to not define themselves primarily as victims, the Global South is restoring their agency in taking responsibility for how their lives can unfold in a different way. As bell hooks puts it in *All About Love*, "Taking responsibility does not mean that we deny the reality of institutionalized injustice . . . but we can choose how we respond to acts of injustice. Taking responsibility means that in the face of barriers we still have the capacity to invent our lives, to shape our destinies in ways that maximize our well-being."[119]

The identity of the merciful is not defined as the victim of a past injustice, because the merciful agent liberates the offender and themselves from their past,[120] and offers a new way forward. There is hope—for oneself and for others. This decision matters not only privately to the victim alone but also publicly because it impacts how we all are collectively deciding to shape the environment and culture around us. And this impacts how we come to think of and design the kinds of institutions we are building presently and will be leaving for future generations.

This is not to imply that only the victims of epistemic injustice carry all the burden of shaping better global health institutions. The responsibility is obviously not only on the shoulders of the Global South. The Global North, as the perpetrators of coloniality, have an important role to play in the full process of mercy, in acknowledging the wrongdoing of epistemic injustices and in asking for forgiveness. It is only by the Global North's sincere repentance that both Global North and South can be given a fresh start and an opportunity to move closer to the reconciliation that would permit them to work together, in authentic international cooperation, and toward a true global solidarity among nations (on this topic, see Chapter 4).

To be sure, it is only human to face the great temptation to cling to anger toward our enemies, to feed ruminations of what happened that imprison us in our own negative thoughts. This is a real obstacle for Global South and North as we move closer to each other with greater (yet prudent) trust that a fresh start for GHG is possible. But when if we don't turn toward our enemy because we are too trapped in our ruminations and too fearful of a possible mistake in trusting someone who wronged us in the past, or because we are unwilling to make ourselves vulnerable as we admit our wrong doing, we also accept that life happens at us, as if we had no agency and no freedom. The power to choose forgiveness and repentance, and to take authorship of a different plot for the future of global health is nevertheless also available. The very difficult choice of mercy, forgiveness, and repentance is one that requires a greater moral strength than the instinctive (easier) choice to remain in anger, resentment, and vengeance. Yet, the path toward the restoration of the authorial voice of all global health actors is available to Global South and north alike. In this respect, forgiveness and repentance are available, enabling tools for decoloniality, that both Global North and Global South can use to take the first, courageous step toward designing a different GHG for the future, one that is grounded in mercy (without forgetting justice).

---

[119] bell hooks, *All About Love*, p. 57.
[120] Nouwen, *Bread for the Journey*, p. 48.

One may still be skeptical of the merciful account of decoloniality that I propose. The fear of the skeptic is that the path of forgiveness and meekness will only generate more epistemic injustice within global health institutions. The path of anger, resentment, and vengeance may feel not only more just but also more reasonable and less vulnerable.[121] There is certainly a place for righteous anger that calls for justice; but mercy also gives us an invitation to move beyond the just option and to have the chance of a fresh start—without being imprudent and trusting unreasonably the untrustworthy. Strengthening relationships by helping people overcome trauma, and reforming institutions by helping communities rebuild after terrible atrocities, are reasonable goals with which most global health actors would agree. In giving global health actors an opportunity to set the stage for something new, mercy provides the necessary tools for us to move forward with the hope that attaining these goals is a real possibility. It might be indeed less vulnerable to remain in the path of anger, resentment, and vengeance, since mercy depends on the mutual vulnerability of the receiver and of the giver of forgiveness. But is it indeed more just and reasonable to remain stuck in fear? In perpetuating the identity of the victim as a victim, the path of anger, resentment, and vengeance blocks the restoration of trust necessary for forming a different more just future.

Of course, to unreasonably trust the untrustworthy is imprudent (see Chapter 6). As discussed in Section 1, mercy does not mean wrong doing is accepted, so this is not about inviting formerly colonized communities, victims of epistemic injustice, to be blindly open to any form of development aid, capacity building, and technology transfer without critically and carefully considering what these would entail. This would be unreasonable because this would expose them to the same injustices of the past. Yet, what mercy teaches us, for example, is that, in forgiving, we from the Global South can be open again to trust—within reason—a form of technology transfer that honors our local knowledge and uses our indigenous wisdom and experience to make adequate decisions for the good of our local communities. This would entail, for example, Global South's scientists critically engaging in the debate with their Global North peers about what to do during a public health emergency of international concern, confidently arguing for their view, and self-assured that their reasoning and unique knowledge are equally relevant for determining the best course of action for the common good. This would in turn necessitate the Global North acknowledging the harmful error they made in the past and correcting it by humbly inviting their Global South peers not only to sit at the decision-making table, but also by giving them a prominent seat where their voices and contributions can be

---

[121] For a critical view of merciful love in the context of racism in the United States, see, e.g., Criss and Asmelash, "The Problem with Always Asking Black People to Forgive."

attentively listened to and carefully considered by all.[122] This loving attention to Global South partners is also the difference between an empty rhetoric of diversity, equity, and inclusion, on the one hand, and the framework of meaningful inclusiveness, on the other (see Chapter 5). The former is a mere check box exercise of simply inviting the marginalized to have access to and sit at the table and then (perhaps even grudgingly) obey some formulaic rules on how to be inclusive. Access is a question of justice, but it does not suffice for healing wounds. The framework offered by merciful love goes beyond access and justice, and it is within this framework of merciful love that shared authority in decision-making, grounded in epistemic justice, and the co-creation of a new future can exist (see further discussion of shared authority and co-creation as important elements of belonging in Chapters 3 and 6).

Mercy allows the Global South and North to enter into each other's peaceful co-existence, sharing their vulnerable presence, growing in trust and closer to the possibility of reconciling and finding a way to work together in cooperation as a team toward a common goal that also upholds the global common good (see Chapter 4 on the principle of solidarity and international cooperation). In other words, mercy in the space of GHG opens the door for international cooperation in solidarity and restored friendship. For example, mercy in GHG might look like Global North and South institutions having to discuss and come to agreement in each other's presence how to define what expertise and scientific evidence should or shouldn't mean considering the plurality of knowledge production systems.[123] The upshot of such interactions moves toward reconciliation and mutual cooperation toward a shared goal because both sides would be building reciprocal trust through the process. The Global South would have to trust that their system would be considered rather than automatically discredited (while not having the certainty it would be necessarily and completely adopted); the Global North would have to recognize and trust that "shared authority in decision making" is the only way forward and that the distinctive way the other authority (the Global South), defines expertise and scientific evidence is a necessary perspective for achieving the common goal.

Only an agent is free enough to trust: the moral agent dares to trust in a reasonable—not unreasonable—manner. Mercy restores agency and can restore such (reasonable) trust, indispensable for an inclusive, effective, and equitable GHG. The current structure of global health clearly lacks in trust and abounds in fearful, self-protective, self-centered behaviors. Examples here range from nationalistic policies of hoarding scarce global health goods necessary for

---

[122] Martins, "Theological Bioethics and Public Health," p. 241; Martins "A escuta como método e os pobres/oprimidos como sujeitos," pp. 270–91.
[123] Mormina, "Knowledge, Expertise and Science," pp. 671–85.

addressing global health threats (see Chapter 4), to relying exclusively on a epistemically narrow way of conceptualizing evidence-based policies that follows a groupthink, monolithic culture of expertise from the Global North, closed to diverse systems of knowledge production from the Global South (see Chapter 6).[124] These were evident during the COVID-19 pandemic, when certain countries in the Global North stored vaccines and other resources necessary to control the spread of the virus (see Chapter 4 for further discussion on vaccine allocation), and where the "follow the science" approach to public health policy was determined by "the views of a relatively small—and arguably homogeneous—group of largely insider advisors" (see Chapter 6 on a critique of the "follow the science" approach).[125] These kinds of behaviors thwart global solidarity and international coordination, ruining global health policies and institutions as they become paralyzed by the lack of cooperation of the members of the international community. While the path of anger, resentment, and vengeance may feel more familiar, it seems to lead to the equally familiar place of distrust, fear, and ineffective GHG.

The path of mercy, forgiveness, and repentance is certainly the one less traveled by, and that perhaps can make all the difference for the restoration of trust and the re-weaving of the unitive fabric of the international community.[126] Mercy would invite Global South actors to forgive the fearful, self-protective, self-centered behaviors that have led to both hoarding resources and epistemic injustice. Mercy would invite Global North actors to repent, by being open not only to share scarce resources following the logic of abundance but also to have their narrow definitions of "expertise" and "scientific evidence" challenged by the diversity requirements of epistemic justice. Mercy opens the door to reconciliation, where both Global South and North could perhaps work together on creating and implementing a new system of global allocation of scarce healthcare resources that fully embraces the shared authority in decision-making that epistemic democracy necessitates.[127]

Conclusion

This chapter defined mercy as a type of love relevant to GHG, focusing on a narrower definition of mercy as forgiveness. It examined mercy's characteristics

---

[124] Ibid.
[125] Mormina, "Knowledge, Expertise and Science," p. 672. See also: Carney, "The UK Government's COVID-19 Policy."
[126] Frost, *The Road Not Taken*.
[127] On epistemic democracy, see: Mormina, "Knowledge, Expertise and Science," pp. 671–85. See also: Anderson, "Epistemic Justice," pp. 163–73.

and its application to global health, arguing that mercy is a decisional process rooted in mutual vulnerability. This involves both the vulnerability of the giver, who risks ridicule for forgiving their undeserving perpetrator, and the vulnerability of the receiver, who depends on forgiveness to be freed from culpability.

Mercy's core feature is this reciprocal gift-of-self. It benefits the receiver but also the giver, as mercy empowers the victim to restore her agency by deciding to make herself vulnerably present to her enemy. While the process of mercy begins with forgiveness, it is only complete when that forgiveness is accepted, creating a peaceful, mutual *presence*. The upshot is the restoration of unity within a community, healing broken relationships and the communal fabric, even if full reconciliation (restoration of companionship) is not achieved.

The chapter responded to objections to this account of mercy and applied the concept to relationships within global health institutions, particularly addressing epistemic injustice caused by coloniality. Mercy, by restoring the agency of victims, directly counters the agency-limiting effects of coloniality in developmental aid contexts. The idea of love as a decisional process through which one makes oneself vulnerably present as a gift of self to another to restore unity in community was introduced here and will be further developed in subsequent chapters. In addition, the theme of trust introduced in this chapter will be explored further in Chapter 6.

2
On Compassion

> If by your art, my dearest father, you have
> Put the wild waters in this roar, allay them.
> The sky, it seems, would pour down stinking pitch,
> But that the sea, mounting to th' welkin's check,
> Dashes the fire out. O, I have suffer'd
> With those that I saw suffer: a brave vessel
> Who had, no doubt, some noble creature in her
> Dashed all to pieces. O, the cry did knock
> Against my very heart! Poor souls, they perished.
> Had I been any god of power, I would
> Have sunk the sea within the earth or ere
> It should the good ship so have swallowed and
> The fraughting souls within her.
>
> Miranda, in Shakespeare's *The Tempest*,
> Act I, scene ii, lines 1–13

> The direful spectacle of the wreck,
> Which touch'd
> The very virtue of compassion in thee
>
> Prospero, in Shakespeare's *The Tempest*,
> Act I, scene ii, lines 27–29

Introduction

In Shakespeare's *The Tempest*, Miranda and her father Prospero, a sorcerer, witness a shipwreck near the island where they live. Upon watching and listening to the great distress of those on board, Miranda immediately feels sympathy for the sailors' anguish. She vividly imagines and thoroughly appreciates their misery. She is then moved by "the very virtue of compassion" in her, as Prospero points out: as she suffers with those sailors in distress, she *effectively chooses* to act, by pleading with her father to stop the storm with their magical powers.

The Rule of Love. Thana C. de Campos-Rudinsky, Oxford University Press. © Oxford University Press 2026.
DOI: 10.1093/9780197762400.003.0003

Feeling sympathy, imagining and appreciating someone's suffering, and then effectively choosing a compassionate course of action are the three stages of the virtue of compassion, or so I shall argue. The first stage of compassion is affective. Call it sympathy (from the Greek *sumpatheia*, *sun* "with," and *pathos* "feeling"). Sympathy is the feeling that is stirred in Miranda, as she sees and listens to the misery of those sailors. The second stage of compassion is intellectual: Miranda vividly imagines and thoroughly appreciates the suffering of the sailors. I call this second stage empathy. The final step of compassion is effective: it leads to a conduct of care. Miranda, for example, chooses to plead with her father to stop the storm. In her judgment, this was the best course of action she could take to love and practically care for those dying men offshore. The effective component of compassion is predicated on a discernment about how to effectively care for the other. I call this third stage compassionate care, where care is the practical, outward expression of compassionate love.[1]

This chapter is laid out in the following manner: I first present my overall conceptual argument that we should conceive of compassion as the three-stage process described above (Section 1). Then I examine in detail each of these three stages, responding to its main objections. In doing so, I put forth my normative argument that the distinctive feature of compassion is the sharing of suffering with another, and that to share in that suffering means to be present (Sections 2–4).[2] My examination of each stage includes an analysis of how each stage is applicable to the relationships that unfold within institutions of GHG. I show why the goal of institutions of healthcare and GHG should be to create communities of mutual care based on friendship and solidarity: the upshots of the applying compassion to healthcare.

Section 1. The concept of compassion and its three stages

Before putting forth a concept of the virtue of compassion as a three-stage process, I should first clarify the terminology I use. I begin here by differentiating compassion to other, similar concepts (namely, mercy and pity), and then by relating compassion to other, similar concepts (namely, sympathy and empathy). There is a general confusion in the usage of all of these terms, which are often employed interchangeably with compassion. The purpose of this first section

---

[1] On the centrality of giving care effectively in practice, see: Herring, *Law and the Relational Self*, p. 51; Lynch, "Love Labour as a Distinct and Non-Commodifiable Form of Care Labour," p. 55.
[2] I define suffering as "a disruption of flourishing that arises when love or justice is violated or absent—and that calls for a communal response" in de Campos-Rudinsky "Flourishing Through Suffering." On medical suffering, see also, e.g., Tate and Pearlman, "What We Mean When We Talk About Suffering"; Tate, "Objective Suffering."

therefore is conceptual clarity in building a common vocabulary of what I mean and do not mean by compassion.

1.1. Differentiating Compassion, Mercy, and Pity

1.1.1. Compassion vs. Mercy

As discussed in Chapter 1, the chief objection to Portia's account of mercy is that it is a top-down, hierarchical, and monarchical concept, which lacks, as philosopher Martha Nusbaum argues, sympathy and empathetic imagination.[3] This chapter continues my reply to Nusbaum, by discussing and defining compassion, predicated on sympathy and empathetic imagination, by way of comparison with mercy.

First, both mercy and compassion are generally conceived as choices made for the benefit of someone who suffers. But mercy and compassion have different applications. As defined in Chapter 1, the narrower case of mercy applies to suffering that can be remedied by forgiveness. The parlance of mercy as forgiveness is more prevalent in the context of law and policy, and especially in the context of criminal justice (as illustrated by Portia's soliloquy in the courtroom discussed in Chapter 1). So, the term mercy is mostly employed, as Nussbaum points out, in a context of suffering that results from bad personal choices leading to culpability, blame, and guilt.[4] Mercy in a nutshell is the type of love that is directed to our enemies, to whom we bestow our forgiveness for their wrongs against us. Compassion, on the other hand, is characteristically the type of love that applies to the suffering resulting from bad luck, chance, and external circumstances—with no fault of the agent—like a shipwreck caused by a tempest, for example. Compassion therefore typically applies to "the suffering that was not caused primarily by the person's own culpable actions."[5] Compassion in this sense is broader than mercy: it is the type of love directed to the other, who suffers, whether such sufferer is enemy or a friend, whether they are complete strangers or someone I know, whether they are someone near or far. Call them "the neighbor." Indeed, the etymology of compassion is the Latin *com-pati*, where *com* means with, and *pati* means to suffer. Compassion then literately means suffering together, and from that togetherness friendship and solidarity unfold, as I will further explain later in this chapter.

Second, mercy and forgiveness are terminologies characteristic of criminal retributive justice, and have only more recently been employed in the contexts of illness, healthcare institutions, and public health structural reforms, as well as GHG, as discussed in Chapter 1. In contrast, we find the terminology of

---

[3] Nussbaum, "If You Could See This," p. 232.
[4] Nussbaum, *Compassion*, p. 31.
[5] Ibid.

compassion abounding in most health-related contexts. It is plentifully used to discuss questions from adequate clinical responses to illnesses in general, as well as adequate structural reforms of healthcare institutions, and satisfactory public health policy changes. Though compassion is not so regularly discussed in the context of global health institutions,[6] this chapter shows that compassion is also relevant to inform discussions on structural reforms at the level of GHG, where stakeholders are faced with the decision to either share in the suffering of the receivers of global health aid or walk away.

Third, though different in application, mercy and compassion have some of the same qualities. It is largely agreed that compassion, like mercy, is an act of the will: a commitment and choice to relieve the suffering of the other.[7] While mercy and compassion share the chief purpose of alleviating the suffering of the other, what is distinct about compassion is that it is a choice and commitment to share in the experience of suffering, for the good of the sufferer—where to share means to be present with the sufferer. Similarly, both mercy and compassion are best appreciated as a process that produces a gift of self. Here gift of self means primarily to be present with another. What this presence requires and entails in each process is different, though. In the case of merciful love, the gift of self through forgiveness restores unity in a broken community. In the case of compassionate love, the gift of self through sharing in the suffering of another builds friendship and solidarity within the community.

1.1.2. Compassion vs. Pity

Several scholars, when conceptualizing compassion, make the distinction between compassion and pity.[8] Pity is an emotion, marked by an asymmetry of

---

[6] Important exceptions include David Addiss, director and founder of The Task Force's Focus Area for Compassion and Ethics (see, e.g., Harrel et al., "Compassionate Leadership," pp. 1450–52) and Liz Grant, director of the Global Compassion Initiative at the University of Edinburgh. See, e.g., Grant et al., "A Compassion Narrative"; Shams Syed, "Unit Head of Quality of Care for the World Health Organizations on Compassion: An Engine for Quality Primary Care"; and WHO, "Compassion and Primary Healthcare."

[7] An important exception is philosopher Martha Nussbaum, who considers compassion (and love in general) an emotion. She defines compassion as "the painful emotion occasioned by the awareness of another person's undeserved misfortune." See Nussbaum, *Upheavals of Thought*, p. 301; Nussbaum, "Compassion: The Basic Social Emotion," pp. 27–41. In contrast, specialists in the science of compassion define it as a process encompassing not only an affective component but also a commitment that leads to a caring action. See, e.g., Herring, "Compassion, Ethics of Care and Legal Rights," p. 159; Dewar et al., "Clarifying Misconceptions about Compassionate Care," pp. 1738–47; Brito-Pons and Librada-Flores, "Compassion in Palliative Care: A Review," pp. 472–79; Jinpa, *A Fearless Heart*; Jazaieri et al., pp. 23–35; Gilbert, "The Evolution and Social Dynamics of Compassion," pp. 239–54; Whitebrook, "Compassion as a Political Virtue," pp. 529–44.

[8] Most authors distinguish pity and compassion by highlighting the asymmetry of power that exists in the former, but not in the latter. (See: Herring, "Compassion, Ethics of Care and Legal Rights," p. 160; and Arendt, *On Revolution*, pp. 80–85; Margalit, *The Decent Society*, pp. 233–4.) The exception is Nussbaum. She uses "pity" and "compassion" interchangeably. As she puts it: "When I use the words 'pity' and 'compassion' I am really speaking about a single emotion." See Nussbaum, "Compassion," p. 29.

power and a vertical relationship: one person (e.g., the healthcare provider or the giver of global health aid) "looks down on the pitiable one"[9] (e.g., the patient or the receiver of global health aid). Pity therefore creates separation, rather than union. On the other hand, compassion, as legal scholar Jonathan Herring observes, "involves a coming-along and a recognition of fellow-humanity, rather than condescending assessment of another."[10] Herring defines compassion as the process of formation of caring relationships. He emphasizes the unitive aspect of compassion between equals. This equality is the key element that allows for the unitive feature of compassion and distinguishes compassion from pity (see discussion in Chapter 4 on equality of dignity and equity of care). Premised, therefore, on inequality of power and vulnerability between the parties, pity sets a gulf between them. But compassion is different as it establishes a horizontal relationship of friendship and solidarity in community. I will come back and develop this point later in this chapter.

1.2. Three Related Concepts in the Process of Compassion: From Sympathy, to Empathy, to Compassionate Conduct of Care

Different scholars explain the process of compassionate love in different ways. The main difference among scholars relates to the number of stages in the process that leads to a compassionate conduct of care. Geshe Thupten Jinpa, a Tibetan Buddhist philosopher and co-creator of the Stanford Compassion Cultivation Training (CCT), defines compassion as a four-step process, particularly useful in clinical settings to help healthcare professionals cope with extreme suffering. For Jinpa, compassion involves four key components[11]: (i) cognitive awareness of suffering, (ii) sympathetic concern (affective response to suffering), (iii) intention to alleviate suffering, and (iv) responsiveness or readiness to help (motivational component).

In this Buddhist approach, compassion unfolds through these four stages leading to an effective response to suffering. In the first, cognitive step, the agent sees and listens to the experience of suffering from the other. This capacity to see and listen depends on what Buddhists call mindfulness.[12] Awareness is the main

---

[9] Herring, "Compassion, Ethics of Care and Legal Rights," p. 160.
[10] Ibid.
[11] Jazaieri et al., "A Randomized Controlled Trial of Compassion Cultivation Training," p. 22. See also: Brito-Pons and Librada-Flores, "Compassion in Palliative Care: A Review," pp. 472–79.
[12] Brito-Pons and Librada-Flores, "Compassion in Palliative Care: A Review," pp. 475–76. Although the practice of mindfulness is typically associated with Buddhism, its concept is universal in that it transcends cultures and religions. In this respect, Psychologists Shauna Shapiro, Ronald Siegel, and Kristin D. Neff define mindfulness as the universal human capacity of awareness. See Shapiro, Siegel, and Neff, "Paradoxes of Mindfulness."

upshot of mindfulness.[13] Second, an emotional response arises, where sympathy is evoked by the other's suffering. Third, intention forms—the agent wills the alleviation of the suffering. Finally, the fourth step is a motivational one, where intention translates into action, responding to the suffering effectively. As the Dalai Lama emphasizes it: compassion is "not just a wish to see sentient beings free from suffering, but an immediate need to intervene and actively engage, to try to help."[14]

The Catholic philosopher Thomas Aquinas provides an analogous yet simpler explanation of this same intellectual process that produces an effective, compassionate response to suffering. Following the Aristotelian tradition, Aquinas defines compassion[15] as a virtue that is produced in a three-stage process: the first is affective and the last is effective. Aquinas explains that for compassion to be virtuous, there is a movement that needs to happen from the affective stage to the effective stage. The affective stage of compassion consists of the emotion of compassion (Aquinas calls emotions in general "passions"). The effective stage of compassion consists of the virtue of compassion, which causes an effect: a conduct of care.[16] To move from emotion (i.e., affective compassion) to virtue (i.e., effective compassion), Aquinas explains that there is an intermediate stage where intellectual judgment (i.e., practical reasoning) takes place.[17] In fact, Aquinas" first stage of compassion (affective compassion) could be better explained if it were to comprise Jinpa's steps 1 (cognitive step) and 2 (affective step). This is because an affective response can only occur after the agent sees and listens to the suffering of another and becomes aware (mindful) of it. Likewise, Aquinas' intermediate stage of compassion (intellectual judgment) seems to correlate with Jinpa's step 3 (intentional step), and Aquinas' final stage of compassion (effective compassion) seems to relate to Jinpa's step 4 (motivational step).

By and large, scholars from disciplines as diverse as psychology, theology, philosophy, law, and healthcare indeed agree that first, the agent of compassion feels an emotion (like sympathy); then, the agent intellectually processes this emotion; and this finally leads the agent to choose a compassionate conduct of care.[18] For simplicity's sake, I will build on Aquinas' three stages of compassion

---

[13] Shapiro, Siegel, and Neff, "Paradoxes of Mindfulness."
[14] Dalai Lama, "Dialogues," p. 225.
[15] Aquinas uses the words "compassion" and "mercy" interchangeably. See: *ST* ii-ii Q 30,1,1; Q30.2, and Supp 94,2.
[16] As Aquinas puts it: "in relation to their neighbor's defects, he should be compassionate in affect (*in affectu*) and provide help in effect (*in effectu*)," *ST* ii-ii Q45, a6, 3. See also: Miner, "The Difficulties of Mercy: Reading Thomas Aquinas on 'Misericordia,'" p. 74.
[17] Aquinas, *ST* ii-ii Q 30.3.
[18] See, e.g., Brito-Pons and Librada-Flores, "Compassion in Palliative Care: A Review," pp. 472–79. Sinclair, Hack, Raffin-Bouchal et al., "What are Healthcare Providers' Understandings and Experiences of Compassion?"; Sinclair, Norris, McConnell et al., "Compassion: A Scoping Review of the Healthcare Literature," p. 6.

(complemented by Jimpa's further explanations of their content) to argue that we should conceive of compassion as a three-stage process. My definition of compassion will build on additional philosophy, law, and healthcare scholarship to provide a definition of compassion that is nuanced enough to be applicable to relationships that unfold within institutions of healthcare and GHG.

For the purpose of clarity, I will call Aquinas' first (affective) stage of compassion sympathy. And the intellectual stage, where the transition from sympathy to compassionate care occurs, I will call empathy.[19] The final (effective) stage, I will call compassionate care.

Section 2. The Affective Stage of Compassion: The Feeling of Sympathy

Although compassion is not a mere emotion, its intellectual process is often triggered by an emotion like sympathy in relation to the suffering of another fellow human.[20] Adam Smith provides a classic definition of sympathy in *The Theory of Moral Sentiments*. He uses "sympathy" and "fellow-feeling" interchangeably, and makes the affective feature of sympathy clear: for him, sympathy is "fellow feeling with passion."[21]

Sympathy happens, for example, when an agent P encounters another agent S (call her the sufferer). To encounter here means not only to meet but also to attentively see, listen to, and become aware of S' suffering. S shares with P an experience of grief and distress. This triggers in P an affective response: P's sensory perception (caused by seeing and listening) generates an emotional reaction in her. Sympathy, therefore, is about the senses and the emotions that follow.

The encounter between P and S becomes P's source of fellow-feeling for S' grief and distress. This communication between P and S creates or strengthens a certain bond between them (of friendship and community) albeit incipient. Their bond is weak and provisional at this stage; the community that P and S

Sinclair, McClement, Raffin-Bouchal et al., "Compassion in Healthcare: An Empirical Model," pp. 193–203; Jazaieri et al., "A randomized Controlled Trial of Compassion Cultivation Training," pp. 23–35; Whitebrook, "Compassion as a Political Virtue," pp. 529–44; Herring, "Compassion, Ethics of Care and Legal Rights," pp. 158–71.

[19] Compassion researcher Shane Sinclair and colleagues also define compassion as a process with three ingredients, including sympathy and empathy. See also, e.g., Sinclair, Norris, McConnell et al., "Compassion: A Scoping Review of the Healthcare Literature," p. 2; Goetz, Keltner, Simon-Thomas, "Compassion: An Evolutionary Analysis and Empirical Review, pp. 351–74; Sinclair, Beamer, Hack et al., "Sympathy, Empathy and Compassion: Palliative Care Patients," pp. 437–47.

[20] For a discussion of compassion in both human and animal relationships, see Nussbaum, *Political Emotions*, Ch. 6.

[21] Smith, *The Theory of Moral Sentiments*, p. 15.

form together in this brief encounter is frail: their bond is conditional upon the duration of P's fleeting sentiment of sympathy. Sympathy is therefore a purely affective stage of compassion: at this early stage, there is no commitment, no act of the will, and no intention yet to effectively choose the good of the other and the amelioration of the other's suffering.[22]

2.1. Sympathy as Self-centered

One could object to my conception of sympathy here, and argue that it is contradictory. On the one hand, sympathy is a fellow-feeling, which means that it is other-directed: P is sympathetic toward the sufferer S. On the other hand, since sympathy is a mere feeling, it is also self-directed: sympathy actually keeps P in the confines of their own fellow-feeling, imprisoned within herself, within how P feels inside. Sympathy, in this sense, is self-centered.[23] But is it not contradictory to say that P's sympathy is both other-directed and self-centered? If the emotion of sympathy is aroused by the suffering of another, then how could sympathy be a self-centered feeling?

In *Love and Responsibility*, phenomenologist philosopher and theologian Karol Wojtyla argues that sympathy is a self-centered emotion due to its subjective nature,[24] as it "exhibits a tendency to divert the subject's attention from the object [the sufferer] and to concentrate exclusively on himself."[25] For example, at the encounter of P and S, when they communicate and P's affective response is triggered, P's attention at that point switches from S to P herself: upon perceiving what it is like to go through S' experience, P starts focusing on how they should feel in that situation. Sympathy is self-centered and subjective because the fellow-feeling is an inward affective response formed by P's own senses in P's own body: sympathy is not outwardly shared with the other.[26] On the contrary, sympathy remains imprisoned within P. Although P's affective reaction was stirred by the sufferer's situation, the fellow-feeling that P feels toward S actually diverts P's attention from the sufferer S to P's inner self and senses.

---

[22] Wojtyla, *Love and Responsibility* (Ignatius, 1981), p. 89.
[23] Anderson and Granados, *Called to Love: Approaching John Paul II's Theology of the Body*, p. 54.
[24] On the subjective quality of sympathy, see also: Post, Ng, Fischel et al., "Routine, Empathic and Compassionate Patient Care," pp. 872–90. For the idea of sympathy as an emotional reaction toward the suffering of another, see, e.g., Sinclair, Norris, McConnell et al., "Compassion: A Scoping Review of the Healthcare Literature."
[25] Wojtyla, *Love and Responsibility*, p. 91.
[26] In contrast, Stephen Darwall argues that sympathy (unlike empathy) is other-directed and adopts the third-person perspective of a caregiver. As Darwall puts it: "sympathy for a person and her plight is felt as from the third-person perspective of one-caring, whereas empathy involves something like a sharing of the other's mental states, frequently, as from her standpoint. This is different from caring about her, even imaginatively. See Darwall, "Empathy, Sympathy, Care," pp. 263–64.

Smith makes a similar point and, like Wojtyla, emphasizes the self-centered character of sympathy:

> As we have no immediate experience of what other men feel, we can form no idea of the manner in which they are affected, but by conceiving what *we ourselves should feel in the like situation*... it is by the imagination only that we can form any conception of what are their sensations. It is the impression of *our own senses only*, not those of their, which our imaginations copy.[27] (*Emphasis added*).

Smith's account of sympathy, like Wojtyla's, emphasizes the subjective perspective of the agent's own impression of their own senses only, not of the feelings and senses of the other. The agent, Smith explains, simply mimics the feelings and senses that the other experiences. Now, here one could raise another, related objection to the concept of sympathy: if sympathy is about a self-centered experience of mimicking what the other feels, as Smith describes it, then sympathy is likely to lead to the problem of emotional contagion (i.e., an emotional convergence among individuals, through an automatic mimicry or spontaneous adoption of the emotional state of another person). Is sympathy then synonymous with emotional contagion?

While sympathy and emotional contagion are not synonymous, sympathy may (and it often does) lead to the problem of emotional contagion. This problem happens when one suffers not only with the other, but in the other,[28] as if one were in the sufferer's body, feeling the sufferer's pain. David Hume, quoting Horace, explained emotional contagion in this way: for Hume, sympathy is the "propensity we have ... to receive by communication [the] inclinations and sentiments of others,"[29] and in this communication "the human countenance ... borrows smiles or tears from the human countenance."[30]

So, for example, if upon encountering the sufferer S, P herself perceives what they should feel in the like situation, then it is possible that P would perceive the sufferer's grief and distress in such a poignant way, that P's perception would lead P to sympathetically feel sorrow for the suffering of S—as if it were their own. But then P would sympathetically feel sorrow for S not so much because of S's suffering, but instead because P, in actuality, would feel their own vulnerability in a

---

[27] Smith, *The Theory of Moral Sentiments*, p. 13.
[28] Dodds, *Thomas Aquinas, Human Suffering, and the Unchanging God of Love*, p. 339.
[29] Hume, *A Treatise of Human Nature*, p. 316.
[30] Hume, "An Enquiry Concerning the Principles of Morals," p. 220.

similar situation.[31] Hence, the self-centeredness of sympathy leads to emotional contagion.

2.2. Sympathy, Emotional Contagion, and Burnout

Although Smith does not employ the term "emotional contagion" when discussing their conception of "sympathy," he seems to suggest the possibility of emotional contagion in the context of sympathy:

> By the imagination we place ourselves in their situation, we conceive ourselves enduring all the same torments, *we enter as it were into their body, and become in some measure the same person with him,* and thence form some idea of their sensations, and even feel something which, though weaker in degree, is not altogether unlike them.[32] (*Emphasis added*).

Emotional contagion—this experience of imagining that one "enters as it were into another's body, and becomes in some measure the same person with the sufferer"—is particularly challenging in the context of healthcare and global health aid, where there are several daily encounters with extreme suffering. Emotional contagion in the healthcare and global health contexts often leads to what is termed burnout.[33]

Symptoms of anxiety, depression, depersonalization, post-traumatic stress disorder (PTSD), suicidal ideation, and secondary traumatization often characterize burnouts. Burnout manifestations are linked not only to daily contact with extreme suffering and inordinate emotional attachment to patients but also (and importantly) to several structural problems within institutions of healthcare and GHG. In other words, burnouts have personal, interpersonal, and institutional causes.[34]

First, burnouts that are the result of a personal cause are often linked to a lack of self-care. Current self-care language is typically self-centered: turn to yourself and prioritize your wellness to avoid burnout. But what I mean by self-care is different: it is not a selfish, but rather an other-directed conduct. You care for

---

[31] Aquinas might describe this experience of emotional contagion as a "union of affection" (*unio affectus*), where "the agent regards his friend as himself; he regards the friend's evil as his own evil, and so, he grieves over the evil of his friend as his own" (*ST* II-II, Q30, a2, co).

[32] Smith, *The Theory of Moral Sentiments*, pp. 13–14.

[33] See: Herring, "Sharing Vulnerabilities in the Woman Patient/Doctor encounter," pp. 223–37. Brooks, Chalder, and Gerada, "Doctors Vulnerable to Psychological Distress and Addictions," pp. 157–64; Shanafelt et al., "Changes in Burnout and Satisfaction with Work-Life Balance in Physicians and the General U.S.," pp. 1600–13; and Dugdale, "Patient as Gift," pp. 4–5.

[34] See, e.g., Vachon, *How Doctors Care—The Science of Compassion and Balanced Caring in Medicine.*

yourself and turn inward introspectively to rest, so that you can recharge and regain balance to be able to love and care for others well in a sustainable way. This turning inward is therefore justified by the practical reason of love (both love of neighbor and love of self) and grounded in the virtue of prudence. A proper love of self enables a proper love of neighbor.[35] What this means is that the primary reason of self-care (as I conceive it as necessary for self-constitution) is to sustainably give myself generously for the good of another. In other words, the primary reason is to fill my cup, so I can continue to pour myself out for others, as no one can give from an empty cup. In short, self-care (as proper love of self, for the purpose of self-constitution) is what allows me to continuously pour myself out to others without burning myself out in the process. This proper love of self stems from a proper sense of self and an appropriate balance in my interactions with others: not overfocusing on myself, my desires, preferences, and wants, but also not completely forgetting to care for myself, by silencing my own agency and obliterating my own needs—I am here drawing a moral distinction between wants, desires, and preferences, on the one hand, and needs, on the other. The lack of the former causes discomfort. The lack of the latter causes disablement.[36]

Second, burnouts that are the result of interpersonal and institutional causes, in turn, are often linked to unbalanced interactions between patients, providers of healthcare and global health aid, and their organizational environment. Typically these burnouts are the result of inadequate institutional design such as lack of institutional structure and incentives for proper self-care, lack of respect for workers' freedom of conscience resulting in their moral distress,[37] caregiver overload (i.e., excessive work due to long working hours and understaffing), lack of adequate communication within the institution,[38] and increased operationalization (e.g., efficiency and productivity) coupled with increased pressure to meet operational targets leading to an inability to spend sufficient time with each patient.[39]

2.3. Addressing Burnout

As sociologist and human flourishing scholar, Matthew T. Lee, summarizes: "much of the disengagement and burnout found in organizations

---

[35] Outka, *Agape*.
[36] MacIntyre, *Dependent Rational Animals*, p. 124.
[37] On moral distress, see: Brito-Pons, Librada-Flores, "Compassion in Palliative Care," p. 475; Bow, Schöder-Bäck, Norcliffe-Brown et al., "Moral Distress and Injury"; Bow, Schöder-Bäck, Norcliffe-Brown et al., "Telling Them 'That's What It Says.'"
[38] Brito-Pons and Librada-Flores, "Compassion in Palliative Care," p. 477.
[39] See, e.g., Kerasidou and Horn, "Making Space for Empathy"; Kerasidou, "Empathy and Efficiency in Healthcare at Times of Austerity."

is likely the result of unskillful expressions of love."[40] In a similar vein, psychologist Gonzalo Brito-Pons and public health scholar Silvia Librada-Flores show that the solution to the problem of emotional contagion and burnout lies in education. They argue for the necessity of educating and training healthcare and global health aid providers on how to transition from the affective stage of sympathy (where emotional contagion takes place and leads to burnout) to the virtue of compassion. For this purpose, they suggest the CCT, based on the Buddhist technique of mindfulness (i.e., the capacity to see and listen and become aware), as a successful tool of self-care.[41] They claim CCT helps healthcare and global health aid providers to be not only givers but also receivers of healing. CCT's vision is mutual giving and receiving, between patients and providers of healthcare or global health aid.[42] CCT aims therefore at building compassionate communities of care, predicated on reciprocity.

Now, if CCT's goal is to build compassionate communities of mutual care, then education would need to be complemented, I would contend, with certain structural reforms of institutions of healthcare and GHG. This is because, as discussed above, burnout manifestations can have a personal/ interactional cause and an institutional cause. CCT seems to be an effective solution for personal and interactional burnout, but it less clear how CCT can also solve institutional dysfunctions and promote the design of compassionate institutions and policies.[43] Without institutional support for compassionate conduct, including compassionate policies at all different institutional levels (from hospital to local healthcare system to GHG), it seems impossible to cultivate compassion sustainably and build resilient communities of mutual care.

Here another objection to my definition of sympathy may be presented. If sympathy may lead to emotional contagion and burnout, and if healthcare and global health aid providers should receive training to move from sympathy to compassion (as CCT and other mindfulness and resilience cultivation programs propose),[44] one might think that sympathy is a negative affection that should be evaded at all costs. On the contrary, I would answer that sympathy and

---

[40] Lee, "Love as a Foundational Principle for Humanistic Management."
[41] Besides the CCT at Stanford University, other examples of compassion training programs include Cognitively-Based Compassion Training at Emory University, the Compassion Integrity Training (CIT), Mindfulness-Based Stress Reduction, the Trauma Resiliency Model and Community Resiliency Models of the Trauma Resource Institute, the Ayeka model, and the Japanese practice of Naikan.
[42] Brito-Pons and Librada-Flores, "Compassion in Palliative Care," pp. 472–79.
[43] Barsade and O'Neill "What's Love Got to Do with It?" pp. 551–98. For a compassion training program that integrates the personal, interpersonal, and organizational aspects, see, e.g., the CIT at: https://www.compassionateintegrity.org/about-the-program/.
[44] Kemper and Khirallah, "Acute Effects of Online Mind-Body Skills Training on Resilience, Mindfulness, and Empathy," pp. 247–53; Mealer, Hodapp, Conrad et al., "Designing a Resilience Program for Critical Care Nurses," pp. 359–65.

sentiments in general are an integral part of the human experience. Without the emotional warmth that sympathy offers, healthcare and global health aid provision become, to use Wojtyla's expression, both "cold and incommunicable."[45] The emotional component of compassion (or sympathy, as I call it) is both welcome and important.[46] However, as the mere first stage of compassion, sympathy should be matured and transformed into the fullness of compassion. Otherwise, sympathy remains self-centered, imprisoned within the subject who feels it, potentially leading to emotional contagion and burnout. For this transformation to happen, sympathy needs to first mature into empathy. The feeling of sympathy alone, as mere sentimentality, can only be transformed into the fullness of compassion, expressed as compassionate conduct of care, if it is accessed intellectually through practical reasoning. This intellectual process of transition from sympathy to compassionate care, I call empathy.

Section 3. The Intellectual Process of Empathy: From Sympathy to Compassionate Care

The concept of empathy is a relatively young one in the history of philosophy and medicine. Healthcare literature has defined empathy as "an ability to understand and accurately acknowledge the feelings of another, leading to an attuned response from the observer,"[47] "while maintaining a self-other distinction."[48] As a search for understanding, empathy has been called "the often-forgotten ingredient of compassion."[49]

Philosopher Martha Nussbaum disagrees. For her, although empathy "is extremely helpful," but it is neither necessary nor sufficient for compassion.[50] Though I disagree with Nusbaum on the role empathy plays in the process of compassion, her definition of empathy is helpful for my purpose of elaborating on the concept. For Nussbaum, empathy is "the ability to imagine the situation of the other, taking the other's perspective."[51] She suggests that merely "thinking

---

[45] Wojtyla, *Love and Responsibility*, p. 91.
[46] For a different perspective, see Soren Kierkegaard, as discussed by Krishek, "How Faith Secures the Morality of Love," pp. 252–63.
[47] Sinclair, Norris, McConnell et al., "Compassion: A Scoping Review of the Healthcare Literature."
[48] Kerasidou and Horn, "Making Space for Empathy," p. 8. Other healthcare scholars discussing empathy include Jeffrey, "Clarifying Empathy," e143–45. Mercer and Reynolds, "Empathy and Quality of Care," S9–S12; Brito-Pons and Librada-Flores, "Compassion in Palliative Care: A Review," pp. 472–79; Hojat, Gonnella, Nasca et al., "Physician Empathy," pp. 1563–69; Decety (ed.), *Empathy: From Bench to Bedside*; Halpen, *From Detached Concern to Empathy: Humanizing Medical Practice*.
[49] Sinclair, Beamer, Hack et al., "Sympathy, Empathy and Compassion," pp. 437–47.
[50] Nussbaum, *Political Emotions*, pp. 145–46.
[51] Ibid.

how one would feel oneself in the other person's place"[52]—which corresponds to my definition of sympathy—is not empathy. Neither is empathy "mere emotional contagion,"[53] because empathy, for Nussbaum, requires the subject not only to distinguish herself from the other, recognizing the other "as a center of experience"[54] but also to "enter into the predicament of another."[55] Alternatively put, for Nussbaum, empathy necessitates a distinct move away from self and toward another. This other-directed movement happens through the intellectual exercise of what she calls "imaginative displacement."[56] This, for Nussbaum, is what constitutes empathy. By suggesting that empathy requires this exercise of "imaginative displacement" Nussbaum seems to mean that empathy is primarily (though not exclusively) objective and intellectual, unlike sympathy, which, as I also define it, is purely subjective and self-centered.

Nussbaum's definition of empathy as an exercise of "imaginative displacement" is compatible with phenomenologist philosopher and theologian Edith Stein's definition that emphasizes the intellectual nature of empathy, while not denying its affective inception.[57] For Stein, empathy is an intentional act of the will—a choice to engage in a process of both ideation and reflection.[58] In her book, *On the Problem of Empathy*, Stein writes that empathy is "the perceiving of foreign subjects and their experience."[59] For Stein, empathy is not subjective and self-centered in the way that sympathy is: empathy is neither a fellow-feeling, nor a "feeling of oneness" that comes from imitation, association, or analogy.[60] For Stein, empathy is a process[61] that begins with an encounter and a communication with the other.

3.1. The Process of Empathy

Let us imagine an encounter with my grandmothers Sadako and Pat. In their encounter, Sadako communicates to Pat that she grieves the loss of her brother in Japan. Naturally, in this initial encounter and communication, some sympathetic emotion is stirred in Pat. But then, with further communication,

---

[52] Ibid.
[53] Ibid.
[54] Ibid.
[55] Ibid.
[56] Ibid.
[57] On both the cognitive and affective aspects of empathy, see also, e.g., Coplan, "Understanding Empathy: Its Features and Effects"; Gruen, "Entangled Empathy"; and Konrath, "The Empathy Paradox."
[58] Stein, *On the Problem of Empathy*, p. 11.
[59] Ibid., p. 1.
[60] Ibid., pp. 14, 16–18.
[61] On the process of empathy, see also: Decety (ed.), *Empathy: From Bench to Bedside*.

further questions, further explanations, further listening, further discernment of Sadako's experience of suffering, Pat's stirred emotions become less central. Here is where Pat intellectually processes the fact that it was not her brother who died, but Sadako's brother: Pat is seeing Sadako more deeply, listening to Sadako more closely, and therefore becoming more fully aware of Sadako's grief, narrated by the sufferer herself. Pat here gradually becomes more mindfully aware[62] of Sadako's lived experiences of suffering, unique to Sadako: the communicated experience that Pat receives, which is foreign to her, is turned into an object of imaginative contemplation and study.[63] Empathy, Stein explains, is this intellectual process by which Pat can objectively reflect on Sadako's suffering as Sadako's experience as a Japanese living in Brazil, lived through the distinctiveness of Sadako's circumstances in the difficulties of travelling to Japan to say her farewell to her brother, the uniqueness of Sadako's character, and the unrepeatability of Sadako's subjectivity. Hence, empathy, for Stein, is both an objective and intersubjective act.

The empathetic act of ideation and reflection allows Pat to thoroughly learn and systematically discern about Sadako's situation, according to what Sadako has shared with Pat.[64] This learning and discernment are possible, according to Stein's account of empathy, because (i) Sadako vulnerably presents and gives herself (her whole self—namely, body, mind, soul, and all that she has experienced)[65] to Pat,[66] and (ii) Pat is open to receive Sadako's gift of self.[67] Upon receiving Sadako's gift of self and going through the emotions of sympathy prompted by it, Pat must then go through an intellectual process of discerning what to do with this gift. This discernment, in Stein's account, is a discretionary act.

As discussed in the previous chapter on mercy, discretionary acts involve a discernment, predicated on the virtue of prudence and exercised through practical reasoning.[68] This discretionary act establishes how Pat will respond to Sadako's gift of self. Pat's response may effectively lead to a compassionate conduct of care (as I discuss in the next section), or it may not. Either Pat decides for empathy followed by compassion or Pat decides against it. If Pat decides against it, Pat walks away at this point and abandons Sadako" gift of self. If Pat decides for an empathetic response that may develop into a compassionate conduct of

---

[62] Shapiro, Siegel, and Neff, "Paradoxes of Mindfulness."
[63] Stein, *On the Problem of Empathy*, p. 10.
[64] Ibid., pp. 95–96.
[65] For Stein, empathy is the process of total self-giving, where one gives their whole person (body, mind, and soul) to another, for the other to assess it and obtain knowledge of the one who gave themselves. Ibid., pp. 41–48.
[66] Stein calls this "primordial experiences," which are shared with the other, and then submitted to the other's discernment and imagination processes. See Stein, ibid., pp. 5–7. See also: McDaniel, *Edith Stein: On the Problem of Empathy*, p. 198.
[67] I borrow the expression "gift of self" from theologian John Paul II, *Man and Woman*.
[68] See my discussion on mercy as a discretionary act in Ch. 1.

care for Sadako, then Pat has also to commit, at this point, to move away from self (and sympathy) and toward Sadako (and her suffering). But how does one move away from self and toward the other's suffering? My answer, as is often the case when it comes to love, is in self-denial, self-sacrifice, dying to self.

3.2. Empathy and Reciprocal Dying to Self

For compassionate care for the other (the third stage of compassion) to be born, sympathy's self-centeredness (the first stage) necessitates dying, so to speak.[69] In other words, the process of empathy requires dying to self, if this process is to be conducive to a compassionate conduct of care. "Dying to self" here means self-denial and self-sacrifice—that is, giving up one's own comforts, preferences, and interests in order to care for another in need.

This experiential process of dying to self that happens here at the second stage of compassion is reciprocal: both Sadako and Pat are required to experience *dying to self* and giving the *gift of self* to the other. Sadako dies to self and presents herself as a gift to Pat when she vulnerably shares her suffering with Pat. This sharing is often not easy: sharing one's suffering is acknowledging one's weaknesses, limitations, and failings, without knowing in advance how the other will respond: *will the other mock me; will the other think I am frail and pathetic; will the other really understand what it means to go through what I am going through?* These are unanswered questions when Sadako shares her experience with Pat. Sharing one's suffering often requires therefore a degree of courage as well as humility. It requires courage because it would be more comfortable and preferable not to share one's grief than to risk ridicule. Since sharing one's suffering necessitates self-denial and self-sacrifice, one needs to courageously choose to communicate their vulnerable experience. Sharing one's suffering also requires humility, meaning self-knowledge or the recognition of the truth about oneself. Sharing one's suffering necessitates acknowledging the truth about one's weaknesses, limitations, and failings.[70] In this sense, Sadako" sharing of her suffering is a gift (of Sadako" courage, Sadako" humility, Sadako" full self, including her good and bad parts) to Pat—regardless of Pat's ability and willingness to appreciate the value of such gift, and fully receive it or not.

Now, Pat, in turn, is invited to die to self and to present herself as a gift to Sadako. This invitation happens when Pat chooses first to overcome her emotional self-centeredness (her sympathy), then to fully receive Sadako" gift of self, and then to fully share (intellectually through discernment) in Sadako"

---

[69] I borrow this expression from John 3:3.
[70] On the correlation between self-knowledge and humility, see: Avila, "Interior Castle."

personal experiences of vulnerability. This is what marks the transition between the first stage of compassion to the second. Interestingly, in doing so, in entering the second stage of compassion by choosing self-sacrificial empathy over self-centered sympathy, Pat learns not only more about the other (as a whole person) but also more about herself, her own weaknesses, limitations, and failings in how she responds (or fails to respond) to others in need. Empathy is in this sense an exercise in humility (i.e., self-knowledge) for both Sadako and Pat.[71] Empathy is also an exercise of courage for both Sadako and Pat. It is not only Sadako who shows courage in choosing to share her vulnerabilities; Pat also needs courage to choose to share in Sadako's suffering. Making this choice to share in the other's suffering is not easy. It requires denying one's comforts, preferences, and interests in order *to be there with* the sufferer, patiently accompanying her in her misery. In choosing self-denial and self-sacrifice to share in Sadako" experience of suffering, Pat is automatically giving something back to Sadako. More specifically, Pat is giving herself, her *presence*, her empathy. This is Pat's gift of self to Sadako.

Empathy therefore is an intellectual process that involves an intentional experience of mutual self-giving and receiving. This process, grounded in the concepts of dying to self and presence, is what fundamentally constitutes the second stage of compassion. As Stein puts it, empathy is premised on intersubjectivity: a mutual exchange and experience of the other. To apply Stein's definition of empathy to my three-stage account of compassion, however, invites us to ask what *dying to self* would require in the specific context of healthcare and global health aid. For example, would *dying to self*" not entail the problem of burnout discussed above?

While I am using dying to self interchangeably with self-denial and self-sacrifice, it does not mean that dying to self necessitates self-annihilation leading to burn out. That is to say, dying to self is not contrary to proper love of self, self-constitution, and self-care, as discussed above. Neither is it contrary to the establishment of healthy boundaries for self-protection, which enables sustainable generosity. To further explain the idea of dying to self and its implications in healthcare and global health aid within the second stage of compassion, I present the phenomenology of a case of medical compassion. As noted earlier, burnout has both personal/interactional and institutional causes. Therefore, the hypothetical case below will explore what dying to self and presence should mean—or not mean—at both levels.

---

[71] Stein, *On the Problem of Empathy*, pp. 114–16. For Stein, empathy nurtures knowledge both of self and of others. In fact, the problem of empathy is the problem of understanding the mind of the other. For a discussion on Stein's views on the knowledge of the other's mind, see: MacIntyre, *Edith Stein: A Philosophical Prologue*, Ch. 9.

3.3. Dying to Self: The Hypothetical Case of Mr. Zangado

3.3.1. The Interaction Setting

Mr. Miguel Zangado is a difficult patient at the Oncology Center of Luanda. A 42-year-old terminal patient, his recurrent colorectal cancer has metastasized to the liver, pleura, and bones. Understandably, he is angry because he is grieving the prospect of dying young. However, his anger primarily manifests as hostility toward his caregivers. He is convinced that the oncology team knows nothing about his unique circumstances and medical condition. Mr. Zangado's behavior is disrespectful: he ridicules doctors, yells at nurses, and frequently refers to the team as "stupid, ignorant, and clueless about me."[72]

Dr. Fatima Sally, the head of the palliative care team, is now tasked with overseeing Mr. Zangado's care. Originally from Brazil, Dr. Sally completed her medical training and specialization in oncology and palliative care there before moving to Angola to support the Oncology Center of Luanda as part of a global health aid initiative. Aware of Mr. Zangado's reputation, she anticipates being mocked for her Brazilian accent while speaking Portuguese with him. One can appreciate how apprehensive she is about introducing herself and her team to this notoriously difficult patient. She is aware of the resilience that she and her co-workers will need to prevent manifestations of burnout, triggered by toxic interactions with Mr. Zangado. Challenging interactions with disrespectful patients can definitely contribute to burnout, as the literature has pointed out,[73] so Dr. Sally instructs her team on how to empathetically interact with Mr. Zangado, how to provide fraternal correction when needed, and how to establish compassionate boundaries when necessary.

3.3.2. The Institutional Setting

The Oncology Center of Luanda collaborates with the Global Oncology Foundation, a US-based global health aid program. The Foundation's mission is to bring high-quality cancer care to underserved patients worldwide. Alongside her role as head of the palliative care team, Dr. Sally serves as vice-director of the Foundation. As a key donor to the Oncology Center, the Foundation's board of directors has significant influence over the Center's institutional reform goals.

Since the partnership began, the Foundation and the Oncology Center have aimed to make the Center a model of compassionate care for other hospitals in Angola. However, initial efforts under a top-down governance model were

---

[72] My hypothetical story of Mr. Zangado was inspired by the true story of Mr. R, a patient of Dr. Dugdale. She writes about Mr. R's story and its impact on her professional life in Dugdale, "Patient as Gift."

[73] Jesse et al., "Professional Interpersonal Dynamics and Burnout in European Transplant Surgeons."

unsuccessful. The Foundation's board, predominantly composed of non-resident foreigners unfamiliar with Angolan medical culture, set compassionate care policies that failed to resonate locally. Their rigid protocols emphasized efficiency and speed, inadvertently neglecting the slower-paced, trust-building practices valued in Angola.

For example, the board introduced a scorecard to measure bedside manners, with one key indicator being that providers listen to patients without interruption for at least 30 seconds. While well-intentioned, this approach led caregivers to focus on timing interactions rather than genuinely connecting with patients. The resulting communications felt shallow and robotic, prioritizing compliance over presence and attentiveness.

Recognizing these shortcomings, the Foundation then adopted a bottom-up approach to foster empathy and compassion more effectively.[74] Decision-making now prioritizes inclusivity and participation. Medical teams and their patients collaboratively deliberate how empathy and compassion are demonstrated in their relationships. Higher authorities, including the Foundation's board, serve now as accountability partners rather than primary decision-makers.

Under this new structure, Dr. Sally's team and Mr. Zangado take the lead in tailoring acts of compassionate care to meet their specific needs. They are free to define what dying to self and presence mean in their daily interactions, fostering a more authentic and culturally appropriate practice of compassion. This participatory process ensures that compassionate care is not only more effective but also personalized for meeting the unique needs of both patients and caregivers.

3.4. Dying to Self at the Interactional Level

One particular need for Mr. Zangado is to be attentively listened to and deeply understood. While all patients share this need, it is especially pronounced for Mr. Zangado, who voices frustration that his healthcare team is unaware of his unique circumstances and medical condition. One can appreciate his frustration, too: questions like, "We are sorry that you feel we don't understand your situation. Would you share more about your perception?" or "What would you like us to know about your specific circumstances?" have not yet been directly posed to him. Such inquiries could bridge the gap between the healthcare professionals' medical expertise and the patient's lived experience. Indeed, both healthcare professionals and patient bring expertise, albeit on different themes. While the former brings medical expertise, scientific knowledge, and clinical skills, the latter brings their phenomenological expertise of their own life, their

---

[74] See Chapter 5 on the principle of subsidiarity and its bottom-up approach applied to GHG.

knowledge of himself, and their discretionary skills in discerning with prudence what is best for their unique practical circumstances. Both types of expertise are necessary to determine the best course of action regarding care options.[75]

To tailor empathy and compassionate care to Mr. Zangado's specific needs, Dr. Sally and her team must attentively turn toward and thoroughly understand his concerns. For example, when one is asked, "What has been the hardest change for you?" one is given the space to reveal one's core struggles and vulnerabilities. The team may need to ask some other clarification questions, paraphrase his account, or reconstruct his narrative to ensure they genuinely understand his perspective. By using their imagination, judgment, and intellectual abilities they can grasp nuances, read between the lines, and validate his experiences while being cautious not to assume too much. For example, they might say, "Do you think this might be because . . . ?" This active, empathetic listening helps Dr. Sally and her team achieve their primary goal: to deeply understand Mr. Zangado's experience of living with metastasized colorectal cancer at just 42 years old.

Empathetically appreciating another's suffering is challenging and demands self-denial from the listener. It requires resisting the urge to interrupt or rush toward solutions, focusing instead on being fully present with the patient. This is a crucial aspect of "dying to self" in the clinical encounter: cultivating courage to share with resilience in the patient's discomfort, with patience to listen to the patient, and humility to learn from their experience. By tempering the urge to fix problems, caregivers can remain present, accompany the sufferer in their misery, and help carry their burden. Dying to self and presence are the foundation of empathy, the second stage in the compassion process.

One might argue that not all healthcare professionals are equipped or willing to act as mental health specialists prepared to die to self in this way. It's true that varying specialties bring different strengths, which collectively enhance a team. However, if healthcare institutions aim to provide holistic care, it is essential for every caregiver—regardless of specialization—to embrace their ethical duty to be present with patients to the best of their abilities, complementing their specialized skills.

Importantly, this self-denial does not equate to tolerating disrespect or condoning bad behavior. While Dr. Sally practices restraint to avoid defensiveness or interrupting Mr. Zangado, she also establishes healthy boundaries to protect her resilience. Boundaries are essential for self-care (which I defined as a proper love of self) and for sustaining the generosity required to care for

---

[75] On the co-expert model, see, e.g., Milo, *Informed Consent to Abortion*," Ch. 3, and Herring, "Sharing Vulnerabilities in the Woman Patient/Doctor encounter," pp. 223–37. For a critical view of the expert model, see, e.g., Watson, "Patient Expertise and Medical Authority," pp. 58–71.

others. Without such boundaries, the three-stage compassion process cannot be maintained.

Dying to self in empathetic interaction means fully sharing in another's vulnerability without succumbing to emotional contagion or burnout. The intellectual discernment integral to empathy allows caregivers to maintain a necessary distance from the patient's emotional intensity.[76] When you, as a caregiver, take a step back to recover and refill your cup, you can then give again (no one can give from an empty cup!). Stepping back enables you to give yourself and your empathy as a gift, marking the transition to the third stage of compassion. Thus, empathy serves as a foundational act of self-care: a proper way to love oneself and uphold one's self-constitution, by preventing burnout and sustaining one's ability to remain compassionate.[77]

This process of building empathy takes time. For example, Mr. Zangado initially shares only disrespectful words with Dr. Sally and her team, withholding deeper vulnerabilities. One can understand: he does not trust them enough to open up.[78] However, by consistently showing presence and availability, the team gradually earns his trust. The key is to avoid false promises of a cure, which would only dismiss his pain, and instead reiterate their commitment: "Mr. Zangado, I know you are suffering, and I will not leave you. I will stay with you during this difficult season. I will keep showing up and asking what matters to you." Over time, Mr. Zangado opens up, he shares his life story, interior world, and lived experiences. And this sharing is in itself a gift. This gradual unfolding is what the second stage of compassion—empathy—looks like at the interactional level.

3.5. Dying to Self at the Institutional Level

Dr. Sally and her team's gift of self—expressed through their consistent presence and availability to Mr. Zangado—was vital for building trust and enabling him to reciprocate the gift of himself. This insight about consistent presence emerged from a conversation that Dr. Sally had with one of the palliative care nurses, who identified the core issue as the caregiver's absence during clinical encounters. The team members were either distracted or focused on other tasks. While personal discomfort with Mr. Zangado played a role, institutional demands, such as the need to maximize the use of their time and to hit daily quotas, also shaped

---

[76] Konrath, "The Empathy Paradox: Increasing Disconnection in the Age of Increasing Connection."

[77] Thirioux, Birault, and Jaafari, "Empathy is a Protective Factor of Burnout in Physicians," p. 763. For an account against empathy, see, e.g., Breithaupt, *Dark Sides of Empathy*. For a skeptical view of empathy in healthcare settings, see, e.g., Samra, "Empathy and Burnout in Medicine," pp. 991–93.

[78] Halpern, "Clinical Empathy in Medical Care," Ch. 13.

their choices. Their choice to be absent, therefore, resulted from both personal and institutional factors.

The Oncology Center of Luanda's focus on efficiency and productivity, driven by quotas and measurable outcomes like patient numbers and shaped by donor and funding-related priorities, directly impacted the quality of care. The Center's emphasis on quantifiable outcomes implicitly devalued essential aspects of compassionate care, like presence and availability, that cannot be easily measured (see Chapter 6 on the incommensurability problem). This prioritization of numbers ultimately made absence and distraction the norm in clinical encounters.[79]

The conversation with the nurse was eye-opening for Dr. Sally. It not only allowed her to empathetically understand the nurse's experience but also prompted reflection on how she herself had often chosen to be absent from others—patients and colleagues alike. In recognizing this, Dr. Sally saw how such absence led to automatic alienation of others. This realization became a lesson in humility, as empathy revealed both her own limitations and the need for change. The nurse's insight made her realize that the entire staff needed to adjust their behavior and interactions. Beyond that, a new policy was needed to sustain such change. Dr. Sally then considered proposing the *Presence Before Efficiency Policy*, as part of the ongoing reforms to make the Center a more empathetic and compassionate institution. The policy would be co-created by Dr. Sally and the palliative care teams, and then presented to the Foundation and Center's board for their approval.

Dr. Sally's decision to involve her co-workers and those under her leadership in crafting the new policy required significant self-denial. Arguably, it would have been more efficient, and less time-consuming, for her to draft the document alone and present it to the board.[80] However, if the goal of the *Presence Before Efficiency Policy* is to promote empathy and compassion at all levels of decision-making, including hospital administration, then meaningful inclusion is essential (see Chapter 1). This process fosters institutional self-reflection.[81] This is an example of what "dying to self," a core element of the second stage of compassion, means at the institutional level: active participation and meaningful inclusion

---

[79] Kerasidou, "Empathy and Efficiency in Healthcare at Times of Austerity," pp. 171–84; Howick, Mittoo et al., "A Price Tag on Clinical Empathy?" pp. 389–93; Howick, Moscrop, Mebius et al., "Effects of Empathy and Positive Communication in Healthcare Consultations," pp. 240–52; Howick, Bizzari, and Dambha-Miller, "Therapeutic Empathy," pp. 233–36; Shanafelt, Gorringe, Menaker et al., "Impact of Organizational Leadership on Physician Burnout and Satisfaction," pp. 432–40.

[80] The claim that a compassionate leadership is less efficient is contested, since there is evidence that it is better for staff and safer for patients, which renders compassionate leadership more efficient in the mid and long-term future. See: de Zulueta. "Developing Compassionate Leadership in Health care," pp. 1–10.

[81] On the importance of participation and self-reflection for creating empathetic institutions, see Kerasidou, Bærøe, Berger, and Caruso Brown, "The Need for Empathetic Healthcare Systems."

within the institution, empathetic appreciation of diverse voices, and an institutional exercise of self-reflection.[82]

3.6. Presence as Active Participation and Cooperation: Meaningful Inclusion in Lieu of Absence, Alienation, and Mere Tolerant Co-Existence

Both at the interactional and at the institutional levels, the dying to self that empathy (the second stage of compassion) requires is fundamentally linked with participation and inclusion, as these activities allow for presence and mitigate absence. Empathy and presence are participatory and inclusive; absence is alienating.[83] Alienation, as phenomenologist philosopher and theologian Karol Wojtyla conceptualizes it, "devastates the I–other relationship, weakens the ability to experience another human being as another I, and inhibits the possibility of friendship and the spontaneous powers of community."[84] By choosing active participation and a meaningfully inclusive governance structure, Dr. Sally rejects alienation and joins others' experiences. This choice cultivates resilience[85] and self-reflection, while welcoming the active participation of those who see and experience the world differently.

I distinguish between active participation and meaningful inclusion. Participation becomes active when it demands more than mere tolerance of another I. While active participation applies to interactions and relationships, its institutional counterpart is meaningful inclusion (defined in Chapter 1) within decision-making processes. By choosing active participation, Dr. Sally attentively sees, listens, and becomes fully aware of the other's needs—whether it is Mr. Zangado, their family, or the members of her palliative care team. Both active participation and meaningful inclusion require empathetic communication: seeing, listening, and being mindfully aware of the other and their voice.

Dr. Sally thought she knew Mr. Zangado—his age, temper, and cancer. But only through consistent presence and availability did he begin to open up. When Dr. Sally asked him, "What has been the hardest change for you?", he let himself feel seen at a deeper level, allowing himself to share his experience with Dr. Sally. He let her in. It was at that moment that Dr. Sally also actually saw and listened for the first time to Mr. Zangado's unique experience of suffering from cancer: his personal journey of isolation, grief, disillusionment, growth, and finally hope and letting go. Infinite new knowledge emerged from Dr. Sally's

---

[82] Tronto, "Creating Caring Iinstitutions: Politics, Plurality, and Purpose," pp. 158–71.
[83] Wojtyla, *Person and Community*, pp. 197–207.
[84] Ibid., p. 206.
[85] Lysaught, Ortega et al., "Building Caregiver Resiliency in Global Health," pp. 184–205.

conversations with Mr. Zangado, as he actively participated by sharing his raw reality. Through this, she glimpsed his interior world for the first time, realizing its richness, depth, and boundless complexity.

Something similar happened as a result of the meaningful inclusion of her team members in the drafting of the *Presence Before Efficiency Policy*. Dr. Sally thought she knew each member of her team—Charles, Maria, Ricardo, Cristina, and Susana. She certainly had knowledge of their individual strengths and weaknesses as professionals, as well as of their complementarity that made that palliative care team robust. She also now recognized the institutional obstacles to fostering empathy and compassion, after her conversation with the nurse about promoting presence over absence during clinical encounters. Convinced of the need for a bottom-up approach to tackle those structural barriers, Dr. Sally invited those under her leadership to actively participate in the drafting process, making the process of building a new governance structure meaningfully inclusive. All collaborated as equals, sharing authority (see Chapter 3 on shared authority in decision-making) in co-creating their shared vision for their organization.

3.7. Presence and the Transcendent Good of Relationality

Dying to self is central to the cultivation of presence, which underpins empathy, the second stage of the compassion process. I have examined how dying to self operates in interactional and institutional settings. Here, I shift focus to the concept of presence itself, highlighting its foundational role in relationality and its continued significance in the third stage of the compassion process.

The significance of presence becomes clearer when considered through the lens of two philosophers: Emmanuel Lévinas and Iris Murdoch. Lévinas defines presence as a face-to-face encounter. In *Totality and Infinity*, he argues that such an encounter with the Other (capitalized to emphasize the other person's uniqueness) creates a responsibility. When the Other calls to me, I am compelled to respond. In this encounter, the Other communicates with me, and in responding, I not only open the space for dialogue but, more importantly, discover my responsibility toward the Other. For example, Dr. Sally, through her conversation with the nurse, realized her responsibility not to alienate those under her leadership and to ensure their meaningful inclusion in decisions that affect everyone.

For Lévinas, it is through communication that I become responsible for responding to the Other and for caring about the good of the Other. In this encounter, the "Face of the Other" reveals their "Infinity" to me. The Other, whom I once saw as merely finite, now opens to me, allowing me to recognize the Infinite within them. What Lévinas calls the "Infinity in the Other" can be understood as the boundless beauty, worth, and dignity of the Other's soul—their Imago Dei, the image of infinite love that resides in each of us, as discussed in Chapter 4.

The face-to-face encounter that Lévinas describes, I would add, also has a transcendent dimension. When my eyes (the windows to my soul) meet the eyes of the Other (the windows to their soul), a communion of souls occurs. In this intersubjective space, we access the spiritual realm of the Other. Lévinas would emphasize the centrality of presence by suggesting that only a face-to-face encounter enables true connection with Infinity, for only the presence of the Other allows such intimate communication and communion with their soul.[86] Lévinas' concept of "Infinity in the Other" awakens in us a desire to understand the Other more deeply and empathetically, to be ever more present with them.[87] This desire, I would suggest, moves us to choose presence over absence, alienation, and mere tolerant co-existence.

Iris Murdoch's account of love further underscores the transformative power of presence. In *The Sovereignty of the Good* (1970), Murdoch defines love as perfected vision: seeing the other person clearly—as they truly are, with both their virtues and flaws, their particularities and idiosyncrasies. In Murdoch's framework, love is not merely a choice to see the other with clarity; it is also a desire to genuinely see the Other and to be seen by them in return.

In this sense, I believe that being present with the Other is a transcendent, participatory experience of alterity. Through empathetic communication and an appreciation of the Other's unique experience, one transcends the alienation of the self and experiences inclusion, belonging, union, and communion with the Other. This transcendent I–Other relationality emerges from a mutual process of dying to self, as I discussed earlier. It is at this point that one faces a crucial choice: whether or not to advance toward the third stage of compassion.

Section 4. The Effective Stage of Compassion: Compassionate Conduct of Care

In the second stage of compassion, where empathy unfolds, the agent encounters the Other's humanity face-to-face,[88] recognizing their equal dignity—their "inner Infinity," as Lévinas describes it (for a discussion of equal dignity, see

---

[86] Lévinas, *Totality and Infinity*, pp. 49–51.
[87] On the importance of curiosity for physicians to understand empathetic accuracy, see, e.g., Halpern, "Clinical Empathy in Medical Care."
[88] It is in this sense that Lévinas compares ethics to optics: the face-to-face encounter with the Other is where ethics happens. Ethics depends on seeing, contemplating the face of the Other, as in an esthetic experience.

Chapter 4). Through this experiential process, the agent learns about the other's needs and is then made responsible to somehow respond to this need. This response begins as a discretionary process of empathy, which may mature into the third stage of compassion—the effective stage—if the agent chooses to advance. At this final stage, the agent's choice is oriented toward effecting compassionate care that addresses the Other's needs.

Both empathy (the second stage) and compassionate care (the third stage) are fundamentally predicated on the idea of presence, meaning being with the one who suffers, sharing in their experience, accompanying, and walking with them. In the intellectual and experiential process of empathy, one learns more deeply and accurately about the other. Empathy then gives one the knowledge required to then effectively respond to the needs of the other. In other words, empathy gives one the capabilities to discern how to tailor care to effectively meet the sufferer's unique needs and particular character. This tailored care may encompass an action or an omission, depending on the patient's needs.

4.1. Effectively Tailored Care

Effectively tailored care is therefore at the core of the third stage of compassion. By effectively tailored care I mean two things. First, it is responsive to the particular needs of the Other, with all their uniqueness. Tailored, personalist care neither too quickly assumes what the needs of the patient are before communicating with them, nor complacently and unthinkingly does whatever the patient wants when such desires are actually harmful for the patient (see Chapter 3 on the definition of authentically beneficent care). To presume too quickly to know what is good for the other and what the needs of the patient are is medical paternalism (see Chapter 6 where I further elaborate on this definition of paternalism). To do whatever the patient wants, either out of laziness in having to go to the trouble of attentively beholding and empathetically communicating with the patient (which takes work) or out of a corrupt understanding of compassion as unfettered acquiescence and acritical niceness (which is easier than respectful disagreement and truthful communication),[89] is to silence one's own conscience, violate one's own agency, and inflict upon oneself moral distress that results in burnout.

---

[89] On a corrupt understanding of compassion as mere acquiescence to the wishes of the sufferer, see, e.g., Hordern, *Compassion in Healthcare—Pilgrimage, Practice, and Civic Life*, p. 41.
    On the definition of truthful communication, see Ch. 6.

Second, as the outward expression of the virtue of compassion, effectively tailored care is a gift of self that is given back in response to a specific person in a particular situation of suffering. As a gift of self, it requires a self-sacrificial act, in giving up one's own comforts, preferences, and interests in order to care well for another in need. But that does not necessarily mean heroic, grand acts of self-denial. Rather, it means a reasonable stretch that pushes one forward to go the extra mile for those in need. Also, grandiosity in care tends to be a symptom of what in the field of humanitarian aid has been called the white savior complex,[90] which typically hides the ulterior motivation of self-congratulatory supererogation (see Chapter 3, where I elaborate on this relation between the savior complex and self-adulation). This is not authentic compassion. What I mean by effectively tailored care, grounded in authentic compassion, is best illustrated by St. Mother Teresa of Calcutta's outlook on care. For her, not all of us can do great things, but we can do small things with great love.

Effectively tailored care often lies in the small details that show attentiveness and presence to others. At the interpersonal level, a simple, everyday example of a small detail that makes a significant difference for those who suffer would include sharing in another's grief by delivering culturally appropriate meals because the sufferer is too overwhelmed to cook for themselves, or sending a thoughtful note and telling the grieving person not to worry about replying back because to respond often requires a mental energy that the sufferer may not have. At the institutional level, a small detail that makes a significant difference would include letting the family stay with the deceased patient for a little longer. Bending certain rules and making some rigid protocols more flexible by accommodating reasonable exceptions is not only a requirement of compassion but also of justice, since reasonable exceptions make for good rules that uphold the common good.[91] Obviously none of these examples at the interpersonal and institutional levels are part of a healthcare professional job description, procedural manual, or hospital policy. But reasonably stretching oneself or an institution to go the extra mile for a suffering patient or their family, attending to small details that are important for them at their particular context is the most appropriate compassionate response. Compassionate love can rarely unfold within one-size-fits-all approaches. Sure, love is universal (we all need love to flourish), but is also deeply personal, and therefore the particulars matter for an authentically compassionate conduct of care.

---

[90] See, e.g., Arguedas, "Te Hundo para Luego Tratar de Salvarte."
[91] I thank Angela Wu Howard for making this point. See her DPhil thesis: Wu Howard, *Religious Exceptions to General Laws*. For a different view, see: Blumental-Barby, "Can Health Care Providers Love Their Patients?"

4.2. Presence as the Absence of Words and Actions

Attentive presence is a fundamental ingredient of an effectively tailored compassionate conduct of care. Now, those small details at the interpersonal and institutional levels, mentioned in the examples above, require that attentive presence be manifested through particular words and actions. Does that entail that words coupled with specific actions are always necessary to effectively care for the other? I would answer no.

Absence of words or actions is not contrary to presence since absence of words or action does not necessarily equate with absence of being. As T. S. Eliot observed, love can be silent.[92] And love, I would add, can also be still. While presence does depend on participative communication, it does not mean that words and actions are always necessary, in particular if these are not what the sufferer needs. While communication is essential to the second and third stages of compassion, spoken words and actions (i.e., doing things) may not be necessary; communication can exist without them (think of the communication between parents and their newborn, as discussed in Chapter 3). Also, words and actions can be empty—especially when they simply try to fill the void of an uncomfortable silence.

Silence is perceived as uncomfortable in most cultures. But a silent, still presence may just be what is most needed in the context of suffering. The urge to always fill the silence with words and actions may come from a misunderstanding of what presence fundamentally is and is not. Being present with patients who suffer does not necessarily entail trying to justify or excuse their difficult situation with certain words. Nor does it necessarily entail trying to take away their suffering by fixing it with certain actions. For example, being present does not require actively bringing a list of suggestions not yet tried but which have worked for others. Neither does presence entail saying things like "everything happens for a reason" or "God has a greater purpose for your suffering and illness," as a way of trying to justify the hardship. These are things that are often said and done with good intention, and these may well be true and helpful in some occasions—but not in every occasion.

Saying words or doing something that will fill the void of the uncomfortable silence is often a desperate response from the agent who is confronted with her own powerlessness to bring alleviation to the sufferer. This is not effectively tailored care. After all, there might not be any easy solution; there might not be a cure, as was the case with Mr. Zangado's cancer diagnosis. But when Mr. Zangado was listened to, he felt noticed, attended to, seen, and appreciated. Not many words or actions were needed afterward. Presence sufficed for Mr. Zangado.

---

[92] Eliot, *The Elder Statesman*.

Presence is at the core of their effectively tailored care. When an abundance of words and actions is a disservice to the sufferer, effectively tailored care requires instead dying to self, which in this situation entails one humbly facing one's own powerlessness and courageously choosing to be present in silence with the powerlessness of the other.

Silent presence is the effective loving response when those who suffer mostly need the other to empathetically listen, quietly appreciate, and compassionately participate in their experience of suffering. Remaining silent yet attentively present, beholding, and directing one's loving gaze[93] toward the sufferer, in a deep eye-to-eye communion, is the most empathetic and compassionate option in many instances of suffering. Just showing up and being there for the other who suffer is an example of an effective tailored care of presence.

4.3. Friendship and Solidarity: The Upshots of an Effectively Tailored Compassionate Conduct of Care

By choosing to die to self and offer tailored care through presence, we are invited to empathetically acknowledge our shared vulnerability in the face of suffering—a universal experience that unites us as a community of mutual care, bonded by friendship or solidarity. This mutual dying to self enables a transcendent and inclusive encounter with alterity. Through empathetic communication and appreciation of the Other's unique experience, we transcend alienation and discover participation, belonging, union, and communion with the Other. Here is where the transcendent I–Other relationality (which marks the third stage of compassion) solidifies, out of a continuous, mutual process of dying to self.

This mutual process of dying to self deepens our appreciation of shared vulnerabilities and draws people closer together. Thus, the third stage of compassion culminates in forming a community of mutual care, grounded in friendship[94] at the interpersonal level and solidarity at the institutional level—solidarity being the "friendship between institutions." Both friendship and solidarity arise from the transition from "I" to "we,"[95] shaped through an encounter with the other's vulnerabilities. This "we" signifies a community of mutual dependence and care, oriented toward the good of the Other and the common good of all.

Suffering isolates the sufferer, creating loneliness and alienation from one's community. This is why the community holds a special responsibility to address

---

[93] Murdoch, *The Sovereignty of Good*, p. 34.
[94] Wojtyla, *Love and Responsibility*, pp. 92, 94.
[95] Ibid., p. 95.

such isolation through presence—by being with the sufferer and tailoring that presence to meet their unique needs through active participation and meaningful inclusion. Presence, in this face-to-face, eye-to-eye, *cor ad cor loquitur*[96] encounter, fulfills the sufferer's deep desire to be seen, valued, and understood.

An effective conduct of compassionate care obtains this by creating a shared experience of belonging, union, and communion, forming a community that transcends the sufferer's sense of alienation. The ultimate product of the third stage of compassion is a strong community of mutual care, grounded in friendship and solidarity. And this should be the precise goal of healthcare and global health institutions (see Chapter 4 for what friendship and solidarity should look like within and among these institutions).

4.4. Presence Before Efficiency Does Not Mean No Efficiency

Now, if the institutional goal is to create a strong community of mutual care, rather than fostering communities of hasty care, then the pragmatic imperatives of efficiency and productivity would need to be deprioritized to allow friendship and solidarity to unfold more organically within organizations. Yet, a strong community of mutual care need not be antithetical to efficiency and productivity.[97] Compassionate care can be offered in simple, non-costly ways: think of those small details that show attentiveness and presence, and which can make a significant difference. Some small details may be even costless and take only a few seconds. In their 2019 book *Compassionomics*, physicians Stephen Trzeciak and Anthony J Mazzarelli, showed that it only takes 40 seconds to give a patient a compassionate gaze, attentive and present enough for the patient to feel seen and acknowledged in their suffering.[98]

While I believe that efficiency is overrated, I am not negating its importance, especially in healthcare and global health contexts where scarcity of resources is a constant reality that often impedes adequate care be delivered. Effectively tailored compassionate care should be consistent with managing resources efficiently (as the principle of stewardship requires, as discussed in Chapter 6). Efficiency is, after all, a pivotal component of any functional healthcare system. Yet, as crucial as efficiency is, compassionate care emerges from the humbling realization that during times of intense vulnerability, such as in illnesses and

---

[96] I borrow this expression from the motto of nineteenth-century theologian and leader of the Oxford Movement, St. John Henry Newman, who adopted *Cor ad Cor Loquitur*—"heart speaks to heart"—as his cardinal motto in 1897.
[97] Brown, "Compassion and Efficiency not Mutually Exclusive in Healthcare," E775–76.
[98] See: Trzeciak "How 40 seconds of Compassion Could Save a Life." See also: Trzeciak and Mazzarelli, "Compassionomics."

death, when our dependence on one another and the need for companionship become magnified, mere efficiency and productivity fall short.[99] They may allow us to have greater access to the basic healthcare goods and services (e.g., essential medication and a hospital bed in the ICU) that meet our basic material needs. Neither efficiency nor productivity can meet our deepest, non-material, transcendent needs to receive and give love in moments of great suffering. In these moments of intense vulnerability and interdependence only the presence that results in true friendship and solidarity suffices.

4.5. Proper Understanding of Love of Neighbor and Love of Self: My Reading of the Good Samaritan

Now friendship and solidarity, as the upshots of compassion, result from "the transition from 'I' to 'we,'"[100] but one may insist here: how does this we and this strong interdependence between subjects not entail their self-annihilation? It seems, one could claim, that the I–Other distinction, on which empathy (the second stage of compassion) was so insistent, has now, in the third stage of compassion, morphed into a we that obliterates the subjects as distinct persons.

I would respond that while the we that comes out of the third stage of compassion indeed requires the mutual dying to self of the subjects involved in the process, the I–Other distinction remains. This dying to self (i.e., the reasonable degree of self-sacrifice that requires a denial of our comforts and preferences) need not—and in fact should not—necessitate the elimination of the I–Other distinction. Dying to self does not entail a complete neglect of one's own needs[101]. This would be self-annihilation. On the contrary, the virtue of compassion, as all other virtues in the Aristotelian tradition, requires a golden mean—meaning, a mean between two extremes: one of deficiency and one of excess. Likewise, for compassion to be a virtue, it requires moderation between (i) the extreme of deficiency in care for the other (and excess in self-care), which leads to the abandonment of the other, and (ii) the extreme of excessive care for the other (and consequently deficiency in self-care), which leads to burnout. The golden mean of the virtue of compassion requires moderation between care for the other (proper love of neighbor) and self-care (proper love of self for self-constitution), as discussed previously.

---

[99] Lamb, Wainstock, and de Campos-Rudinsky, "Ethics of Love for End-of-Life Care," pp. 76–78.
[100] Wojtyla, *Love and Responsibility*, p. 95.
[101] Earlier in this chapter, I have drawn a moral distinction between wants, desires, and preferences, on the one hand, and needs, on the other. The lack of the former causes discomfort. The lack of the latter causes disablement.

The formation and sustainability of a strong community of mutual care require both compassionate care for the good of the other and also for my own good. That is to say, the purpose of a community of mutual care is not only the good of the other who is suffering but also the common good of all, including myself. The common good demands not only the dying to self in the service of the other but also the establishment of reasonable boundaries in the provision of such service, for the attainment of proper self-care (for self-constitution). Simply put, without healthy boundaries there is no proper love of self, and without proper self-care there is neither mutual care nor common good. This is because one cannot give what one does not possess: one needs to love and care for herself to be able to give love and care for those in need.

The theme of self-care has increasingly become prominent in the context of healthcare, particularly when it comes to defining what compassion means and necessitates from healthcare providers and institutions. The theme has in fact become urgent because of the many instances of burnout of healthcare providers, and the difficulty that healthcare professionals and institutions face in reasonably differentiating what compassion requires and does not require from them. This distinction can only be clarified when the boundaries in the provision of healthcare services are plainly defined. This chapter has sought to clarify several of the confusions related to compassion, self-care, and their corrupted forms.

However, misinterpretations regarding the delineations or even the morality of these boundaries abound. For example, an opponent of self-care may insist that compassion in the service of the other may require a complete opposition to the selfish idea of self-care, because self-care by definition cannot be other-directed or service-oriented, but rather self-directed and therefore egotistic. The opponent of self-care may here invoke the parable of the Good Samaritan,[102] as exemplary of how virtuous healthcare professionals and institutions should strive to treat their patients compassionately and selflessly.

In the parable, the Good Samaritan passes by a half-dead man who had fallen into the hands of robbers, has been beaten, stripped of their clothes and left to die. The Good Samaritan, having compassion on this man, stops on their way, moves toward him, and cares for him by bandaging their wounds. Then, the

---

[102] Luke 10:30–37.
The idea of compassion is frequently associated with the idea of the "Good Samaritan." The idea has spurred a protracted debate on the scope of the general duty to aid and rescue the needy, of which the duty of care for the ill (in a healthcare context) is a specific type. On the debate of the duty of aid and rescue, see, e.g., Fabre, *Whose Body is it Anyway?—Justice and Integrity of the Person*, pp. 40–54; Feinberg, *Harm to Others—The Moral Limits of the Criminal Law*, pp. 126–85; Weinrib, "The Case for a Duty to Rescue," pp. 247–93; Ripstein, "Three Duties to Rescue: Moral, Civil, and Criminal," pp. 751–79; Malm, "Bad Samaritan Laws: Harm, Help, or Hype," pp. 707–50; Mack, "Bad Samaritanism and the Causation of Harm," pp. 230–59; McIntyre, "Guilty Bystanders? On the Legitimacy of Duty to Rescue Statues," pp. 157–91; Malm, "Liberalism, Bad Samaritan Law, and Legal Paternalism," pp. 4–31.

Good Samaritan puts the man on their donkey, brings him to an inn, to continue to care for him. The next day, the Good Samaritan pays the innkeeper to provide the services and the care that the man needs, guaranteeing the innkeeper that any extra-costs of care would be later reimbursed.

Invoking the parable, the opponent of self-care would here likely claim that healthcare providers have a moral duty to care for their patients as the Good Samaritan did: going beyond the call of duty and serving their patients as generously and selflessly as possible. True, virtuous healthcare professionals should strive to treat their patients as compassionately as the Good Samaritan did. This is hardly debatable. However, I would contend that there is nothing in the parable that leads to the conclusion that proper self-care (for self-constitution) is immoral, or that the moral duty to love and care for patients and the moral duty to love and care for oneself are mutually exclusive. In fact, I would maintain that the parable shows that the virtue of compassion requires the fulfillment of both duties, as a golden mean.

It is right to say that the Good Samaritan goes beyond the call of duty and serves the half-dead man generously and selflessly by caring for him on the road and then taking him to an inn. However, the Good Samaritan also establishes certain boundaries and cares for himself by then leaving the ill man in the inn to take care of their own business and needs. He also arranges with the innkeeper the continued care of the man (see Chapter 5 where I argue that a good leader is able to delegate certain tasks, empowering those under her leadership rather than centralizing power and control by doing it all herself).

Establishing boundaries should never mean abandoning or neglecting (see Chapter 5 where I elaborate on the requirement of non-abandonment), and the Good Samaritan makes sure that the man is cared for adequately. However, establishing boundaries does mean being able to create a certain detachment or attitude of surrender in relation to the suffering of another, since the caregiver is not (and cannot be) the sufferer's savior (see the discussion on the so called "white savior complex"[103], above and in Chapter 3). The creation of a healthy detachment or posture of surrender is a compassionate and virtuous choice, because it depends on the humble acknowledgment of one's own limitations and on the prudent recognition of one's need take care of oneself and one's own businesses too. Neither the identification of one's own limitations, nor the choice to leave a person in need under the care of another is easy. Both require a discernment and discretionary process, predicated on the virtues of prudence, humility (i.e., self-knowledge), and courage to act on that deliberation. Only then can one more clearly draw the reasonable boundaries that define how a virtuous healthcare professional and institution should strive to treat their patients and

---

[103] See, e.g., Arguedas, *Te Hundo para Luego Tratar de Salvarte*.

other professionals compassionately while treating herself compassionately, too. It is in this sense that compassion is a discretionary process, predicated on those virtues, and exercised through practical reasoning.[104] The parable of the Good Samarian offers lessons that illustrate the morality of these boundaries in care and aid, when it comes to the social application of love, not only in personal interactions but also in institutional dynamics, as I have sought to show in this chapter. (In Chapter 5, I elaborate further on the necessity of such reasonable boundaries applied to good leadership and institutional governance, particularly the WHO leadership of GHG.)

In sum, the Good Samarian has a proper sense of self: not overfocusing on himself and his comforts or preferences, but also not completely forgetting to care for himself, by violating his agency, conscience, freedom, own needs, and other commitments or responsibilities of care, which would only lead to self-annihilation, exhaustion, and burn-out. In his integrity (inner integrity of character) and authenticity (outer authenticity of action), the Good Samaritan is a model of what proper love of self for the purpose of self-constitution (or self-possession) should look like.[105] It is precisely because of his self-possession that he can love fully by giving himself totally as a his gift to the half-dead man in need (again, one cannot give what one does not possess).

Conclusion

In this chapter, I defined the second type of love that applies to the context of GHG, namely *compassion*, or love of neighbor. I provided a general analysis of compassion and applied it to the interpersonal relationships that unfold within institutions of healthcare and GHG. Building on Chapter 1, I demonstrated that the common feature between mercy and compassion is that both are best understood as processes that culminate in a gift of self, given in response to suffering. However, I argued that compassion's distinctive feature is the choice to *share* in the sufferer's suffering through accompaniment or presence.

Specifically, I proposed that compassion is a three-stage process that results in presence. The first stage is *affective*, which I termed *sympathy*. The second stage is *intellectual*, which I referred to as *empathy*. The third stage is *effective*, producing a conduct of care, which I called *compassionate conduct of care*. After applying this three-stage conception of compassion to the context of medical suffering,

---

[104] See my discussion on discretionary acts in the previous Chapter 1 based on H.L.A Hart's definition of discretion.

[105] On the practical reasonableness of self-constitution as integrity and authenticity, see: Finnis, *Natural Law and Natural Rights*, p. 169.

I responded to its main objections (applicable not only to each stage individually but also to my argument of compassion as a three-stage process more generally).

The central idea of compassion as a process that culminates in presence introduced several key tensions explored throughout this chapter. These include the tension between *being with* the sufferer and *doing things with or for* the sufferer, a theme I clarify further in Chapter 3. It also introduced the tension between *equality of dignity* and *equity of care*, a topic I expand on in Chapter 4. Finally, this chapter introduced the theme of *proper self-care* and the establishment of reasonable boundaries to allow for sustained generosity, a discussion I develop further in Chapter 5.

Compassion, as conceptualized in this chapter, is a discernment process focused on how to be present in adequately caring for the other. It is fundamentally *other-directed*, involving mutual discernment and a mutual commitment to *die to self* for the good of the other—as *Other*, respecting their uniqueness and agency. The following chapter elaborates on the idea of love as willing the good of the other—as Other, a notion I borrow from theologian Hans Urs von Balthasar and from philosopher Emmanuel Lévinas. The outcome of the process of compassion at the interactional level I called friendship, which requires the active participation of the Other in deliberations. At the institutional level, I referred to this outcome as solidarity, which requires the meaningful inclusion of the Other at the negotiation table (see Chapters 1 and 5 on the definition of meaningful inclusion). The upshot of friendship and solidarity is the creation of strong communities of mutual care. The central takeaway from this chapter is that the creation of communities of mutual care—grounded in the friendship and solidarity that arises when compassion is applied across relationships, policies, and structures of healthcare and GHG—should be the primary goal of these institutions. Such communities stand in contrast to "communities of hasty care," which arise from an exclusively utilitarian understanding of efficiency. Instead, compassion-driven institutions foster meaningful presence, equity, and care, forming the backbone of a truly humane and sustainable GHG system.

3
On Beneficence

> A friend should bear his friend's infirmities.
> Caius Cassius, in Shakespeare's *Julius Caesar*,
> Act IV, Scene iii, line 89

Introduction

One may exercise the virtue of prudence in questioning anything that Cassius ever said to Brutus about friendship. After all, they plot to betray and kill their mutual friend Julius Caesar. This act of treason led both, according to Dante, to hell, where they were eternally placed in the mouth of Lucifer (together with Judas, who betrayed Jesus).[1] As Shakespeare recounts in *Julius Caesar*, Cassius convinces Brutus to join their group of friends in their plot to assassinate Julius Caesar. Cassius persuades Brutus that the purposes of their plans were righteous and that they would betray Julius Caesar only to defend a greater cause, namely to remain loyal to their political ideal of the Roman Republic. To enhance his trustworthiness and ease Brutus' hesitancy, Cassius makes some true claims about friendship. One of them is the claim that "a friend should bear his friend's infirmities." True, a friend is indeed expected to bear with another. But what does that mean? Does it mean to do things for the other? In this sense, was Brutus then expected to do something for Cassius in order to help Cassius advance his presumably well-meaning plans? Or does bear with mean to have a shared end and do things together with the other in order to reach that common object? If so, would Brutus then be expected to join Cassius and their group of friends in pursuing together their common goal to defend the Roman Republic at all costs? Or does "bear with" a friend actually mean something much simpler, namely to be present by accompanying the friend on his journey—especially when the road gets rough and his infirmities, frailties, limitations, vulnerabilities, and flaws become more difficult to tolerate? Throughout this chapter, I defend this latter interpretation.

---

[1] Dante, *Inferno*, p. 34.

I will argue that the core feature of beneficence is being with, and not only actively doing things for or with the other. The chapter is laid out in three sections. In the first, I will present a conceptual analysis, justifying that we should conceive of benevolence (i.e., willing the good of the other—as Other, where the good encompasses the uniqueness of the other, their agency, and freedom) as a step toward beneficence (i.e., a conduct—either an action or an omission—that effectively benefits the other). Put differently, benevolence is an intentional intellectual step toward the effective step of beneficence. Like the move from empathy to compassionate care that characterizes compassion as described in Chapter 2, this move from the intellectual step of benevolence to the active step of beneficence also produces an effective conduct of care, grounded on genuine love. After presenting this conceptual analysis relating benevolence and beneficence (Section 1), and responding to its main objections (Section 2), the chapter then proceeds with its normative claim, namely that the core feature of beneficence is the state of simply being with another and not actively doing things for or with the other (Section 3). I call this core feature the contemplative component of a beneficent conduct.

As discussed in Chapters 1 and 2, and now in this chapter, the common feature among these different types of love (i.e., mercy, compassion, and beneficence) is that they are best appreciated as a process that produces a gift of self. Here, gift of self means primarily to be present with another, bearing with one another, and discerning together how to best care for each other. In other words, gift of self is the contemplative component of good care. For care to be good, it has to be attentive to the uniqueness of the cared for. This loving attention—where the caregiver beholds the cared for to learn about her uniqueness and know her more deeply—is the caregiver's gift of self to the cared for. Good care in the context of illnesses and suffering may—more often than not—necessarily entail doing certain tasks for and with the other who is unwell. While these active components of care are necessary, they may be neither sufficient nor the most essential feature of good care. The ill surely needs to be cared *for*; but above all cared *about*.[2] The contemplative component of care is, I contend, fundamental, because it is the basis for experiencing genuine love and authentic (rather than paternalistic) care. While this contemplative component is the most essential for love to be truly experienced, there is a complementarity between the contemplative and the active features of care. I will explain how this complementarity is key to designing good institutions of healthcare and GHG that strive to build strong communities of mutual care. By further developing the idea of presence in the context of GHG, this chapter (together with the previous chapters on mercy and

---

[2] For this distinction, see: Herring, *Law and the Relational Self*, p. 51; Tronto, *Moral Boundaries*, pp. 127–34.

compassion) continues to challenge the design of existing institutions and to show how love could reform them.

Section 1. A Conceptual Analysis of Beneficence

Mercy, as I define in Chapter 1, is a specific type of love concerned about how to love the enemy. Compassion, as I define in Chapter 2, is a more encompassing type of love: it is about how to love those neighbors who suffer, whether the sufferer is an enemy, a friend, or a stranger, whether they are near or far. In this chapter, I discuss beneficence, a third type of love whose scope is even broader. As I define it, beneficence is concerned about how to love the Other—where the Other is as an enemy, a friend, a stranger, a family member, or a beloved one—in times of suffering and beyond. Beneficence answers the question of how to love the Other who is in front of me, whoever they are, whatever their life circumstances (i.e., whether in seasons of suffering or not). Because of this all-embracing nature of beneficence, I often use "beneficence" and "love" interchangeably in this chapter, as do most scholars with whom I will dialogue. Different from most scholars, however, I do differentiate the ideas of "beneficence" and "benevolence."

Although in the bioethics and philosophy literatures the terms "benevolence" and "beneficence" are by and large used as synonymous, strictly speaking, these words do not signify exactly the same. The philosopher Thomas Aquinas, for example, makes their distinction clear.[3] Benevolence, or *bene volere*, means to will the good of the other.[4] Beneficence, or *bene ficens*, means to do the good (through such good-will).

But who knows what the good of the other truly is? A paternalist benevolent agent is quick to presume they know what the good for the other is. A truly benevolent agent wills the good of the other but is not so quick to assume anything. Instead, they recognize through self-reflection that they may not always know what is good without first attentively contemplating[5] the other in their uniqueness, learning more about that person and their particular life circumstances, and above all respecting the freedom of the other as a moral agent.[6] I would therefore slightly modify Aquinas' definition, and conceive of benevolence as willing the good of the other—as Other—that is, honoring the Other's uniqueness and

---

[3] Kant makes a similar distinction, when affirming that active benevolence results in beneficence. See: Kant, *Metaphysics of Morals*, II, 1.1. 25–30 (450).
[4] Aquinas, *ST* ii-ii, Q 27, a2. See also: Wojtyla, *Love and Responsibility*, p. 83.
[5] For philosopher Josef Pieper, contemplation is a process of knowing the Other, inspired by love. See: Pieper, *Happiness and Contemplation*.
[6] I thank Lauren Woodside Alegre for making this point clear.

respecting their freedom, by attentively beholding[7] them in an attempt to getting to know them at a deeper level.[8] Hence, my addition of "as Other" is not trivial: it serves the purpose of differentiating a paternalistic kind of benevolence from true benevolence.

(True) benevolence is, more specifically, a virtue. The virtue of benevolence predisposes the agent to attentively learn to choose thoughtfully, form a commitment, and then perform a certain conduct that will benefit the other while respecting their agency.[9] Benevolence is then an intellectual process of attentive observation, careful reflection, and resolute commitment to contribute to the other's well-being in a thoughtful manner. The actual conduct (the action or omission) that effectively contributes to one's well-being, however, is an act of beneficence.[10]

As the effective component of (true) benevolence, beneficence represents the "outward gift"[11] from benefactor to beneficiary. Beneficence is a practical principle[12] that justifies certain actions and omissions that benefit other people,[13] promoting their flourishing. In bioethics, beneficence is understood as a principle that requires healthcare professionals to act in their patients' best interests.[14] Some, like the bioethicist Edmund Pellegrino, have argued that beneficence is the most fundamental bioethical principle of professional medical ethics.[15] Beneficence clarifies both the nature and the ultimate purpose of healthcare professions, especially medicine.[16] It focuses on care (synonymous with healing) as opposed to cure (which may not always be possible) and aims to prioritize the patient's good. Importantly, the good of the patient is truly good when care respects the patient's freedom, and therefore aligns with the bioethical principle of autonomy.[17]

---

[7] Philosopher Stephen Darwall also talks about the action of beholding the beloved in his presence. As Darwall puts it: "beholding is a distinct form of attention that we can give only to what is present to us in some way or another." Darwall, "Love's Second Personal Character," p. 104.

[8] I am borrowing the expression "the other—as Other," from theologian von Balthasar and philosopher Lévinas. For von Balthasar, mutual love is "where the other as other is encountered." See: von Balthasar, *Love Alone Is Credible*, p. 53; Lévinas, *Totality and Infinity*, pp. 49–51.

[9] See: Aquinas, *ST* ii-ii, Q31, a4. See also: Beauchamp and Childress, *Principles of Biomedical Ethics*, p. 166.

[10] Ibid.

[11] Aquinas, *ST* ii-ii, Q31, a4.

[12] Practical principles provide reasons for action. See: Grisez, Boyle, and Finnis, "Practical Principles, Moral Truth, and Ultimate Ends," p. 102.

[13] Aquinas, *ST* ii-ii, Q31, a1.

[14] Besides the principle of beneficence, bioethicists Tom Beauchamp and James F. Childress list the principles of non-maleficence, autonomy, and justice. Their theoretical account is also known as "principlism." See: Beauchamp and Childress, *Principles of Biomedical Ethics*.

[15] Pellegrino, "The Four Principles and The Doctor-Patient Relationship"; Pellegrino and Thomasma, *For the Patient's Good*.

[16] Ibid.

[17] For bioethicists Edmund Pellegrino and David Thomasma ("The Conflict between Autonomy and Beneficence in Medical Ethics"), care and agency are not at odds but mutually consistent. However, philosopher Onora O'Neill (*Autonomy and Trust in Bioethics*) argues that the dominance

While the three types of love discussed, respectively, in Chapters 1 and 2, and now here are different, what mercy, compassion, and beneficence share in common, however, is that they all involve this "internal dynamic process"[18] within the agent who loves. In this process, a feeling or perception awakens an intellectual choice that then moves the agent to form an effective commitment to perform a particular conduct of care, in the name of the good of another—as Other. That is to say, the good cannot simply be quickly assumed but must be the result of choosing to be present with the Other, contemplating them, and thinking deeply about what is needed to care for them in their unique circumstances and in a manner that upholds their agency, freedom, and dignity. This internal, intellectual dynamic process moves the agent from a convenient, comfortable position (the status quo) to a self-sacrificial choice (a gift of self) that changes the status quo. Here, by gift of self I mean that love is a self-sacrificing gift: it requires the giver (of mercy, compassion, or beneficence) to choose to change the status quo and share in by thinking deeply about the experience of the other (especially in those difficult experiences of suffering and infirmities)—for the good of the other. This is precisely the distinctive feature of love: the sharing of life (more often than not characterized by seasons of deep suffering and severe infirmities) with another.[19] To share in the experience of the other is to be with them, to accompany them in their journey. In one word, it means to be present. And this is what gift of self fundamentally is: presence.[20] This presence is not merely physical when the agent does something for or with the Other; but is instead a full presence that engages the body, mind, and soul of the agent in attentively contemplating and learning about the other—as Other. Whether the agent makes herself present by performing a forgiving conduct of care (as in the case of mercy), or a compassionate conduct of care (as in the case of compassion), or a beneficial conduct of care (as in the case of beneficence), the agent effectively changes the status quo, and thus fosters communion and community with the other.[21] These are the upshots of love.

of autonomy rights has made it "difficult to find clear affirmations of traditional models of medical beneficence." For a historical perspective on the rise of autonomy and its impact on beneficence in bioethics, see Faden and Beauchamp's *A History and Theory of Informed Consent*.

[18] I am borrowing this expression from legal scholar Adam Perry, who makes a similar point when he remarks that mercy involves an "an internal dynamic process" from anger to forgiveness. See: Perry, *Mercy*, in *Philosophy and Public Affairs*, pp. 62, 87.
[19] As discussed in Chapter 1, mercy may not always lead to the full restoration of a shared life in companionship, although it always restores union in community.
[20] In his discussion of love, Darwall also uses the term "presence" (to be with another). However, Darwall explores this idea within the context of reciprocal love and his theory of the second-person standpoint, rather than in the broader realm of agapic love that I define in this book as encompassing a multidirectional care network. For Darwall, to love and be present is "to be in second-personal rapport with each other." (See: Darwall, "Love's Second Personal Character," p. 93; Darwall, "Being With," pp. 4–24.)
[21] Aquinas, *ST* ii-ii, Q31, a1.

To be clear, willing the good of the other, committing to it, and directing one's conducts to benefit the other are not simply based on an emotional perception (e.g., sympathy, pity, delight of attraction, and desire). A feeling or perception may awaken this internal process, but the exercise of the virtue of benevolence coupled with the practical effects of beneficence are chiefly grounded on a decisive and deeply contemplative act that leads to a committed choice to care well and respectfully for another in their uniqueness. The philosopher Harry Frankfurt describes this internal dynamic that I refer to, when defining love as the practical reason that justifies conducts of care for the beloved's benefit, in a self-sacrificial, rather than self-interested way:

> [Love] is a species of caring about things... To love differs from having feelings of a certain type, such as those of powerful attraction or of intense desire or of compelling delight. [Love] is volitional... What a person loves helps to determine the choices that he makes and the actions that he is eager or unwilling to perform.... Loving of any variety implies conduct that is designed to be beneficial to the beloved object.... His primary goal is not to receive benefits but to provide them. He is motivated by an interest in serving the interests and ends of his beloved rather than an interest in serving his own.[22]

Frankfurt's conception of love is close to the Thomistic definition of benevolence that ensues beneficence, which I provided at the beginning of the chapter: both love and benevolence signify willing the good (i.e., the well-being and flourishing) of another, in a "disinterested" way.[23] By "disinterested love," Frankfurt means the opposite of self-interested concern. For Frankfurt, the best (or at least closest) example of disinterested love, among all types of human relationships, is the loving concern that parents have for their infants or small children. The reason is that this is the clearest example, for Frankfurt, of a total self-donation, where there is a total gift-of-self from the caregiver to another in complete need and utter dependance. This, Frankfurt thinks, "is the mode of caring that comes closer—much closer than romantic or erotically based devotion—to provide pure instances of ... love."[24] Frankfurt's pristine model of disinterested love is contentious, though,[25] and I will come back to discuss it in more detail later in

---

See also: Wojtyla, *Love and Responsibility*, Ignatius, p. 90. For Beauchamp and Childress, although "obligations of beneficence to society are typically derived from some form of reciprocity," "we certainly cannot justify all forms of virtue of benevolence in terms of reciprocity." Beauchamp and Childress, *Principles of Biomedical Ethics*, p. 174.

[22] Frankfurt, "Autonomy, Necessity, and Love," pp. 129, 133. See: Frankfurt, "On Caring," p. 165.
[23] Frankfurt, "On Caring," p. 165.
[24] Ibid., p. 166.
[25] For different perspectives, see, e.g., John Paul II, *Man and Woman*; Ebels-Duggan, "Against Beneficence," pp. 142–70.

the chapter. But first, I want to complete the presentation of my concept of (true) benevolence resulting in beneficence.

Combining both Frankfurt's concept of love and my (slightly amended) Thomistic definition of (true) benevolence, one concludes that beneficence to be authentic cannot be primarily motivated by self-interest. However, in real life, because neither of us is perfect, there is normally some degree of self-interest or self-centeredness that blinds us to perfectly see, behold, contemplate the other in front of us, and therefore perfectly know the Other and what is truly good for them, in their uniqueness. We all have our blind spots, after all! As I explained, benevolence is not always true benevolence and can at times be paternalistic in spite of the good motivations of the agent. If one acknowledges the possibility of paternalistic benevolence, I believe benevolence (to will the good of the other) is best appreciated as an Aristotelean virtue. As a virtue, there are at least three general degrees of benevolence. There can be too much benevolence (i.e., excessive eagerness to care to the point of overpowering the other's agency),[26] or too little (i.e., indifference leading to negligence). True benevolence, as a virtue, ought to seek the golden mean. It means caring for the good of another—in his uniqueness and with respect for his agency, in a committed yet "disinterested"—or detached enough—manner. By detachment here I mean the recognition of the other's agency along with my willingness and decision to care for their good. That is to say, being dedicated to meeting the needs of the other, but neither to the detriment of one's own good, agency, and freedom, nor with a fixated motivation to save the other as if one could be the other's hero or savior.

In correlation to these three degrees of benevolence, there are three degrees of beneficent conducts. The first degree relates to self-interested acts that result in excessive, overpowering beneficence toward the other. When this happens, one's conduct may be called paternalistic in some cases or self-congratulatory supererogation in others. A paternalistic conduct disrespects the agency of the beneficiary, by acting in a patronizing and demeaning way (see Chapter 6 where I elaborate on this definition). The paternalistic benefactor presumes that he knows more and better, and therefore has a duty to save the cared for from her ignorance by trying somewhat to control her choices. Paternalism is self-interested because it is blind to the other; it is also self-indulgent as it makes the benefactor feel good about himself as the savior or hero. A self-congratulatory supererogatory conduct, in turn, goes beyond what is morally required and good: it is a praiseworthy conduct that brings the benefactor applause and admiration, aggrandizing their *amour proprio* (in the Rousseaunian sense).

---

[26] See my definition of paternalism in Chapter 6: paternalism often, but not always, stems from a good motivation and belief that one is caring for another. However, such care is exercised in a manner that disrespects the other's agency and undermines their freedom.

Self-congratulatory supererogation is therefore laudable and often masks the ulterior motives of the benefactor in desiring mostly to gain a reputation for generosity.[27] In other words, self-congratulatory supererogation is also self-interested or self-indulgent. Both paternalism and self-congratulatory supererogation are the contrary of "disinterested love" in Frankfurt's sense.

Although the words charity and philanthropy should not automatically entail paternalism or self-congratulatory supererogation, these words now typically bring such pejorative connotations.[28] This is particularly true in the context of GHG, where a donor-centered model of international development assistance is prevalent.[29] This model has been highly criticized for conforming first and foremost to the interests and political agendas of global heath donors rather than the actual health needs of the recipients of aid.[30] In so doing, the contemporary model of global health philanthropy and charity is defined as both paternalistic and self-congratulatory supererogation. It is paternalistic because it wrongly assumes that donors know best what the recipients' health needs and priorities should be (see Chapter 5 where I discuss this problem at length). This has been called white savior complex.[31] It is also self-congratulatory supererogation because it is primarily self-interested rather than other-directed.

The second degree of beneficence, at the opposite side of the spectrum, corresponds to self-interested conducts that result in insufficient beneficence. The agent who acts with insufficient beneficence is often called a "Bad Samaritan": his conducts fall below of what is morally—and at times legally—required as a duty.[32] For example, there are the so-called "Bad Samaritan" laws in certain jurisdictions,[33] typically involving cases of easy rescue and nonfeasance.[34] These are controversial laws that penalize the person who denies rescue

---

[27] Not all supererogatory conducts are self-congratulatory. For a general definition of supererogation, see: Aquinas, *ST* i-ii, Q 107, Q 108; and *ST* ii-ii, Q106; Finnis, *Aquinas—Moral, Political, and Legal Theory*, p. 142; Feinberg, "Supererogation and Rules," pp. 276–88; Gewirth, "Private Philanthropy and Positive Rights," pp. 56–78; Raz, "Permissions and Supererogation," pp. 161–68; and Raz, *The Morality of Freedom*, pp. 196–97.

[28] The terms charity, philanthropy, donation, and altruism are often used interchangeably. See, e.g., Waldron ("Welfare and the Images of Charity," p. 463), defining charity as "a person giving part of his wealth to others who are less well-off than he is." However, in moral theology, charity carries a broader meaning, signifying love in general—including love of God, neighbor, and self.

[29] Gostin and Mok, "Innovative Solutions to Closing the Health Gap between Rich and Poor," p. 451; Ruger, "Global Health Governance as a Shared Health Governance," p. 654.

[30] Ibid.

[31] See, e.g., Arguedas, "Te Hundo para Luego Tratar de Salvarte."

[32] For a discussion on the stringency of duties of beneficence, including prospective duties of beneficence, see: Cordelli, "Prospective Duties and the Demands of Beneficence," pp. 373–401.

[33] For a list of jurisdictions applying Bad Samaritan laws, see: Feinberg, p. 126.

[34] In jurisdictions that enforce "Bad Samaritan" laws, failing to throw the rope or neglecting the suffering child to the point of death would be legally wrong. However, in some countries following the Common Law tradition, such nonfeasance would generally be legally permissible, though this has been extensively debated for decades. (In tort law, "nonfeasance" refers to inaction causing harm to a person or property, which can result in liability if there was a duty of care toward the injured person.)

to those in need, when the risk to the life of the rescuer is minor.[35] It is argued that a duty of (easy) rescue is not only a stringent moral duty but also a legally enforceable one.[36] The reasoning behind this argument is that insufficient beneficence is wrong and should not be tolerated because it prioritizes one's own comfort above any willing of good for another.[37]

The third degree of beneficence corresponds to disinterested, detached conducts of care displaying an appropriate level of beneficence. It is the Aristotelian golden mean between the other two extremes. Let's call this *authentic* beneficence for the sake of clarity. This authentic beneficence is the right reason that should guide the practical conduct of a virtuous agent, committed to the true good of the cared for. Good Samaritan-type conducts set the standard here for ordinary morality. Although Good Samaritan-type conducts may not be legally obligatory, they are morally required: they define how one should generally love their neighbors.[38] Importantly, the Good Samarian, as discussed in Chapter 2, has a proper sense of self: not overfocusing on themselves, their comforts, and their preferences but also not completely forgetting to care for themselves, by silencing their agency, freedom, and their own needs,[39] leading to self-annihilation, exhaustion, and burnout (see Chapter 2 for my reading of the parable of the Good Samaritan in how he goes an extra mile to care well for the injured man but also delegates care tasks to others, who can do it as well or better than them, so he can leave the injured man under good care to take care of his own business without neglecting the cared for).

These are, in broad stokes, the three general degrees of benevolence and beneficence. Their specific contours and moral stringency, however, are not so easily defined. These often spur protracted debates in philosophy.[40] But generally speaking, the more closely related the benefactor and the beneficiary are, the more stringent the moral duties of benevolence and beneficence are. For *prima facie* the closer the relationship, the greater the responsibility to care for one's

---

[35] Singer, "Famine, Affluence, and Morality," pp. 229–43.
[36] On the controversies involving "Bad Samaritan" laws and their enforceability, see, e.g., Fabre, *Whose Body Is It Anyway*, pp. 40–54; Feinberg, *Harm to Others*, pp. 126–85; Weinrib, "The Case for a Duty to Rescue," pp. 247–93; Ripstein, "Three Duties to Rescue: Moral, Civil, and Criminal," pp. 755–79; Malm, "Bad Samaritan Laws," pp. 707–50; Mack, "Bad Samaritanism and the Causation of Harm," pp. 230–59; Alison McIntyre, "Guilty Bystanders?" pp. 157–91; and Malm, "Liberalism, Bad Samaritan Law, and Legal Paternalism," pp. 4–31.
[37] I thank Lauren Woodside Alegre for making this point clearer.
[38] Luke 10:30–37.
[39] I have drawn a moral distinction between wants, desires, and preferences, on the one hand, and needs, on the other. The lack of the former causes discomfort. The lack of the latter causes disablement. See Chapter 2.
[40] See, e.g., the debate between Peter Singer ("Famine, Affluence, and Morality," pp. 229–43) who argues for a stronger principle of beneficence, and Liam Murphy ("The Demands of Beneficence," pp. 267–92) who argues for a "limited principle of beneficence."

good—other things being equal (see Chapter 5 on the idea of *ordo amoris* within the discussion of the principle of subsidiarity).[41]

Section 2. Objections to My Conceptual Analysis of Benevolence and Beneficence

2.1. Response to the Problem of Paternalism

I have defended the view that the virtue of benevolence coupled with the practical principle of beneficence give the agent the right reasons to choose and then act for the true good of the other—as Other—where the true good encompasses the uniqueness of the other and as well the other's agency and freedom. The caveat the Other with capital O, signifying their unique identity, is not a frivolous addition. As I explained in the previous section, care to be truly good necessitates a loving regard from the agent, that is, an attentive, contemplative, full presence with another that allows the agent to more closely learn about and more deeply get to know the Other, and their unique needs. This loving regard enables the agent to avoid paternalistically presuming too much, and override the other's agency. But the problem of paternalism in the context of loving care is so insidious and grave that some may likely object to this conceptual analysis that I provided. My opponents may contend that this transition from willing the good of other (i.e., virtue of benevolence) to acting in a beneficent way may not be so straightforwardly accomplished in practical terms. Simply willing the good of the other—as Other, they would insist, does not necessarily lead to acts of care grounded on genuine love. It can also lead, my opponents would repeat, either to acts of paternalism and condescension or to acts of self-serving and self-congratulatory supererogation. For example, if one accepts Frankfurt's parent–infant example as the paradigm of benevolence and beneficence, then one has also to understand genuine love as providing practical reasons for the agent to care for those entrusted to their care. But care may not always be loving and desirable, my opponents would insist. Given that small children are dependent on others and not able to do things for themselves, one important way in which parents care for their small children is by doing things for them. However, as philosopher Kyla Ebels-Duggan argues, doing things for others, under the excuse of caring for them, assumes that the cared for are merely "a passive object of care."[42]

---

[41] This idea will be further developed in Chapter 6 where the principle of subsidiarity will be discussed. See also: Aquinas, *ST* ii-ii Q26, a6, and Q31, a3.
[42] Ebels-Duggan, "Against Beneficence," p. 145.

Ebels-Duggan argues that love must respect the autonomy of the beloved as a self-governing agent. Following this argument, in doing things for others, one disrespects the agency and freedom of those for whom one cares. Instead, interactions in a loving, respectful relationship, one should do things with and not for one another, deciding together what to do in partnership.

Philosopher Stephen Darwall makes a similar point on the central role of interactions between two agents in a loving relationship. For Darwall, "caring... neither requires the context of a relationship, nor essentially involves any such relating."[43] For Darwall, therefore, care and love are not connected concepts. While care aims at one's well-being, love "includes desires to support each other in their goals and dreams, even at the cost to their friend's well-being."[44] For Darwall, love must respect one's agency and freedom, but care does not.[45] Furthermore, he notes that interactions with small children are too limited (given their very limited ability to make reasonable choices and therefore have agency and autonomy)[46] to justify the parent–infant example as the pristine model of love.

I agree with Darwall that love, in its genuine sense, must respect the Other's agency and freedom, being therefore incompatible with abuse. bell hooks also defends the view that "love and abuse cannot coexist."[47] Similarly by respecting the other's agency, love is incongruent with paternalism. As discussed in Chapter 1 and further elaborated in Chapter 6, paternalism occurs when a presumably well-intentioned individual, who arguably wills the good of the other, subtracts or robs the other's agency in the name of the other's well-being, presuming that they know best what the good of the other is. The paternalistic agent therefore is neither sufficiently attentive to nor properly respectful of how the Other practically conceptualizes the good, as applicable to their unique life circumstances. While I agree that love must respect the other's agency and never override it, even at the cost of what the loving agent may see as best for the well-being of the other, I disagree with Darwall's concept of love and care in two important ways:

First, for Darwall, respecting the autonomy of the beloved should come before anything else. Therefore, for him, love requires an absolute respect of the

---

[43] Darwall, "Reply to Griffin, Raz, and Wolff," pp. 441–42.
[44] Ibid.
[45] Other disability scholars have also voiced the same critique that care is disrespectful to one's agency and freedom. See, e.g., Jenny Morris ("Care or Empowerment," p. 64), for whom care itself is a form of oppression against disabled people. See also: Kelly, "Making 'Care' Accessible," pp. 562–64. For a postmodern critique of care, see also: Bauman, *Postmodern Ethics*, p. 11. For a different view within the critical disability studies literature, however, see, e.g., Feder Kittay, *Learning from My Daughter*, pp. 208–12, where she presents a defense of care that is respectful to one's agency and freedom.
[46] Darwall, *Welfare and Rational Care*, p. 15.
[47] hooks, *All About Love*, p. 6.

beloved's autonomy to choose and author their life as they see fit. Darwall calls this requirement of love the "upholding" of the beloved.[48] To uphold or to support the beloved, for Darwall, is not simply to care for their well-being, but rather to empower and enable them to pursue their own projects, dreams, and pursuits.[49] Also, for Darwall, "we uphold people... when we are loyal to them."[50] So from Darwall's love requirement to uphold the beloved's desires, one would deduce that Brutus, for example, would indeed be expected to join Cassius and their other friends in being loyal to their shared end to defend the Roman Republic at all costs.

But if we were to accept Darwall's concept of love, premised on a respect for unfettered autonomous choices as the highest moral imperative, then we would obtain that love would require the person who loves to potentially silence their own conscience and violate their own agency for the sake of upholding (or better said, conceding) the beloved's desire, simply because the beloved wants it. It seems to me, however, that this interpretation of love and its consequences would contradict the very concept of reciprocity (as mutual recognition of people's equal moral agency and authority as equal members of the moral community) so fundamental in Darwall's theory of the second-person standpoint.[51] To unthinkingly enable the beloved to achieve their desires, whatever they might be, simply because they want them, is not love if it requires the lover to obliterate their will and remove their agency out of the way. Love, as I define it, is a discretionary process that results in a free choice, which cannot exist if the lover must deny their own conscience.

Here, Darwall might argue that without complete respect and "upholding" of the other's desires, the loving agent risks becoming paternalistic. However, I do not think that avoiding paternalism necessitates the person who loves to be a doormat, who does whatever the other wants, simply to please them, be nice, and avoid confrontation. Love, as I define it, is the mark of a fully-fledged moral agent, who thinks deeply, carefully, and critically about what the good of the Other, in their uniqueness, requires and does not require. Love is therefore not acritical niceness and automatic people-pleasing attitudes. Sure, there is tenderness and a reasonable submission of self in loving attention and caring response. But there is also thoughtfulness and discretion. Love (as I define it in the concluding remarks of Part 1) and authentic beneficence (as I am defining it here in this chapter) are not mechanical conducts void of critical judgment, but

---

[48] See Darwall, "Love's Second Personal Character," pp. 105–6.
[49] Ibid.
[50] Ibid.
[51] What Darwall calls "the second person" is the idea that morality is fundamentally about the demands that particular people are entitled to make on each other. See, e.g., Darwall, *Morality, Authority, and Law*.

rather the result of an attentive contemplation of the Other, through a careful intellectual examination of what are the needs of this Other in front of me.

Love does not mean satisfying all of the beloved's wants, desires, and preferences without discretion (the judgment and discernment process based on practical wisdom and prudence, as defined in Chapter 1). I am here drawing a distinction between needs, on the one hand, and wants, desires, and preferences, on the other.[52] When the former is lacking, there is a disablement.[53] When the latter is lacking, there is discomfort. Needs are objectively necessary to the Other to flourish in their uniqueness and particular circumstances. Wants, desires, and preferences may or may not objectively lead to the person's flourishing; in fact, they may even cause them harm. So, to support, without discretion, all of my beloved's projects, dreams, and pursuits, simply because they want them, is not love. It is complacency. Love requires the lover to behold the other, evaluate what their real needs are, and discern whether and how she can meet them through a thoughtful, tailored response. True love—or agape as I will refer to it—is indeed unconditional. But unconditional love does not mean unconditionally tolerating bad behavior (see discussion on Chapter 1 about mercy and abuse) or giving whatever the beloved wants. Unconditional love instead means to give love that is unmerited, without expecting anything in return (see concluding remarks of Part 1 on the definition of agape).

2.2. Response to the Problem of Love, Care, and Doing for Another

The second point in Darwall's concept of love with which I take issue is his distinction between love and care, in that care is paternalistic, and unrelated to love. Granted: care, as a practical, outward expression of love, manifests itself within a spectrum of beneficence. In this sense, it is possible to care too much (to the point of overriding the other's agency) and care too little (to the point of neglecting and abandoning the other in need). But I would contend that genuine care, grounded in true benevolence and authentic beneficence is possible. The Aristotelian golden mean of care, where the agency and freedom of both caregiver and cared for are respected, is possible—even when there is a perceived asymmetry of power, vulnerabilities, and dependencies between the two (such as in the parent–infant and the doctor–patient cases that I further discuss shortly).

Sure, genuine love can at times be inconsistent with care, when care is excessive or deficient, such as in the cases of paternalism, self-congratulatory supererogation, or neglect. But when both love and care are genuine, they are mutually

---

[52] I discuss this distinction at length in de Campos, *The Global Health*, Ch. 1.
[53] MacIntyre, *Dependent Rational Animals*, p. 124.

reinforcing (*viz.*, when their purposes are aligned toward the good of the other—as Other—that is, where the good encompasses the other's uniqueness, agency, and freedom). When care and love are consistent with each other, care is the effective aspect of love. In other words, love (to will the good of the other—as Other) is manifested and experienced through a caring conduct that is authentically beneficent. That is to say, it is a caring conduct that effectively meets the needs of the other while fully respecting the other's dignity, freedom, and agency. For love and care to be mutually reinforcing, the caregiver has to attentively learn who the other agent is, respecting their personality, observing their limitations, and identifying their needs by interacting with them, and then serving them by meeting such needs. In other words, the caregiver has to be committed to giving their loving regard,[54] their personal attentiveness to the other, and to receiving the gift of the other in return. This is the contemplative practice that true benevolence (love) and authentic beneficence (care) require.

Love and care are not passive. Both necessitate the active participation of (i) the one who vulnerably shares their needs with another and (ii) the one who contemplates and receives the gift of the other, in attentively getting to know, learn, and love the other—as Other. Love and care are not passive therefore because both necessitate interaction based on mutual respectful consideration and loving regard (see Chapter 4 on the definition of equality). Care here is a loving act of service where the caregiver loves the other person by encountering them in their needs. True, this service often entails doing things for the other—things that neither violate the agency and freedom of the person being cared for, nor violate the agency and conscience of the caregiver. Despite doing things for the other that often characterizes the care given in the parent–infant example, and also in the caregiver–ill patient example, care expressed as doing something for the other does not mean it is passive, disrespectful of one's agency, and demeaning.

2.3. Response to the Problem of Asymmetries of Vulnerability and Dependence

Although Ebels-Duggan argues that love that respects the autonomy of the beloved as a self-governing agent is only congruent with doing things with the other and is incongruent with doing things for the other, I would contend that this is not necessarily the case. As I explain below by discussing the parent–infant and the caregiver–ill patient examples, doing things for another can be an expression of authentic beneficence and is congruent with a love that respects

---

[54] Murdoch, *The Sovereignty of Good*, p. 34.

the agency of the other. In fact, what these two examples can teach us, when they are experienced in a disposition of authentic love and care, is the lesson of what it fundamentally means "to bear with" a friend's infirmities, frailties, limitations, and vulnerabilities. To explain this point, I will analyze in greater detail these two examples and defend their moral instructive authority in response to Ebels-Duggan's and Darwall's objections.

2.3.1. The Parent–Infant Model

Both Ebels-Duggan and Darwall argue that love must respect the autonomy of the beloved as a self-governing agent. So, for both, parent love does not exemplify well what love requires as a moral value. In the parent–small child example, the recipient of beneficence (i.e., the infant) has very limited capacity to autonomously choose and care for herself. This gives reasons for their benefactors (i.e., parents) to care for the infant, by choosing on the child's behalf and in their best interest. Is it morally permissible for parents to care for small children in this way? Or should this not be tolerated because it is oppressive, disrespectful, and demeaning to the infant? Few would contend that this is an inappropriate form of care for an infant or small child. In being completely vulnerable and dependent on their caregivers, they are indeed receivers of care. Also, by virtue of being children, they are—and should be—subjected to adequate parental authority, where such authority (defined in Chapter 6 as service) is justified by the parents' special duty of care for their children. However, parental authority and parents' special duty of care do not automatically make children mere "passive objects of care,"[55] as Ebels-Duggan contends. For one thing children communicate with their caregivers—even if not with words. And in response the caregivers should enter into a contemplative practice that enables them to better discern what the child needs. For another thing because relationships of care—all of them—have the potential to be reciprocal, making both the giver and the receiver of care "gifts of self" to one another.[56] Sure, the caregiver primarily gives care, and the child, as the recipient of care, primarily receives it. This is tautological. What is not tautological, though, is the fact that the caregiver may also receive something incommensurably valuable (e.g., love, joy, humility, and wisdom), perhaps not directly from the newborn (who may not even be able yet to smile back in grateful appreciation), but from the contemplative and active interactions with the child. The parent must engage in the contemplative practice of being attentive, listening,

---

[55] Ebels-Duggan, *Against Beneficence*, p. 145.
[56] I borrow this expression from John Paul II, *Man and Woman He Created Them*, p. 4. Although JP II uses the expression "gift-of-self" to explain reciprocity as an element of love in general, and more specifically of divine and spousal loves, the idea of gift of self can serve as an analogy to other types of relationships of love, including the one I am discussing here (the relationship between parents and children, based on love in general and on beneficence specifically). The same rationale applies, as I discuss below, to the relationship between caregivers and patients.

and discerning when the newborn cries because they are tired, or hungry, or in pain, and what exactly they need their parents to actively do for them. This contemplative interaction is necessary for ensuing an active care of authentic beneficence that does not simply assume that parents know it all without first gazing lovingly at their child. In these contemplative and active interactions, the caregiver may receive something and may also be nurtured by the infant, if the caregiver is open to perceiving and receiving the child, in all their neediness, limitations, and vulnerabilities, as a gift. As in any other healthy human relationship, there is here, too, the potential for a rich interaction and exchange of gifts of self that can be mutually nurturing. But whether the caregiver does receive something back or not is not really the main point. Children, even the smallest ones, are not mere passive objects of care because the contemplative practice of loving attention that allows the caregiver to discern what the child is trying to communicate is vital. Love and good care require parents to not be too quick to presume that they always know what their children need without beholding them contemplatively first and thoughtfully discerning what is best for each specific situation.[57]

One may still insist, however, that the parent–small child model does not perfectly exemplify love (meaning, the virtue of benevolence that leads to an authentically beneficent conduct of care), chiefly because of the great asymmetries of vulnerabilities, dependence, and capacities to autonomously choose that exist between an infant and their parents. There is an obvious (yet justifiable) asymmetry of authority between parents and children, which may indeed render this model insufficient to fully explain beneficence in the context of other types of love relationships. Some, like Ebels-Duggan herself and the theologian Karol Wojtyla,[58] contend that a better analogy would be the love relationship between spouses. For Wojtyla, as equals and friends, spouses have a reciprocal duty of care, where one is a gift (of self) to the other.[59] This reciprocal responsibility to love would require both spouses to will the good of the other—as Other— and act according to such practical reason of beneficence. While it may seem more accurate to say that the spousal relationship better reflects what is really at stake in authentic beneficence, all analogies fall short, one way or another. Also, while it is true that spouses are equals and friends, it is not true that there are no asymmetries of vulnerabilities, dependence, and capacities to autonomously choose over the course of their marriage. It is a myth to believe that there is a perfect 50–50 ratio in marriage or in most lifelong partnerships. These asymmetries will be more evident, for example, when one of the spouses

---

[57] I thank Lauren Woodside Alegre for making this point clearer.
[58] Wojtyla, *Love and Responsibility*.
[59] See, e.g., Waldstein, "Introduction," in JP2, *Man and Woman He Created Them*, pp. 24, 33.

becomes ill and is therefore more vulnerable and dependent and less capable of autonomously choosing what is best for them. But in any case, whether the parent–infant model, or the spousal model, or the caregiver–ill patient model (to be explored next) is the best to demonstrate what the moral value of love and authentic beneficence entail is somewhat beside the point for me here. My argument transcends this debate in acknowledging that while all analogies and models fall short one way or another, they are all helpful in showing that across the board, genuine love, expressed through an active conduct of authentic beneficence, requires first a contemplative practice of being fully present with the other.[60] This is the main lesson of love and beneficence that I draw from discussing the parent–infant model: being present is what fundamentally means "to bear with" another's infirmities, frailties, limitations, and vulnerabilities. Let us now turn to the caregiver–ill patient model and see what is the lesson of love and beneficence that stems from it.

2.3.2. The Caregiver–Ill Patient Model

Both Ebels-Duggan and Darwall hold the view that true love cannot be expressed by caring conducts that are given in a context of asymmetries of power and authority between the parties. My counter-argument to them involve two steps: (i) to acknowledge the natural reality of asymmetries of dependence and vulnerability throughout our life spam (especially in moments of illnesses but not restricted to these), which will pave the way for me; and (ii) to reveal the opportunity (and lesson of love and beneficence) that lies within these naturally occurring asymmetries. First, however, let me go back to Ebels-Duggan's discussion of the caregiver–ill patient model.

Ebels-Duggan contends that caring for others by doing things *for* them is "a corrupt view of love" that cannot be morally justifiable.[61] For her, doing things *for* others is a disrespectful and condescending form of care that treats the recipient of care as a mere "passive object," thereby creating or enlarging the asymmetry of power between the parties.[62] She does allow for an exception, though. Ebels-Duggan acknowledges that certain medical conditions are so debilitating that they do legitimately call for the kind of love and care centred around doing things for another. She gives the example of a severely depressed man, who

> like a child, is not competent to take care of [themselves] ... the depressive although chronologically an adult, is practically a child. It's just on the basis of a judgment that he's not a full-fledged agent, not well-functioning enough to

---

[60] I thank Lauren Woodside Alegre for making this point clearer.
[61] Ebels-Duggan, *Against Beneficence*, p. 153.
[62] Ibid., p. 148.

have sovereignty over his own life, that you think it appropriate to adopt the role of benefactor toward him.[63]

In her example, Ebels-Duggan mentions that the patient's wife, as his primary caregiver, makes certain choices on his behalf, in his best interest. The wife has her husband's good in mind when making decisions. That is to say, the good of her husband is the practical reason guiding the wife's decisions. This is, for Ebels-Duggan, an acceptable exception, where a beneficent conduct of care, in which one does things for another, can be reasonably justified by the exceptional circumstances of extreme debilitation of the cared for. For Ebels-Duggan, only when someone is so severely ill that his agency is deficient to the point of being comparable to an infant or a small child in terms of vulnerability, dependence, and autonomy to choose, can his caregiver justifiably act beneficently by doing things for them.

True, in real-life situations of ill-health and death, vulnerabilities become greater, mutual dependence (rather than individual independence) become the norm, and the capacity to autonomously and self-sufficiently choose becomes reduced. In this sense, there are certain unavoidable asymmetries between a patient and their caregivers (e.g., their family and friends, healthcare providers, and immediate community). So, Ebels-Duggan is right in recognizing the critically ill patient–caregiver model is a valid example of love and authentic beneficence. On the other hand, Ebels-Duggan seems to be wrong in interpreting her example as a very exceptional case. Asymmetries are part of anyone's life in a community: all of us are vulnerable and dependent on others, though in different ways and to different degrees throughout our life span.[64]

2.4. Normalizing Asymmetries of Dependence and Vulnerability: An Opportunity to Grow in Maturity

All human beings face periods of profound vulnerability[65] (including seasons of serious diseases, weakening, or suffering). These are experienced by each and every one of us, often in seasons of great dependence on others and reduced capacity for exercising autonomy and self-sufficiency.[66] The different degrees of vulnerability and the varying spectrum of dependence that exist among us are

---

[63] Ibid., p. 147.
[64] See, e.g., MacIntyre, *Dependent Rational Animals*, p. 73; Snead, *What It Means to Be Human*, p. 88.
[65] On the concept of vulnerability, see, e.g., Herring, *Vulnerable Adults and the Law*, Ch. 1.
[66] For a definition of the vulnerability approach to care, see, e.g., Fineman, "The Vulnerable Subject," p. 168.

contingent on a number of considerations, and these differences in vulnerabilities and dependencies justify different levels of responsibility to care for one another (I further discuss these different levels of responsibility in Chapter 5).

One such consideration may be, for example, differences in age, which typically correlate to differences in vulnerability and dependence. When a patient is very young, they are more vulnerable and dependent. Caregivers (e.g., their family and friends, healthcare providers, and immediate community) have therefore a greater role and responsibility to care for the very young. As one advances in age and becomes an adult, one also normally (though not necessarily) becomes less vulnerable and dependent on others' care. In fact, adults who have become less vulnerable and dependent on other's care often become caregivers themselves, especially of those who once took care of them (their parents) and/or of those who will likely take care of them in the future (their children). Here, we are back again at the parent–child paradigm of love and care.[67] In defending this paradigm as the fullest expression of our human interdependence, both communitarian philosopher Alasdair MacIntyre and feminist ethics of care philosopher Eva Feder Kittay go even further to argue that the parent–*disabled* child example is actually the most perfect model of unconditional love and non-contingent care.[68] And later in one's life, as bioethicist and legal scholar O. Carter Snead points out, the same need for unconditional love and non-contingent care will rise again as patients move toward the end of their lives.[69] Near death, the patient is naturally as vulnerable and dependent as the patient once was at the moment of their birth. Indeed, there is a beautiful resemblance that marks the beginning and the end of life: life begins and ends with great vulnerability, dependence on others, and need for love and presence.

Another consideration that influences the different degrees of vulnerability and dependence is not difference in age *per se*, but more precisely differences in stages of development. Age and stage of development are often correlated: younger people are in their early stages of development, making them more vulnerable and dependent on others' care. The earlier in the stage of development, the greater their vulnerability and dependence, and therefore, the greater the responsibility to care for them. *Prima facie*, then, the community in general and the primary caregiver in particular have stringent duties of love and care for those patients at the earliest stages of development. In this sense, the community in general and the mother and father in particular have the most stringent duties of love and care for their child in the womb, when the person/patient is at their earliest stages of development. This duty gradually becomes

---

[67] Besides Frankfurt (discussed above), another philosopher who also uses the parent/child example as the paradigm of love and care is the Feminist Care Ethicist Nel Noddings (*Caring*).
[68] MacIntyre, *Dependent Rational Animals*, p. 108; Feder Kittay, *Learning from My Daughter*.
[69] Snead, *What It Means to Be Human*, p. 89.

less stringent as the child develops into an adult and becomes less vulnerable and dependent. But stage of development may not necessarily correlate with age. For example, some adult patients with severe mental disabilities can be as vulnerable and dependent as infants, as Ebels-Duggan points out in her example. But here, too, the community in general and the primary caregiver in particular have stringent duties to love and care for the disabled patient: the greater the disability, the greater the duty to love and care for the disabled—noting here the reality that all human beings without exception exist on a "scale of disability"[70] that justifies duties of mutual (or more specifically, multidirectional) care.[71]

But the degrees of vulnerability and dependence may be neither a question of age nor of stages of development. Greater vulnerability and dependence can be suddenly faced by any autonomous, self-sufficient adult in unexpected ways. In these cases, an external circumstance that fall outside of one's control determines the different degrees of vulnerability and dependence. Unforeseeable illnesses or accidents are the obvious examples here. They may happen to any fully-fledged agent at any time, abruptly increasing their levels of vulnerability and dependence, and unexpectedly imposing on others (without their previous consent) a stringent duty to care for them. Others may—and likely will—feel unprepared to fully take on this unchosen duty of care. But their commitment to the good of those they love will so require of them, giving them a stringent moral duty and no actual moral right to choose differently.[72] This might make the once autonomous, self-sufficient adult who is now deeply vulnerable and profoundly dependent on others feel uncomfortable and perhaps even humiliated for having to impose such heavy burden on others. Most importantly, however, this situation might also be a lesson of humility and wisdom in acknowledging our shared dependence on others and our co-responsibility to care for one another. What this lesson can teach is that "to bear with" a patient's and friend's serious infirmities, frailties, limitations, and vulnerabilities, though difficult and burdensome, can give both the patient and their caregivers an opportunity to fully mature in their humanity, *viz.*, to grow in humility and wisdom in discharging their co-responsibility to love and care for one another.

My point with this discussion is to show that the caregiver–ill patient model should not be seem as such a rare exception, as Ebels-Duggan contends. The

---

[70] MacIntyre, *Dependent Rational Animals*, p. 73.

[71] On a phenomenology of caregiving that discusses the theme of responsibility in community, engaging with the Feminist Ethics of Care tradition in dialogue with Emmanuel Lévinas, see the work of Philosopher and Disability Studies Scholar Joel Michael Reynolds ("Infinite Responsibility in the Bedpan," pp. 779–94; *The Life Worth Living: Disability, Pain, and Morality*).

[72] The idea that there are unchosen obligations is supported by both communitarians [including Sandel ("The Procedural Republic and the Unencumbered Self," p. 86), Taylor (*The Malaise of Modernity*, p. 16), and Goodin (*Protecting the Vulnerable*, p. 27)] and feminist care ethicists [including Held (*The Ethics of Care*) and Herring (*Law and the Relational Self*, pp. 26–27, 29, 60)].

asymmetries of vulnerability and dependence are a reality and are part of anyone's life in a community: all of us are vulnerable and dependent on others, though in different ways and to different degrees throughout our life span. In trying to normalize the acceptance of these asymmetries I am in no way saying that injustices (especially structural injustices) that spur from such asymmetries are to be tolerated. Quite the contrary: this is the point of equity (see Chapter 4 for a discussion of equity and equality). My point here is just that the acceptance of these asymmetries as a normal part of any life can give us a more hopeful perspective of how these difficulties also offer opportunities for our growth in community as we mature to become fully fledged agents together (again, by fully fledged agent I mean the agent who is capable to love; that is, to discharge their responsibility to give and receive love, contributing to their community of mutual care).

2.5. From Objections to the Lessons of Love and Beneficence

Arguably, to mature and become a fully-fledged agent is not to grow into an independent, self-sufficient adult. As Kittay points out,

> in our modern industrial and postindustrial world, where independence is construed as the mark of adulthood, it is difficult for many to acknowledge that dependency may be a permanent feature of a life, and that dependency can recur (to various degrees and in different ways) throughout our lives, so that we are always vulnerable to onceagain becoming fully dependent.[73]

As Communitarian philosophers Jean Vanier and Alasdair MacIntyre have also argued, to mature and become a fully fledged agent is, instead, to grow in dependence. That is to say, to become responsible for others in one's community.[74] This entails becoming more able to think for oneself in deciding how to best love and care for others while receiving love and care from others.[75]

---

[73] Feder Kittay, *Learning from My Daughter*, p. 147.
[74] Both Feminist Ethics of Care and Communitarianism challenge the mainstream, individualistic, Rawlsian understanding of justice centered on individual rights and autonomy. Other Feminist Ethics of Care philosophers emphasizing our vulnerable, interdependent nature include Gilligan (*In a Different Voice*), Robinson ("After Liberalism in World Politics," p. 148), Held ("Care and Human Rights," pp. 634–35), Fineman (*The Autonomy Myth*, p. 263), Herring (*Law and the Relational Self*), Engster (*The Heart of Justice*), Feder Kittay and Meyers (eds., *Women and Moral Theory*), and Tronto (*Moral Boundaries*). Other Communitarian philosophers making similar arguments against individualism include Taylor (*Sources of the Self*), Goodin (*Protecting the Vulnerable*), and Sandel ("The Procedural Republic," pp. 81–96).
[75] Vanier, *Becoming Human*, Chs. 1 and 4; MacIntyre, *Dependent Rational Animals*, p. 120.

To mature is then to gradually learn to take responsibility for one's choices and their impact on others, and to come to realize that one's life is less about personal accomplishments (as important and valuable as they are) and more about promoting the good of those entrusted to one's love and care. So, to mature into adulthood seems, I would suggest, to involve two basic ingredients. The first ingredient is self-knowledge (wisdom) about one's strengths (i.e., one's unique contribution to one's communities) and one's limitations. This requires humility in acknowledging one's needs and fragilities.[76] In learning about one's own strengths and weaknesses, one can more responsibly decide how to care for others and how to receive care from others. That is to say, in growing in self-knowledge, one can more fully participate in one's community of mutual care, where one's strengths meet the needs of others and one's needs are met by the strengths of others. This is the second ingredient of maturity or adulthood, then: growing in capacity to give and receive love and thereby become a fully-fledged member of a community of mutual, multidirectional care (see Chapter 1 on the idea of the multidirectional web of giving and receiving). Maturity therefore entails embracing the complementary responsibilities of love and care that come with adulthood. This is the point in one's life when one becomes less self-absorbed and more other-directed; when one contributes to one's community as an active member who meets the needs of other members and complements their strengths while also being assisted in one's own limitations.

In a nutshell, maturing into adulthood means learning to give and receive love more fully within community, and to both belong to and depend on others. One belongs when one actively participates—by contributing what one can and engaging collaboratively in decision-making about care. One depends on others when one receives their love and care, having one's own infirmities, frailties, limitations, and vulnerabilities tended to. In giving and receiving love—meaning, in belonging to and depending on others—one fulfills the co-responsibility "to bear with" one another, building a community that nurtures self-knowledge, humility, and a shared commitment to choosing the good for each other. This is the moral authority of a complementarity model of unconditional love and non-contingent care.

This is also the central lesson I draw from the caregiver–ill patient model, which builds upon the insights of the parent–infant model. From the latter, I deduced that "to bear with" a friend's infirmities, frailties, limitations, and vulnerabilities fundamentally means to be present with the Other. In exploring what it means to be truly present, I showed here that it requires learning to belong to one another in a state of interdependence and mutual, multidirectional care.

---

[76] On the correlation between self-knowledge and humility, see: St. Teresa of Avila, Saint, "Interior Castle," Ch. 1.

Asymmetries of vulnerabilities, dependence, and capacity to autonomously choose are naturally occurring in all human relationships and should, I contend, be embraced in this spirit of self-knowledge, humility, and complementarity. Again, this is not to say that asymmetries are not to be corrected: infirmities, frailties, limitations, and vulnerabilities are to be properly addressed; and oppressive, disrespectful, and demeaning conducts are not to be tolerated. Yet, acknowledging these asymmetries provides an opportunity to recognize our differing strengths and weaknesses and to strive for complementarity in building a community of mutual, multidirectional care (for a discussion on how this idea applies to global health institutions see Chapters 4 and 5). This complementarity does not mean disrespecting agency, as Darwall and Ebels-Duggan caution. On the contrary, agency and freedom are fundamental for forging loving interactions and loving institutions that are conducive to cooperation, participation, and mutual care: the agent freely chooses to love others and to be cared for by others. Even when the agent is completely vulnerable and fully dependent, they still communicate (even without words) and express their will to the caregiver, using their agency to choose how to love others and be cared for by others.

I explained why infirmities, frailties, limitations, and vulnerabilities are not exceptional, but rather cyclical events in every human life. However, Ebels-Duggan might want to insist that by and large caring for another by doing things for them is an expression of distorted love (with some specific exceptions) because such acts do not reflect respect for their agency. But what my discussion of the caregiver–ill patient model has hopefully shown is that naturally recurring asymmetries need not lead to a demeaning, vertical relationship. This is not to say that one should not be vigilant against occasions leading to paternalism and oppression—particularly in the context of healthcare and global health aid. In these contexts (routinely marred by power imbalance and subjugation of patients and global health aid recipients), meaningful inclusion in decision-making is key (the concept of meaningful inclusion was introduced in Chapter 1 and will be further developed in the next section). My point is to show that genuine love and authentic beneficence—that honor the Other's uniqueness and respect their agency and freedom—can yield a radically different outcome. Rather than paternalism, oppression, and abuse, the upshot is a horizontal relationship of mutual care, where caregiver and patient nurture one another, forming a community of friendship and solidarity that may at times even blur the once clear distinction between who the caregiver and cared for originally were.[77]

In what follows, I articulate a normative claim: the core of authentic beneficence is not merely doing things for or with another, but simply being present

---

[77] Herring, *Caring and the Law*, p. 5.

with the Other—bearing with their weaknesses and suffering. This commitment to presence is the essence of genuine, transformative care.

Section 3. The Core Feature of Beneficence: Being Present

To present my normative claim on being present with another, I first further discuss Ebels-Duggan's critical take on beneficence as doing things for another and her view of love as doing things with another. My critical analysis of Ebels-Duggan's theory of love will pave the way for the presentation of my argument that the core feature of (authentic) beneficence and love is simply being present with—indispensable for doing truly beneficial things for and with the other.

3.1. Doing For, Doing With, Being in Each Other's Presence: A Critical Analysis of Ebels-Duggan's Theory of Love

Ebels-Duggan's theory of love has two main, interlinked components: shared authority and shared ends. For Ebels-Duggan, to be authentic, rather than corrupted, love needs to respect the autonomy of the beloved as a self-governing agent, who has "authority to set [their] own path."[78] Each party in a love relationship therefore has authority to set their own, individual ends. And all parties in a love relationship have joint authority to set their shared ends.[79] Her idea of the shared authority of the partners in a relationship focuses on co-deliberation: "a substantive judgement about what you jointly have most reason to do, taking into account all of the considerations that bear on the decision."[80] It is through this shared authority that the partners in the relationship can co-deliberate and set their shared ends. Now, for Ebels-Duggan, "sharing ends" means specifically "doing things with each other."[81] This involves actively participating in each other's life projects, making decisions together, and working jointly as a team to successfully accomplish such shared vision for the future.[82] In a word, it means companionship (a concept introduced and discussed in Chapter 1).[83]

While Ebels-Duggan paradigm of love does not account for the frequent asymmetries that exist in relationships not only between children and parents but also between adults of differing power, capabilities, and dependencies due

---

[78] Ebels-Duggan, *Against Beneficence*, p. 155.
[79] Ibid., p. 158.
[80] Ibid., p. 165.
[81] Ibid., p. 156.
[82] Ibid., pp. 157, 165.
[83] As discussed in Chapter 1, mercy in the form of forgiveness may not always restore a shared life journey in companionship, although it always restores union in community.

to illness or phase of life, her idea of "shared authority" seems indeed to be an important ingredient of loving relationships, especially in the context of healthcare and global health institutions. Shared authority is crucial for addressing the problem of vertical, paternalistic relationships both between healthcare professionals and patients, and between global health institutions and beneficiary local communities. There is little disagreement about the need for greater participation of patients and inclusion of local beneficiary communities in decision-making related to best medical treatments, healthcare resource allocation, and priority setting in local recipient communities:

(i) At the interpersonal level of *provider–patient* relationship, the co-expert model has been defended as a remedy against medical paternalism (as discussed in Chapter 2). The model is predicated on the understanding that both provider and patient bring expertise, albeit on different themes. While the former brings their technical expertise of medicine, scientific knowledge, and clinical skills, the latter brings their phenomenological expertise on their own life, their knowledge of themselves, and their discretionary skills in discerning with prudence what is best for their unique practical circumstances. Both types of expertise are necessary to determine the best course of action regarding care options.[84]

(ii) Likewise, at the level of global health institutions-beneficiary local communities, the decoloniality model of global health has been advocated (as discussed in Chapter 1).[85] It is predicated on the understanding that global health institutions and local communities contribute different things to the process of international development assistance. The former brings international resources, international medical expertise, global scientific knowledge, and foreign clinical skills. And the latter also brings their local resources, local medical expertise, local scientific knowledge, and local clinical skills. If authentic human development is the goal, then these have to be integrated and harmonized. Crucially, global health institutions need to incorporate local communities in their decision-making processes regarding healthcare resource allocation and priority setting, because local communities know best what their epidemiological reality, medical culture, circumstances, social problems, and priorities are (I elaborate on this

---

[84] On the co-expert model, see, e.g., Milo, *Informed Consent to Abortion*, Ch. 3; Herring, "Sharing Vulnerabilities in the Woman Patient/Doctor Encounter," pp. 223–37. For a critical view of the expert model, see, e.g., Watson, "Patient Expertise and Medical Authority, pp. 58–71.

[85] Atuire, "Some Barriers to Knowledge from the Global South"; Khan, Abimbola, and Aloudat et al., *Decolonising Global Health in 2021*; Abimbola and Pai, *Will Global Health Survive Its Decolonization?* pp. 1627–28; Koum Besson, *Confronting Whiteness and Decolonizing Global Health Institutions*, pp. 2328–29; and Ekeocha, *Target Africa: Ideological Neocolonialism in the Twenty-First Century*.

point in Chapters 1 and 5). The lack of such integration and harmonization has been identified, as discussed above, as one of the chief problems of GHG, currently reliant on a donor-centered model of international development assistance (see Chapter 5 on the donor-centered model of GHG).[86]

While there is little disagreement about the need for greater participation of patients and inclusion of local beneficiary communities in decision-making processes in healthcare and global health contexts, one may promptly object here that shared authority is practically unfeasible: intractable impasses happen in interpersonal and institutional decision-making processes and the pressure for rapid solutions—especially in life and death situations—would justify a degree of paternalism and unilateral decision-making, in both the healthcare and global health contexts.

True, integrating and harmonizing the (often opposing) views of different stakeholders are difficult. It could even be costly, burdensome, and time-consuming, and time is indeed pressing, especially in contexts of health emergencies. However, the fact that shared authority is practically challenging does not mean that it is not the right thing to do, or that it should not be pursued. Oppression, domination, and coercion should not be tolerated in the name of practical efficiency (on the problem of an excessive emphasis on efficiency within healthcare and global health institutions, see Chapter 2).

While Ebels-Duggan's idea of "shared authority" seems indeed to be an essential ingredient of love relationships—especially in the context of healthcare and global health institutions, her idea of "sharing ends"—by which she means specifically "doing things with each other"[87]—seems to me to be important but not essential. To focus exclusively on "shared ends" is, I believe, a limited view of love. Her idea of "doing things with each other" is not the only loving expression of good care: as I have previously contended, "doing things for" another can also be an expression of genuine love and need not be a paternalistic form of care.

Ebels-Duggan's concept of shared ends, nevertheless, finds strong support among others who emphasize collaboration. Pope Francis, in *Fratelli Tutti*, highlights the importance of working *with* the poor—such as co-designing public policies—rather than acting *for* them.[88] Healthcare practitioners similarly stress that effective care is less about what we choose to do for others and more about what we do *together* with them. This relational approach fosters reciprocity, interdependence, and mutual care.[89]

---

[86] Gostin and Mok, "Innovative Solutions to Closing the Health Gap," p. 451; Ruger, "Global Health Governance," p. 654.
[87] Ebels-Duggan, *Against Beneficence*, p. 156.
[88] Pope Francis, *Frattelli Tutti*, para. 169.
[89] Belinda Dewar, Elizabeth Adamson, Stephen Smith, Joyce Surfleet, and Linda King, "Clarifying Misconceptions about Compassionate Care," pp. 70, 8, 1738–47, p. 1741.

True, love is a relational concept. Setting a shared vision for the future together and working jointly to successfully accomplish the goals toward such vision are certainly part of maturing and growing together in love. This is part of making daily choices of commitment to one another. The sharing of lives is indeed a vital component of love and authentic beneficence: without daily choosing (and committing to choose) the good of the other—as Other, and without striving together to perfect and attain a shared end toward the common good, no communion and no community can be built. Communion and community depend therefore on authentic beneficence. Communion and community begin when people come together, communicate, share an end (i.e., a purpose and a vision), and then choose and commit to coordinate their interactions with a view to a shared future of a common good[90] (on how communication leads to communion and community, see Chapter 6).

Ebels-Duggan's idea of love as co-deliberating projects and successfully completing tasks and goals together with a view toward a shared dream, while gripping and true in many ways, makes me ask whether there is more to love than doing things together in the pursuit of a common vision of success. This question arises as I reflect upon and experience the limitations of real life, where, more often than I would have wanted, I cannot do what I had originally planned or as I had initially dreamed of. Real life, for most people, involves: endless boring everyday chores, unexpected changes that only add up to daily chaos, difficult relationships, flawed human beings, poor communication, sickness, accidents, discontents, fatigue, and loss. It seems to me, though, that it is precisely in this everyday madness that love and communities of mutual care are formed, shaped, and strengthened. Love is embedded in cluttered real-life; yet, love transcends all of these (e.g., the tiresome routines, the disappointments, the less than perfect reality, as well as the carefully planned and idealistic agendas for the future) to slowly yet surely form communion and community.

For example, during the 2020 COVID-19 pandemic, schools were shut for several months, and many parents had to home-school their children. Some parents, together with their children, made beautiful plans for their school year. They carefully planned every lesson, set shared educational goals, and established an agenda for some virtual activities in coordination with other children and their families in the local community. But then life happened and the beautiful plan fell apart several times. For example, Jordan's daughter, Isabel, got upset every time she could not complete a task. Jordan had to interrupt the project he was working on multiple times to attend to his child. But surprisingly enough, what was lost in accomplishment was gained in communion. It is precisely in being present with his daughter—in rocking her in silence, in helping her deal

---

[90] See, e.g., Finnis, *Natural Law and Natural Rights*, p. 152.

with her frustration, in asking her to be patient with herself after failing a lesson, and in drying her tears—that community blossoms.[91] It is in the messiness and difficulties of daily life, which thwart those perfect plans for an envisioned success, that love indeed occurs and matures. It is precisely in these repetitive and inconvenient acts of care that father and daughter learn how to fully belong to and depend on one another. This is how love occurs and matures: in the giving and receiving of care in community, in bearing with one another's journey of infirmities, frailties, limitations, and vulnerabilities.

The emphasis of love, therefore, should not lie solely in the doing of tasks—whether for or with the other—or in the successful accomplishment of shared ends, projects, and dreams. To be sure, these are important; but their failure is not a sufficiently strong reason to dissolve communion. Rather, the focus should be, I would contend, on experiencing togetherness, belonging, and mutual dependence amid the ongoing struggles of shared lives. In other words, love is about the daily choice to renew our commitment to bear with one another in sickness and health, in poverty and riches, through failures and successes, in weaknesses and strengths, in amid both chaos and calm as the seasons of life unfold. To love is, fundamentally, to bear with one another through all these seasons. Depending on the circumstances, this may entail doing things for or with the other; yet, the core of true love and authentic beneficence transcends mere action.

3.2. Contemplation as the Foundation of Beneficence

If the essence of love is to bear with one another through all seasons—good and bad—then the point of authentic beneficence is not so much in being together for the sake of attaining some desired shared end, but in being together first and foremost for the sake of being together. Belonging to and depending on the other are therefore not only instrumentally but also, and more fundamentally, intrinsically good.

The core feature of authentic beneficence is therefore to be present with the Other (whether the other here is the patient or the caregiver). And presence entails attentive accompaniment, where (i) to accompany is to share the good things of life as well to bear with the infirmities, frailties, limitations, and vulnerabilities of one another; and (ii) to be attentive is to love and behold the other, to contemplate the other's humanity—meaning, the beauty, goodness, and truth reflected in their dignity (see Chapter 4 for the definition of dignity), but also their flaws, weaknesses, and failings. Love is indeed, as philosopher Iris Murdoch puts it, vision perfected: love is seeing the other person

---

[91] I thank Angela Wu Howard for making this point clearer.

with clarity—that is, as the other truly is, with their virtues and flaws, in their particularities and idiosyncrasies.[92]

The internal dynamic process that moves the agent to an authentically beneficent conduct of care starts and is grounded in a contemplative benevolence. It is only through a contemplative benevolence that authentic beneficence and genuine love can unfold. It is this contemplative component what makes benevolence and beneficence appropriate care and therefore neither overpowering/controlling nor negligent. Also, it is in experiencing this contemplative component of authentic beneficence, in attentively accompanying the other in their journey through life, that the patient becomes a gift to the caregiver and the caregiver becomes a gift to the patient. One makes oneself a gift to the other by offering one's loving regard[93] to the other. This means giving one's personal attentiveness to the other, in carefully observing their needs, intently learning their character, and thoughtfully choosing how to best tailor one's care to effectively meet this patient's unique needs and particular character. And in return, the patient gives their loving regard and personal attentiveness back to the caregiver, in beholding and contemplating the humanity of their caregiver in her virtues as well as vulnerabilities. This reciprocal gift-of-self, which takes place in the medical encounter and through a mutual exchange of presence, is the very substance of love and authentic beneficence in the context of healthcare and global health institutions.

As vital as it is to actively strive to attain a shared end (e.g., to cure an infirmity through the competent administration of a certain medical treatment), the communal aspect of togetherness that comes through care (not cure)[94] is fundamental. Likewise, as key as it is to hit the targets of development goals defined by global health institutions to advance the important cause of global public health, experiencing belonging and dependence together with local communities receiving global health aid is essential. Love and authentic beneficence necessitate both: its active as well as its contemplative components.

While the active component of beneficence (i.e., doing things with and for the other, coordinating interactions in pursuit of a common end and the common good) is necessary for building communion and community, it is not in itself sufficient as an expression of genuine love. The contemplative component (i.e., being present with one another) is essential for an authentically beneficent conduct of care, which is neither paternalistic nor neglectful. Doing too much can be distracting, isolating, and alienating: it robs the other of one's real presence, of one's attentive accompaniment. Love requires being attentive to just one

---

[92] Murdoch, *The Sovereignty of Good*, p. 34.
[93] Ibid.
[94] On the difference between care and cure, see Pellegrino, "The Internal Morality of Clinical Medicine," p. 72.

thing—to the one in front of us, who we are accompanying.[95] This is the requirement of authentic beneficence: one cannot love what one is not attentive to and what one does not attentively accompany. This does not entail, however, that the contemplative component of beneficent care is a mere passive attitude of inaction. Of course, doing too little is not admissible. Being present requires attentively discerning with the other how to best care for them (and for oneself).

Presence may, for example, be at times silent and still. Remaining silent and still yet attentively present, beholding the other and directing one's loving gaze[96] toward the sufferer, in a deep eye-to-eye, soul-to-soul, *cor-ad-cor* communion, is often times the most loving option in many instances of healthcare involving grave infirmities and abject suffering. Caregivers (healthcare providers and the patient's family and friends) do have a stringent duty to attend to the patient's basic material needs in striving to do all that is in their capacity to cure the illness and alleviate the pain. But love goes beyond and deeper than the material realm. Love transcends the material realm (where things are done with and for the other) to be more fundamentally established in the transcendent relationality between persons, *viz.*, in the participation of each other's suffering and in the sharing of our powerlessness in the face of such suffering. Love as presence is thus a transcendent, participatory, shared experience of "alterity."[97]

3.3. Complementarity of the Active and Contemplative Aspects of Beneficence in Healthcare and Global health

How can the philosophical concept of beneficence—as a process rooted in contemplation that informs and complements action—be applied to real-world healthcare and global health institutions? While these theoretical discussions may seem abstract, they offer valuable insights into reforming institutions to prioritize presence and mutual care over transactional or purely material approaches.

There are at least two examples, one at the level of healthcare institution and another at the level of global healthcare institution, where the complementarity between what I called the active and the contemplative components of beneficence is sought after. These are not perfect examples. Serious critiques of both models have been raised and should be taken into careful considerations, as I will allude to below. While imperfect and in need of reform, these two examples are, currently, those that come closer to the kind of love-based institutions,

---

[95] I thank Fr Toby Lees OP for making this point clearer.
[96] Murdoch, *The Sovereignty of Good*, p. 34.
[97] See Ch. 2 on the transcendent good of relationality.

where presence (and the contemplative component of an authentic beneficent care) is at the core of the institutional architecture, complementing the active/material aspects of care. These examples hint to, albeit in imperfect ways, how presence with those in need is often silent, always attentive, and never assuming. These examples give a glimpse of what authentic beneficence could look like in reformed institutions that take presence seriously.

The first example, at the level of healthcare institution, refers to the *L'Arche* Community, founded by the philosopher Jean Vanier, together with Raphaël Simi and Philippe Seux, in Trosly-Breuil, France, in August 1964.[98] Their mission focuses primarily on the mentally or intellectually disabled. While the material provision of medical treatments is certainly necessary, the *L'Arche* model emphasizes primarily the need to simply be present, generously present, with another by sharing life (in all its messiness) with the disabled. In the *L'Arche* model caregivers and cared for live together: they share meals, they share the ugly aspects of everyday life, but they also share the good and the beautiful aspects of daily encounters in community life. In so doing, caregivers and cared for form a sense of belonging in community.[99] To give someone else the gift of my full presence (body, mind, and soul) is not only a way to love another in a generous way and build a mutual sense of belonging but also a way to respond to a culture of "ableism,"[100] which centers around doing things and accomplishing tasks successfully. In his lived experience with the disabled, Vanier realized the central relevance of accompanying the other, generously and tenderly bearing with one another's infirmities, frailties, limitations, and vulnerabilities, and thereby fostering horizontal relationships of mutual care, friendship, and solidarity.[101] It could be claimed that the *L'Arche* model ultimately fails in crafting perfectly horizontal relationships in their communities, since cases of abuse have been recently reported. However, the fact that the *L'Arche* model needs to include better accountability mechanisms for shared authority does not completely negate the potential of the model, in what it does well. The *L'Arche* model has embodied an effective, though not perfect, way to harmonize what I have called the active and the contemplative aspects of love and authentic beneficent care. In this sense, it can serve as a guide in helping one reimagine healthcare institutions that are able to transcend the material, in fostering a culture of generous presence and a community of mutual, multidirectional care.

The second example, at the level of global healthcare institution, refers to the *Partners in Health* initiative, founded by Paul Farmer, Ophelia Dahl, Thomas

---

[98] Wright, *Summer in The Forest*.
[99] Spezio, Peterson, and Roberts, "Humility as Openness to Others," p. 27.
[100] For the idea of "ableism," see, e.g., Kumari Campbell, *Contours of Ableism*; Reynolds, *The Life Worth Living*.
[101] Cushing and Lewis, "Negotiating Mutuality and Agency in Care-Giving Relationships," p. 173.

J. White, Todd McCormack, and Jim Yong Kim in 1987.[102] Their mission focuses on ensuring that quality healthcare is available in some of the world's most vulnerable communities. Their mission started in Haiti, and from there spread to Peru and Russia, and then across Africa. While the material provision of quality medical treatments is certainly crucial for their mission, the *Partners in Health* model also strongly emphasizes the need to accompany the patient.[103] For the effective accompaniment to take place, a partnership (hence the name *Partners in Health*) is established. Doctors and nurses partner with community healthcare workers in caring for patients. These community healthcare workers regularly visit the patients, their families, and friends with the purpose of not only accompanying the patient between medical appointments but also integrating patients, their families, and friends in the partnership of care. Like Vanier, Farmer also realized, in his experience of living with the local communities in these developing countries, the central relevance of accompanying the other, generously and tenderly bearing with others their infirmities, frailties, limitations, and vulnerabilities, and thereby fostering horizontal relationships of mutual care, friendship, and solidarity. Both generous material provision and generous accompaniment of the patient are complementary in attaining the goal of ensuring quality healthcare. It could be claimed that *Partners in Health* ultimately fails as a global health institution, since it is an inefficient model of international development assistance: quality healthcare based on generous material provision and generous accompaniment is unfeasible, takes too much time, and cannot be extended universally given the scarcity of trained healthcare personnel and adequate healthcare goods. Here again, however, the fact that the *Partners in Health* model faces practical challenges when scaled up does not completely negate the potential of the model, in what it does well. The *Partners in Health* model has embodied an effective, though not perfect, way to harmonize what I have called the active and the contemplative aspects of love and authentic beneficent care. In this sense, it can serve as a guide in helping one reimagine global healthcare institutions able to transcend the material (while not neglecting their institutional need for efficiency in allocating scarce resources), in fostering a culture of generous accompaniment of patients.

Though not perfect examples, both *L'Arche* and *Partners in Health* demonstrate how generous presence (i.e., being fully present—mind, body, and soul—and being fully attentive to the other) can be incorporated and fostered within healthcare and global healthcare institutions, in a way that nurtures communities of mutual, multidirectional care. Both examples emphasize the need to

---

[102] Davidson and Kos, "Bending the Arc."
[103] Griffin and Weiss Block, *In the Company of the Poor*; Weiss Block OP, Lysaught, and Martin, "A Prophet to the Peoples," Ch. 9–11.

complement the material (in the doing of tasks and in the provision of medical treatments) with the most fundamental need of giving one's generous, full presence to those who suffer. These are two examples of what authentic beneficent care should primarily seek. Care in contemporary society has been reduced to the performance of contracted and commodified tasks: there is a price for each activity of care.[104] In emphasizing the idea that care should be concerned with the provision of generous presence/accompaniment, without neglecting the patient's material needs for medical treatments and the institutional needs for efficiency in allocating scarce resources, both *L'Arche* and *Partners in Health* defy the priced activity model of care.[105]

Both *L'Arche* and *Partners in Health* concretely illustrate my theoretical argument that caring relationships that are authentically beneficent are mutual or, more precisely multidirectional. Genuine care that comes from authentic beneficence is not to be reduced to activities done for or with another, but is part of the complementary dynamic of giving and receiving care, which challenges the traditional divide between us (i.e., the competent, able caregivers, including the healthcare providers and the global healthcare donors) and them (i.e., as mere passive receivers or objects of care,[106] including patients and global health aid recipients). Also, the complementarity between what I have called the active and the contemplative components of beneficence serves the purpose of explaining why one should conceive the doctor–patient relationship not simply as about the doctor doing something for or with the patient, but chiefly about being together—sharing life and *being fully present* with one another. Likewise, one should conceive the global health benefactor–local community beneficiary relationship not simply as the benefactor doing something for or with the beneficiary, but mostly about belonging to and depending on one another.

Conclusion

This chapter built on Chapters 1 and 2 and defined a third type of love that applies to the context of GHG, namely beneficence, by putting forth a conceptual and normative argument. I first presented the conceptual part of my argument that we should conceive of benevolence (i.e., willing the good of the other—as Other) as a step toward beneficence (i.e., the conduct, meaning either an action

---

[104] Herring, "Sharing Vulnerabilities in the Woman Patient/Doctor Encounter."
[105] The priced activity model has also been generally criticized by other disability rights activists alongside Jean Vanier. Jan Morris, for example, has argued that care itself is a form of oppression against disabled people. True care is not doing an act for someone, but living with someone. For Kane, it is a relationship of care. See: Kane, "Childhood, Growth, and Dependency in Liberal Political Philosophy," pp. 156–70.
[106] Ebels-Duggan, *Against Beneficence*, p. 145.

or an omission, which effectively benefits the other). Put differently, benevolence is an intentional intellectual step toward the effective step of beneficence. Like the move from empathy to compassionate care that characterizes compassion (Chapter 2), this move from the intellectual step of benevolence to the effective step of beneficence also produces a conduct of care, grounded on genuine love. Chapter 3 defended this concept of genuine love expressed through authentic beneficence while responding to its main objections. It also resolved the tension raised in Chapter 2 between "being with" and "doing things" for or with the sufferer. In doing so, I presented the normative part of my argument that the core feature of authentic beneficence is being present with, and not actively doing things for or with the other. I called this core feature the contemplative component of a beneficent conduct of care.

As discussed in Chapters 1 and 2, and in this chapter, the common feature among these different types of love (i.e., mercy, compassion, and beneficence) is that they are best appreciated as a process that produces a gift of self. Here, gift of self means primarily to be present with another, bearing with them and their infirmities, frailties, limitations, and vulnerabilities, and discerning together how to best care for each other. It is this gift of self that is the contemplative component of loving care. Good care in the context of illnesses and suffering may—most often than not—necessarily entail doing certain tasks for and with the other who is unwell. While these active components of care are necessary, they may be neither sufficient nor the most essential feature of good care. The ill surely needs to be cared *for*; but above all *about*.[107] The contemplative component of care is, I contended, fundamental. While this contemplative component is the most essential for genuine love and authentic beneficence to be experienced, the complementarity between the contemplative and the active features is also key to design good institutions of healthcare and GHG that strive to build strong communities of mutual, multidirectional care. In the concluding remarks of Part 1 that follows next, where I define the concept of agape, I further elaborate on such complementarity. In further developing the idea of presence in the context of GHG, this chapter (together with the previous chapters on mercy and compassion and the following concluding remarks on agape) continued to challenge the design of existing institutions and to show how love could reform them.

---

[107] For this distinction, see: Herring, *Law and the Relational Self*, p51; Tronto, *Moral Boundaries*, pp. 127–34.

Concluding Remarks—On Agape

> Love hath reason
> Shakespeare, *The Phoenix and the Turtle*

> Love is not love
> Which alters when it alteration finds,
> Or bends with the remover to remove.
> O no! it is an ever-fixed mark
> That looks on tempests and is never shaken;
> ...
> Love alters not with his brief hours and weeks,
> But bears it out even to the edge of doom.
> Shakespeare, Sonnet 116

It is not easy to define love. Overused, misused; it has a plurality of meanings.[1] Classically, the Greeks differentiated its four main types: romantic love (*eros*), love of friends (*philia*), familial love (*storge*), and universal love (*agape*).[2] But there are other types: love of country, love of one's profession, love of work, obsessive love, love of animals, love of guests, love of strangers, love of enemies, love of God, and love of neighbor. There are also many terms that are commonly used interchangeably with love: care, affection, kindness, mercy, compassion, pity, sympathy, empathy, tenderness, benevolence, beneficence, altruism, and charity.

Part I offered a conceptual analysis of the three types of love that most often apply within the context of healthcare and global health, namely: merciful love (or love of enemy, featured in Chapter 1), compassionate love (or love of neighbor, near and far, discussed in Chapter 2), and beneficent love (or love of the Other before me, whoever he is—an enemy, friend, stranger, neighbor, family member, or beloved—as presented in Chapter 3). Together, these three chapters of Part I offer a typology of love, applicable to the interpersonal and institutional dynamics that unfold within healthcare organizations, at the local and global levels alike.

---

[1] Lee, "Love as a Foundational Principle," p. 10.
[2] See, e.g., Lewis, *The Four Loves*; Cicero, *Tusculan Disputations*.

I have defined and differentiated each of these types of love—mercy, compassion, and beneficence—but I have also highlighted the common features among them. They all comprise an internal dynamic process of reasoning that leads to the deliberation of an effective giving of oneself as a gift. These common features will now serve the purpose of defining the umbrella term of love applicable to the contexts of clinical, public, and global health. For the sake of clarity, I will call this umbrella *agape*, since it is the most encompassing type of love. Different from other, more specific types, agape is typically understood as universal (it extends to all human beings) and unconditional (it is not merited and it expects nothing in return).

1. What Agape Is and Is Not

By agape I do not mean mere sentiments of love. As discussed throughout Chapters 1–3—and as recognized by thinkers as diverse as Aquinas, Shakespeare, Dr. Martin Luther King Jr., and bell hooks—love is not simply an emotion "which alters when it alteration finds." Rather, it is a complex, discretionary process, guided by prudence and exercised through practical reasoning, and that involves a steadfast commitment to repeatedly choose the good of the other—a firm commitment "that looks on tempests and is never shaken."[3] While love is often awakened by our senses and stirred by emotions, this initial, raw feeling—typically self-centered, imprisoned within the self—must mature through an intellectual process of discernment that engages the agent's discretionary powers and will. Although the affective ingredient of love is only the beginning, it is not irrelevant: without it, love is "cold and incommunicable."[4] To be sure, contemporary culture tends to overrate feelings. Yet, emotions should not be completely dismissed, suppressed, or invalidated, for they serve the purpose of moving the agent toward an effective conduct of care, tailored to the other in need.

Chapters 1–3 examined this internal dynamic process (typically not linear—like most things in life!), dedicating special attention to the often ignored intellectual component through which love matures. Across all three types of love, the exercise of intellectual, discretionary powers and the will is what shifts us from a self-absorbed state—where emotions engulf us and cloud our vision—to an other-directed posture of learning. In this state, the intensity of emotions subsides, giving way to prudence and practical reasoning, which enable us to see the Other attentively and appreciate his uniqueness as a gift. In dialogue with

---

[3] On agape's permanent stability, see also: Outka, *Agape*, p. 11.
[4] Wojtyla, *Love and Responsibility*, p. 91. For a different perspective, see: Soren Kierkegaard, as discussed by Krishek, "How Faith Secures the Morality of Love," in *The Routledge Handbook of Love in Philosophy*, ed. A.M. Martin (New York: Routledge, 2019), pp. 252–63.

thinkers as diverse as novelist and philosopher Iris Murdoch (who stresses the importance of gaze and attention), to philosopher Emmanuel Lévinas (who emphasizes the encounter with the Other), to theologian Karol Wojtyla (who highlights the gift of self), I conceptualize love as a journey—a shared one.

This journey involves the agent's attentive contemplation of the Other,[5] leading to deeper knowledge and genuine appreciation of him in his totality—both the beautiful and the ugly parts. This contemplative, intellectual process represents the epistemic function of love: it fosters, through attentive presence and thoughtful reflection, a clearer and more profound understanding of the Other's unique reality. From there, the agent must decide how to respond to the gift received: either to reject it and let go or to accept, keep, and care for it. This deliberation constitutes the practical function of love. Thus, the internal process of agape reaches its fulfillment: the mature agent freely chooses to accept, keep, and care for the gift of the Other, not only by committing to his ultimate good but also by reciprocating with her own gift of self. In this way, the shared journey of agape embodies the logic of gift (discussed in Chapter 1) where a gratuitous, vulnerable, yet sustainable generosity underpins effective care.

Throughout Part I, I have also clarified what it means to will the good of the other—as Other. The capital "O" is not a frivolous detail. I borrow the expression "the other as other" from theologian Hans Urs von Balthasar, for whom mutual love is "where the other as other is encountered."[6] I follow Lévinas in capitalizing "Other,"[7] in order to underscore the uniqueness of the Other in his unrepeatability and his infinite dignity (on the concept of human dignity as the image of infinite love in us, see Chapter 4). This means that to will the good of the Other is to seek what truly promotes their flourishing and well-being, rather than simply imposing the agent's interpretation of the good, or passively accepting the Other's desires.

These two flawed approaches—paternalism and passivity—stand in stark contrast with the reasonable, reciprocal nature of agape. In the paternalistic approach, the agent is too quick to presume she knows what is best for the Other. Without first engaging in attentive presence and empathetic communication to understand the Other's perspective (see Chapters 2 and 6), she thereby denudes him of agency. In the passive approach, she acquiesces to every demand the Other makes, without going to the trouble of critically engaging, reasoning, and communicating with honesty and discretion (see Chapter 6). Such passivity, a self-annihilating attitude, subjugates the agent's own agency, reducing her to a mere doormat (as discussed in Chapters 1 and 3). Both extremes distort love, for

---

[5] See Chapter 3 on the idea of contemplation as a loving attainment of awareness, that is, a process of knowing the other, inspired by love. See also: Piper, *Happiness and Contemplation*.
[6] Von Balthasar, *Love Alone Is Credible*, p. 53.
[7] Lévinas, *Totality and Infinity*, pp. 49–51.

agape requires respect for our equal agency (see Chapter 4 on human dignity as equality of respectful consideration and loving regard).

I define agape first as a practical reason—a reason to act for the good of each and every Other before me (see the Introduction). To discern what is genuinely good for another, the agent must engage in an attentive process of deliberation, being fully present to the Other. Thus, to love is to offer a reasonably self-sacrificial gift of presence for the good of the Other and for the flourishing of the community. This offering culminates in the choice of a tailored conduct of care for the unique person before me. Second, I also define agape as a virtue: a stable disposition of character to see and understand the Other deeply, cultivated through the habitual choice to be present for the Other's good.

Specifically, the normativity of agape—as both a practical reason and a virtue—establishes love as a directive for individual and institutional deliberations, grounding a universal yet personal responsibility to care for those suffering from serious illnesses that transcend political borders. To truly care for *all* who suffer, one must journey with each and every sufferer *personally*. Ultimately, as a shared journey of presence, agape nurtures a community of mutual, multi-directional care.

2. The Reasonableness of Agape

Agape—and the shared journey of presence that it entails—is practically reasonable. In other words, the individual and institutional deliberations that agape justifies are not arbitrary (hence, the term "Rule of Love," reminiscent of the "Rule of Law," as explained in the Introduction). Agape calls for a shared journey of presence amid the messiness and real tensions of daily life: the tension between love of self (essential for self-constitution) and love of neighbor, as well as the further tension among distinct neighbors—those who are near versus far, in dire need versus less desperate, and closely bound versus less connected.

The *Rule of Love* orders our priorities of care by helping us discern, with prudence, which gifts and caring responsibilities to relinquish and delegate—not abandon! (Chapter 5), and which to accept and nurture (Chapter 4), all while engaging in shared decisions and truthful communication about our limitations and boundaries (Chapter 6). Although agape requires never abandoning those in need, its unconditional nature does not require giving from an empty cup. Rather, agape permits—and at times necessitates—the agent to reject certain demands. This refusal is neither arbitrary nor selfish; it is an exercise in agapic discernment, predicated on prudence and practical reasoning that carefully considers our current commitments and duties (Chapter 4), our limited capacity and resources (Chapter 5), and our proper understanding of the Other's needs (Chapter 6) as distinct from mere desires, preferences, and wants.[8] Agape is a labor of love that demands effort; yet, the self-sacrifice it requires is reasonable.

It is reasonable to decline additional responsibilities when I am overextended and overcommitted (Chapter 5), and to prioritize those whose needs are more pressing and have been directly entrusted to my care (Chapter 4). It is equally reasonable to disclose my limitations with honest vulnerability tempered by discretion (Chapter 6). At the institutional level, it is reasonable to de-prioritize a singular focus on productivity and efficiency (Chapter 2) when such goals foster dehumanizing interactions, and instead to emphasize active participation, meaningful inclusiveness, and shared decision-making (Chapters 1 and 3). Indeed, as Shakespeare reminds us, "love hath reason."

Agape is both reasonable and challenging. To give my full, undivided, attentive presence[9] as a gift of self to the Other—while accompanying that person on his journey—may seem unfeasible. Indeed, perfect love is impossible. Consistently showing up, through good and bad seasons, is arduous, and to "bear it out [with the Other] even to the edge of doom," as Shakespeare notes, is not for the faint of heart. Yet, to love is to share *unconditionally* in life's messiness and uncertainty. This is what forces our love to mature as we learn to depend more vulnerably on one another and belong more deeply in communion—to belong is to co-deliberate and co-create in community.

Again, the unconditionality of agape does not mean unconditionally affirming the Other's feelings, acquiescing to whatever he wants, and ignoring my own agency or needs (this would be unreasonable!). But it probably demands a greater self-sacrifice of my own comforts and preferences than I initially anticipated. So, agape calls for a reasonable degree of self-sacrifice, inviting the agent to walk an extra mile (or two, even!) with and for the Other.[10] Agape "is not an occasional act, it is a constant attitude"[11] of pouring myself out to the Other, without emptying myself completely—giving generously yet sustainably, with

---

[8] I draw a distinction between needs, on the one hand, and mere desires, preferences, and wants, on the other. While the lack of former causes disablement, the lack of the latter causes only discomfort.

[9] The idea of presence "as being with" the other has been discussed in fields as distinct as theology, philosophy, sociology, nursing, and medicine. In theology, see, e.g., Stump, *Wandering in Darkness*, pp. 108-28. In philosophy, see, e.g., Darwall, "Love's Second Personal Character," pp. 101-2; Darwall, "Being With." In sociology, see, e.g., Cousiño and Valenzuela, *Politizacion y Monetarizacion en America Latina*. In nursing ethics, see, e.g., Benner, 1984. *From Novice to Expert*; Zyblock, "Nursing Presence in Contemporary Nursing Practice"; Boeck, "Presence." In medicine, see, e.g., Verghese, "The Importance of Being"; Zulman et al. "Practices to Foster Physician Presence and Connection with Patients in the Clinical Encounter."

[10] By saying that agape requires a *reasonable* degree of self-sacrifice, I am responding to feminist critics of the conception of love such as theologian Barbara Hilkert Andolsen, who contends that the self-sacrificial overtones of agape often reinforces female submission (see Andolsen, "Agape in Feminist Ethics").

[11] King, "Love in Action."

proper boundaries. Through this ongoing process, love occurs and love matures. It occurs through the daily renewal of the choice to give and receive presence. It matures through the daily commitment to bear with one another's infirmities, limitations, and vulnerabilities, while contemplating each other's unique beauty, goodness, and truth (see Chapter 3 for an elaboration of the idea of bearing with one another).

Agape, as a shared journey of presence, unfolds in two interdependent dimensions: a contemplative (intellectual, epistemic) dimension and an active (effective, practical) dimension. In its contemplative aspect, the agent employs practical reasoning to understand what it truly means to fully accept the gift of self from the Other, clarifying the commitment required and its transformative potential. Should the agent choose to embrace this gift, the active dimension emerges: I offer my full being—my presence—as a tailored conduct of care in response to the unique needs of the Other (see Chapter 2 on the concept of "effectively tailored care"). Within the *Rule of Love* framework, care is not synonymous with love[12]; rather, it is the outward expression of the gift of self, given in response to the Other's needs. For this caring response to be authentically grounded in agape—and not in paternalistic assumptions—it is crucial that the agent engages in attentive contemplation, which inherently includes empathetic listening (Chapter 6), to truly honor the Other's uniqueness. In short, while attentive contemplation is fundamental, it works in tandem with the active dimension of care, together completing the full circle of love as a reciprocal gift-of-self.

3. A Vision of Agape: The Complementarity between the Active and the Contemplative

If you were to ask me for a practical depiction of agape's contemplative and active components in daily life—within and beyond healthcare—I would point you to Caravaggio's *Seven Works of Mercy* (1607). Housed in the Church of Pio Monte della Misericordia in Naples, this altarpiece was commissioned to depict the "corporal works of mercy" described in Matthew 25:35-36. Caravaggio's composition captures the messy reality of life by presenting several independent yet interconnected scenes, each illuminated through his masterly use of chiaroscuro.[13]

Although titled *Seven Works of Mercy*, the painting embodies, I believe, more than mercy (which I define in Chapter 1 as forgiveness); it also portrays acts of compassion and beneficence. These seven "works of agape"—as I would call

---

[12] bell hooks makes the same point differentiating love and care; she sees care as an ingredient of love, not the same as love: hooks, *All about Love*.

[13] Caravaggio, *Seven Works of Mercy*.

them—demonstrate, I believe, the active component of agapic love, the outward expression of our gift of self to those in need.

The first scene exemplifies compassionate love where the gift of self is manifested in sheltering the homeless—the first work of agape. Caravaggio depicts St. James of Compostela talking with an innkeeper, symbolizing the act of hospitality (derived from the ancient Greek concept of *philoxenia*, or love of strangers).[14]

The second scene, depicts another form of compassionate love, clothing the naked—the second work of agape. Here, Caravaggio portrays St. Martin of Tours tearing his robe in half to share it with a naked beggar. According to custom, knights owned only half of their garments, with the other half belonging to the state. Thus, St. Martin sacrifices his own share for the beggar, who shivers in the cold. Caravaggio's use of chiaroscuro highlights St. Martin's compassionate expression as he provides "effectively tailored care" (as defined in Chapter 2) to the physically disabled, naked man on the street, doing all he can to alleviate the beggar's suffering in the dead of winter.

The third scene represents merciful love, where the gift of self is shown in refreshing the thirsty—the third work of agape. Caravaggio depicts Samson drinking water from a hollow in the desert of Lehi after his battle with the Philistines.[15] It has been argued that this may also serve as Caravaggio's self-portrait, expressing his own thirst for mercy and forgiveness.[16] Facing a death sentence for murder, Caravaggio fled from Rome and worked on the *Seven Works of Mercy* in Naples, hoping for a more lenient sentence that would allow his return. The water not only quenches his thirst for mercy but also symbolically cleanses him of his victim's spilled blood—washing away guilt and sin in an act of forgiveness and reconciliation with Rome (see Chapter 1 for definitions and distinctions between forgiveness and reconciliation).

The fourth scene exemplifies beneficent love, where the gift of self is manifested in two acts: healing the sick and burying the dead (the fourth and fifth works of agape). Here, Caravaggio depicts a deacon assisting in the rapid transportation of a corpse while leading mourners in the *Ars Moriendi*. Originating during the fourteenth-century bubonic plague as a set of texts guiding a "good death" within the community, the *Ars Moriendi* evolved into broader practices eventually adopted by non-Christian traditions.[17] In this scene, beneficence is expressed not only in caring for the deceased's soul but also in comforting mourners and preparing both individuals and the community to die well—a service to the common good.

[14] Ward, *The Guardian of Mercy*, p. 4.
[15] Judges 15:19.
[16] Ward, *The Guardian of Mercy*.
[17] Dugdale, "Dying, a Lost Art," p. 7; Lysaught, "Ritual and Practice," p. 81.

The fifth scene, in my view, exemplifies all three types of love in my typology. It combines mercy, compassion, and beneficence, as the gift of self is actively expressed through two works of agape: visiting the prisoner (the sixth work) and feeding the hungry (the seventh work). Caravaggio portrays the story of Roman Charity, where Pero, having just given birth, visits her aged, famished, and imprisoned father, Cimon. Moved by compassion and guided by her beneficence, Pero mercifully forgives her father and, with a total gift-of-self, offers him her breast milk. Caravaggio emphasizes her tender, unconditional love through a subtle detail: while scared for prison guardians, and watchful of their moves, Pero lifts up her skirt to place it under Cimon's chin, ensuring he can drink more comfortably through the iron bars. This small yet powerful gesture highlights her attentive love for her father (on the key importance of small details that show presence and attentiveness to those in need, rather than grandiose and heroic acts of sacrifice, see Chapter 2).

These seven actions are known in the Catholic tradition as the "corporal" works, emphasizing their bodily, material nature. Caravaggio's depiction illustrates how we can meet our neighbors' most basic material needs through simple yet profound acts of loving care—that is, by doing something for or with them (see Chapter 3). However, as I argued in Chapter 3, for these active works of agape to be fully effective, they ought to transcend the material: love goes beyond doing things for or with the other. While meeting material needs is vital, works of agape must also nurture our non-material, transcendent need of relationality, met when we transcend ourselves to meet the other in a profound, transformative encounter (see Chapter 2). Interestingly, I believe Caravaggio's work here seems also to reflect this higher dimension: his depiction of the Madonna and Child with two angels, positioned above scenes of material care, suggests, I think, our transcendent good of relationality, realized through our encounter with these heavenly figures.

The Madonna and Child are not actively doing anything to alleviate people's suffering.[18] Instead, they are simply there: they "show up" for the sufferers through their silent presence. And I believe this is key: it is precisely this silent presence that is the standard by which we should measure our love, for it demonstrates how to genuinely will the good of the Other—as Other. Instead of demonstrating passivity or indifference toward the suffering of their people by not miraculously providing the material cure they desire, the Madonna and the Child—in their own humanity, limitations, and vulnerability—offer an utterly fundamental (yet non-material) good: their attentive accompaniment through their silent human presence.

---

[18] On medical suffering, see, e.g., Tate and Pearlman, "What We Mean When We Talk about Suffering"; Tate, "Objective Suffering."

The Madonna and Child personally encounter each sufferer right where they are: in the raw, chaotic tapestry of everyday life. There, they listen with empathy when we choose to speak. There, they patiently bear our unjust, angry outcries when, in our weariness, pain, and grief, we lose all control over our emotions. There—in that sacred space of intense vulnerability and interdependence—they remain with us in tender silence, mercifully forgiving our shortcomings, consoling our wounds, and strengthening us to persevere in our daily battles with hope. In that quiet, unspoken presence, they extend an invitation without words—a call for an encounter that blossoms into communion and community. This is the trinity of relationality—communication, communion, and community—that will be explored further in Part II.

With unwavering attentiveness, the Madonna and the Child behold each of us, as they accompany us on our singular journeys. They see us—fully, deeply—embracing every nuance of our being, while our material needs are met by our communities. They are ever present, and yet they are never intrusive and they never overpower our agency or freedom. They never abandon us in our suffering. Even when we are too overwhelmed by our own misery to sense their nearness, they remain—silent, steadfast, merciful. It is in these quiet, intimate encounters that they reveal their own humanity, their own vulnerabilities and wounds, inviting us to recognize the sacred worth of every soul.

My point here is this: in its silent potency, presence unveils the transformative power of love. It is love that can transmute suffering into a space of encounter with the transcendent—that which transcends us and helps us rise above self-pity and self-centeredness. The presence of the Other may not solve my problem, cure my infirmity, or take away my pain, but it invites us to transcend ourselves and receive the gift of human presence. In this shared journey, we find an opportunity to nurture genuine friendship and solidarity. The Other who walks beside us—whether a member of our community or the Madonna and Child—may not offer the quick fix or the miracle we long for, yet what they do offer is the very essence of agape: presence. A silent, unwavering presence that does not remove the storm but cradles us within the warmth of their loving, attentive gaze.[19]

It is in our personal encounter with suffering, in the willingness to share our vulnerabilities, that a community of mutual care is born. Such community depends on acknowledging our interdependence—our need for one another, both in the material and in the transcendent realms. The complementarity of agape's active and contemplative dimensions allows communion to take root in the messiness of real life, as my reading of Caravaggio's *Seven Works of Mercy* has sought to show. Communion, nourished through communication, is the fruit of agape—the web that binds a community of mutual care.

---

[19] Murdoch coins the term "just and loving gaze" in *The Sovereignty of Good*, p. 34.

Yet, this community of mutual care is not built as the mere exchange of favors, as though love were a transaction to repay in kind. As discussed in Chapter 1, the logic of the gift is not one of measured reciprocation, but of superabundance: one does not pay back, but pays forward in gratitude.[20] This is what makes agape universal and unconditional, weaving together a multi-directional web of "uncalculated giving and graceful receiving"[21] (as explored in Chapters 1 and 3). The upshot of agape is, in the end, the formation of a community shaped by love—a community of mutual, multi-directional care. For agape is both a virtue and a practical reason, ordering our choices toward the flourishing of such communities. It reshapes not only our personal relationships but also the very institutions we build, guiding them toward justice and love.

4. Institutional Agape

In Part I, I have shown how different types of agape unfold within healthcare institutions at both local and global levels. My concept of agape therefore has an important institutional element. I do not doubt that love as presence is deeply personal and most clearly manifested in interpersonal relationships. But the choice to foster presence within institutional dynamics—nurturing spaces of encounter where communities of mutual, multi-directional care can thrive—is also an essential part of my concept of agape.

Based on the complementarity between the interpersonal and institutional components of love explored in these chapters, I propose the following working definition:

> Agape is a directive for both individual and institutional deliberations that grounds a universal yet personal responsibility to care for those suffering from serious illnesses that transcend political borders. To care for *all* who suffer, one must journey with each sufferer *personally*. Ultimately, as a shared journey of presence, agape nurtures a community of mutual care—this co-responsibility requires the firm commitment to accompany the sufferer by offering the reasonably self-sacrificial gift of one's presence.

Part I provided a conceptual analysis of three types of agape, most frequently manifested in healthcare: merciful love, compassionate love, and beneficent love. Part II will provide a normative analysis of the three practical principles that arise from my working definition: the principles of solidarity (Chapter 4),

---

[20] Ricœur, "Love and Justice," p. 34.
[21] MacIntyre, *Dependent Rational Animals*, p. 121.

subsidiarity (Chapter 5), and stewardship (Chapter 6). Practical principles provide reasons for actions.[22] So Part II will present agape-based reasons for actions that will help us reimagine the conventional way of doing GHG and of leading its institutions. In establishing agape as a journey of shared presence, Part I has already introduced some normative considerations that challenge the design of existing healthcare institutions at the local and global levels. Part II will further elaborate on these normative requirements to show more fully how agapic love can reform these institutions. Together, the chapters of Part II will present an agapic vision for future GHG and leadership—one that fosters communion (Chapter 4) and community (Chapter 5) through communication (Chapter 6).

Part I raised some normative challenges to GHG that Part II will further examine. Three, in particular, merit some preliminary attention. They are the agapic moral requirements, first, to de-prioritize productivity and efficiency (as discussed in Chapter 2); second, to emphasize active participation (Chapter 2) and meaningful inclusion (Chapter 1); and third, to respect the agency of the other through shared decision-making authority (Chapter 3). These are three normative challenges that agape presents to traditional institutional design.

Agape—as a shared journey of presence that fosters communion and community through communication—morally requires global health institutions to be reformed by way of creating and then nurturing genuine spaces of encounter, where communities of mutual, multi-directional care can thrive. But to achieve this, GHG must move beyond a singular focus on productivity and efficiency. While these metrics are conventional hallmarks for a functioning healthcare system, especially amid scarce resources (Chapter 4), agape requires that deliberations center first on the responsibility to care effectively, before grounding the duty to manage cost-effectively (see Chapters 5 and 6 on the difference between good leadership and management). Agape can only be nurtured in spaces where encounter is not rushed; being attentive to the person in front of me is an act of contemplation. An excessive preoccupation with doing tasks in a productive and efficient manner robs people of that contemplative attention and dehumanizes both self and other.[23]

But to deemphasize productivity and efficiency so that active participation and meaningful inclusion can be institutionally prioritized is not easy. The second normative challenge that agape presents requires a reasonable degree of self-sacrifice from leaders, as illustrated by the hypothetical case of Mr. Zangado in Chapter 2. Here, the *Presence before Efficiency Policy* was co-created and co-deliberated with participation from all levels of the hospital community,

---

[22] Grisez, Boyle, and Finnis, "Practical Principles, Moral Truth, and Ultimate Ends," p. 102.
[23] On the dehumanizing nature of modern, post-industrial healthcare, see Tate and Clair, "Love Your Patient as Yourself."

including patients and staff directly affected by hospital protocols. This required Dr. Sally, the hospital director, to practice self-denial, to "waste her time" empathetically listening, humbly learning, and deeply seeing those under her leadership, before assuming things and making decisions based on those assumptions. Active participation and meaningful inclusion, allowing for institutional self-reflection and empathetic appreciation of different voices from all levels of hospital administration, were vital for the success of the *Presence before Efficiency Policy*.

But choosing this agapic way of governance and leadership may not be the most efficient and productive option. Sure, as sociologist and human-flourishing scholar Matthew T. Lee rightly emphasizes, love-based governance and leadership "need not be financially reckless."[24] Yet, active participation and meaningful inclusion would probably still be more time-consuming and therefore more costly in the short term (although there is evidence that it is not true of the long term).[25] Though apparently not cost-effective, active participation and meaningful inclusion are essential for creating and then nurturing spaces of encounter where communities of mutual, multi-directional care can thrive, especially because they allow for shared authority in decision-making to unfold. This leads to the third normative challenge that institutional agape poses to GHG.

For shared authority to be a real thing and not simply a fake performance, participation and inclusion need to be real, too. They cannot be a mere checkbox exercise of bedside manners where an unengaged listening to patients counts as participation (see Chapter 2). Neither can a parade of empty diversity, equity, and inclusion rhetoric count as inclusion (see Chapter 1). These are not only inauthentic but also alienating, instead of genuinely participatory and inclusive. Shared authority, to be real, needs to tolerate some degree of inefficiency and slowness that characterize a process of true co-deliberation and co-creation of a shared vision for life—and for a new governance structure (see Chapter 3).

The three normative challenges that institutional agape poses to GHG—de-prioritizing productivity and efficiency, emphasizing active participation and meaningful inclusion, and respecting the agency of the Other through shared decision-making—are essential ingredients for reforming global health institutions toward decolonization—a central theme in GHG that was introduced in Chapter 1 and which will be further examined in Chapter 5. These challenges illustrate what equal respectful consideration and loving attention to Global South partners should look like, as Chapters 4 through 6 will demonstrate.

---

[24] Lee, "Love as a Foundational Principle."
[25] Trzeciak and Mazzarelli, *Compassionomics*; Brown, "Compassion and Efficiency."

For shared authority to be a reality in GHG, it is crucial that the typically silenced voices of local communities from the Global South actively participate and are meaningfully included at the negotiation tables. Empathetic (not rushed) listening to these voices require a reasonable degree of self-sacrifice from leaders—especially those from the Global North, who with greater resources, often control rapid decision-making. A reasonable degree of epistemic humility would be required to counter their impulses to presume knowledge and jump into global health interventions. This expresses not good leadership, but rather paternalism. Reframed in the light of agape, good leadership calls for less control over the process and the outcome, and more of a posture of mutual learning.[26]

In this agapic journey of mutual learning, uncertainties, failures, and frustrations are inevitable. Yet, it is within this quotidian messiness, as Caravaggio illustrates, that love is truly forged and matured. Through our silent presence—bearing one another's infirmities and vulnerabilities—we come to discern the unique beauty, goodness, and truth in the Other. This silent presence is the true measure of our institutions. It reveals how genuinely global and public health leaders can will the good of the other—as Other. By embracing this quiet presence without fear, we uncover the essence of humane leadership and transformative care, illuminating a path toward a world where love becomes the guiding force in all our endeavors.

---

[26] Martins, "Bioética e saúde global a partir de baixo," p. 113; Martins, "A escuta como método e os pobres/oprimidos como sujeitos," pp. 270–91.

PART II

A PRINCIPLED TRIPARTITE FRAMEWORK—A NORMATIVE EXAMINATION OF AGAPIC LOVE IN THE CONTEXT OF GLOBAL HEALTH GOVERNANCE

> Thus there are three things that endure:
> Faith, hope, and love,
> And the greatest of these is love
> 1 Cor. 13:13

Part II builds on Part I's conceptual analysis of love as the greatest gift. Chapters 1–3 established agape as a both virtue and practical reason, requiring individuals and institutions to embrace a shared journey of presence. Specifically, this means reforming institutions to create and nurture spaces of encounter where communities of mutual, multidirectional care thrive. Chapters 4–6 now introduce an agapic framework for GHG and leadership, fostering communion and community through communication. Together, these chapters offer a reimagined vision of GHG, rooted in love (alongside justice): a tripartite framework of GHG based on three practical principles of love.

Practical principles provide reasons for actions.[1] From my working definition of agape (outlined in the Conclusion of Part I), three key principles emerge: solidarity, subsidiarity, and stewardship. Widely recognized in human rights, international law, and global health discourse as principles of justice, these principles will be reinterpreted in Chapters 4–6 through the lens of agape. By integrating its core element of presence with the demands of justice, I will explore what these principles require in practice.

---

[1] Grisez, Boyle, and Finnis, "Practical Principles, Moral Truth, and Ultimate Ends," p. 102.

Chapter 4 examines what love requires of developed nations when less developed neighbors face a public health emergency. What does agapic love as a shared journey of presence require in the face of suffering? The answer lies in the principle of solidarity, operationalized in complementarity with subsidiarity (explored in Chapter 5). Solidarity, paired with subsidiarity, guides a good leader how to prioritize with reason, enabling her to love well those under her leadership while remaining attentive to those in need beyond her jurisdiction or direct sphere of influence. This is the leadership lesson of solidarity, which calls for union and communion with those in need.

Chapter 5 explores what love requires of higher-level institutions in decision-making processes impacting local communities. How does agapic love guide leaders like the WHO when designing public health interventions? The answer lies in the principle of subsidiarity, operationalized in complementarity with stewardship (covered in Chapter 6). Subsidiarity, paired with stewardship, guides a good leader to humbly discern and truthfully communicate her strengths and those of her team, fostering collaboration toward a shared vision of the common good. In guiding leaders to relinquish control, subsidiarity empowers those under the leader's care and uphold their dignity, agency, and responsibility. This is the leadership lesson of subsidiarity, which calls for strong communities.

Chapter 6 addresses how love shapes the way global and public health authorities communicate laws and policies affecting vulnerable populations. How should leaders share decisions about public health measures? The answer lies in the agapic principle of stewardship, which complements and operationalizes subsidiarity and, by extension, solidarity. Stewardship guides leaders to communicate truthfully, with a reasonable degree of vulnerability, about what expert authorities know—and do not know—regarding a global health threat. This fosters trustworthiness. This is the leadership lesson of stewardship, which calls for good communication—the process by which community is formed and communion maintained.

Ultimately, Part II asks: if nurturing spaces of presence with those who suffer became the hallmark of institutions, what would GHG look like? Solidarity, subsidiarity, and stewardship provide the agape-based reasons for reimagining GHG and its leadership. Together, these principles anchor an agapic vision of governance centered on communion, community, and communication—the trinity of relationality.

4
On Solidarity and Communion

> Everyone is really responsible to all men for all men
> and for everything
> Father Zossima, in Fyodor Dostoyevsky, *The Brothers Karamazov*,
> Book VI, Chapter ii.a

Introduction

Fr Zossima, the wise elder in Dostoyevsky's *The Brothers Karamazov*, had important teachings on faith, humility, courage, and love. He advocated a universal love and responsibility, grounded on the fact that every good and every evil that each of us does, even our most private choices, have consequences on everybody's lives. One could stretch Fr Zossima's claim to suggest that his idea of universal love grounds a universal and an undifferentiated responsibility for all of God's creations. For those who support this extension, this is what to love one another means: to be equally responsible to all for all and for everything without any discrimination or differentiation among God's creatures.[1]

If one believes such a theory of universal love and responsibility, one cannot avoid the question of whether the moral value of love, while requiring the universality of loving all, would indeed also require an undifferentiated, homogeneous responsibility to care for all equally. Many would contend that this is precisely what the idea of global solidarity entails: a radical cosmopolitan responsibility to care for all neighbors equally. I will, however, argue against this conception of solidarity and defend the position that this normative conception of love is neither feasible nor reasonable.

I will present this argument by first introducing my interpretation of the principle of solidarity, as the first principle of love. I shall examine what solidarity requires and does not require in the context of global allocation of scarce healthcare resources, such as life-saving medicines. Debates on universal access to costly, patent-protected, essential treatments are perennial: they are revived with every new declaration of a public health emergency of international concern[2]

---

[1] Some content of this chapter is based on a previously published chapter: de Campos-Radinsky, "Solidarity and Global Allocation of COVID-19 Vaccines."

[2] See fn. 5.

The Rule of Love. Thana C. de Campos-Rudinsky, Oxford University Press. © Oxford University Press 2026.
DOI: 10.1093/9780197762400.003.0006

that necessitates access to such healthcare resources. Some prominent modern examples are the HIV/AIDS epidemic in the 1980s, the ongoing global health crisis caused by poverty-related diseases,[3] and the COVID-19 pandemic in 2020. While I have chosen the global allocation of scarce COVID-19 vaccines as my case study in this chapter, the theoretical debate and questions it spurs are applicable to past and future cases of public health emergency of international concern that require universal access to costly, patent-protected, essential treatments.

If one were to defend the view that universal love grounds undifferentiated responsibilities for all, and then apply that view to the allocation of scarce healthcare resources, one would endorse a view of radical vaccine cosmopolitanism in the context of the COVID-19 pandemic. However, as I believe that Fr Zossima's wisdom on universal love does not entail undifferentiated responsibilities of care, I will propose a revised theory of moderate vaccine cosmopolitanism, grounded in an agapic interpretation of the principle of solidarity, tempered by the principle of subsidiarity, the second principle of love (to be further discussed in Chapter 5). Agapic solidarity, as I interpret it, calls for a love of neighbor that is universal. By universal, however, I do not mean homogeneous. Rather, I mean a love that extends to all. Grounded in this understanding of universal love, my concept of agapic solidarity is predicated on the idea of equality of dignity (introduced in Chapter 2)—meaning equal respectful consideration and loving regard among persons and nations. Agapic solidarity thus calls for global responsibilities of mutual care among nations and peoples. While my concept of solidarity calls for a universal love of neighbor and equality of dignity, it necessitates neither equality of treatment and resources, nor equality of care and concern. Instead, it necessitates equity of care that requires preferential, differentiated treatment for the most vulnerable in our community.[4] By equity of care, I mean that love requires shared yet differentiated duties to care for those in need, according to their needs and our relationships to the most vulnerable. Love allows, and in some cases even requires—as this chapter demonstrates—some partiality in first taking care of those closest to us, in our own community, and prioritizing those with greater need, without abandoning outsiders to their fate. Though it may seem contradictory, equality of dignity is consistent with treating, caring, and being concerned with different people in different ways, according to their different needs and their different relationships to us, as the principle of subsidiarity suggests (and as will be further discussed in Chapter 5).

---

[3] de Campos, *The Global Health Crisis*, Ch. 4.
[4] On the idea of equity as a preferential option for the most vulnerable, see, e.g., Martins "Ethics and Equity in Global Health," pp. 96–105. See also: Martins, "The Preferential Option for the Poor as an Existential Commitment," pp. 59–75.

Through a test case of pandemics (since one should not just think of 2020 COVID-19 as an idiosyncratic event), I identify the limitations of mainstream conceptualizations of solidarity, especially in the international law and human rights literature. This case clearly demonstrates why the international order needs a more robust understanding of solidarity among nations and international institutions and of the obligation to cooperate.

In this chapter, I first offer an overview on how solidarity has been conceptualized in the relevant literature and interpreted within the specific context of my case study: that is, the global distribution of scarce COVID-19 vaccines (Section 1). Then, I shall discuss the controversies surrounding the case and the two rival theories behind them (Sections 2 and 3 on radical vaccine cosmopolitanism and moderate vaccine cosmopolitanism, respectively). Then I present my revised agape-based theory of moderate vaccine cosmopolitanism (Section 4). In asking what agape would require of developed nations in relation to their less developed neighbors, my agapic interpretation of the principle of solidarity defends that love requires equality of dignity and equity of care. My interpretation of solidarity based on agape will offer a new way of understanding communion[5] in community and of responding to the current backlash against multilateralism by substantiating the need for more complementarity and cooperation among global health stakeholders in times of public health emergency of international concern (like pandemics) and beyond. This is the leadership lesson of solidarity, which I identify as the first practical principle of agapic love. The principle of solidarity, along with subsidiarity (further discuss in Chapter 5), guides a good leader to order their priorities with reasonableness, so that they can love well those under their leadership and care, without abandoning those in need who are outside their sphere of jurisdiction.

Section 1. Background on Solidarity and Its Application to Scarce Health Resources

1.1. Relevant Conceptions of Solidarity

Solidarity is often regarded as a structural principle of international law, shaping international relations alongside principles like sovereignty.[6] It has even proposed it as a human right.[7] For years, the UN has been working on a declaration to establish the human right to international

---

[5] On the theological dimensions of communion, applied to the context of healthcare, see: Lysaught, *Caritas in Communion*.
[6] Carozza and Crema, "On Solidarity in International Law," p. 8.
[7] Ibid.

solidarity.[8] It defines solidarity as "a central principle in contemporary international law,"[9] emphasizing unity among individuals, peoples, states, and international organizations to achieve common goals,[10] and requiring states to cooperate in addressing global challenges.[11]

Legal scholars have criticized such overly broad and underspecified definitions. Hurst Hannum has argued that a new human right requires precise content and meaning,[12] and Paolo Carozza and Luigi Crema note that the proposed right to international solidarity remains too general and ambiguous.[13] Despite this vagueness, recent discussions have sought to refine the concept, particularly in healthcare ethics.[14]

Bioethicists Barbara Prainsack and Alena Buyx define solidarity as "an enacted commitment to carry 'costs' (financial, social, emotional, or otherwise) to assist others with whom a person or persons recognize similarity in a relevant respect."[15] Ruud ter Meulen's historical analysis shows that solidarity has traditionally been a principle of mutual aid, particularly for those in need among the members of a community, linking it to justice—another inherently relational concept.[16]

Philosophers Lisa Eckenwiler, Christine Straehle, and Ryoa Chung emphasize solidarity's connection to structural vulnerabilities.[17] They argue that solidarity arises not just from affective ties, such as sympathy for fellow community members, but also, and more fundamentally, from an awareness of mutual interdependence. (I arrived at a similar conclusion in Chapter 2, where I define compassion as a three-stage process.)

---

[8] United Nations Human Rights (UNHCR), *Independent Expert on Human Rights and International Solidarity*.
[9] UNHCR Council, A/HRC/53/32, *Revised Draft Declaration on Human rights and International Solidarity*, Annex, Art. 1, p. 14.
[10] UNHCR Council, A/HRC/35/35, *Report of the Independent Expert on Human Rights and International Solidarity*, Annex, Art. 1, p. 17.
[11] UNHCR Council, A/HRC/53/32, *Revised Draft Declaration on Human rights and International Solidarity*, Annex, Art. 7, p. 16.
[12] Hannum, *Rescuing Human Rights*, p. 9
[13] Carozza and Crema, "On Solidarity in International Law," p. 11.
[14] See, e.g., Dawson and Verweij, "Solidarity: A Moral Concept in Need of Clarification," pp. 1–5; Gould, "Solidarity and the Problem of Structural Injustice in Healthcare," pp. 541–52; Davies and Savulescu, "Solidarity and Responsibility in Health Care," pp. 133–44; West-Oram and Buyx, "Global Health Solidarity," pp. 212–24; Jennings, "Relational Ethics for Public Health," pp. 4–12; Kolers, "What Does Solidarity Do for Bioethics?" pp. 122–28; Domingo-Osle and Domingo, "Redefining Nursing Solidarity," pp. 651–59; Jennings and Dawson, "Solidarity in the Moral Imagination of Bioethics," pp. 31–38.
[15] Prainsack and Buyx, *Solidarity in Biomedicine and Beyond*, p. 52.
[16] ter Meulen, *Solidarity and Justice in Health and Social Care*.
[17] Eckenwiler, Straehle, and Chung, "Global Solidarity, Migration and Global Health Inequity," pp. 382–90. For a definition of structural health vulnerability, see: Chung "Structural Health Vulnerability," pp. 201–16.

These discussions clarify that solidarity is not just an emotional response to suffering but a commitment to aiding those in need. Such commitment does entail certain "costs,"[18] as Prainsack and Buyx describe, but I find this term inadequate. Rather than framing solidarity in transactional terms, I propose understanding it as a commitment to love those who suffer—one that necessarily involves a reasonable degree of self-sacrifice (see Chapters 1–3). Solidarity, in this sense, is an act of love—one that operates *in tandem* with justice rather than in opposition to it. It is a gift-of-self, expressed through the giving of aid to those in need.[19] Grounded in the logic of generosity, solidarity directly challenges the logic of scarcity and fear—an outlook that, for instance, justifies stockpiling scarce resources for national use rather than sharing them with those in more urgent need (see Chapter 1). I will return to these ideas later in the chapter.

As discussed in Chapter 2, I use solidarity and friendship almost interchangeably, both arising from the three-stage process of compassion—moving from affective sympathy to intellectual empathy to effective compassionate care. Friendship describes this dynamic at the interpersonal level, while solidarity applies at the institutional level; in essence, solidarity is friendship between institutions. Both reflect a shift from "I" to "we,"[20] a community forged through encounters with vulnerability. This "we," as I explored in Chapter 2, forms a strong community of mutual care, oriented toward both individual and common good.

This initial iteration of my conception of solidarity is closest to the account of philosophers and global health ethicists Caesar Atuire and Nicole Hassoun, which draws on the African philosophy of personhood.

They describe solidarity as "a primary ethical duty" arising from our inherent relationality rather than merely a means of assisting the worse off.[21] They ground solidarity in the interdependence intrinsic to personhood—and, I would add, to the notion of human dignity, as I will discuss in Section 4. Expanding on Prainsack and Buyx's definition, they characterize solidarity as "a sympathetic and imaginative enactment of collaborative measures to enhance our given or acquired relatedness so that together we fare well enough."[22]

Atuire and Hassoun appear to use "sympathy" as a synonym for compassion, broadly meaning "to suffer with." In Chapter 2, however, I distinguished sympathy as an initial emotional response—a fellow-feeling—while compassion is the enacted commitment to share in another's suffering for their good.

---

[18] Prainsack and Buyx, *Solidarity in Biomedicine and Beyond*, p. 52.
[19] For a discussion on the logic of gift, see Chapter 1.
[20] Wojtyla, *Love and Responsibility*, p. 95.
[21] Atuire and Hassoun, "Rethinking Solidarity Towards Equity in Global Health," p. 3.
[22] Ibid., p. 4.

Compassion, as a gift-of-self, requires making oneself present to the other, actively accompanying them in their suffering.

While my understanding of sympathy differs from Atuire and Hassoun's, our definitions of solidarity share fundamental elements: relationality, mutual vulnerability, interdependence, and enacted compassionate measures that meet the needs of the other and lead to the common good of all Thus, I propose the following definition of solidarity:

> a sympathetic perception and an empathetic understanding of the suffering of another leading to an enacted commitment to a compassionate conduct that meets the needs of the sufferer and enhances our sense of belonging to a community of mutual care.

The key to understanding what this kind of solidarity requires is appreciating our relational dignity, expressed in our intrinsic interdependence, and how, in belonging together in the same human family, we can all also flourish together, since your good and the common good of all depend on my good too.

Now, if we are all equal members of the same human family, and all equal in human dignity, what does such equality morally require of each of us, in the way we treat and care for one another? One may think that all concepts of solidarity should entail an idea of equality that requires equality of treatment, resources, care, and concern within a community. We are, after all, brothers and sisters in the same human family. Perhaps the extended version of Fr Zossima's claim would support this view. However, different philosophical conceptions of solidarity are grounded in different theoretical conceptions of equality, and these differences have important practical implications for how laws and policies establish what are reasonable or unreasonable ways, for example, of distributing scarce resources among members of a community. In what follows, I outline two different conceptions of the principle of solidarity, chosen as being the most relevant to debate on global allocation of scarce healthcare resources. Each conception entails different ethical requirements.

One concept of solidarity requires equality of treatment and resources among nation states. A second concept of solidarity rejects this idea of equality of treatment and resources among nations, and requires instead equality of care and concern across nations and between members of the international community. While the ideas of equality of treatment and resources and equality of care and concern may look at a first glance synonymous, they are not: they require different things.

Equality of treatment and resources asserts that all nations are equal members of the international community; it therefore requires equality of treatment, in terms of distribution of resources, between the nationals and non-nationals of each particular nation. That is to say, under this first concept of solidarity the citizens of Zimbabwe, Japan, Argentina, and Sweden are all equals, and must be treated equally by receiving the same amount of a particular resource (e.g., a scarce anti-viral that is vital to control a pandemic afflicting all of these countries equally), if their needs and levels of risks are also all equal.

Equality of care and concern, on the other hand, while acknowledging that all nations are members of the international community, and deserve to be equally cared for, denies that all members are the same. There are some important differences across and between members that need to be taken into account when distributing scarce resources. More precisely, there are differences in closeness and in community ties, both within and among the nations. So, this second concept of solidarity argues that the citizens of Zimbabwe, Japan, Argentina, and Sweden, while all deserving to be cared for, can be treated unequally. For example, if Sweden has an extra amount of the vital but scarce anti-viral, Sweden is allowed, according to the concept of equality of care and concern, to treat its own people differently from non-citizens, prioritizing ill people in Sweden before sending the remaining anti-viral to other countries. This second concept of solidarity, therefore, allows for an unequal distribution of resources, while requiring equality of care and concern across nations.

Now, my proposed conception of the principle of solidarity enunciated above and further developed throughout this chapter requires neither of these forms of equality. Instead, I argue that the principle of solidarity requires equality of dignity and equity of care.[23]

1.2. Implications of Different Conceptions of Solidarity for Global Allocation of COVID-19 Vaccines

The COVID-19 pandemic revived an important, perennial debate on the ethics of distribution of patent-protected, life-saving treatments among countries. In both the international human rights law and the global bioethics literatures, the debate has centered around whether states (and developed nations in particular) have an obligation of solidarity to cooperate with and assist other countries in addressing a public health emergency that has spread across borders. This question is grounded on the protracted moral tension between protectionism and

---

[23] A clarification note on the different concepts of equality and equity. Equality generally means giving everyone the same amount of something (e.g., resources, treatment, care, concern, opportunities, and freedoms), reflecting a justice ideal focused on uniformity. Equity, however, acknowledges that each person has different needs, vulnerabilities, and circumstances. While recognizing that we are all equal in dignity, equity allows for tailored treatment—allocating resources or support based on what's necessary to achieve the most just outcome.

multilateralism, linked to the rival theories of nationalism versus cosmopolitanism, with a moderate form of cosmopolitanism based on communitarian values as the middle ground between the two. In the context of COVID-19 vaccines, these rival theories have given rise by and large to two opposite approaches to solidarity: vaccine nationalism and vaccine cosmopolitanism.

The crux of the controversy lies in the existence of two competing duties, each grounded on one of these two opposite approaches to solidarity. States have jurisdictional duties to care for those under their jurisdiction. Yet, states also have cosmopolitan duties to assist and care for the vulnerable population of other nations in need. The former is grounded in a narrower interpretation of solidarity, where a community can only be formed under the jurisdiction of the nation-state and membership depends on national ties. The latter is grounded in the much broader interpretation of solidarity provided by international human rights law, where community refers to the international community that all nation-states form.

Those who defend protectionism and vaccine nationalism typically defend jurisdictional duty over and above cosmopolitan duty, based on the criterion of membership of the nation-state community. They therefore espouse a narrower interpretation of solidarity, according to which the duty to assist is not applicable to those outside a state's jurisdiction. Those of the opposite view by and large defend cosmopolitan duties to assist and care for the vulnerable population of other nations, based on a broader idea of solidarity and equality between the basic health needs of those within and outside a certain jurisdiction. Now, there are different versions of vaccine cosmopolitanism based on different conceptions of solidarity and equality, depending on how broadly solidarity and equality are defined. These different theoretical conceptions of solidarity, and the different kinds of equality they justify, have important practical implications for establishing reasonable (and unreasonable) ways of distributing COVID-19 vaccines among countries.

Putting aside vaccine nationalism (the 'my country first' approach), based on the narrower interpretation of solidarity, this chapter discusses two different versions of vaccine cosmopolitanism. The first, more radical form is grounded in an understanding of solidarity as effective altruism among nations. Effective altruism is a philanthropic movement founded on the ideas of the utilitarian philosopher Peter Singer. Applying a consequentialist lens to the problem of global poverty, it proposes that we should act in ways that will do the most good for the greatest number of people. Specifically, we should direct our philanthropy through effective organizations that spend money efficiently and make the greatest possible impact.[24] When it comes to resource distribution, effective

---

[24] See, e.g., Singer, "The Why and How of Effective Altruism." https://www.effectivealtruism.org/peter-singer-ted.

altruism requires equality of treatment and resources between nationals and non-nationals. Nation-state community membership is, according to this view, an arbitrary and morally irrelevant consideration.[25]

The second, more moderate version of vaccine cosmopolitanism (supported, for example, by bioethicists Kyle Ferguson and Arthur Caplan) is grounded in an underspecified interpretation of solidarity as love of neighbor. Call this "the insufficient theory of moderate cosmopolitanism." It requires equality of care and concern within the international community, while allowing for unequal distribution of resources between nationals and non-nationals. Again, while the terms equality of treatment and resources and equality of care and concern may look at first glance synonymous, they are not. Unlike radical cosmopolitanism, moderate cosmopolitanism does not defend equality of treatment and resources among countries. While seeking to justify a fair global distribution of coronavirus vaccines based on the different concept of 'equality of care and concern' among nations, the moderate view acknowledges that a degree of national partiality is ethically justifiable. It can thus establish a common ground between radical vaccine nationalism and radical vaccine cosmopolitanism: while it generally agrees with my country first, it also accepts that there are stringent cosmopolitan duties to aid other countries in need.

In what follows, I will critically examine how these two versions of vaccine cosmopolitanism answer the question of what human rights obligations of solidarity and international cooperation are required in the COVID-19 context. By juxtaposing them, the chapter will, first, reveal the shortcomings of the radical view and, second, substantiate the theoretical underpinnings of the insufficient theory of moderate cosmopolitanism, based on an underspecified love of neighbor. Hence, I will propose a revised, more theoretically robust moderate view of cosmopolitanism, grounded on an agapic interpretation of the principle of solidarity, and tempered by the principle of subsidiarity (to be further discussed in Chapter 5). Call it "the agapic theory of moderate cosmopolitanism." Furthermore, I will develop the concept of solidarity enunciated above, specifically how it is predicated on an agapic understanding of equality as equality of dignity among persons and peoples. This understanding leads to the factual and normative basis for human rights obligations of solidarity among persons and nations that clarify real-world questions concerning global health laws and policies.

---

[25] See also: Herlitz, Lederman, Miller et al., "Just Allocation of COVID-19 Vaccines," e004812.

Section 2. Radical Vaccine Cosmopolitanism: Solidarity as Effective Altruism among Nations

For Singer and other supporters of the effective altruism utilitarian tradition,[26] everyone's suffering counts equally. Their understanding of solidarity is predicated on equality of treatment and resources between people of different nationalities, races, or religions. As Singer puts it: "[e]ffective altruists do not discount suffering because it occurs far away or in another country or afflicts people of a different race or religion."[27] For Singer, therefore, the principle of equal treatment and resources for people at an equal level of risk should guide COVID-19 vaccine allocations across countries. With the goal of saving more lives worldwide and reducing the years of life lost,[28] scarce resources should be distributed only on the basis of need or level of risk, with no regard to citizenship. Indeed, Singer argues that getting vaccines to the Global South, most affected by global poverty and therefore, in his view, at higher risk from contagious disease, should actually be the highest priority.[29]

For Singer, an understanding of solidarity as effective altruism requires equality of treatment among people of different nationalities, which entails equality of resources to be distributed between nations. Solidarity as effective altruism requires an efficient and equal distribution among countries. One practical upshot of Singer's argument is the need to abolish intellectual property protections. This would achieve globally efficient and equal distribution through sharing patent-protected medical knowledge on coronavirus vaccines, and scaling up the production of generic vaccines. However, Singer's argument for the production and distribution of generic COVID-19 vaccines, grounded on an understanding of solidarity as equality of treatment and resources, raises both a theoretical and practical problem.

2.1. Theoretical Objection to Singer: Solidarity as Equality of Treatment and Allocation of Resources among Nations?

Questions about the nature of equality—whether it pertains to equality of treatment and resources, care and concern, opportunity, respect, or freedom—are central to contemporary debates on solidarity and human rights, especially in defining justice in the context of the human right to health. Scholars employ

---

[26] Singer, "The Logic of Effective Altruism." See also: MacAskill, "Effective Altruism."
[27] Singer, "The Logic of Effective Altruism."
[28] Singer, "The Ethics of Prioritizing COVID-19 Vaccination."
[29] Bazelon, "People Are Dying. Whom Do We Save First with the Vaccine?"

various terms as justificatory bases for health rights and responsibilities, but these terms remain highly contested.

Debates around equality of treatment and resources are particularly contentious. It is unreasonable to expect everyone to treat all individuals everywhere in the exact same way or allocate identical resources universally. Different kinds of relationships and needs justify varying responsibilities, which in turn justify unequal treatment or distribution of resources.[30] Legal philosopher John Finnis argues that giving "equal concern to the interests of every person anywhere"[31] is both unreasonable and unjust. Certain distinctions—such as those based on different needs, relationships, or responsibilities—are not only defensible but also necessary. For instance, distinctions between nationals and non-nationals may be justifiable in particular contexts.

I will revisit this issue later to further analyze the problems of basing solidarity on equality of treatment and resources, or equality care and concern. For now, it suffices to highlight the theoretical shortcomings of these interpretations and their practical implications.

2.2. Practical Objection to Singer: Abolition of Intellectual Property Rights for Production of Generic COVID-19 Vaccines

Solidarity as effective altruism requires an efficient and equal distribution of coronavirus vaccines among countries. For Singer, this could be practically accomplished through the abolition of intellectual property protections for coronavirus vaccines, resulting in an efficient and equal distribution of shots among countries.

Elsewhere, I have argued that private property (including intellectual property) is not an absolute right.[32] In exceptional scenarios, the common good requires that certain private properties become public for a certain period of time. I have used the same rationale as the justificatory basis for legal exemptions from intellectual property rights.[33] In exceptional scenarios, the global common good requires that intellectual property rights over certain medical knowledge be suspended in certain countries and for a certain period of time.[34] While the COVID-19 pandemic easily qualifies as such a catastrophe, it is not clear that abolishing property protection over coronavirus vaccines would be sufficient to suppress it, as Singer seems to suggest. Waiving medical patents by way of

---

[30] de Campos, *The Global Health Crisis*, p. 83.
[31] Finnis, *Natural Law and Natural Rights*, p. 177.
[32] de Campos, *Global Health Crisis*, Ch. 4.
[33] See *Agreement on Trade-Related Aspects of Intellectual Property Rights (TRIPs)*, Arts. 30 and 31.
[34] de Campos, *Global Health Crisis*, Ch. 4.

intellectual property licenses is a necessary first step to address some public health crises, such as the HIV/AIDS epidemic in the 1980s and the ongoing global health crisis caused by poverty-related diseases.[35] Access to previously protected medical knowledge may then enable scaled-up production of a generic version of the effective medicine, which subsequently needs to be adequately distributed and administered. With COVID-19, however, there are specific complications related not only to the particular kind of medical knowledge that these vaccines contain but also to the requirements for their production scalability, adequate distribution, and safe administration.

First, it has been argued that existing COVID-19 vaccines are not as easily replicable as other drugs.[36] This is presumably because vaccines are more difficult to correctly replicate than drugs like the antiretrovirals used to contain the HIV/AIDS epidemic in the 1980s or other pharmaceuticals utilized to treat poverty-related diseases such as malaria and tuberculosis.

Second, even if the knowledge gap between the patent holder and licensees was overcome, and the COVID-19 vaccine could be technically replicated by licensees, production and distribution/administration complications would remain. Three main difficulties have been pointed out: (i) most countries (i.e., the licensees) have insufficient manufacturing capacity, and these infrastructure limitations are not easily addressed during a pandemic that requires immediate action;[37] (ii) Throughout the COVID-19 pandemic there was a shortage of the raw materials necessary to manufacture the vaccines (a global supply chain problem); and finally (iii) COVID-19 vaccines need to be kept at ultra-cold temperatures, making distribution/administration logistics more difficult. None of these complications existed in, for example, the HIV/AIDS epidemic.

In the case of the COVID-19 pandemic, it seems therefore that while licensing the vaccines' intellectual property was a necessary first step, more was required.[38] A true solidaristic pandemic suppression strategy would involve, as I have argued elsewhere, a reciprocal cooperation strategy applied to global pharmaceutical supply chains, predicated on complementary manufacturing, export, and import of COVID-19 treatments and vaccines under license.[39] Such coordination would involve, for example, some countries producing certain generic, affordable pharmaceutical products to treat and prevent COVID-19, and other countries producing other such products, all according to a complementary

---

[35] Ibid.
[36] Rutschman and Barnes-Waise, "The COVID-19 Vaccine Patent Waiver: The Wrong Tool for the Right Goal."
[37] Ibid.
[38] For a different perspective, see: Venkatapuram and Zielinska, "Covid Vaccine Patent Waivers are for Health Sovereignty."
[39] de Campos-Rudinsky, "Intellectual Property and Essential Medicines in the COVID-19 Pandemic," p. 534.

cooperative strategy of exchange. This is what global solidarity and friendship among nations should look like during public health emergency of international concern like pandemics. This division of labor would be morally justifiable, strategically helpful for the international community, and consistent with the existing intellectual property rights legal regime.

Singer is not wrong to argue for the need to waive intellectual property protection over coronavirus vaccines. However, this would be insufficient to ensure solidarity where countries need to coordinate responses to help each other in a workable, complementary way. So, Singer's argument for a solidarity based on equality of treatment among people of different nationalities entailing no more than equality of resources (by limiting itself to abolition of the intellectual property protections and saying that nothing further is to be done) does not hold up practically.[40] A complementary division of labor among nations, according to countries' different production capacities, would, in my view, be necessary to develop and distribute these vaccines not only effectively but also ethically among diverse populations across the world—according to their different vulnerabilities and epidemiological needs.[41]

Section 3. The Insufficient Theory of Moderate Vaccine Cosmopolitanism: Solidarity as Underspecified Love of Neighbor

Both radical and moderate approaches to vaccine cosmopolitanism seek to find a model of fair global distribution of coronavirus vaccines. But while the radical approach judges discrimination between nationals and non-nationals to be morally arbitrary, the moderate approach judges that a limited national partiality is not only reasonable but also just. Ferguson and Caplan explain that equality of care and concern among nations allows for unequal treatment and resources, due to "role-based and community-embedded responsibilities to take care of one's own."[42] So for defenders of a moderate vaccine cosmopolitanism, community membership justifies nation-states special obligations to prioritize their own people. Both moderate vaccine cosmopolitanism and vaccine nationalism therefore share the common ground of my country first.

The moderate approach therefore makes a distinction between the nation-state's duty to care for outsiders and its duty to care for one's own (i.e., those

---

[40] I thank Fr Iain Matthew for making this point clearer.
[41] I have put this argument forth at: de Campos-Rudinsky, "Intellectual Property and Essential Medicines in the COVID-19 Pandemic."
[42] Ferguson and Caplan, "Love Thy Neighbor? Allocating Vaccines in a World of Competing Obligations." For other moderate vaccine cosmopolitan views, see Emanuel et al., "On the Ethics of Vaccine Nationalism: The Case for the Fair Priority for Residents Framework," p. 543; Lie and Miller, "Allocating a COVID-19 Vaccine," p. 450; Jecker et al., "Vaccine Ethics," p. 308.

citizens and residents under their jurisdiction). I will call the former "cosmopolitan duties of beneficent care" and the latter "jurisdictional duties of beneficent care." The moderate version of vaccine cosmopolitanism is grounded on an interpretation of solidarity as love of neighbor. Ferguson and Caplan never define what they mean by "love of neighbor."[43] This is the reason I am calling their account "the insufficient theory of moderate cosmopolitanism," grounded on an underspecified interpretation of solidarity as love of neighbor. While Ferguson and Caplan never define what they mean by love, they present it in the context of cosmopolitan duties of benevolence and their view of solidarity.[44] I would therefore suggest that their reading of "love of neighbor" is friendship among nations, where one should love all neighbors, near and far, but one is allowed to treat one's own (those neighbors who are near) and one's friends from outside (those neighbors who are far) differently. That is to say, solidarity requires both cosmopolitan and jurisdictional duties of care for neighbors, yet these different duties have different moral weights.

The moderate approach defended by Fergunson and Caplan distinguishes between these two duties by making a distinction between neighbors: while all neighbors (nationals and non-nationals) are equally worthy and deserving of benevolent care and concern, this does not mean all neighbors are entitled to receive equal treatment and resources from a certain nation-state. Each nation-state has a moral obligation to treat in a special way those neighbors within its own jurisdiction—without abandoning those neighbors who are outside its jurisdiction to their own luck. In other words, the nation-state has a special obligation to prioritize the basic health needs of those under its jurisdiction who share in community membership. It is the associative ties, shared by all (national) neighbors within a jurisdiction, that justify such priority, without contradicting the state duty to cooperate with and assist other countries in need.

Moderate vaccine cosmopolitanism is grounded therefore on an interpretation of solidarity as love of neighbor, requiring both cosmopolitan and jurisdictional duties of care for neighbors (universal and particular therefore are not an oxymoron for moderate cosmopolitans). Most proponents of the moderate approach (like Fergunson and Caplan) make this claim based on equality of care and concern among nations, which allows for unequal treatment between national and non-national neighbors regarding resource distribution.[45] However, Fergunson and Caplan do not provide a thorough theoretical justification for equality of care and concern among nations in the context of the COVID-19 pandemic. Nor have they systematically explained why a limited national

---

[43] Ferguson and Caplan, "Love Thy Neighbor?"
[44] Ibid., p. 3.
[45] Ferguson and Caplan, "Love Thy Neighbor?" p. 3; Emanuel et al., "An Ethical Framework for Global Vaccine Allocation," p. 1310.

partiality and prioritization of national over non-national neighbors is reasonable and just when it comes to global vaccine allocation. In what follows, I will supplement the insufficient theory of moderate cosmopolitanism by addressing these shortcomings and further elaborating the idea of love of neighbor.

3.1. A Supplementary Theory: Dworkin on Partiality, Prioritization, and Equality of Care and Concern

Legal philosopher Ronald Dworkin's canonical theory of equal concern is helpful in providing part (but not all) of the missing theoretical justifications for the moderate version of vaccine cosmopolitanism.[46] In other words, while the defenders of moderate cosmopolitanism will need additional theories to fully explain their view, they could use Dworkin's theory of equal concern to start explaining what equal care and concern among nations means or does not mean. Dworkin believes that "No government is legitimate unless [it shows] equal concern for the fate of every person over whom it claims dominion."[47] Importantly, though, he argues for a political principle of equal concern within the nation-state and does not address the question of equality of concern among nations. Nevertheless, Dworkin's conception of equality of concern as an idea that is morally compatible with certain partialities and prioritizations is exactly what moderate cosmopolitans, like Ferguson and Caplan, need to make their claim more theoretically robust.

While Dworkin, in some earlier works, generally argued that equal concern within a nation-state entails equal treatment of all those under the same jurisdiction,[48] in later work, he shows how his principle of equal concern is actually compatible with certain partialities and prioritizations.[49] To put it in another way, it does not entail equality of treatment. Instead, certain preferences in how you treat different people are legitimate. Dworkin gives two main examples. In one, three swimmers face an imminent shark attack; a rescuer is only able to rescue one swimmer. Dworkin believes it is justifiable for the rescuer to save a swimmer with whom they have special ties (say, a friend or spouse) or a swimmer who has special personal qualities (who is, say, much younger, or an exceptional teacher, or a particularly virtuous person). Dworkin justifies these differential treatments without "implying or assuming that the lives of the two [swimmers] you *abandon* [to the sharks] are objectively less important than' the life of the swimmer you rescue" (*emphasis added*).[50] The other example involves treating

---

[46] For a different approach on equal concern, see: Scanlon, *Why Does Inequality Matter?*
[47] Dworkin, *Justice for Hedgehogs*, p. 2.
[48] Dworkin, *Sovereign Virtue*, p. 6. See also: Scanlon, *Why Does Inequality Matter?* Ch. 2.
[49] Dworkin, *Justice for Hedgehogs*, p. 13. See also: Finnis, "Equality and Differences," p. 21.
[50] Ibid. Dworkin, p. 281; Finnis, p. 21.

one's own child differently. As Dworkin puts it: "I can accept with perfect sincerity that your children's lives are no less important objectively than the lives of my own and yet I dedicate my life to helping my children while I *ignore* yours. They are, after all, my children" (*emphasis added*).[51]

These two examples complement the main claims of moderate vaccine cosmopolitanism. Dworkin gives a theoretical insight not only into their claim of equality of care and concern (without entailing equality of treatment) but also into their claim of limited national partiality. He also gives a theoretical insight into a disputed claim that some—though not all—supporters of the moderate view maintain on the need to prioritize the vaccination of those who are younger and for whom a premature death would be, presumably, more tragic.[52]

3.2. Shoring-up the Shortcomings of the Dworkinian Account

While Dworkin's canonical theory of equal concern is certainly helpful in providing some of the missing theoretical justifications for the moderate version of vaccine cosmopolitanism that Ferguson and Caplan defend, his idea of equality of care and concern among members of the same national community has, in my view, two main shortcomings.

Dworkin's account allows for certain individuals outside of my jurisdiction to be abandoned (to the sharks) and children who are not my own to be ignored.[53] However, abandoning and ignoring certain individuals contradict the very idea of solidarity as love of neighbor. To abandon and ignore cannot therefore be permissible within the moderate approach to vaccine cosmopolitanism that claims to be grounded on love of neighbor. Although Dworkin justifies abandoning and ignoring certain persons so that others can be prioritized, solidarity as love of neighbor would insist, I believe, on never abandoning and ignoring those in need, albeit allowing for certain partiality and prioritization. This is where, I think, solidarity needs to be tempered and complemented by subsidiarity. Subsidiarity offers a clear justification for differentiation of treatment, care, and concern without leading to abandonment or ignoring.

In this book, I conceptualize both solidarity and subsidiarity as practical principles of agapic love. This agapic interpretation of solidarity calls for responsibilities of mutual care among neighbors. Subsidiarity, as it will be further developed in Chapter 5, specifies how different neighbors and their different communities are to love one another by cooperating with and assisting

---

[51] Ibid.
[52] See, e.g., Emanuel et al., "Ethical Framework for Global Vaccine Allocation."
[53] Dworkin, *Justice for Hedgehogs*, p. 281.

one another when problems emerge. That is to say, subsidiarity operationalizes solidarity. Like solidarity, subsidiarity is also a structural principle of global governance and international human rights. It proposes a bottom-up structure that allocates duties of aid, first to local neighbors and communities and then to higher levels of governance only insofar as the lower-level neighbors and local communities need aid.[54] Subsidiarity basically establishes that where families, neighborhoods, and local communities can effectively address their own problems, they should do so, and only where they cannot, should governments and other higher-level structures of authority intervene and provide aid (i.e., *subsidium*). The term sub-sid-iary—which literally means to seat (sid) an activity down (sub) as close to the problem as possible[55]—recognizes the value of first trying to solve social problems locally and moving up to higher levels of governance only as necessary. Subsidiarity therefore provides a moral justification for differentiated treatment, concern, and care when implementing the principle of solidarity.

In the context of epidemics, local stakeholders typically have better knowledge of the epidemiological reality and the medical culture in a particular country, and are therefore *prima facie* best positioned to more effectively solve public health problems that require the coordination of persons and institutions across sectors and across nations.[56] Subsidiarity then requires coordinated interaction between higher- and lower-level neighbors, as well as between national and international communities, for their mutual aid, while giving leadership roles to locals, who know best.

Three requirements of subsidiarity provide additional insights that strengthen the justification for the moderate cosmopolitan argument:

(i) It encompasses the idea of non-abandonment: aid should be provided when lower-level neighbors and local communities cannot pursue their own ends by themselves;
(ii) It comprises the idea of respect for the agency of those in need of aid: the legitimate freedom of lower-level neighbors and local communities (to exercise their leadership role) ought to be honored if development assistant is to be authentic; and
(iii) It necessitates coordination among stakeholders: development aid should be directed toward pursuit of a common end (shared between lower-level neighbors/local communities and higher-level/international community) as well as the common good of all. This coordination is defined according

---

[54] de Campos, *Global Health Crisis*, Ch. 3.
[55] Vischer, "Subsidiarity as a Principle of Governance," p. 103.
[56] de Campos, *Global Health Crisis*, Ch. 3.

to the closeness between stakeholders—where closeness refers to not only geographical nearness but also the capacity to meet the need. In principle, the closer the stakeholders, the more capable they are to provide aid effectively and ethically to those in need.

As practical principles of agapic love, solidarity and subsidiarity complement one another and ought to be read in conjunction. Together, they justify an understanding of international cooperation and assistance that is inimical to the abandonment of those in need, while allowing for a reasonable[57] degree of partiality toward and prioritization of certain individuals and communities, based on closeness of community ties. In this way, my agapic reading of solidarity coupled with subsidiarity responds to the first shortcoming of the Dworkinian account, and makes the moderate cosmopolitan argument more theoretically robust. Now, how would my theoretical idea apply to a real-world scenario?

Agapic solidarity justifies a cosmopolitan duty to love and care for all neighbors. While this duty is universal and falls on everybody everywhere, the duty to love and care is also personal and differentiated, depending on the closeness of the relationship and the needs to be met. Take, for example, the different degrees of closeness and needs that I, a Brazilian living in Chile, have in relation to four different people with different kinds of needs: (i) my infant son; (ii) the Venezuelan doorman, Norfran, who works at my university campus; (iii) an elderly person convalescing with COVID-19 in the rural parts of my home country Brazil; and (iv) a woman in Sub-Saharan Africa who sacrifices for her community and chooses to eat less to be able to nourish more people in her village, especially those most vulnerable to COVID-19.

My son, Norfran who drives me home from campus most days; the elderly person who is my fellow citizen; and the virtuous African woman are all my neighbors. But my duty to love and care for each of them is different, according to my degree of closeness to them and their specific needs. My primary responsibility is to love and care for my son, who was directly entrusted to me. My son comes first. This does not mean that I should not care for Norfran, who is facing financial hardship during the COVID-19 pandemic and whose wife, Mariajesus, has just lost her job. Norfran has protected me and has become a friend over the years. My closeness to him and my capacity to meet some of his material needs, without unreasonably overburdening our household income or taking away from my family duties, justify my duty to care for him in a special way. This however does not give me license to abandon, ignore, or not care for my

---

[57] There are distinctions that are reasonable and others that are not because they are arbitrary. On the difference between reasonable distinction and discrimination, see: Ewa Rejman, *International Law as a Tool to Protect Mother's Rights*, Ch. IV.

fellow citizens in Brazil who have suffered greatly during the COVID-19 pandemic. Communal ties to my home country, Brazil, and the basic health needs of my fellow Brazilians, justify my duty to care for them in some way, too. This does not mean, however, that I should not care at all for the virtuous African woman who is saving her village. She is also my neighbor, albeit the most distant among these four people.

There are different degrees of closeness to me, and there are also different degrees of needs. These two factors determine how I should love and care for each of these four people. Subsidiarity therefore helps me to discern and specify how I should assist and act in solidarity to each one of these people in need. While solidarity requires loving each and every one of them, subsidiarity helps to clarify important differentiations in my commitment to love and practically care for each of them in particular. These differentiations make solidarity to all possible. Subsidiarity therefore operationalizes solidarity by ordering our loves.

3.2.1. Ordo Amoris as a Guide to Solidarity

The Augustinian concept of *ordo amoris* helps me explain why and how the principle of subsidiarity guides agents to love well, meaning: with the right will and in the right way, respecting our moral priorities. *Ordo amoris* has been pictured (in Book 19 of Augustine's *City of God*) as a set of expanding concentric circles, representing our different relationships and our different duties toward each of those relations. It expresses the legitimate moral preference that ought to be given to those closer to us: namely, our family, friends, and fellow citizens. Importantly, it shows us that duties to distant strangers in need ought to be trumped by the unique claims of these closer special relations.[58]

Augustinian theologian Eric Gregory adds that Augustine's moral psychology, grounded in his account of "rightly ordering loving focuses not only on the 'what' of loving, but also on 'how.'"[59] *Ordo amoris*, he explains, is based on the understanding that agape, while "unconditional and universal, begins 'at home' and extends 'outward'"[60]—in Augustine's words:

> All people should be loved equally. But you cannot do good to all people equally, so you should take particular thought for those who, as if by lot [*quasi quadam sorte*], happen to be particularly close to you in terms of place, time, or any other circumstances.[61]

---

[58] Gregory, "Agape and Special Relations in a Global Economy," p. 23.
[59] Gregory, *Politics and Order of Love*, p. 41.
[60] Ibid., p. 294.
[61] Augustine, *On Christian Teaching*, p. 294.

Gregory clarifies that Augustine, realistically recognizing that our embodied, finite nature places some constraints on our capacity to practically love others in need, endorses the partiality that comes from special relations of closer connections.[62] Dworkin would probably agree. Yet, Gregory also emphasizes that such endorsement does not entail a type of partial preference that *abandons* strangers in need, by *ignoring* their claims.[63] Here Dworkin and Gregory would seem to disagree.

The Augustinian concept of *ordo amoris*, therefore, in the way it conveys and further clarifies my idea of agapic love, informed by both solidarity and subsidiarity, contradicts Dworkin's two examples of duty to assist. In both of Dworkin's scenarios, my proposed idea of agapic love would first and foremost object to Dworkin's permissibility of abandonment of outsiders who are not my own. While subsidiarity would justify prioritizing the swimmer who is my friend or spouse and my own child, solidarity would not permit me to simply abandon/ignore the remaining swimmers/children. If it is in my capacity to save them or at least ask for assistance, I have a stringent moral duty to do so. Solidarity so requires. Subsidiarity justifies differentiating neighbors according to my relationship to them and their needs, but abandoning or ignoring is not an option within the love of neighbor framework.

Furthermore, my idea of agapic love, informed by both solidarity and subsidiarity, would contradict Dworkin's prioritization of the younger over the older. While subsidiarity justifies certain partiality and prioritization according to associative ties, it does not *prima facie* and *ceteris paribus* justify prioritizing the younger over the older simply because the younger presumably has more quality and quantity of life to live, as the Dworkinian principle of equality suggests.[64] Agapic love allows me to prioritize the younger if the younger is closer to me in relationship and has a greater need or vulnerability in comparison to an older person. However, this is different from prioritizing exclusively based on estimation of someone's quality and quantity of life to live.

Although the concept of *ordo amoris* clarifies how the principle of subsidiarity guides agents on how to operationalize solidarity in loving others well by respecting our moral priorities, Gregory argues that globalization has changed the concept of neighbor.[65] Global economic reality, he suggests, calls us to revisit the concept of distant strangers, given that our "economic life draws each of us into ever closer and more compact connection with 'near and distant neighbors.'"[66]

---

[62] Gregory, "Agape and Special Relations in a Global Economy," pp. 35–36.
[63] Gregory, *Politics and Order of Love*, p. 295.
[64] The Dworkinian principle of equality would concur with the utilitarian view on the QAYS (Quality-Adjusted Life-Year, a measurement of the length and quality of life of patients). See, e.g., Savulescu et al., "Utilitarianism and Pandemic," p. 620.
[65] Gregory, "Agape and Special Relations in a Global Economy," p. 16.
[66] Ibid., p. 23.

In this sense, Gregory, like Singer, might conclude that nation-state community membership is an arbitrary and morally irrelevant consideration in conceptualizing solidarity.[67] Love of neighbor, for Gregory, would now require equality of treatment between nationals and non-nationals when it comes to resource distribution, as per Singer, because the practical opportunities to provide immediate aid are not constrained in the way they once were.

True, practical opportunities may not be as constrained as before, but resources still may be limited. Also true, our heightened sense of interconnectedness resulting from globalization gives us much more awareness of distant others and an increased knowledge about how our local actions affect distant others to a much greater extent than before. Yet while distant strangers today are less distant than centuries ago when global communication, transportation, and economic interaction were not as easy and efficient, it still holds that each of us has different degrees of closeness to different people. We may all be much closer neighbors than before, but still not all neighbors are exactly the same. Sure, I am closer now in distance and time to the virtuous African woman: I could jump on a plane and get to her village in a matter of days or perhaps hours. But this enhanced accessibility does not negate the fact that I still have closer ties, and therefore greater responsibilities, to care for my own son first, then to Norfran, and then to my elderly Brazilian fellow citizen—if questions on needs were equal for all four people. The order of love remains the same. While modern technologies have expanded my opportunities to love all universally, they have not changed our embodied, finite nature that restricts our capacity to practically love all individuals in need in the exact same way.

3.2.2. Conceptual Clarity: Equality of Respect as a Response to Shortcomings with Equity of Care

The second shortcoming in Dworkin's account of equality relates to the terminology of equality of care and concern. This terminology causes confusion, and the confusion is made explicit when one analyses more closely the first problem (namely, abandoning and ignoring those in need). If the Dworkinian conception of equality of concern allows for some to be abandoned and ignored while others are cared for, then it cannot actually claim to require equal concern for all. There cannot be equal concern in theory if in practice some members of the community are left abandoned or ignored. The Dworkinian idea of equality presents therefore a problem of nomenclature and conceptual clarity that inevitably leads to practical confusions.[68]

---

[67] Gregory ("Agape and Special Relations in a Global Economy," p. 17) carefully argues for a Christian defense of Singer's moral argument on the universal duty to aid the poor. Charles C. Camosy (*Peter Singer and Christian ethics: Beyond Polarization*) comes to the same conclusion.

[68] See also: Waldron, *One Another's Equal*, Ch. 1.

Acknowledging that it is morally wrong and practically impossible to care for and be concerned with all members of a community equally, Finnis prefers, instead, the terminology of equality of respect (more specifically, equality of respectful consideration)[69]:

> No one can reasonably treat with equal concern everybody whose interests one could ascertain and affect; not only is it permissible for an individual or a government not to treat everyone as entitled to equal concern, it is wrong for individuals or governments to treat everyone with equal concern; the proper principle is, rather, that everyone is equally entitled to respectful consideration, a consideration that can instantly warrant treating different people very differently and with very great differences in the concern one shows for their well-being.

Finnis' conception of equality, while averting the nomenclature and conceptual clarity problem, is not totally divergent from Dworkin's conception of equality. Both believe that justice requires a kind of equality that allows treating different neighbors differently. But Finnis prefers the term equality of respectful consideration as it is does not mislead one into thinking that it is morally right and practically possible to care for and be concerned with all members of a community equally. In what follows I will discuss some of the implications of Finnis's conception of equality of respect for solidarity in global vaccine allocation, putting Finnis in dialogue with authors to explain my own revised theory of moderate cosmopolitanism, based on agape (see my definition of agape in the Concluding Remarks of Part I).

Section 4. My Proposed Agapic Theory of Moderate Vaccine Cosmopolitanism: Solidarity as Agapic Love of Neighbor

One could think, stretching Fr Zossima's claim from *The Brothers Karamazov*, that an understanding of solidarity as "love of neighbor" would require equality of care and concern.[70] But I have shown it does not. For one thing, it is impossible to care for and be concerned with everybody, everywhere, in the same way. (We are humans, not God!) For another thing, it is unreasonable to expect equal measures of care and concern for all. To counter the unfeasible presumption of equality of care and concern, Finnis proposes equality of respect. Equality of

---

[69] Finnis, "Equality and Differences," p. 22.
[70] Theologian and bioethicist Charles Camosy (view *Peter Singer and Christian Ethics*, p. 160) defends this view.

respect is premised on the idea that all human beings are equal in human dignity: since human dignity is the image of God (*imago Dei*) in each of us, we are all equally worthy of respect, being equal in *imago Dei*. This is our most fundamental or equality (where "radical," Finnis clarifies, comes from the Latin *radix*, meaning "root").[71]

The conception of equality of respect recognizes therefore our radical equality as *imago Dei*. Alternatively put, we are equals because we are all children of God, made equally in God's image and likeness. Now, while we all have equal dignity, each and every one of us also has, as the Personalist philosopher and theologian Karol Wojtyła emphasized, an "irreducible, unique, and unrepeatable" personal dignity.[72] In this sense, our *imago Dei* (or human dignity) is both universal and particular. This universality and particularity reflect, I would suggest, the way we ought to love one another: the duty to love and care for neighbors is both universal (as solidarity requires) and particular (as subsidiarity requires), because love itself is both universal and particular (see the Concluding Remarks of Part I of the book for my definition of love). The ethical commandment to love all is also realized in the deeply personal experience of loving the person in front of me. While agape's universal quality grounds equal respect for human dignity, its particular quality grounds equity of care, according to one's specific needs and relational responsibilities. So, agapic love necessitates equality of respect[73] and equity of care—meaning shared yet differentiated duties to care for those in need, according to our relationships to the most vulnerable and their specific needs.

4.1. Theoretical Grounds for Solidarity as Agapic Love of Neighbor: Friendship among Persons and Nations

Finnis presents his conception of equality by first explaining what the factual basis for equality is, and then exploring what its normative basis entails. I will further develop his ideas by juxtaposing them against other schools of thought. The factual basis gives a descriptive account of the equality between oneself and others. And this factual, descriptive basis then justifies the normative, prescriptive basis—the norms that are "needed to instantiate the good of being reasonable and the good of friendship"[74] (among persons and, I add, among nations). In short, what Finnis refers to as the normative basis of equality are the norms for loving one another, and "to love" is (as defined in the Concluding Remarks of

---

[71] Finnis, "Equality and Differences," p. 18.
[72] Wojtyła, *The Acting Person*.
[73] On respect as an approximation of agape, see: White, "Love First."
[74] Finnis, "Equality and Differences," p. 19.

Part I of this book) to choose the good of the other (e.g., your friend)—as Other (with capital O, meaning, as defined in Chapter 3, to choose the good not in a paternalistic way, but instead in a way that is attentive to the uniqueness of the Other who I am called to love as a friend).

4.1.1. Factual Basis of Equality

For Finnis, the factual basis of equality lies in the fact that all humans have equal radical capacity to love from the moment of their conception (or ensoulment).[75] This is when God imprints *imago Dei* in one's unique, unrepeatable soul. But what could this possibly mean? In what follows, I will try to unpack the idea of *imago Dei* in its relation to love. Before I do that, I shall respond to two common objections about this "factual basis of equality."

First, why does Finnis call it factual, when what he is referring to is not material, but metaphysical? This is a fair point; perhaps, indeed, it would be better to call it the ontological basis of equality. Second, are not the ideas of *imago Dei* and agapic love of neighbor traditionally Christian and therefore Western and Eurocentric? If so, these ideas cannot be universally accepted. While they are indeed traditionally Christian, it would be a mistake to jump to the conclusion that therefore they cannot also be universally appreciated. This is precisely why I will be further developing Finnis's Natural Law view by putting it in dialogue with non-Christian schools of thought that have also made contributions to the concepts of human dignity and love of neighbor.

Several philosophical schools of thought accept that we owe each other equal respectful consideration for our equal human dignity, whether the precise definition of human dignity is as *imago Dei* or not. The same can be said about love of neighbor, sometimes also called the Golden Rule,[76] an idea embraced by diverse cultures, including multiple faith traditions and atheists. While atheists will likely challenge the theological idea of agape as love of God, neighbor, and self,[77] they can and do accept the Golden Rule based on reason alone. The capacity to love, to be compassionate, and to act in solidarity with those who suffer obviously does not depend on divine revelation. Theists may accept the idea of agapic love of neighbor based on reason alone, but additionally have religious grounds on which to embrace the Golden Rule.

---

[75] Ibid.
[76] The Golden Rule is a practical principle. There are slightly different formulations of it, but generally it establishes that we should treat others as we would have them treat us. Some have claimed that this formulation is not exactly the same as the idea of agapic love of neighbor (Duxbury, "Golden Rule Reasoning, Moral Judgment, and Law," p. 1583). But here I am using the Golden Rule generally as a synonym of agapic love of neighbor, as Finnis does. (See Finnis, *Aquinas: Moral, Political, and Legal Theory*, pp. 126–28.)
[77] Outka, *Agape*.

A myriad of religious traditions upholds the idea of love of neighbor. The three Abrahamic religions (Judaism, Islam, and Christianity) endorse the view that we ought to be moral and respect the Golden Rule because God created us all in His image and likeness.[78]

Non-Abrahamic religions are also grounded on the Golden Rule. For example, in Hinduism, the idea of *namaste,* meaning "the divine/sacred within me bows to the same divine/sacred within you," seems to echo the concept of *imago Dei,* in the equality of respect for human dignity that it grounds Hinduism is based on the idea of universal love and compassion as the way to achieve the highest good: since all forms of life are a manifestation of the divine, all forms of life are part of a large universal family (*vasudaika kutumbam*). This evokes the Christian idea of solidarity as love between brothers and sisters, as sons and daughters of the Heavenly Father, who are equal members of the same human family.

Likewise, universal love and compassion is at the core of Buddhism. As the Dalai Lama puts it: "the liberation of mind by love is practiced with universal pervasion by extending it to all beings, then all breathing things, all creatures, all persons, and all those with a personality."[79] There is an interesting common ground between the Christian understanding of agapic love of neighbor and the Buddhist understanding of compassion. A compassionate action, as an instance of neighborly love, does good to others, by alleviating their suffering, and it also does good to the agent who chooses to act with compassion, for compassion to others leads to transcendence and enlightenment.

Although not strictly speaking religions but philosophies, Confucianism and Taoism are also grounded on the virtue of compassion, and focus on developing characters of loving kindness in doing good to others, as in the Christian concept of agapic love of neighbor. Confucian ethics, for example, emphasizes the responsibilities we have to care for one another: "the family is the unit of the practice of solidarity," where "the responsibility for care in a family is differentiated according to the closeness of family members, using a concentric circle as a metaphor."[80] This is an interesting parallel with my conception of subsidiarity based on the Augustinian *ordo amoris* discussed above.

Taoism is equally centered on the cultivation of virtues, especially the three treasures of compassion, frugality, and humility. To have a compassionate heart is to turn toward all creatures, living in harmony and unity with the Tao. This

---

[78] Although the Qur'an does not explicitly instruct "love your neighbor as yourself," it expresses this command in different terms: for example, "Show kindness and do good to parents, relatives, and orphans—to the near neighbor and the distant neighbor who is a stranger—to the companion by your side and the traveler that you meet" (Qur'an 4:36).
[79] Dalai Lama XIV and Chodron, *Buddhism: One Teacher, Many Traditions*.
[80] Yeh, "Confucian Welfarism," p. 4.

entails, for example, regarding your neighbor's gain as your own gain, and your neighbor's loss as your own loss[81] (reminiscent of Romans 12:15: rejoice with those who rejoice, weep with those who weep).

Last but not least is the conception of human dignity or moral personhood in African religions and philosophical traditions. There are many examples across the African continent: (a) the Kenyan Mbiti's understanding that "I am, because we are; and since we are, therefore I am";[82] (b) Nigerian thinker Menkiti's[83] conception of personhood in community; (c) the idea of Sawugona, an indigenous form of greeting in South African Zulu, meaning "the God in me sees the God in you";[84] (d) the Southern African Ubuntu philosophical value system, grounded on the maxim *umuntu ngumuntu ngabantu*—meaning— "to be a human being is to affirm one's humanity by recognizing the humanity of others and, on that basis, establish humane relations with them,"[85] which has been further developed by thinkers such as Ramose,[86] Ramphele,[87] Sindane,[88] and Khoza[89]; and (e) the Ghanaian tradition that highlights how persons are defined as *nurbiik*—meaning—"a son or daughter of a person and therefore one who matters deeply to someone,"[90] most recently developed by philosophers Wiredu,[91] Gyekye,[92] and Atuire.[93] The common ground among all these richly diverse schools of African thought is the view that relationality is essential to the notion of dignity and the human person cannot be conceived in isolation.[94] This idea that our personal identity is utterly dependent on our relationships with other persons echoes clearly the idea of *imago Dei,* in God's agapic relational love for us, since our primary identity, in the Christian tradition, is as sons and daughters of God (and therefore a person who matters deeply to someone).

This very brief overview of diverse faith and philosophical traditions is meant to show why I do not think that the concept and rationale behind the ideas of *imago Dei* and agapic love are exclusively Christian. Very diverse cultures share a

---

[81] Suzuki and Carus (trans.), *T'ai-Shang Kan-Ying P'ien* ("Treatise of the Exalted One on Response and Retribution").
[82] Mbiti, *African Religions and Philosophy*. pp. 108–9.
[83] Menkiti, "Person and Community in African Traditional Thought," pp. 171–81.
[84] Caldwell and Atwijuka, "'I See You!'—The Zulu Insight to Caring Leadership," Art. 13; Kaunda, "Sawubonda: A Theo-Ethic for Everyday Decolonial Gestures," pp. 41–59.
[85] Juma, "Catholic Social Justice Principles," p. 107
[86] Ramose, "The Philosophy of Ubuntu and Ubuntu as a Philosophy," pp. 230–38.
[87] Ramphele,"Citizenship Challenges for South Africa's Young democracy," pp. 1–17.
[88] Sindane, *Ubuntu and Nation Building*.
[89] Khoza, *Let Africa Lead*.
[90] Atuire and Hassoun, "Rethinking Solidarity Towards Equity in Global Health," p. 52.
[91] Wiredu. "The Moral Foundations of an African Culture," p. 155.
[92] Gyekye. *Tradition and Modernity*.
[93] Atuire, Kong, and Dunn, "Articulating the Sources for an African Normative Framework of Healthcare," pp. 216–27.
[94] Atuire and Hassoun, "Rethinking Solidarity Towards Equity in Global Health." See also: Kizito and Juma, "Catholic Social Justice Principles," p. 107.

basic understanding of human dignity and love of neighbor, which should at least hint that these concepts are more universally shared and appreciated than not.

In what follows I will present my reading of *imago Dei* based on the relationality that the idea of agapic love of neighbor introduces paving the way for better grasping what Finnis means by the factual (or ontological) basis of equality. I interpret human dignity in relation to agapic love, against this background of the multiple faith and philosophical traditions throughout the world that also espouse these values.

4.1.2. Imago Dei and Agapic Love of Neighbor

In the Christian tradition, God is love.[95] If so, then one can read human dignity or *imago Dei* literally as the image of love in us. For Christians, one has the radical capacity to love like God, and should strive to do so. Yet one can only love like God because God Himself has first chosen to love us. Our radical human capacity to love, then, totally depends on God, who has given us the example of how to love well. In the Christian tradition, the fullest example of love is Christ's death on the cross, where God lays down His own life for all of humankind.[96] Every human being has a thoroughly particular, non-replicable individual call (or vocation) to self-sacrificially love all, universally, while also loving certain people in special ways. Again, love is both universal and particular; likewise the duty to love and care for neighbors.

For me, the factual (ontological) basis of equality resides in the requirement to equally respect the dignity of all human beings, since each and every one of us has a unique, non-replicable sign of the cross imprinted in our souls. This sign of the cross is the universal and particular call, received in the moment of our conception, to vulnerably love the Other in front of us, as God vulnerably loved them, to the point of dying for them. I should love this person in front of me with reverence, knowing that, as the daughter of God and as the sister of Christ, who died for them on the cross, she is a person who matters deeply to them both (this echoes the Ghanaian tradition of seeing each person as *nurbiik*).[97]

By saying that the sign of the cross is imprinted in each human soul, I mean that we should revere and respectfully consider the humanity of each particular person in front of us, for whom God has particularly chosen to make Himself vulnerable to the point of death. This is how I interpret Finnis' idea of equality of respect or equal respectful consideration for the dignity of each human being: we all have a duty to respect and revere the universal image of vulnerable love (the cross) imprinted in a particular, personal, unique way in each of us.

---

[95]
[96] 1 John 3:16.
[97] Atuire and Hassoun, "Rethinking Solidarity Towards Equity in Global Health," p. 52.

The persistent objector would insist, though: to what extent does this interpretation of equal human dignity that you provide rest on a theological (and more specifically Christian) premise? I believe that those who do not acknowledge the validity of the theological concept of agape as love of God, neighbor, and self[98] can still accept the reasonableness of the concept of equality of respect for human dignity, and even the reasonableness of the concept of agapic love, as I define it in the Concluding Remarks of Part I, where love here need only mean agapic (universal, unconditional) love of neighbor. Human dignity, as I have defined it, is a relational concept, like the concept of love itself. It is no mere individualistic value, but a relational, communal experience of our mutual vulnerability and interdependence. Our shared experience of vulnerable love confirms our dignity as members of the human family.

I should also add in response to my persistent objector that skepticism about the factual (or ontological) basis of equality need not undermine the epistemic independence of the normative, prescriptive basis of equality, which can be grounded on the practical reasonableness of agapic love of neighbor alone.[99] I turn to this point now.

4.1.3. Normative Basis of Equality

What Finnis calls the normative basis of equality is the set of practical norms required by the general duty to love others by choosing their good. It answers the question: how, in practice, do we make choices to promote friendship, not only among persons, but also, I would add, among nations?

(i) The Call for Communion: Solidarity as Friendship among Persons

For Finnis, respectful consideration for all is key.[100] In conceptualizing equality as equal respectful consideration, Finnis means that we all should regard others with equal respect. This is what agapic love of primarily requires. Equality of respect or equal respectful consideration requires us to regard others with respect, reverence, I would add, love—seeing all persons unique and unrepeatable dignity, and their individual virtues and flaws as well. That is to say, equality of respect requires equal respectful consideration, compounded with equal loving *regard* for all.[101] In adding the idea of loving regard I am distilling what it means, in practice, to meet others with equal respectful consideration, and thus further developing Finnis's theory of equality.

---

[98] Outka, *Agape*.
[99] I thank Mark Retter for making this point clearer.
[100] Finnis, "Equality and Differences," pp. 19–20.
[101] For a different interpretation of what *agapic* love of neighbor requiring "equal regard" means, see: Outka, *Agape*, p. 309.

Loving regard here is not a mere sentiment (e.g., pity or sympathy, defined in Chapter 2). Irish novelist and philosopher Iris Murdoch talks about loving regard or loving attention as "a just and loving gaze directed upon an individual reality."[102] This, she believes, "is the characteristic and proper mark of the active moral agent."[103] A loving regard happens when one's eyes "the windows of one's soul"[104] encounter another soul. In this encounter, both souls are fully present with one another. And it is in this communion of souls that a community of friendship is established. Loving regard is a choice to give oneself generously (body, mind, and soul), through one's full presence, for the other. I discussed this idea of love as presence, where I give myself (and my presence) as a gift to the other, in Chapters 1–3: loving regard involves a choice to make oneself a present to the other (pun intended!).[105] And it is in this choice to share the gift-of-self with each other that a communion, leading to a community of mutual care and belonging, is formed. This is friendship: in this encounter and communion of souls, one surrenders one's "I" to enable a transition to "we."[106]

So, to talk about equality of human dignity as the normative basis of the duty to love one another is to talk about equal respectful consideration and loving regard for all neighbors. This requires considering and regarding every neighbor (nationals and non-nationals) as a gift to be received, accepted, and revered in the process of forming a we. While each of these individual presents can only be encountered personally, the duty to consider and regard neighbors as gifts extends to all neighbors, universally. This is friendship among persons. This is how solidarity is lived and communion is formed among individual souls. But solidarity and communion can also be established among institutions. I turn now to the friendship that nations should cultivate among themselves to realize their call to love their neighbors.

(ii) The Call for Communion: Solidarity as Friendship among Nations
Solidarity has the purpose of respecting, protecting, and fulfilling the human dignity of every human being, in the reality of our vulnerabilities and mutual dependency.[107] It is the recognition of our shared human dignity, vulnerability, and dependence that calls for persons—including the communities and institutions they form—to commit to mutual care and flourishing. This means that solidarity requires, as a matter of justice and most fundamentally of love, that both individuals and institutions be committed to promote the good of each

---

[102] Murdoch, *The Sovereignty of Good*, p. 34.
[103] Ibid.
[104] Finnis, "Equality and Differences," p. 19.
[105] Biehl and Velasco (eds.), *Pedro Morande*, p. 30.
[106] Wojtyła, *Love and Responsibility*, pp. 95–96.
[107] de Campos, "Guiding Principles of Global Health Governance in Times of Pandemics," p. 212.

and every person (i.e., the common good). More specifically, solidarity entails, in the reality of global health threats, a shared commitment that unites all global health stakeholders and institutions in upholding the good of each person in every community (i.e., the global common good).[108]

Martin Luther King Jr understood solidarity as love of neighbor in terms of a creative force for change in pursuit of unity in community.[109] The goal of solidarity is to pursue a shared commitment to unity among equals—from I to we—both within and among communities. This communion within and among nations can be ensured, among other things, by human rights responsibilities.

Typically, there are three types of human rights responsibilities: the duties to respect, protect, and fulfill.[110] The equality of human dignity unites all human beings by serving as the very foundation of human rights[111]—it is the fundamental basis of one's duties to respect, protect, and fulfil the good of each and the good of everyone (the common good). To put it another way, the capacity to love is the factual (ontological) foundation of human rights.[112] This capacity to love is, I contend, the foundation of human rights in general and, in particular, of the international human rights law principle of solidarity.[113] This is solidarity or friendship among nations.

Friendship among nations predicated on the idea of equality of human dignity is ordered, as I discussed above, by the principle of subsidiarity, which allows different people to be loved and cared for in different ways, according to their needs and relationships. To talk about equality of dignity is, in sum, to talk about equal respectful consideration and loving regard. This entails neither equality of treatment and resources, nor equality of care and concern. Instead, equal respectful consideration and loving regard entail equity of care: shared yet differentiated duties to care for those in need, according to the degree of vulnerability and relationship to the vulnerable, as the principle of subsidiarity establishes. As Finnis puts it, our duties are "summed up in the normative justice

---

[108] Finnis defines the common good as "a set of conditions which enables the members of a community to attain for themselves reasonable objectives, or to realize reasonably for themselves the value(s) for the sake of which they have reason to collaborate with each other (positively and/or negatively) in a community." Finnis, *Natural Law, Natural Rights*, p. 155. I have elsewhere defined the global common good as "a set of conditions that enables all members of the global community or whole human family to attain for themselves reasonable objectives or to realize reasonably for themselves the value(s) for the sake of which they have reason to collaborate with each other (positively and/or negatively) in a global community." See de Campos, *The Global Health Crisis*, pp. 147–48.
[109] King, "An Experiment in Love," para.16.
[110] Shue, *Basic Rights: Subsistence, Affluence, and US Foreign Policy*.
[111] Rizki, *Report of the Independent Expert on Human Rights and International Solidarity*, para. 58.
[112] On the relation between love and Human Rights, in the context of the UK Human Rights Act of 1998, see Douglas, "Love and Human Rights," pp. 273–97
[113] Human Rights Council, *Promotion and Protection of All Human Rights, Civil, Political, Economic, Social, and Cultural Rights, Including the Right to Development*, para. 19.

principles: 'Like cases are to be treated alike'. And relevantly different people are to be treated differently."[114]

4.2. Practical Implications of Solidarity as Agapic Love of Neighbor: Application to the COVID-19 Pandemic

What does this all mean in the complex reality of a public health emergency of international concern, like the 2020 COVID-19 pandemic? My revised theory of moderate vaccine cosmopolitanism presents an agapic interpretation of solidarity, tempered by subsidiarity. It would never require nations to prioritize care for outsiders at the cost of neglecting the most vulnerable under their own jurisdiction. This would be contrary to the principle of subsidiarity. However, my account would impose extra-territorial obligations to care for vulnerable outsiders, when the state has the capacity to do so without abandoning its vulnerable nationals. Solidarity would so require. But how to discharge both jurisdictional and cosmopolitan duties of beneficent care, given the reality of the scarce initial supply of coronavirus vaccines and impossibility of meeting global demand?

Specifying how scarce coronavirus vaccines ought to be distributed within and among nations would require careful integration of a principled account and updated empirical epidemiological knowledge of COVID-19 (scientific data continued to change and develop for several years). Here, therefore, I only suggest a few, necessary differentiations and principles that would help domestic and international policymakers when considering how to discharge human rights obligations of international cooperation and assistance in the 2020 COVID-19 context. These differentiations and principles would equally apply to other instances of allocating scarce healthcare resources.

My agapic theory of moderate vaccine cosmopolitanism would start by trying to define a spectrum of vulnerability,[115] both domestically and across global populations. This is a practical way to show equal respectful consideration and equal loving regard. It would identify where domestic and global immunization priorities should lie (in a context of vaccine scarcity, which remained the case years into the COVID-19 pandemic). The most vulnerable populations to which lexical priority should *prima facie* be given would include, for example, the elderly in nursing homes, those with co-morbidities and a compromised immune system, the homeless or inadequately housed, the incarcerated, essential workers—including, here, frontline healthcare and supply chain workers. Call

---

[114] Finnis, "Equality and Differences," p. 20.
[115] Sam, "Redefining Vulnerability in the Era of COVID-19," p. 1089; Ahmad, Chung, Eckenwiller et al., "What Does It Mean to be Made Vulnerable in the Era of COVID-19?" p. 1482.

them Priority Group #1, composed fundamentally of all those who were hit the hardest during the pandemic, in every country.

All members of Priority Group #1, in all nations, should be offered, *prima facie* and *ceteris paribus* the chance to get vaccinated before the members of Priority Group #2, first domestically and then internationally. Priority Group #2 could include, for example, other health professionals not included in the first group (perhaps because their services could be provided through telehealth, for example), school teachers, and other less vulnerable populations. Once all members of Priority Group #2 in all nations are vaccinated, the immunization of members of Priority Group #3 would follow, first domestically and then internationally, and so on for subsequent groups, lowest in vulnerability and thus least in priority. In sum, agapic solidarity tempered by subsidiarity would *prima facie* and *ceteris paribus* justify allocating vaccines first to all #1 priority people in my country, then to all #1 priority people in the world; then to all #2 in my country, then to all #2 in the world, before offering vaccines to #3 in my country, and so on.[116] My proposed Agapic Theory of Moderate Vaccine Cosmopolitanism is not about ignoring certain people domestically or abandoning others internationally, but instead it is about justifying why not all people are to be prioritized in the same way when vulnerabilities and relational responsibilities are different. Some groups, lowest in vulnerability and thus least in priority, are asked to wait a bit longer, and this reasonable degree of self-sacrifice is justifiable. Countries are also called to love in a reasonable self-sacrificial way by sharing more of the vaccines they possess with other countries in need, before they offer them to their groups of people who are lowest in vulnerability and thus least in priority.

As the principle of subsidiarity would call for, the exact composition of each priority level should be defined by each government, according to the country's changing epidemiological, cultural, and economic needs.[117] To be clear, given that each country determines the makeup of each group, my proposal really is about giving equal moments of prioritization, not necessarily prioritizing specific groups equally across the globe. For example, in some places younger people in an urban setting might be vaccinated in a higher priority group than young people in a rural setting.[118] All nations have the same number of priority groups and everyone in their group #1 (domestically defined) is treated first and before anyone in their group #2 (also nationally determined). Each government should decide which specific populations are to compose their Priority Group #1 so that the country is able to maintain a noncrisis level of mortality domestically.[119] Likewise, each government should decide which neighbor countries

---

[116] I am grateful to Fr Iain Matthew for making this point clearer.
[117] Sam, "Redefining Vulnerability in the Era of COVID-19," p. 1089.
[118] I am grateful to Lauren Woodside Alegre for making this point clearer.
[119] Emanuel et al., "On the Ethics of Vaccine Nationalism," pp. 543–62.

should receive the remainder of vaccines, according to needs and relationship. The rationale for differentiating groups according to a spectrum of vulnerability (from the most vulnerable in group #1 to the least vulnerable in groups #3 and beyond) is to help coordinate both jurisdictional and cosmopolitan duties of beneficent care, in an effective and ethical manner. No doubt this is logistically much more difficult than it might sound. Nevertheless, the fact that something is practically difficult does not mean it is not ethically justifiable and necessary.

On 2 December 2020, COVID-19 vaccines started to be distributed in the UK, followed shortly after by other developed countries. It was claimed in the beginning of 2021 that high-income countries—such as the UK, the US, and Canada—had the economic capacity to vaccinate not only their Priority Groups #1 and #2 but also #3 and beyond. They were offering COVID-19 vaccines to the least vulnerable (such as fit, wealthy white-collar workers, and others who could easily work remotely from their homes), while some neighboring countries continued to struggle to immunize their priority group #1. Some accused these countries of vaccine nationalism; they hoarded not only vaccines but also personal protective equipment, such as masks and gloves.

My agapic account applied to global vaccine allocation would indeed challenge these countries' policies, given their lack of coordination with neighboring countries which long continued to have insufficient means to offer vaccination to their Priority Group #1. If solidarity in the context of pandemics justifies duties of mutual care among nations, based on their shared vulnerability to epidemics; and if solidarity justifies extra-territorial obligations to care for and assist outsiders, when the state has the capacity to help, and even when it is costly or inconvenient to do so, then solidarity would require these high-income countries, having vaccinated all their Priority Group #1, to self-sacrificially allocate any surplus to other countries for their Priority Groups #1, before offering vaccines to their own Priority Group #2, enabling all the most vulnerable global populations to be vaccinated as soon as possible.

Solidarity would also require the least vulnerable in countries like the UK, the US, and Canada to continue to make reasonable sacrifices (e.g., by hygiene measures, wearing masks, and respecting lockdown measures when required) for the sake of the global common good, until all the most vulnerable populations worldwide had been given the chance to get the vaccine. Love does require some degree of self-sacrifice for the good of others, especially those in more urgent need (for a discussion of what a reasonable degree of self-sacrifice entails, see Chapter 2).

One may ask: why is it illegitimate to prefer all nationals before Priority Group #1 non-nationals? Why not define the threshold as Priority Group #2 or even #3? Retaining COVID-19 vaccine doses for residents is *prima facie* morally justifiable. However, in the context of scarce vaccines and a global health crisis that justify emergency measures globally, this is morally permissible only insofar as doses are needed to maintain a noncrisis level of mortality domestically.[120] To go beyond Priority Group #1 in the knowledge that other nations are suffering is to ignore or abandon a neighbor in need; the principle of solidarity as I have laid it out cannot justify this. My proposal here is also consistent with the principle of subsidiarity, since to care for the most vulnerable outsiders is not to neglect the national population, whose most vulnerable members are cared for first.

Subsidiarity should always be in tandem with solidarity, requiring a multilateral, global co-responsibility of care in the face of common threats. Subsidiarity would not validate claims of self-sufficiency, extreme protectionism, or vaccine nationalism that entail the abandonment of the most vulnerable in other countries. Now, this bottom-up approach requires a coordinated interaction between higher- and lower-level communities, both internationally and locally (see Chapter 5), and necessitates effective communication among all stakeholders (see Chapter 6). This is a role for an international organization like the WHO, in coordination and communication with local authorities.

A key element of this co-responsibility of care is truthful, evidence-based, consistent, and timely communication with stakeholders and the general public (see Chapter 6 for further discussion of the communicative duties of global and public health authorities).[121] Without this kind of communication, there can be no trust in relationships of care. Global and public health authorities should have communicated their COVID-19 vaccine allocation plans truthfully, explaining: the spectrum of vulnerabilities; the different priority groups, and how/why their composition will differ from one country to another; a realistic timeline for each group to receive the vaccine; and justifications for changing plans. Undoubtedly, the operational frameworks to ensure this kind of communication among institutions at different levels pose a logistical challenge, on top of existing difficulties, such as lack of capacity and poor infrastructure, especially in low-income countries. This is a real difficulty, but not an argument against doing the right thing.

A government respects its people when it provides truthful, timely, and sufficient information about vaccination plans (and justifies any changes), and also when it educates them about the vital importance of multilateral collaboration with other nations for effective pandemic suppression worldwide. Truthful, evidence-based, consistent, and timely communication has surely been lacking in the context of public health emergencies of international concern. This has resulted in the erosion of public trust in authorities in general and global and

---

[120] Ibid.
[121] de Campos-Rudinsky and Undurraga, "Public Health Decisions in the COVID-19 Pandemic Require More Than 'Follow the Science,'" p. 296.

public health experts in particular, leading to further polarization, disunion, and a backlash against cooperation at all levels of communities, as I discuss in Chapter 6. But the language of love, and its principles of solidarity, subsidiarity, and stewardship, may help restore union in community.

One way love can move things forward is by establishing common ground between opposing views, such as vaccine nationalism and radical vaccine cosmopolitanism. My agapic theory of moderate vaccine cosmopolitanism identifies this common ground in justifying equity of care as shared yet differentiated duties to care for those in need, according to their needs and our relationships to the most vulnerable. Solidarity as agapic love of neighbor justifies this kind of global co-responsibility of care among persons and nations—a kind that allows for unequal treatment, unequal distribution of resources, and unequal care, while maintaining equal respectful consideration and loving regard for all.

Conclusion

Chapter 4 wrestled with the question of what agape requires of developed nations in relation to their less developed neighbors. More precisely, what agapic love as a shared journey of presence require (or does not require) of certain nations when their neighbors experience medical suffering. This chapter proposed for a revised theory of moderate cosmopolitanism, grounded in an agapic interpretation of the principle of solidarity, tempered by subsidiarity. Agapic solidarity does call for love of neighbor, and therefore global responsibilities of mutual care among nations (also known as the duty of international cooperation). However, agapic love necessitates, I argued, neither equality of treatment and resources, nor equality of care and concern. Instead, it requires equity of care: shared yet differentiated duties to care for those in need, according to their needs and our relationships to the most vulnerable. So, love allows—and in some cases even requires—some partiality in taking care first of those in one's own community, without abandoning outsiders to their own luck. This agapic understanding of solidarity is predicated on the idea of equality of dignity—meaning, equal respectful consideration and loving regard among persons and nations (an idea introduced in Chapter 2 and further developed here in Chapter 4). The concept of human dignity has been obscured and the idea of *imago Dei* has been forgotten. But, as Victor Hugo famously puts it in the conclusion of *Les Misérables,* "to love another person is to see the face of God." The COVID-19 pandemic, which if only the most recent of a myriad of public health emergencies of international concern that happened and will continue to happen in the future, has given us yet another opportunity to deepen our understanding of the image of God—of love—in each of us. The problem of global allocation of scarce, patent-protected, costly yet essential healthcare resources that are vital to contain catastrophes like public health emergencies of international concern is a recurrent one. Every pandemic reminds us that we have a duty to love and to act in solidarity with those who suffer the effects of catastrophes. And this responsibility to love and care for one another is grounded in the reality that we are all made in the image and likeness of love—in all the vulnerability and interdependence that such love represents.

5
On Subsidiarity and Community

> Go now; with your persuasive word, with all
> that is required to see that he escapes,
> bring help to him, that I may be consoled.
>
> For I am Beatrice who send you on;
> I come from where I most long to return;
> Love prompted me, that Love which makes me speak.
> Beatrice to Virgil in Dante's *Inferno*, Canto 2 lines 67–72

Introduction

Although Beatrice only appears briefly and speaks a few words in *Inferno* and then again in *Paradiso*, where she directly guides Dante through the spheres of heaven, Beatrice is a central character in Dante's *Divine Comedy*. Beatrice symbolizes the love of God in union with the human soul. She therefore embodies agape. A woman of vision and action, Beatrice has a pivotal leadership role. Love moves her to descend all the way from Heaven into the dark woods of Limbo to call upon the Roman poet Virgil for his aid. Beatrice asks Virgil to guide and walk with Dante, the pilgrim, throughout his journey to Heaven, his final destination, where she could then personally take on the task of accompanying Dante herself. Beatrice therefore delegates her guiding role to Virgil: she humbly acknowledges her own limitations and the fact that Virgil was more apt than her at that point to assist the pilgrim to reach his destination (not only Virgil, as a poet, had greater ability with words to persuade his fellow poet, Dante, but I would also add that Virgil was much closer geographically to Dante).[1]

This delegation of roles, however, may invite a skeptic to question the authenticity of Beatrice's love as well as her leadership abilities. Sure, love moves her to descend all the way to Limbo, but would love not compel her to do more than

---

[1] Some content of this chapter is based on three previously published papers: de Campos-Rudinsky and Canales, "Global Health Governance and The Principle of Subsidiarity"; de Campos, "A European Take on Global Public Health"; de Campos-Rudinsky et al., "Decolonising Global Health."

The Rule of Love. Thana C. de Campos-Rudinsky, Oxford University Press. © Oxford University Press 2026.
DOI: 10.1093/9780197762400.003.0007

simply delegate her guiding role to Virgil? Was this not a form of negligent care or even abandonment? Was Beatrice not using Virgil's greater persuasive capacities and his geographical closeness to Dante as mere excuses for not accompanying Dante all the way in his arduous journey from Limbo to Hell to Purgatory to Heaven? Would love not require Beatrice to do more for her loved one?

As discussed in Chapter 3, love does not necessarily entail doing more for or with the other. Often, love requires establishing boundaries that allows for proper self-care (for self-constitution), as defined in Chapter 2, and sustained generosity. I provided an illustration of proper self-care also in Chapter 2 by offering my own reading of the Parable of the Good Samaritan: he leaves (not abandons) the ill man in the inn, under the care of the innkeeper, so he can attend to his own business. In the present chapter where I introduce subsidiarity as a practical principle of agapic love, I want to make the point that good leadership, grounded in love, requires vision and action, as embodied by Beatrice, and the Good Samaritan. It requires the leader to show up and be present to those under one's leadership and care, so they can jointly pursue the shared vision, but it also requires, as Beatrice did: (i) recognizing, in humility, our limitations as leaders; and (ii) delegating, in prudence, certain roles of care to others who can perform them well or better. The principle of subsidiarity encompasses all of these attributes of good leadership grounded in love.

To demonstrate how these lessons of good leadership, grounded in agape, apply to GHG, I will use the WHO, the global health leader par excellence, and its institutional reform proposals as a case study. This chapter will show how my conception of leadership grounded in love would challenge the conventional wisdom of most global health experts in how they want to reform the WHO.

Debates on how to reform GHG, in general, and the WHO, in particular, are perennial.[2] They flare up with every new declaration of a public health emergency of international concern.[3] Global health scholars have typically argued that the WHO's mandate should be reformed by way of expansion and centralization. In other words, they argue that in order to be a better global health leader, the WHO should expand its financial resources and further centralize authority and decision-making power, in order to be able to do more, to have more operational capacities, and thereby to offer better care for those in need under its leadership. Call this the centralization approach to GHG reform, grounded in the conventional wisdom of what leadership should traditionally look like. Defenders of the centralization approach think the WHO would be more effective with more resources. This of course does not address the issue of scarcity of resources that was discussed in Chapter 4 and was a major reason why

---

[2] Villarreal, "The Law of the WHO and the COVID-19 Pandemic Reformism," pp. 11–40; Lee, Pang (Pangestu), "WHO: Retirement or Reinvention."
[3] See fn. 5.

solidarity must be complemented with subsidiarity. As contended in Chapter 4, however, even if the finitude of resources were not a problem, resources are still not sufficient to provide good, loving care: incommensurable values like presence and accompaniment are paramount. So, in opposition to the centralization approach, I present an alternative: the robust decentralization approach to GHG reform, predicated on the principle of subsidiarity.

Chapter 5 wrestles with the questions of what agape requires of certain global health stakeholders with leadership position when it comes to decision-making that affects communities experiencing medical suffering. More specifically, what does agapic love as a shared journey of presence require (or does not require) of certain global health authorities like the WHO? In confronting these questions, Chapter 5 introduces the principle of subsidiarity. Subsidiarity, as a principle of love as well as justice, solves the tension between caring too little (by being indifferent to and abandoning the loved one in need of care and aid) and caring too much (by paternalistically overstepping the agency of the loved one). Agapic love calls for the Aristotelian golden mean between these two extremes, to which the principle of subsidiarity points by necessitating both non-abandonment and respect for the agency of those in need of aid.

I argue that agapic love does not require the centralization of power and control coupled with the expansion of resources to enable good care. Instead, I argue that love requires a decentralization that leads to the decolonization of global health institutions: love requires (as discussed in Chapter 3) shared authority in decision-making processes with the active participation and meaningful inclusion (as defined in Chapter 2) of the recipients of care—namely, patients and local communities that benefit from international aid. The voice of the patient is vital in discerning the best medical option for that particular person. Likewise, the voice of local communities is crucial in discerning the best way to allocate healthcare resources and set the priorities that meet the specific needs of that particular local community. So, love allows—and in some cases even requires—a reasonable degree of delegation of the authority to care for those in need, which permits the integral human development[4] of those who are cared for.

To argue for the robust decentralization approach to GHG reform, this chapter begins by providing some background information on what GHG is and what its main problems that call for the institutional reform of the WHO are (Section 1). Then, the chapter will critically examine the solution that the centralization approach proposes and uncover its shortcomings (Section 2). In showing how the centralization approach fails, I then present the robust decentralization

---

[4] In recognizing that human flourishing is not solely about economic growth or material possessions, integral human development proposes a holistic approach that aims to promote the well-being of every person and the whole person, encompassing all aspects of life, including social, economic, political, cultural, personal, and spiritual dimensions. See, e.g., Sedmak, *Enacting Integral Human Development*. See also: Debeulin and Sedmak (eds), *Integral Human Development*.

approach, by first introducing the theoretical concept of subsidiarity and then applying it to the context of GHG (Section 3).

The upshot of my robust decentralization approach is a different understanding of good leadership in GHG, one which fosters global solidarity (discussed in Chapter 4) through interdependence and mutual self-giving (two central attributes of agapic love as describes in the three types of agapic love introduced in Part 1), by counteracting the negative consequences of centralized authority, power, control, and resources, notably paternalism and the subtraction of agency from global health aid recipients. The take away message of my proposed approach is that to be a better (meaning more loving) leader, the WHO should do much less and have a much narrower mandate. The humble (and wise) recognition of its true strengths and limitations should lead the WHO to delegate most of its many functions and focus exclusively on coordination efforts among other global health stakeholders, because the WHO is uniquely placed and equipped to do this well. In providing a principled approach to GHG reform, based on the principle of subsidiarity, this chapter not only offers the global affairs literature a new way of theorizing the long-standing debate on the WHO reform, but it also offers a new lens for philosophically justifying the claim for the need to decolonize GHG. These are the leadership lessons of subsidiarity, which I identify as the second practical principle of agapic love.

Section 1. Background Information: GHG, WHO, and Core Problems

GHG is the existing structure that seeks to regulate a wide range of global health stakeholders, through laws and policies. While independent, these stakeholders are generally willing to cooperate when coordination is required to solve global health challenges.[5] These stakeholders include a variety of global health institutions (comprising state and non-state actors alike), with different capacities, budgets, mandates, and agendas.[6] While it is agreed that global cooperation is good and that coordination is required to solve global health problems effectively, in actuality the laws and policies that each of these institutions produce are typically not coordinated. They address isolated aspects of global health in a self-interested and fragmented way.[7] As a result, these laws and policies do not usually lead to the best outcomes.[8]

---

[5] See: Harman, *Global Health Governance*.

[6] For a thorough description of all global health stakeholders, see: Youde, *Global Health Governance in International Society*, pp. 75–94; Clinton and Sridhar, *Governing Global Health: Who Runs the Worlds and Why*, pp. 48–82.

[7] Ruger, "Global Health Governance," p. 653.

[8] Gostin and Mok, "Innovative Solutions to Closing the Health Gap," pp. 451, 453.

Although independence, self-interest, and fragmentation constitute the chief features of today's GHG, if one is asked which global health institution is the main stakeholder or global health leader, the answer that immediately comes to mind is the WHO. Presumably this is because the WHO is expected to exercise the coordinating authority for global health necessary to effectively and efficiently address global health threats, like pandemics and major epidemics, such as plagues, cholera, flu, severe acute respiratory syndrome (SARS), HIV/AIDs, Ebola, Zika, and COVID-19.

The WHO was founded in the aftermath of World War II as an international organization and specialized agency of the UN responsible for global public health. The 1948 WHO Constitution establishes the agency's governance structure. Article 45 of the WHO Constitution establishes that regional organizations are an integral part of the WHO. Since its inception, the WHO governance structure includes six semi-autonomous regional offices (i.e., Africa, the Americas with the Pan American Health Organization (PAHO), Southeast Asia, Europe, Eastern Mediterranean, and Western Pacific) and 150 field offices worldwide.[9] That is to say, since its inception, the WHO's structure has followed a decentralized governance model. Arguably, the WHO's six regional and 150 field offices have been created for the purpose of directly serving local communities affected by global health threats, with the idea that such geographical closeness would allow for the inclusion of these local communities in the WHO's decision-making processes. This reading of the WHO Constitution regarding WHO's regional and field offices is consistent with the general purpose of the organization.

The preamble to the WHO Constitution establishes the WHO for "the purpose of cooperation to promote and protect the health of all peoples."[10] Its article 1 further specifies the purpose of the WHO as a coordinating authority for global health as follows: "the objective of the WHO shall be the attainment by all peoples of the highest possible levels of health," where health is "a state of complete physical, mental and social well-being and not merely the absence of disease or infirmity." While it is reasonable to understand the WHO's purpose as the coordinating authority for GHG, the WHO's unworkable definition of health makes one question how feasible the WHO's ambitious objective is.[11] In addition to WHO's overly ambitious objective, article 2 subsequently lists a lengthy list of twenty-two functions that the WHO ought to perform as the coordinating authority for global health.

Since its inception, the WHO has been expected to serve as the coordinating authority for global health; however, its ambitious objectives and numerous

---

[9] WHO Constitution 1948, arts. 45, 46.
[10] Ibid., preamble.
[11] de Campos, *The Global Health Crisis—Ethical Responsibilities*, Ch. 1.

functions, as defined in its constitution, have contributed to expansion of their work as a global health leader. Expectations around its objectives and functions have particularly expanded since the 1990s, when global health initiatives (such as Global Alliance on Vaccines and Immunization; the Global Fund to Fight HIV/AIDS, Tuberculosis, and Malaria; the Bill and Melinda Gates Foundation, etc.) proliferated. In this new scenario, the WHO has to compete with all of these new global health institutions for limited funding.[12] Also, since donors now get to stipulate how the capital they invest in the WHO and other global health institutions ought to be spent, the WHO has lost the autonomy to define its own institutional priorities.[13] Donors' interests are numerous, ranging from pandemic preparedness and response to non-communicable diseases, such as obesity and mental health, to reproductive rights, to regulation of tobacco use, to poverty-related illnesses and social justice, to traffic accidents, to air pollution and environmental issues, and so on. As WHO's financial sustainability increasingly depends on the voluntary contributions from other powerful global health institutions and donors, the WHO's autonomy to define how healthcare resources are allocated and how priorities are set has significantly diminished.[14]

In short, the current GHG scenario is one where the WHO and a plethora of global health institutions act according to the individual goals of their respective donors, acting independent global health stakeholders, in an uncoordinated manner. The result is a donor-centered GHG that excludes local community perspectives. As global health scholars Lawrence O. Gostin and Emily A. Mok put it, "international development assistance for health tends to be framed by donor countries in terms of their geostrategic and philanthropic interests. Donors often focus on the most visible, high-profile diseases, or dramatic events requiring rescue, which receive prominent media attention and provoke widespread public concern."[15] As a consequence, it is ultimately the multiple interests of donors, rather than the actual health needs of the affected local populations, that presently determines GHG priorities.

The WHO's original governance structure, based on a decentralized model, where regional offices, field offices, and local communities would work together toward the common goal of "cooperation to promote and protect the health of all peoples"[16] has not materialized. On the contrary, with the proliferation of global health institutions and divergent donor focused agendas, GHG today suffers from (i) a total lack of coordination among its different stakeholders and their

---

[12] Lee and Pang (Pangestu), "WHO: Retirement or Reinvention," p. 120.
[13] Liden, "The WHO and Global Health Governance," pp. 141–42.
[14] Mackey and Liang, "A United Nations Global Panel for GHG," p. 13.
[15] Gostin and Mok, "Innovative Solutions to Closing the Health Gap," p. 452.
[16] WHO Constitution, 1948, preamble.

diverse goals, and (ii) an exclusion of local communities in the decision-making processes where such goals are defined.

1.1. Lack of Coordination

The philosopher and global health scholar Jennifer Prah Ruger has carefully examined the problem of lack of coordination and the fact that global health institutions follow their own agendas and individual preferences. For her, this stems from the donors-centered model of GHG. Global health institutions typically focus on their own goals by complying first and foremost with their donors' expectations, rather than focusing on the specific health needs of the local communities to whom they provide assistance.[17] In other words, there is a dissonance between the help provided and the help needed.[18]

Lack of coordination among all the multiple global health stakeholders (including global health institutions and local communities alike) gives rise to other problems. Firstly, lack of coordination creates duplication of health services as well as unnecessary competition among stakeholders who could be instead working together in cooperation and solidarity, in more efficient and complementary ways.[19] Secondly, lack of coordination also creates confusion and delays in decision-making processes dealing with healthcare resource allocation and priority setting. Stakeholders who do not communicate well with one another (in an effort to cooperate and complement each other's strengths) cannot be clear on what needs to be prioritized. Confusing priorities inevitably lead to delays in decisions, and delays, especially in the case of global health threats, can be catastrophic. Ruger described a calamitous situation created by the lack of coordination in underdeveloped countries:

> In 2006 the World Bank estimated that half of the aid for health in Sub-Saharan Africa fails to reach intended clinics and hospitals. Another study of children's immunization programs found that confusing priorities and polices at the global and country level delayed new vaccine delivery, and recommended that overlap among the WHO, the World Bank, the Gates Foundation's Children's Vaccine Program and other organizations be addressed. Conflicts among actors create competition and duplication of health activities that stress developing

---

[17] Ruger, "Global Health Governance," p. 654.
[18] Ibid.
[19] Ibid.; Gostin and Mok, "Innovative Solutions to Closing the Health Gap," p. 452; Mackey and Liang, "A United Nations Global Panel for GHG," p. 13.

country governments to manage each donor's project in terms of organizational accounting and reporting requirements.[20]

Ruger refers to the uncoordinated global health structure, based on independence, self-interest, and fragmentation, as an ongoing "chaos and disorder."[21] Crises such as the HIV/AIDS pandemic in the 1980s to which she refers to as particularly calamitous in sub-Saharan Africa, exemplify in her view the bad outcomes brought about by a lack of coordination among stakeholders. This was again exposed, for example, during the 2014 Ebola outbreak, when many scholars criticized the WHO for its lack of good leadership in coordinating global health stakeholders that led to delayed, inadequate, and duplicative responses to the epidemic.[22] Similar issues were also experienced during the 2020 COVID-19 pandemic, leading to a delayed inadequate and duplicative response.[23]

The WHO attempted to lead by trying to centralize various global health interventions aimed at containing the spread of the SARS-CoV-2 virus. However, it failed in its coordination role, because it did not always ensure that global health stakeholders communicated with each other in a truthful, evidence-based, consistent, and timely manner.[24] The lack of good leadership on the part of the WHO has led to an erosion of trust in the international organization and in global health expert authorities (as I discuss in Chapter 6), and to a general backlash against multilateralism and international cooperation.

Ruger contends that GHG's coordination problem is made evident in the fact that the help provided does not meet the actual needs of the recipients.[25] There is therefore a conflict between, on the one hand, the goals that global health institutions estipulate based on their perception (assumption, perhaps) of what would be most beneficial for local communities, and on the other, the recipient's true good (on the definition of true benevolence as both attentive to the uniqueness of the recipients of aid and respectful of their agency, see Chapter 3). This conflict reveals, I would suggest, not only dissonant agendas but also dissonant voices in global health that speak different languages.

The language of donors and global health institutions is the language of measurable efficiency (i.e., cost-effectiveness) and quantifiable productively, with a narrowly defined success criteria[26] (e.g., performance results based

[20] Ruger, "Global Health Governance," p. 654.
[21] Ruger, "Global Health Justice and Government."
[22] Mackey, "The Ebola Outbreak"; Gostin and Friedman, "Ebola: A Crisis in Global Health Leadership," p. 1323; Gostin, Sridhar, and Hougendobler, "The Normative Authority of the WHO," p. 855.
[23] Ruger, "The Future of Global Health Governance"; Gostin, "9 Steps to End COVID-19 and Prevent the Next Pandemic"; Eccleston-Turner, "COVID-19 Symposium."
[24] Ruger, "Positive Public Health Ethics," pp. 44–54.
[25] Ruger, "Global Health Governance," p. 654.
[26] Ibid.

on organizational measures—number of loans disbursed, dollars provided, number of people saved, and numerical decline of mortality). Call it "the language of commensurability." The preferred language of the local communities is different. It is not that recipients of aid negate the importance of those calculable aspects of their health needs. It is instead that these are not the exclusive or first priority when one's life is hit by a catastrophe that causes great suffering. For local communities face to face with suffering, numbers, though important for an evidence-based solution, are cold and incommunicable and do not suffice as an effective response to the lived experience of suffering. Suffering can only be fully met by love, through the giving of one's presence, encounter, and accompaniment, as I have established throughout Part I of the book. Thus, as discussed in Chapter 2, suffering cannot be effectively addressed without also a fair dose of compassion (e.g., presence, accompaniment, attention, empathetic listening, shared vulnerability, and truthfulness), where a relationship of solidarity and friendship is established between those who are supposedly coming to provide care and those who are suffering. For local communities this relationship of solidarity and friendship is what most fundamentally (though not solely) defines success in global health aid partnerships. These not so easily measurable values related to compassion are best expressed through what I call "the language of incommensurability."[27] I will further elaborate on this dichotomy of languages in Chapter 6. But some concrete examples would be helpful here upfront to understand this tension and dissonance.[28]

Physician and medical anthropologist Eugene T. Richardson recounts of his lived experience in West Africa during the Ebola epidemic between 2014 and 2016, when he realized the limitations of the clinical practice. Clinical practice follows public health guidelines based on epidemiological studies developed by outside experts mostly from Western countries of the Global North, like himself, who typically assume that the priority #1 is (or should be) a no-brainer: to control the spread of the disease as efficiently as possible.[29] In presumptuously assuming that this was also the priority shared with the afflicted locals, foreign aid providers were not attentive to local customs and other structural and historical factors that were contributing to the spread and to how people were reacting to the epidemic. If the goal was to successfully control the epidemic and efficiently reduce the numbers of contagion, then these cultural, systemic, and historical aspects nevertheless needed to be taken into consideration

---

[27] On the concept of incommensurability, see, e.g., Urbina, *A Critique of Proportionality and Balancing*.
[28] Alexandre A. Martins also points to this dichotomy in priorities. See: Martins, "Theological Bioethics and Public Health," p. 241.
[29] Richardson, *Epidemic Illusions*, p. 39.

A similar perception was shared by another physician and medical anthropologist, Paul Farmer, who also served during the Ebola epidemic. Farmer reflected on the emphasis that outsiders put on controlling the spread of the disease and how this made them blind to other crucial aspects of care.[30] Farmer observed this tension between the Western outsiders' urge above all else to control the spread in the most cost-effective (efficient) way, and the locals' preoccupation with containing the spread efficiently, while also caring adequately for those already infected and for the rest of the community by respecting values and traditions, such as those around death and burial.

Richardson and Farmer explain that Western outsiders considered it more cost-effective to allocate scarce healthcare resources exclusively to control the spread rather than to care for those who were already infected and would die anyway. Outsiders also considered the preoccupations with traditional values not only trivial but also unreasonable in the context of a public health emergency that could quickly escalate to a pandemic if drastic measures were not taken.

By way of exemplifying the Western exclusive emphasis on control rather than care, Richardson mentions that he was not allowed to even use a catheter to care for a dying Ebola patient since the protocol permitted him only to provide electrolytes with a spoon.[31] Sure, in a context of catastrophe, where resources are extremely scarce, this kind of rigid guideline may show the most rational way to manage the crisis, but one does question the reasonableness of making all decisions based on cost-effectiveness alone. For example, while adequate palliative care for the dying might not be the most cost-effective in a crisis situation, or might not be an option in extreme situations such as epidemics, one does still question whether it would ever be ethically justifiable to deny care by abandoning the dying or to disrespect the local traditional religious values around death. These considerations show how the language of incommensurability—of presence, accompaniment, cultural traditions, religion, relationships—can be easily dismissed.

Global public health decisions are typically imposed in a top–down manner, since they are made predominantly by authorities and experts with little and no direct contact with or knowledge of the local communities' reality. This top–down imposition is too quick to invalidate the reasonableness and credibility of the local language of incommensurability. It is therefore too quick to silence the voices of local communities, which should instead be included in the public health decisions that affect them directly and which depend on their cooperation to succeed. This points to a more fundamental structural problem within

---

[30] For Farmer, there is a false conflict between prevention and care. Farmer, *Fevers, Feuds, and Diamonds*, p. 19.

[31] Richardson, *Epidemic Illusions*, p. 39. See also: Martins, "A escuta como método e os pobres/oprimidos como sujeitos," p. 281.

GHG: a lack of good leadership able to empathetically listen[32] to different voices that speak different languages, and able to bring them all together in a constructive cooperation with active participation and meaningful inclusion[33] that leads to a shared vision of global public health assistance. I will come back to this point later on this chapter, but now it suffices to understand how the coordination problem (made evident by the fact that the help provided does not meet the actual needs of the recipients in their particular context and culture) relates to the second chief GHG problem, namely lack of inclusion of local communities.

1.2. Lack of Inclusion of Local Communities

By local communities I refer here chiefly to the recipients of global health aid, and more specifically I mean local institutions, comprising not only national governments but also and most fundamentally various civil society organizations and non-governmental organizations (NGOs)—especially women's groups, faith groups, and other groups that represent key minority populations.[34] Typically, though not always, these local communities, who are the recipients of global health assistance, are located in the Global South, while aid typically comes from global health institutions and donors located in Western developed countries of the Global North.

Presently, in the donor-centered model of GHG, local communities have little or no freedom to choose how the financial assistance is to be allocated. By constraining local communities' freedom to choose the best course of action for their own public health reality, global health institutions and donors overstep local communities' agency and sovereign right to self-determination.[35] The perspectives of local scientists, epidemiologists, medical researchers, healthcare professionals, and traditional healers are typically ignored by Western outsiders in their benevolent motivations to solve the local public health problem as efficiently as possible and to take away the locals' pains as quickly as possible.

While filled with good motivations for doing good, the outsiders' urge to be efficient and quick, however, does not meet, as discussed above, the real needs of the locals, because Westerns do not take the time to attentively listen to the locals' perspective and learn from them what they actually need. In their haste to do good and take away the pain of those suffering, outsiders do not wish to "waste" time learning from locals what they assume they already know, and building their trustworthiness which they assume they already have. Typically, outsiders

---

[32] See: Chapter 6 for the definition of empathetic listening.
[33] See: Chapter 2 for the definitions of active participation and meaningful inclusion.
[34] Byanyima, Lauterbach, and Kavanagh, "Community Pandemic Response," pp. 253–55.
[35] de Campos-Rudinsky et al. "Decolonising Global Health."

ignore the credibility of local phenomenological knowledge of their own medical reality. With such rushed attitude, well-motivated outsiders neglect the reality that the locals' perspective is paramount for the success of their mission.

During the time he served in Uganda, Brazilian theologian and global health scholar Alexandre A. Martins recounts a conversation he had with Archelo, a local from Buganda. Martins did take the time to listen, learn, and build trust. What Archelo reveals confirms this paradox of well-motivated, yet not authentically benevolent outsiders (as defined in Chapter 3). As Archelo puts it:

> I am a Buganda person and I don't think like you. Foreigners and missionaries come here to help us, just like you. They do a good job, but they don't trust us. They treat us as if we were incapable of doing anything right. All the cool, good work is then attributed to foreigners who are then acclaimed by their international circle of people.[36]

The phenomenological knowledge and expertise of the local community should be taken into detailed consideration not only because, practically speaking, local communities are best positioned to assess their own epidemiological needs, knowing better what their epidemiological reality, medical culture, circumstances, social problems, and priorities are, but also because, morally speaking, their healthcare landscape should no longer be exclusively shaped by the foreign interests of global institutions and donors, from the top–down, as has been historically the case.

As discussed in Chapter 1, GHG has a colonial history. Anthropologists João Biehl and Adriana Petrina and legal scholar Matiangai Sirleaf argue that global health has its roots in colonial practices, where Western powers imposed their biomedical models and systems on colonized regions, often disregarding local knowledge and practices.[37] Arguing along similar lines, global health scholars Ilona Kickbusch and K. Srikanth Reddy add that "global health could be defined mainly by Western countries and big donors as building issue focused alliances of the willing rather than negotiating global health agreements and dealing with structural issues prioritized by developing countries."[38] In this vein, it has been argued that this imposition of a Western/Global North agenda upon decisions about health care resource allocation and priority setting in local communities that receive assistance is, in actuality, a form of white supremacy and neocolonialism.[39]

---

[36] Martins, "A escuta como método e os pobres/oprimidos como sujeitos," p. 278.
[37] See, e.g., Biehl and Petryna, "A Critical Global Health," pp. 1–20; Biehl, "Theorizing Global Health," p. 128; Sirleaf, "White Health."
[38] Kickbusch and Reddy, "Global Health Governance," p. 839.
[39] See, e.g., Khan, Abimbola, Aloudad, et al., "Decolonising Global Health in 2021"; Abimbola and Pai, "Will Global Health Survive its Decolonization?" pp. 1627–28; Koum Besson, "Confronting

The colonial origins of GHG have ongoing implications. It is this colonial history of global health that explains, as analyzed in Chapter 1, the present call to decolonize global health institutions. While the colonial era is over, coloniality nevertheless persists. Coloniality, as philosopher Caesar Alimsinya Atuire conceptualizes, is the *modus operandi* that perpetuates the injustices of colonialism—even in the absence of evident colonizers. Coloniality therefore perpetuates the power imbalance between center and periphery, which has been coupled with a lingering sense of superiority and inferiority. Atuire defines the specific moral wrong of coloniality as the subtraction of the agency of communities and peoples, where their agency is removed in the service of the interests of colonizers.[40] To recognize and incorporate local communities in the decision-making processes, Atuire emphasizes therefore the need to focus on local agency.[41]

While this movement to decolonize GHG is not new, it is only starting to gain traction.[42] Not all global health scholars endorse it or understand it in the same way, as I will explain below. Yet, scholars generally agree with the, need to address the coordination problem in GHG and include local communities in the decisions that directly affect them. Although there is no dispute that donors should step back so that local communities can step in and share decision-making authority with other global health stakeholders at the negotiation table, global health experts disagree on the best strategy to solve the coordination and inclusion problems. In what follows, the chapter will present two alternatives. One, further elaborated in Section 2, I will call the centralization approach to GHG reform, contends that the best strategy is to centralize more authority, power, and resources in the hands of the WHO. This would presumably allow the WHO to be a better leader, more able to coordinate global health stakeholders and enforce the inclusion of local communities in global health dynamics. In Section 3, I will propose a second alternative solution, the robust decentralization approach to GHG reform, that challenges the centralization approach, and is grounded in what I understand that love requires of good leaders, namely the application of the principal of subsidiarity.

Whiteness," pp. 2328–29; Ekeocha, *Target Africa: Ideological Neocolonialism in the Twenty-First Century*.

[40] Atuire, "Some Barriers to Knowledge from the Global South," p. 335.
[41] Ibid.
[42] Sekalala, Forman, Hodgson et al., "Decolonising Human Rights," e006169; Affun-Adegbulu and Adegbulu, "Decolonising Global (public) Health," e002947; and Shamasunder, Holmes, Goronga et al., "COVID-19 Reveals Weak Health Systems By Design," pp. 1083–89.

Section 2. The Centralization Approach to GHG Reform

The wisdom conventionally shared by global health experts is that the solution to the coordination and inclusion problems lies in making the WHO stronger. By stronger, they essentially mean a WHO that has greater centralized authority and decision-making power. This would presumably enable the WHO to do more, and to more easily take steps toward not only expanding their operational capacities (their boots on the ground, so to speak) but also their monitoring and compliance mechanisms (their teeth). With more boots on the ground, the WHO would be more capable of directly managing and efficiently coordinating global health stakeholders to avoid delayed, inadequate, and duplicative responses. With more teeth, the WHO would be more capable of directly enforcing the inclusion of local communities. Presumably, this centralized authority and decision-making power would allow the WHO to do all of these, and thus, offer better care for those under its leadership—particularly for those local communities in urgent need of global health aid.[43] Obviously, as the defenders of the centralization approach emphasize, the WHO can only do more if it expands its current budget.

As global health scholars Lawrence O. Gostin and colleagues explain, without increased and sustainable financing, it is impossible for the WHO to do all it is expected to do today and continue to grow in impact as the central leader of global health.[44] Recalling the WHO Constitution, Gostin and colleagues highlight that "WHO's first stated constitutional function is 'to act as the directing and coordinating authority on international health work.'"[45] This means, as global health law scholars Benjamin Mason Meier, Allyn Taylor, Mark Eccleston-Turner, Roojin Habibi, Sharifah Sekalala, and Lawrence O. Gostin further explain, that the "WHO was created to be a *centralized authority* to coordinate international responses to rising health threats" (*emphasis added*).[46] Supporters of the centralization approach, nevertheless, emphasize that the existing WHO funding is wholly insufficient to fulfill all of the twenty-two functions (listed in

---

[43] Gostin, "Ebola: Towards an International Health Systems Fund," e49; Gostin and Friedman, "Ebola: A Crisis in Global Health Leadership," p. 1323; Kickbusch and Reddy, "Global Health Governance," p. 838; Mackey, "The Ebola Outbreak?" p. 699; Gostin, Sridhar, and Hougendobler, "The Normative Authority of the WHO," pp. 857–67. Gostin, "COVID-19 Reveals Urgent Need"; Gostin and Wetter, "Using COVID-19 to Strengthen the WHO"; Burci, "The Outbreak of Covid-19 Coronavirus: Are the International Health Regulations Fit for Purpose"; and Moon, Leigh, Woskie et al., "Post Ebola Reforms," j280.

[44] Gostin, Sridhar, and Hougendobler, "The Normative Authority of the WHO"; Gostin and Friedman, "Ebola: A Crisis in Global Health Leadership"; Gostin, "Ebola: Towards an International Health Systems Fund."

[45] Gostin, Chirwa, Clark et al., "The WHO's 75th Anniversary," e012344.

[46] Mason Meier, Taylor, Eccleston-Turner et al., "The World Health Organization in Global Health Law," pp. 796–99.

art. 2 of the WHO Constitution) that the WHO ought to perform as the central authority for global health. To demonstrate WHO's deficient budget and its discrepancy in relation to what is expected of WHO's global leadership, they estimate that WHO's budget is currently "less than the size of a single large teaching hospital in the United States of America."[47]

Criticizing "the WHO's decentralized structure [which] hampers the WHO's ability to speak with a single voice and exercise global leadership,"[48] the defenders of the centralization approach, in a nutshell, advocate for a stronger WHO with more "boots on the ground,"[49] more "teeth,"[50] more financial resources,[51] and a single centralizing authoritative voice. For them, decentralization hinders leadership, arguably because it fosters an environment of dissonant voices, rather than a unitive atmosphere of solidarity, conducive to cooperation. This is the reason why the defenders of the centralization approach also advocate for the creation of a single platform for dialog, to be led by the WHO's single centralizing voice.[52] The purpose of this platform would be to bring WHO member states together with multiple global health stakeholders, including local communities, other international organizations, public–private partnership initiatives, foundations, etc. Under the WHO's leadership, these stakeholders would discuss global health problems, sharing their views and specific needs. For the defenders of the centralization approach, giving the WHO a single authoritative voice in global health is the most efficient way to coordinate and to give voice and representation to all stakeholders, particularly to the marginalized local communities whose voices have been silenced for so long in the GHG dynamics.[53]

While this single platform for dialog to be led by the WHO's single centralizing voice has been recurrently proposed as a solution, it has been repeatedly rejected. For example, in 2011, as a response to the influenza A/H1N1 pandemic of 2009-10, it was proposed under the name of World Health Forum: a "multi stakeholder meeting under WHO auspices to increase effectiveness, coherence, and accountability, and reporting to formal governing structures."[54] In 2020, in the wake of the COVID-19 pandemic, it was proposed again and this time also as "forum

---

[47] Gostin, Chirwa, Clark et al., "The WHO's 75th Anniversary," e012344. See also: Daugirdas and Burci. "Financing the World Health Organization," pp. 299–338; Gostin, Klock, Clark et al., "Financing the Future of WHO," pp. 1445–47.
[48] Gostin, Sridhar, and Hougendobler, "The Normative Authority of the WHO," pp. 857–67.
[49] Moon, Leigh, Woskie et al., "Post Ebola Reforms: Ample Analysis, Inadequate Action," j280.
[50] Mason Meier, Taylor, Eccleston-Turner et al., "The World Health Organization in Global Health Law," pp. 796–99.
[51] Gostin, Chirwa, Clark et al., "The WHO's 75th anniversary," e012344; Daugirdas and Burci, "Financing the World Health Organization," pp. 299–338; and Gostin, Klock, Clark et al., "Financing the Future of WHO," pp. 1445–47.
[52] Gostin, Sridhar, and Hougendobler, "The Normative Authority of the WHO," p. 860.
[53] Gostin, Sridhar, and Hougendobler, "The Normative Authority of the WHO," pp. 857–67.
[54] Ibid.

for international health law making."[55] This would allow WHO to exercise its single centralizing voice in global health and its "expansive international legal authority to codify international treaties, regulations, and recommendations to address any matter of public health importance."[56] As global health law scholars Benjamin Mason Meier, Allyn Taylor, Mark Eccleston-Turner, Roojin Habibi, Sharifah Sekalala, and Lawrence O. Gostin contend, "WHO's leadership in global governance for health is supported by an expansive mandate to serve as a forum for the codification of international law."[57] For them, it is therefore the proper role of the WHO, as the single authoritative voice in global health and as "the legal authority, to serve as a platform for conventions and agreements,"[58] helping to further centralize the solutions of the coordination and inclusion problems related to global health threats.

2.1. Limitations of the Centralization Approach

My main concern with this proposal of the centralization approach is this: in becoming the single authoritative voice in global health and the central coordinating and legal authority of GHG, the WHO could certainly enforce that diverse voices sit formally together at the WHO treaty negotiations table. But would this not entail that the desired coordinated unity in GHG is imposed top–down by the WHO itself? I believe it would. With an expansive law-making power as the centralization approach defends, the WHO would presumably have the final say in deciding how divergent opinions are "reconciled" and how "consensus" in international law-making is achieved. It continues to be highly debatable whether diverse voices and wide-ranging views coming from different countries with varied negotiation power have ever been able to be indeed reconciled in a way that truly achieved consensus in treaty making. To be more precise, it is not clear how a more powerful WHO would be able first to tackle the perennial international law problem of power imbalance in the history of treaty making and negation processes, and second be sure that it is truly giving voice to the voiceless and including their views in the making of international health law. Is the WHO the most able among global health stakeholders to ensure the meaningful inclusion of those who have been historically silenced in treaty making and negotiation processes? Can authentic participation and meaningful inclusion even be mandated from a centralized top–down approach? I find this hard to believe

---

[55] Mason Meier, Taylor, Eccleston-Turner et al., "The World Health Organization in Global Health Law," pp. 796–99.
[56] Ibid.
[57] Ibid.
[58] Ibid.

given the great distance (not only geographical but also in priorities) between the WHO and the local communities directly affected by the global public health interventions being negotiated and potentially codified.

To be sure, it is certainly the virtue, and the ethical duty of a good leader to welcome diverse voices. It surely is also desirable to foster a culture of unity, global solidarity, interdependence, and cooperation in GHG. However, it is not clear how the centralization approach and its proposed centralized platforms or forums with a bigger and stronger WHO would actually foster a true dialogue, where the coordination and inclusion problems are addressed. Specifically, it is not clear how the creation of centralized platforms or forums, to be managed by the WHO as the single authoritative and centralizing voice of global health, would automatically lead to better communication between global health institutions and local communities.

To be a manager is not the same as being a good leader (see Chapter 6 on the difference); neither is having authority and power synonymous with exercising good leadership (see also Chapter 6 for my definition of good leadership). While a manager exercises control over operations and focuses on enforcing regulations, the good leader is primarily the one with a vision of the common good, who also has an eye for the complementary strengths of each stakeholder and for the flourishing of each and every stakeholder through the pursuit of their common vision. This entails that the good leader is one who not only welcomes diverse voices but also, and more fundamentally, one who is able to meaningfully include them.

The concept of meaningful inclusion—introduced in Chapter 1 and further developed in Chapter 6—contrasts sharply with the empty rhetoric of diversity, equity, and inclusion. The empty rhetoric reduces inclusion to a checkbox exercise, where marginalized individuals merely have access to the negotiating table and are then expected to adhere to formulaic rules of inclusion. Do not get me wrong: access is good; it a question of justice. But access alone does not suffice. This is where the complementarity of love comes in. Agapic love offers a framework for meaningful inclusion where the Global South is given a prominent seat at the table, where their perspective receives the loving attention, it deserves. This goes beyond access and justice. And it is within this framework of love that shared authority in decision-making, grounded in epistemic justice, and the co-creation of a new future can exist (see further discussion of shared authority and co-creation as important elements of belonging in Chapters 3 and 6). In sum, the good leader creates space for diverse voices to be meaningfully included by listening empathetically to their different pleas, understanding the nuances of the different languages that diverse stakeholders speak, and then bringing them all together, facilitating a constructive dialogue toward co-creating a shared vision of global public health aid.[59] A good leader therefore hones her empathetic

---

[59] See: Martins, "A escuta como método e os pobres/oprimidos como sujeitos," pp. 270–91.

skills in recognizing the different languages (i.e., priorities) of each stakeholder, listening, understanding, and meeting each stakeholder where they are. In the case of global health, the good leader would need to help each stakeholder recognize and appreciate both the priorities of measurable efficiency and quantifiable productivity (the primary language of global health institutions and donors—and what I have called the language of commensurability), and the priorities of relationality (the primary language of local communities—and what I have called the language incommensurability). In short, the good leader must serve as a translator between these different languages—careful to represent each side accurately— so that all voices can be meaningfully included in the dialogue and co-creation process.

Within the centralization approach, it is not clear how there would be much room for this kind of love-based leadership. In becoming the single authoritative voice in global health and the central coordinating and legal authority of GHG, the WHO would be imposing a top–down decision-making structure. This is not conducive to the needed love-type leadership in GHG where shared (rather than top–down imposed) decision-making authority is nurtured. In a nutshell, the centralization approach to leadership does not leave much room for the love and empathy necessary for shared authority in decision-making. Furthermore, it is not clear that the WHO, itself a global health institution, being so far removed from the reality and lived experiences of local communities, is capable of speaking and understanding the local language of loving attention, empathetic listening, presence, accompaniment—the language of incommensurability, which is locals' primary language. Without the ability to speak and understand their primary language, it is unlikely that the WHO would successfully create a negotiation environment where the local voice is meaningfully included.

Although there is no evidence that the WHO is unable to speak the language of incommensurability, it is reasonable to say that the primary language of the WHO, as an international organization that strives to be functional, is—and reasonably should continue to be—the language of productivity and efficiency, especially given the reality of scarce global health resources. My point here is this: it is not a given that the WHO would be the best mouthpiece for both global health institutions and local communities. There is no evidence that the WHO could legitimately channel the concerns of both sides. As a global health institution itself, dependent on donors, it is unreasonable to presume that the WHO can legitimately represent the actual needs of local communities and speak on behalf of, or even alongside local communities. It could be argued that doing so would be overstepping and, in some cases, robbing local communities of their agency, and therefore another example of a paternalistic, top–down global policy that perpetuates coloniality.

2.2. Limitations for Decoloniality

True, the defenders of the centralization approach do, by and large, endorse the decolonization of GHG as a movement. However, as mentioned earlier, not all global health experts endorse it or understand it in the same way. Some like legal scholars Lawrence Gostin, Danwood Chirwa, and colleagues, in describing the beginning of the decolonization movement, mentioned how "developing states pushed WHO to advance health equity through medical technology transfers and public health system."[60] Legal scholars Sharifah Sekalala, Lisa Forman, and colleagues also underscore the theme of equity and technology transfer when putting forth a decolonial approach to the intellectual property laws that hinder universal access to essential medication, by stressing the need for "sharing technology and building manufacturing capacity" and also calling for the fulfillment of "the ethical and legal obligations of corporations in global health."[61] However, while philosopher Gabriela Arguedas-Ramirez is also critical of "corporations that profit from those normalized historically-rooted privileges," she understands the decolonial approach to deeply challenge this "white savior industrial complex" which the concept of technology transfer may entail:[62] in possessing all the solutions to the poverties afflicting the Global South, Global North "heroes" have the moral duty to "save" those in the margins and help them grow into achieving progress and development. In a similar vein, philosopher Caesar Alimsinya Atuire questions the concept of technology transfer based on outsourcing manufacturing capacity and exporting tools to help the marginalized develop. Before transferring, outsourcing, and exporting, or even instead of these, "what about letting [the global south be] free to develop their own tools? Why do they have to be a periphery at the service of big industries?"[63] In posing these questions, Atuire is, in actuality, challenging the true purpose of technology transfer by critically evaluating who is producing such technology, which voices are involved in the production of such technology, and who truly is benefiting from such technology transfer.

Not all global health scholars agree on decolonizing GHG, which underscores the need to assess coloniality from the lived experience of local communities receiving assistance. While the WHO and other global health institutions may be motivated by the desire to aid those in urgent need efficiently and cost-effectively, their focus on measurable efficiency raises important questions. Can the WHO truly represent the diverse priorities of local communities? When global health institutions presume they know best, they risk caring in ways that may overstep

---

[60] Gostin, Chirwa, Clark et al., "The WHO's 75th anniversary," e012344.
[61] Sekalala, Forman, Hodgson et al. "Decolonising Human Rights," e006169.
[62] Arguedas-Ramírez, "Build That Wall!" pp. 375–87.
[63] "A Decolonial Framework for Thinking about Sustainable AI," at 21:15.

and undermine the agency of the cared for. As discussed in Chapter 3, there is a constant tension between caring too much—thereby overpowering the Other's agency—and caring too little, which results in neglect. The boundaries between these extremes are often unclear. The principle of subsidiarity offers a solution. Grounded in agapic love, subsidiarity identifies a mid-point between overbearing and insufficient care by upholding both non-abandonment and respect for the agency of those in need. Consider Dante's Beatriz, who humbly recognizes her limitations by delegating tasks to Virgil, while remaining actively present for Dante—attentively, yet silently accompanying him throughout his journey. Building on this principle, in the following Section 3, I propose an alternative approach to GHG reform: the robust decentralization approach.

Section 3. The Robust Decentralization Approach to GHG Reform

To present the robust decentralization approach, I will first discuss its foundations by introducing the principle of subsidiarity and then applying it to the reality of GHG.[64]

3.1. The Principle of Subsidiarity

Subsidiarity functions as a structural principle that clearly determines the appropriate level of decision-making authority among stakeholders operating at various levels, favoring a bottom-up approach.[65] According to this principle, the authority closest to the issue or the needs of the community is best positioned to address it.[66] Subsidiarity therefore acknowledges the value of initially attempting to solve problems at the local level and escalating to higher levels of governance only when necessary.[67] By providing the necessary structures, subsidiarity operationalizes solidarity by guiding coordination; implementing cooperation

---

[64] My reliance on the principle of subsidiarity makes my robust decentralization approach morally and practically distinct from the original decentralized governance model outlined at the creation of the WHO in 1948.

[65] de Campos, "Guiding Principles of Global Health Governance in Times of Pandemics," pp. 212–14; Atuire, "Some Barriers to Knowledge from the Global South," p. 5.

[66] Gosepath, "The Principle of Subsidiarity," pp. 157–70; Cahill, "Theorizing Subsidiarity," pp. 201–24; Höffe, "Subsidiarity as a Principle," pp. 56–73; Chaplin, "Subsidiarity: The Concept and the Connections," pp. 117–30.

[67] da Silva, "Subsidiarity and the Allocation of Governmental Powers"; Besson, "Subsidiarity in International Human Rights Law," p. 69; Finnis, "Subsidiarity's Roots and History," p. 134; Carozza, "Subsidiarity as a Structural Principle," p. 38; and Vischer, "Subsidiarity as a Principle of Governance," p. 142.

among individuals; ensuring accountability in the pursuit of the common good for all members of the community, while leaving no one behind; and empowering lower units to play an active role in decision-making.[68]

The principle of subsidiarity is a principle of justice:[69] it orders relations within communities toward the common good. But it is also a principle of love: it orders relations and therefore our loves by differentiating the levels of responsibility that each sphere of care owes (or does not owe) to another (see the discussion on *ordo amoris* in Chapter 4). More specifically, subsidiarity provides a justification for decentralization of decision-making authority and for allocation of different levels of responsibility to different spheres of cares.

Originally articulated by Catholic social teaching,[70] the principle of subsidiarity was adopted as part of European Union law to prevent excessive centralization within the European system of government.[71] The principle of subsidiarity has been debated mainly in the contexts of constitutional law (on the themes of federalism and EU governance) and international law (on a variety of themes, from intercountry adoption to international human rights), but I believe it is very helpful in the context of GHG. In using a language and rationale that the Global North may appreciate, the structural principle of subsidiarity then becomes a practical tool to decolonize GHG and operationalize global solidarity.

In its original catholic articulation, subsidiarity literally meant to "seat a service down" as close to the need as possible.[72] In other words, subsidiarity holds that individuals, families, neighborhoods, and local communities should address problems when they are capable. Only when they prove ineffective should bigger, higher-level governance structures intervene and provide aid (subsidium).[73] In short, the principle calls for social problems to be addressed from the bottom-up rather than imposed from the top down.

The chief reasons for avoiding unnecessary interference are both justice and love-based, that is, aimed at respecting the agency, freedom, and dignity of those in need of aid, and therefore at empowering these individuals. These reasons of justice and love create an environment conducive to integral human development, at both the individual and the community levels. Every individual has their particular goals in life to flourish, and it is good and legitimate for them to

---

[68] de Campos, *The Global Health Crisis*, Ch. 3.
[69] Finnis, *Natural Law and Natural Rights*, p. 146; Carozza, "The Problematic Applicability of Subsidiarity," pp. 51, 53.
[70] Ortúzar, "Prólogo," *Subsidiariedad*, p. 11. See also: de Campos, "A European Take on Global Public Health," pp. 141–51.
[71] Treaty of Lisbon, Art. 3b.
[72] Vischer, "Subsidiarity as a Principle of Governance," p. 103.
[73] The principle of subsidiarity is fundamentally not about efficiency. A higher structure should not intervene in the activities of a lower one solely based on efficiency. In some cases, even if a lower structure operates inefficiently, interference from a higher authority may still be unjust.

pursue these personal goals—so long as they do not violate the common good of the community. Also, strong communities are formed and sustained over time when individuals flourish and collaborate to attain a common end, which serves both their own good and their common good. As explained in Chapter 4, by properly ordering our loves and the relationships of care among the plurality of individuals in the community toward achieving the common good, the principle of subsidiarity therefore enables strong and sustainable communities.[74]

Communities grounded in the principle of subsidiarity are as diverse as the individuals who compose them. That is to say, subsidiarity orders our loves and the plurality of communal relationships in which we are involved: from non-political (e.g., families, churches, and businesses) to political (i.e., states), from national (e.g., government), to regional (e.g., the African Union, the European Union, North Atlantic Free Trade Agreement, the Association of Southeast Asian Nations, the Southern Common Market—Mercosur, and the PAHO), to international (e.g., the WHO, the UN). The principle of subsidiarity can operate therefore within a plurality of diverse institutional arrangements. The general requirements of subsidiarity will apply to all the different types of communities, albeit in various specific ways.

3.2. Objections to the Application of Subsidiarity

One may object and contend that the specific institutional framework of each of these communities is too different, to an extent that their dissimilitude renders an across-the-board application of the principle of subsidiarity impossible. The principle of subsidiarity has been conventionally discussed and applied in the contexts of the nation-state and the European Union. So, to try to apply it to a transnational context, as is the case with GHG, might be stretching it too far. My opponent might compare, for example, the institutional framework of a state and of the WHO, to name the two which are directly relevant for a discussion about GHG. A state's governance structure and the WHO's governance structure are completely different. The state is vested with institutional capacities, prerogatives, and duties that allow it to advance the well-being of its citizens.[75] This structure provides specific conditions for subsidiarity to operate. For example, states have legislatures that ultimately decide the laws governing citizens. There is also a clear chain of administrative authority known to all citizens. Civil society usually knows what the state authorities' prerogatives are and in what fields they operate. But at the international or global level, my opponent would

---

[74] Barber and Eckins, "Situating Subsidiarity"; Cahill, "Theorizing Subsidiarity," pp. 201, 213.
[75] Barber, *Principles of Constitutionalism*, Ch. 5.

rightly point out, none of these conditions are wholly present. In the international realm, there is no supra-national sovereign that would have "the final say about the rights and obligations of those within its territory."[76] No one has a definitive decision-making responsibility for solving subsidiarity questions at the global level. Within the institutional framework of a nation-state, however, the opponent would conclude, there is someone who clearly possesses the final say in allocating decision-making authority.

However, the fact that the governance structure of a nation-state is different from GHG's fragmented structure, from the European Union's regional structure, or from the non-political structure of a family does not defeat my argument for the application of the principle of subsidiarity to these different forms of community. The three general requirements of subsidiarity, which will be discussed below, can apply to each of these different types of community and, in each case, provide a general structure that orders our loves, our communal relationships, and our responsibilities of care. While the application of the principle of subsidiarity is context-specific and different for each type of community, the general framework is applicable across the board.

The applicability of the principle of subsidiarity is made possible not by the existence of a government with a head of state. While the institutional capacities, prerogatives, and duties, vested in the state are necessary to the proper application of the principle of subsidiarity within the state community, they are not requisite in other contexts and communities. Neither the European Union nor the family have the institutional structure of a nation-state. Rather, what makes the application of the principle of subsidiarity possible is the existence of a community, with different levels or spheres of decision-making responsibilities that impact the stakeholders and community members. The core purpose of the principle of subsidiarity is to provide a normative structure for decision-making processes within a community by identifying the proper level of decisional authority among multilevel stakeholders.[77] And it does so according to a bottom-up perspective; that is, from local to regional to global.[78]

3.3. The Requirements of Subsidiarity

Legal scholar Paolo Carozza describes the principle of subsidiarity thus:

---

[76] Ibid., p. 208 and Chs. 2, 7.
[77] de Campos, "Guiding Principles of Global Health Governance in Times of Pandemics," pp. 212–14.
[78] de Campos, *The Global Health Crisis*, Ch. 3.

[The principle of subsidiarity] requires larger communities to protect the legitimate autonomy of smaller communities, to provide them with the assistance (*subsidium*) needed to fulfill their ends, and to coordinate and regulate their activities within the common good of the larger community, of which they are part and which is also necessary to the flourishing of their individual members.[79]

If I unpack and further develop Carozza's explanation, the principle of subsidiarity can be understood as threefold: (i) it encompasses the idea of no-indifference or non-abandonment, according to which assistance (*subsidium*) is to be provided when the smaller, lower-level community is unable to meet its needs and goals on its own and has asked for help; (ii) it comprises the idea of respect for the agency, dignity, and freedom of the smaller, lower-level community, which ought to be honored if development assistance is to be authentically beneficent rather than paternalistic (see Chapter 3 on the definition of authentic beneficence); and (iii) it includes the idea of coordination among the stakeholders involved in the process, since development assistance ought to be directed toward the pursuit of a common vision (shared by the smaller, lower level community and the bigger, higher-level community) that upholds the common good of all, requiring the active participation and meaningful inclusion of all.

In what follows I further discuss these three ingredients or requirements of the principle of subsidiarity and explain how subsidiarity responds to the two problems of current GHG, namely lack of coordination and lack of inclusion of local communities. I contend that the solution offered by the principle of subsidiarity (and by my robust decentralization approach to GHG reform) is more reasonable than the solutions advanced by the centralization approach to GHG reform.

3.3.1. Non-abandonment: Assistance in the Pursuit of a Common Good

The first requirement of the principle of subsidiarity is non-abandonment. Non-abandonment requires that a bigger, higher-level community provides aid to a smaller, lower-level community, when the latter cannot solve a certain problem by itself and has asked for assistance. In other words, it requires higher-level communities not to be indifferent to a lower-level community's plea for help. While a higher-level community should never be indifferent to the lower-level community in need of assistance, the requirement of non-abandonment also necessitates a clear identification of who the responsible higher-level community should be. The answer is not simple; several higher-level communities

---

[79] Carozza, "The Problematic Applicability of the Principle of Subsidiarity," p. 53.

might have the capacity and be willing to care and provide assistance. But should all qualify equally as aid providers?

A further analysis of the requirement of non-abandonment helps to narrow down the list of candidates. Non-abandonment identifies those higher-level communities that have the same goals and values as the lower-level community in need. Only those higher-level communities that are able to appreciate and share the objectives of the lower-level community, while upholding the common good, should be permitted to step in and intervene in the lower-level community's affairs. In other words, higher-level communities that are capable and willing to assist, but do not share or support the purposes of the lower-level community should be disqualified.

As I discussed in the previous sections, dissonant agendas and goals, which are also not consistent with the common good, are indicative of stakeholders that are too dissimilar, with different voices and who speak different languages. These may create communication problems, which hinder a healthy partnership for authentic, integral human development. The principle of subsidiarity in general, and its requirement of non-abandonment in particular, is therefore predicated on a common purpose, shared by the lower-level and the higher-level communities, and consistent with the common good of all. The common goal (i.e., the provision of a specific *subsidium*, as it has been asked and as it is needed) is precisely what unites the two parties in pursuit of a common vision of cooperation through friendship and solidarity. Without a shared goal, this partnership of assistance, friendship, and solidarity could not be formed. In this joint venture, the higher-level community unites itself with the lower-level community to help the latter help itself,[80] and in the process of giving care, it also receives care from the relationships that unfold, in a process of mutual communication, learning, and growth. This new association and community is a necessary condition for the integral development of the lower-level community as well as of the higher-level community: the partnership is formed to achieve the common vision of friendship and solidarity, which cannot be achieved otherwise.

The non-abandonment requirement helps to answer the who question by identifying the higher-level communities eligible to care and provide better assistance, that is, communities that share a common goal with the lower-level community and are attentive to the common good at large. The identification of the common goal is therefore a necessary condition for the identification of the short-listed candidates. Yet, in itself, it is insufficient to identify the best candidate for *subsidium* provision. The other requirements of subsidiarity, as will be discussed shortly, will provide further criteria for a more precise identification.

---

[80] Finnis, *Natural Law and Natural Rights*, p. 146.

The principle of subsidiarity in general, and its requirement of non-abandonment in particular, helps to bring greater clarity to GHG because it demands precision about the common goals to be pursued, even before a partnership for development is established. Such clarity is welcome, among other things, because it allows the communities to collectively choose to either invite or exclude from their association those who do not share their ends. This would potentially lead to a more effective GHG structure, since only those committed to the common end and the common good would remain as strong candidates for a particular association. The requirement of non-abandonment therefore provides the tools necessary (though not alone sufficient) for a good triage.

The non-abandonment requirement better addresses the two problems of current GHG than the solution provided by the centralization approach. As discussed in Section 2, the root cause of the coordination and inclusion problems, and more specifically of the dissonance between the assistance provided and the actual health needs of local communities is, I have suggested, the fact that these diverse stakeholders in fact speak different languages. The centralization approach's solution to these two problems was the creation of a centralized platform for dialogue that would give the WHO the "ability to speak with a single voice and exercise global leadership."[81] In contending that the WHO should be the single authoritative voice in global health, the centralization approach's solution would also presumably expect the WHO to authoritatively define and clarify the particular ends that different global health institutions and local communities should pursue together and under the WHO's leadership. But if I am right in saying that the root cause of the absence of clear common goals between global health institutions and local communities is that they in fact speak different languages, then, as also discussed in the previous section, it is unclear that the WHO, as a global institution itself, is the most suitable stakeholder to bridge that gap and singlehandedly define the common goals to be pursued by other global health institutions and local communities under its leadership. By contrast, the robust decentralization approach that I propose suggests a different arrangement and assigns a different responsibility to the WHO in setting unified goals.

By positing the need for clear common goals, the principle of subsidiarity in general, and its requirement of non-abandonment in particular, also fosters a culture of good communication between and within communities even before a partnership for development is established: a clear common goal can only be defined if all parties involved are able to communicate in a truthful and responsive manner (see next Chapter 6 on the principle of stewardship that focuses on good

---

[81] Mackey, "The Ebola Outbreak," p. 700; Gostin, Sridhar, and Hougendobler, "The Normative Authority of the WHO," p. 855.

communication and therefore operationalizes the principle of subsidiarity). A global health leader such as the WHO could certainly facilitate truthful communication by fostering (not top–down imposing) a global health culture of assessability, reasonable transparency, and meaningfully inclusive dialogue. However, this culture need not involve—and in fact, should not involve—the centralization of all communications and decisions about common ends in the hands of the WHO. The (love) type of leadership that the robust decentralization approach presents does not recommend that the WHO authoritatively define any specific set of goals on behalf of the stakeholders involved, but rather that it facilitates the dialogue in a non-authoritative way. The different agents involved should be more than passive observers that accept without critique whatever goal-setting decisions are brought to them by the WHO. Instead, all agents should truly own those decisions, and for that their active participation and meaningful inclusion are central (see Chapter 2 for the definitions and difference between active participation and meaningful inclusion). Integral human development requires from both the higher-level and the lower-level communities alike. The higher-level community that provides assistance is called actively give their loving presence, by doing, making, or simply attentively being there for the recipient community by accompanying those in need throughout the development process (see Chapter 3 on the active and contemplative ingredients of love). The lower-level community that receives care is called to actively participate in the process by taking ownership of the decisions and sharing the authority and responsibility for them (see Chapter 3 on the concept of shared authority). The solution proposed by the centralization approach falls short regarding this active aspect of shared authority to care. In the centralization approach, it is ultimately the WHO, as the single authority, that has the last word.

While subsidiarity runs counter to the centralization of power in the hands of a single institution, the robust decentralization approach is not at odds with good leadership. A good leader, as I define it, is a just and loving leader: they never needlessly step in and interfere, but respect the agency, self-determination, and the pace of development of those who they assist and are under their mandate of care, by fostering an assessable, reasonably transparent, and meaningfully inclusive culture of communication among all participants (see Chapter 6 on what good communication for leaders looks like). Think of Beatrice in Dante's *Divine Comedy*: she is neither indifferent to Dante's needs, nor does she abandon him. Quite the contrary: she is present, attentive, and she shows up. She contemplates and beholds Dante with loving attention to understand his needs and does not presume that she already knows. She also does what needs to be done. But she doesn't care for him excessively by interfering too much and disrespecting Dante's own pace of development throughout his journey. She self-sacrificially chooses self-restraint in letting Dante proceed with the journey that is best suited for him at that point. She self-sacrificially gives part of her power in respect for the agency of her beloved. This self-sacrificial act is a gift of self (a gift of her power). Beatrice did hold the power to change things efficiently and quickly but she is a good steward: she holds off and waits in respect of Dante's own time, until he asks for it, giving him a chance to figure things out by himself first. Therefore, from the point of view of the power holder (the steward), subsidiarity looks like a reasonable degree of self-sacrifice. Sure, it would probably be easier and more efficient if Beatrice were to step in and directly interfere. But love commands her to be patient and kind: love commends her to tolerate some degree of inefficiency for the good of Dante. Subsidiarity, therefore, as an act of love, is a gift of self through the self-restraint and reasonable self-sacrifice, required for letting go of one's own preferences and comforts for the good of the other, shaped within the context of his uniqueness, his pace of development, and his individual journey. Good communication (meaning communication with loving attention, a reasonably vulnerable honesty, and empathetic listening) is key for the identification of clear common goals and the operationalization of subsidiarity as an act of love (this is how the principle of stewardship, grounded in good communication, operationalizes subsidiarity, as Chapter 6 discusses).

By necessitating the identification of clear common goals, the principle of subsidiarity in general, and its requirement of non-abandonment in particular, provides the basic framework for a cooperative and equitable relationship between lower-level and higher-level communities. The shared vision in the area of global public health should therefore inform the way higher-level communities (i.e., global health institutions) self-sacrificially fulfill their responsibility of care. It should also inform how the needs of lower-level communities, in their uniqueness, are met—according to what they communicate and request, to avoid paternalistic assumptions that lead to colonialism. Because the principle of subsidiarity will not specify the particulars of the assistance to be provided and received, it is the task—and responsibility—of all parties involved to co-deliberate through good communication the specific scope of assistance and set the boundaries of the shared objectives (e.g., the specific development goal in the area global public health) in accord with the common good (on co-deliberation as part of the idea of shared authority, see Chapter 3; on how good communication shapes shared authority, see Chapter 6). Subsidiarity, as a principle of justice and love, only provides a general guidance for a just and loving association between the parties. The specific blueprint for development assistance in global public health would still have to be thoroughly discussed and carefully crafted by those involved, respecting each stakeholder's agency to identify the good for their local context. This leads us to the second requirement of the principle of subsidiarity.

3.3.2. Respecting the Agency of Those in Need: Subsidiarity as a Decolonial Tool

Respect for the agency of those in need of assistance is the second requirement for subsidiarity. It requires that higher-level communities respect, protect, and fulfill the right to freedom and self-determination of lower-level communities by meaningfully including them in aid-related decision-making processes that directly affect them. Shared decision-making authority therefore is crucial for fully respecting the agency of those receiving assistance. Such respect thus contributes to a proper, just, and loving dynamic of care in international development assistance that has friendship and solidarity as the common vision. The requirement of respect for agency also provides a further answer to the who question, because only those higher–level communities that not only (i) share a common goal and work toward the common good with the community in need but also (ii) are able to honor the agency of that community, by fostering their meaningful inclusion and sharing their authority in decision-making should be eligible for association.

Respecting, protecting, and fulfilling the agency of lower-level communities require that higher-level communities not absorb, obliterate, or subsume lower-level communities. In other words, it requires not caring excessively by presuming that the higher-level organization holds the only solutions and then overpowering lower-level organizations in the name of (a false) benevolence (see Chapter 3 for the definition of true benevolence). This requirement thus not only allows but also necessitates lower-level communities to be free to make their own the decisions and develop their own goals on their own time (there cannot be genuine love without genuine freedom). The reason behind this requirement is that individuals and communities can only develop capacities to their full potential if they freely own their decisions.[82] To be more precise, the respect for agency requirement is grounded in the understanding that the kind of empowerment that leads to integral human development can only be attained if lower-level communities are meaningfully included to freely discern and then own the decisions concerning the assistance they receive.

The freedom to take charge of and be responsible for one's goals in life is therefore not only empowering but also crucial to one's active participation in one's community (see Chapter 2 on the definition of active participation). This conviction is at the core of the principle of subsidiarity in general, and of its component of respect for agency in particular. As Finnis puts it: "anyone who is never more than a cog in big wheels turned by others is denied participation in an important aspect of human well-being."[83] Although it is true that freedom is crucial

---

[82] Carozza, "The Problematic Applicability of the Principle of Subsidiarity," pp. 53–54; Carozza, "Subsidiarity as a Structural Principle," p. 43.
[83] Finnis, *Natural Law and Natural Rights*, p. 147.

for love, integral human development, and active participation, it does not mean that the autonomy to define one's goals is absolute and unconstrained. Neither does it mean that the provider of assistance has an obligation to give whatever the local community asks for in order to respect the locals' agency. Freedom can only be legitimate if it is consistent with both the good of the recipients of care making the choice and the common good of all—which also includes the assistance provider. So, for example, freedom to do harm to oneself and to others in the community is not to be tolerated, and is therefore not to be considered legitimate. The principle of subsidiarity in general, and its component of respect for agency in particular, is predicated on a freedom that is legitimately consistent with the good of the person and the common good of all (see Chapter 3 for a detailed discussion of this requirement and its objections).

Furthermore, to say that the requirement of respect for agency is based on legitimate freedom does not contradict the general purpose of the principle of subsidiarity to form strong communities and sustainable partnerships. When individuals and communities adopt a course of action, they are choosing the means for achieving specific ends. When common goals are identified, individuals and communities have the freedom to decide whether or not to achieve those goals by means of association, friendship, and solidarity. When individuals and communities choose to associate, however, they do not lose their freedom. Instead, they are making use of it. And the same freedom that has led to their association, friendship, and solidarity may also be used to justify its dissolution, when reconciliation, the restoration of the relationship, and the restitution of companionship signify an imprudent course of action (see Chapter 1 on mercy and forgiveness).

Respect for agency requires higher-level assistance providers (i.e., global health institutions—and particularly donors) to honor the legitimate freedom of local communities receiving assistance. This is a requirement of justice as well as love, since there can be no love without freedom (as an intellectual, discretionary process that culminates in a deliberation, love necessitates freedom to unfold—see the Concluding Remarks of Part 1 on the definition of agape). The freedom to take charge of and responsibility for one's goals is not only empowering for local communities but also crucial for their active participation and meaning inclusion in the new community that they are building together with the higher-level community while receiving aid. The principle of subsidiarity requires lower-lever communities to be free to choose the means by which they achieve their ends by participating and being included in aid-related decisions. The goals of partnerships aimed at providing assistance should therefore not be primarily equated with the donors' philanthropy agenda driven by strategic self-interests; rather, the assistance partnership is a common end, established jointly by the recipient community and the global health institution. They equally share the authority in the decision-making processes regarding the provision of care (see Chapter 3 for the definition of shared authority as a core ingredient of love).

As discussed previously, local communities are disempowered by the donor-centered model of international development assistance, which calls for decolonizing GHG. While the centralization approach does by and large endorse decolonization, not all global health scholars who support centralization share the same understanding of decoloniality. Many favor a decolonial model implemented through WHO's centralized authority of the WHO, but I have argued that the WHO is constrained by its donor-driven agenda and top-down impositions, limiting its ability to effect decolonization. In contrast, a robust decentralization approach—grounded in the principle of subsidiarity—offers a practical means to decolonize GHG by positioning local communities, rather than the WHO, as the primary protagonists in operationalizing global solidarity.

By empowering lower units to play an active role in decision-making, subsidiarity enables more informed and contextually appropriate responses to the global public health threats. Subsidiarity recognizes that local communities have a deeper understanding of their own circumstances and can contribute valuable knowledge and expertise.[84] This approach also fosters a sense of ownership and responsibility among community members, as they are actively involved in shaping the solutions that directly impact their lives.[85] By restoring agency within the context of tailored assistance driven by community needs, subsidiarity provides practical means to decolonize GHG. Subsidiarity thus takes WHO's centrality and directs it to local communities.

In doing so, the principle of subsidiarity seeks to avoid the criticized practice of imposing "one size fits all" prescriptions executed by centralized global organizations like the WHO. This not only reduces reliance on a limited number of powerful private and public actors who hold significant sway over the world but also directly empowers local communities, which includes, as mentioned earlier, not only national governments but also various civil society organizations and NGOs—especially women's groups, faith groups, and other groups that represent key minority populations.[86]

It is crucial to strike a golden mean between the first two ingredients of subsidiarity to avoid detrimental outcomes. A disproportionate emphasis on non-abandonment while neglecting agency can result in paternalistic, patronizing, and condescending forms of assistance by overpowering care. Similarly, an excessive focus on agency alone, as exemplified by vaccine

---

[84] Wainstock and Katz, "Advancing Rare Disease Policy in Latin America."
[85] Atuire, "Some Barriers to Knowledge from the Global South," p. 5; Jecker, Atuire, and Bull, "Towards a New Model of Global Health Justice"; Atuire and Rutazibwa, "An African Reading of the COVID-19 Pandemic."
[86] Byanyima, Lauterbach, and Kavanagh, "Community Pandemic Response," pp. 253–55.

nationalism and hoarding (as discussed in Chapter 4), promotes an individualistic approach that undermines collaborative efforts, coordination, and cooperation among different communities, ultimately impeding global solidarity. The element of respecting agency grants local units the freedom and responsibility to generate, utilize, and rely on their own knowledge and expertise as a primary resource.[87] They are empowered to identify when and what type of assistance and association they require from other units in a collaborative effort.

The AIDS pandemic in the 1980s serves as a prominent example where agency has been harnessed to influence and shape global health policy, particularly in disease prevention and treatment. Community activists, including individuals living with AIDS, became partners and collaborators rather than mere constituents or subjects, fundamentally altering the course of research and treatment approaches.[88] Denying agency to people and communities, even under the guise of efficiency, constitutes an injustice. Respect for agency necessitates the acceptance of some degree of inefficiency in how individuals and local communities choose to utilize assistance. It also necessitates the acceptance of peoples' different pace of development. This tolerance of diversity is essential to uphold the unity that justice and love seeks through meaningful inclusion and active participation of local communities in decision-making processes at all levels.

The ingredient of non-abandonment complements the ingredient of agency in that local authorities should be given the freedom to exercise their agency, but are not abandoned by higher units when assistance is needed. In other words, non-abandonment means that local units are provided with support when they make an explicit request based on their actual needs and how they want these needs to be met, rather than on what the agenda of other countries, the market, or global health donors stipulate.[89] It also means that corrupt local units are not left free to use the help they receive for fraudulent, self-serving purposes. While the agency of local governments ought to be respected, the voices of civil society organizations and NGOs are key in the fight against corruption. Non-abandonment together with respect for agency therefore places shared yet differentiated responsibilities on both the local and higher-up units to operate in solidarity under a global health framework of justice and love (on the definition of equity as shared yet differentiated responsibilities of care, see in Chapter 4). For shared yet differentiated responsibilities to be allocated equitably to different global health stakeholders, the robust decentralization approach requires

---

[87] Atuire, "Some Barriers to Knowledge from the Global South," p. 5; Abimbola, "The Uses of Knowledge in Global Health."
[88] Brandt, "How AIDS Invented Global Health," pp. 2149–52.
[89] Ruger, "Global Health Governance," pp. 653–61; Gostin and Mok, "Innovative Solutions to Closing the Health Gap," pp. 451–58.

donors and bigger, higher-level global health institutions to indeed step back to allow other smaller, lower-level global health stakeholders to take the lead in providing assistance.[90] To be sure, the robust decentralization approach to GHG reform does not justify the involvement of a higher-level authority with much bigger bureaucracy, such as the WHO, unless all lower-level stakeholders prove incapable of providing the assistance being requested by the local community in question. There are a myriad of lower-level global health stakeholders that are more capable than the WHO of fostering local communities' meaningful inclusion and legitimate freedom. They are more capable because they are closer to these local communities. I analyze the concept of closeness next.

3.3.3. Ordering Our Loves According to Closeness

In order to simultaneously ensure both non-abandonment and respect for agency, there is a third requirement of the principle of subsidiarity: assistance activities must be carried out in such a way as to make these activities conducive not only to the flourishing and integral human development of each and every member of the lower-level communities but also to advancing the common good of all with the active participation and meaningful inclusion of beneficiaries. But how can higher-level communities coordinate—that is, organize and order—their assistance activities to this end? It is the concept of closeness that furthers such coordination dynamics by helping us to order our loves, so to speak (on the Augustinian idea of *ordo amoris*, see discussion in Chapter 4). The concept of closeness also provides an additional answer to the question of who provides aid by narrowing the candidate list. The eligible candidate should (i) share the common goals with the community in need and support the common good; (ii) be able to respect, protect, and fulfill the agency and legitimate freedom of the local community by fostering their inclusion; and (iii) be closely related to the afflicted community and the nature of their affliction.

In the context of GHG, closeness may have two possible meanings: the first meaning of "closeness" is relatedness to the afflicted people based on the criterion of geographical proximity. Think of Virgil, who, in being more geographically close to Dante, was also better positioned to guide him through his journey through hell and purgatory all the way to heaven, when Beatrice could then take over. Accordingly, lower-level communities should first seek association with those higher-level communities that are closer, in terms of both territory and jurisdiction.[91] And only when the closer communities are unwilling or unable to help should the more distant communities (or higher spheres of power) step in and intervene in their affairs. Closer communities are typically more familiar

---

[90] See also, for the same conclusion: Ruger, "Global Health Governance," p. 655.
[91] Evans and Zimmermann, "The Global Relevance of Subsidiarity."

with, and more knowledgeable about, the context and the problems faced by lower-level communities.[92]

In other words, neighbor communities, being proximally close to one another, and more familiar with the epidemiological context and the medical problems faced by their closer neighbors, have primary responsibility to assist. The more distant a community (or the higher the sphere of governance), the less familiar and less knowledgeable it is of the local problem, and therefore the lesser their responsibility to assist. Sure, in the case of a pandemic (which spreads globally across borders, rather than an epidemic which is localized) one ought to think about prevention, preparedness, and response at a global level and not just locally. Multilateral cooperation among all countries and global solidarity are paramount in the case of public health emergencies of international concern public health emergency of international concern. So, when subsidiarity stipulates that closer neighbors have primary responsibility to assist, it does not mean that when a public health emergency of international concern is declared, farther neighbors are freed from any responsibility to assist and care. This would contradict subsidiarity's first requirement of non-abandonment. It would also contradict the principle of solidarity, discussed in Chapter 4.

The second meaning of "closeness" is relatedness to the problem[93] based on, I would suggest, the criterion of capacity to address such a problem. Think here again of Virgil, who, in being a pagan poet acquainted with the challenges one goes through when in hell or purgatory, was more capable than Beatrice at that initial point to guide Dante in his incipient journey of spiritual growth. Accordingly, the lower-level communities should first seek association with the higher-level communities that have experience and knowledge of the types of problems that the lower-level communities are facing. Presumably, by having means of dealing with a related problem, they are by extension capable of better addressing it effectively. In other words, if a community is facing a public-health crisis, communities with related experience and relevant expertise are best suited to provide assistance. This experience and expertise confer the responsibility to assist. The more capable, experienced, knowledgeable, and well equipped to address a community's problem, the more stringent the responsibility to assist.

The two possible meanings of "closeness" in the context of GHG should ideally be taken together to reinforce one another. They help identify with greater certainty the higher-level communities that could hold primary responsibility for providing assistance to an afflicted community. However, these two interpretations of "closeness" may not apply simultaneously in a concrete case.

---

[92] John Paul II, *Centesimus Annus*, para. 5, n. 48.
[93] Evans and Zimmermann, "The Global Relevance of Subsidiarity," p. 2.

How then should one identify the primary responsible stakeholder? For example, if a higher-level community is geographically remote from the lower-level community in need of assistance but happens also to be the most capable to address the problem: should this higher-level community have the primary responsibility for addressing the situation in a remote lower-level community? What if, on the other hand, the afflicted community's nearest neighbor, well familiar with and knowledgeable about the situation, is unable to offer assistance: is this neighboring community justified in shirking its responsibility to assist?

Like the other two components of subsidiarity (i.e., non-abandonment and respect for agency), closeness is *prima facie* a necessary condition for justifying the choice either to accept or to reject the responsibility to assist. At the same time, like the other two, closeness on its own is an insufficient condition to determine responsibility to assist. Although all three components are necessary, none is sufficient in itself; they must be taken together. Perhaps additional criteria will need to enter the equation, when identifying the community best suited to provide assistance. The criterion of closeness will nevertheless still be fundamental in determining whom the lower-level community should primarily ask for assistance, because closeness can very quickly and clearly indicate the neighbors who are better placed to address the problem at hand. This is especially relevant in crisis situations when decisions must be made speedily—which is often the case when tackling global health threats. The principle of subsidiarity helps the decision-making process to be principled, clearer, and therefore also faster and more efficient.

The principle of subsidiarity in general and the requirement of closeness in particular tackle the lack of coordination among different global health stakeholders by identifying those global health institutions that are most closely related to (and therefore most effective in assisting) the afflicted community, based on either their geographical proximity or their capacity to remedy the problem at hand. As previously discussed, the centralization approach proposes to address the problem of coordination by centralizing decision-making authority in the hands of the WHO. However, this alternative would only expand their bureaucracy, raise their operational costs, and lead to more inefficiency. Although the WHO is typically considered the global health leader *par excellence*, the principle of subsidiarity would not justify necessarily investing the WHO with the primary responsibility of directly addressing and managing a global health threat in a specific local community. This is because there are other global health institutions that may be nearer and/or more capable of handling the localized problem at hand. This conclusion, however, does not rob the WHO of its global health leadership. On the contrary, it frees the WHO of excessive global health functions that could be performed more effectively by other lower-level global health institutions. What role and sphere of influence should the WHO occupy then?

3.4. Implications of Subsidiarity on the Role of the WHO

The WHO itself has recognized its limitations by proclaiming itself "overcommitted, overextended and in need of reform."[94] The organization itself has also acknowledged that it "lacks a clear grasp of its comparative advantage, including at country level, at times taking on what others might do better."[95] The WHO's overcommitments and overextensions impede the organization to be a good leader by pulling it in different directions. This provides further evidence that the application of the principle of subsidiarity and its requirement of closeness, which would allow the WHO to do less and have a much narrower mandate, is reasonable not only ethically but also for practical reasons. The key for the WHO to serve more effectively as a global health leader would be to delegate several of its twenty-two functions (listed in art. 2 of the WHO Constitution) to lower-level stakeholders and focus on coordinating (through policies and laws) the general course that GHG should take. By focusing on good coordination, I mean, more precisely, to focus exclusively on ensuring truthful, evidence-based, consistent, and timely shared communications regarding public health emergencies of international concern among WHO member states and other global health stakeholders, including those at lower levels (see Chapter 6 for what this kind of communication entails). Coordination and communication are not synonymous. Coordination is WHO's core purpose, and communication is a condition for coordination to ensue. But if sharing truthful, evidence-based, consistent, and timely communications is a necessary condition for good coordination, then by focusing on ensuring such kind of communication among stakeholders, the WHO would be focusing on performing its core purpose (i.e., coordination) well. As Chapter 6 on the principle of stewardship (the third practical principle of agapic love) will show, good communication-—truthful, evidence-based, consistent, and timely-—is a gift of self from the leader to those under her care. This kind of communication is the mark of a good leader. Just as the principle of solidarity is complemented by the principle of subsidiarity (as discussed in Chapter 4), the principle of subsidiarity must to be complemented by the principle of stewardship, namely the stewardship of information. In other words, stewardship operationalizes subsidiarity by facilitating a structure of truthful, evidence-based, consistent, and timely shared communications.

[94] WHO, *Draft Twelfth General Programme of Work*, para. 50.
[95] WHO, *Task Force on Resource Mobilization and Management Strategies*.

An objector would content that limiting the WHOs mandate to public health emergency of international concern is excessive. Given that it is not only infectious, communicable diseases that spread across borders but rather non-communicable diseases (including heart disease, stroke, cancer, diabetes, and chronic lung disease) that are collectively responsible for 74% of all deaths worldwide,[96] one might argue that this would be an overly narrow mandate for a global health leader. What is more, my objector would add, more than three-quarters of all non-communicable disease deaths occur in low- and middle-income countries.[97] It is therefore unreasonable, my objector would conclude, to make the global health leader *par excellence* responsible for only coordinating communications about public health emergency of international concern among stakeholders, while seemingly ignoring 74% of diseases that are killing people globally.

It is undeniable that non-communicable diseases (and I would add mental health conditions to the list) can be as severe and debilitating as communicable diseases. Their severity is not in question. However, when it comes to evaluating the WHO's capability to address different diseases effectively, one can also recognize that while the WHO, as the chief coordinating body for global health threats, is in a unique position to coordinate communication and therefore facilitate action to tackle public health emergency of international concern quickly and effectively, the organization has not been in a comparably advantageous position to address non-communicable diseases (like cancers of different sorts) as quickly and effectively as other stakeholders (such as local or other global health actors who are better positioned or equipped to meet the basic health needs of local populations in need of cancer treatments of different sorts). It has been argued that the most commendable work that the WHO has done since its inception is on infectious diseases.[98] This is because the WHO is uniquely placed to facilitate international coordination among different stakeholders, a role that is fundamental to contain the spread of epidemics worldwide. Focusing on public health emergency of international concerns, while delegating the many other serious basic health needs that arise outside of public health emergency of international concern (e.g., cancers) to other local and global health actors in a better position to address them efficiently and effectively with the inclusion of local communities is, I contend, justifiable for the purpose of WHO's priority setting. Furthermore, to focus exclusively on the subset of basic health needs that qualify as public health emergency of international concern and to delegate the other basic health needs that are not public health emergency of international concern

---

[96] WHO, *Health Topics—Noncommunicable Diseases.*
[97] Ibid.
[98] Jha, "A Race to Restore Confidence in the World Health Organization."

is ethically and practically reasonable. By differentiating these two types of basic health needs (i.e., those that are public health emergency of international concern and those that are serious non-communicable diseases) and by arguing that only public health emergency of international concern should fall under WHO's remit, I am not saying that public health emergency of international concern is more morally relevant than serious non-communicable diseases. Nor am I saying that non-communicable like cancers should not be a priority at all. Serious non-communicable diseases are and should be a priority of local and global health stakeholders better equipped than the WHO to address these severely debilitating illnesses in an efficient and effective manner. The WHO, however, has never been in a position to do so well.

In a nutshell, in the context of GHG, the principle of subsidiarity in general and its requirement of closeness in particular justify that the WHO should focus its global leadership on coordinating communications pertaining public health emergency of international concern because its expertise and experience allow it to fit the second definition of closeness to lower-level communities impacted by communicable diseases. Delegating their many other responsibilities related to non-communicable disease demonstrates their humble acknowledgment that they do not fit the closeness criteria for these health issues, respecting the agency of lower-level communities or other global health institutions that are better equipped to address these issues. In this way the WHO, in its leadership, would strike the right moderation between non-abandonment and respect for agency. Humbling restraining itself to being only a conversation coordinator and doing it well, while delegating other functions to other global health institutions that can do those better, would be a way for the WHO to practice the kind of institutional self-sacrifice that agapic love requires. In practical ways the WHO could do this, for example, by focusing on coordinating the discussions on the definition of common goals among diverse global health stakeholders (e.g., local communities, donors, and other global health institutions providing assistance) within the context of public health emergency of international concerns: ensuring truthful, evidence-based, consistent, and timely shared communications among stakeholders, enabling recipient communities to be sufficiently informed to freely choose how to best use the donated resources. By focusing on truthful, evidence-based, consistent, and timely shared communications among stakeholders, the WHO could step more fully into its leadership of facilitating local communities' empowerment, meaningful inclusion, and active participation in global health decisions.

The upshot of the application of a robust decentralized approach does not undermine the WHO's role as a global leader. On the contrary, it encourages good leadership that is able to step back from and delegate their authority to others who are best positioned to address an issue. Love allows—and requires—a reasonable degree of delegation of authority to care for those in need, permitting the integral human development of those who are cared for. While this may require self-sacrifice and self-restraint from the leader, it also fosters solidarity, interdependence, and mutual self-giving (as introduced in Chapter 2), by counteracting the top–down centralization of authority, power, control, and resources. Think, once again, of Beatrice, who humbly accepts her limitations and delegates the guiding role to Virgil until she then becomes the one better placed to directly guide Dante himself. By humbly acknowledging one's limitations and other's strengths, a good leader not only serves and empowers those under their leadership to become less reliant on the leader's direct guidance but also fosters more reciprocal relations of mutual giving within their community.[99]

Conclusion

Chapter 5 discussed subsidiarity, the second practical principle of agapic love, using the WHO's institutional reform as a case study. Global health scholars typically argue that the WHO should further centralize authority and decision-making power including over financial resources, in order to be able to do more, to have more operational capacities, and thereby to offer better care for those in need. I called this position the centralization approach to GHG reform, and I have argued against it. Instead, I have argued for a robust decentralization approach to GHG reform, predicated on the practical principal of subsidiarity, which gives a normative structure to decision-making processes by locating the proper level of decisional authority among multilevel stakeholders according to a bottom-up perspective—that is to say, from personal to local to regional to global.

The practical implications of my approach respond to two main problems of GHG by (i) requiring better, bottom-up coordination among different stakeholders, in helping clarify common goals, and thus uniting global health stakeholders through a shared mission, and (ii) fostering the meaningful inclusion of local communities and shared authority in the decision-making process (see Chapter 3 for the definition of meaningful inclusion and shared authority). Subsidiarity as a practical principal of agapic love calls for non-abandonment, respect for the agency of those in need of aid, and an ordering of love based on closeness that determines in part who is responsible to provide assistance. The balance between these three ingredients is reached through a decentralization that leads to the decolonization of global health institution where love requires shared decision making authority through the active participation of patients

---

[99] See: MacIntyre, *Dependent Rational Animals*, pp. 119–39.

and the meaningful inclusion of local beneficiary communities. These are the upshots of applying the practical principal of subsidiarity to GHG.

Applied to the reform of the WHO as a GHG leader, the practical application of subsidiarity should lead the WHO to be a better leader, one that is humble in recognizing its true strengths and limitations, and focus exclusively on supporting coordination efforts among global health stakeholders. Essential to effective coordination is good communication and stewardship of information, and this will be the focus of Chapter 6. Just as subsidiarity discussed in this chapter complements the principal of solidarity (discussed in Chapter 4), stewardship (to be further discussed in Chapter 6) complements subsidiarity. These are the elements of my tripartite account of a love-based GHG and leadership.

to 1950s Japanese norms, intentionally misdiagnoses terminal cancer as a "mild ulcer" to spare the patient distress.[2] However, this deception only isolates Mr. Watanabe, depriving him of understanding and agency.

In both Bandeira's poem and Kurosawa's film, the dynamics of the communication of truth in healthcare are explored. The caregivers' intentions are seemingly good. In Bandeira's poem, the physician strives to tell the terminal tuberculosis patient the unvarnished truth, aiming to honor the patient's autonomy and allow him to choose how to live his final days—perhaps enjoying Argentine tango. Yet, this blunt honesty leaves the patient disoriented, isolated, and abandoned rather than empowered. Conversely, in Kurosawa's film, the physician opts to withhold the truth about Mr. Watanabe's terminal stomach cancer, adhering to norms that prioritize shielding patients from painful realities.[3] Though intended to spare him distress, this deception instead leaves Mr. Watanabe feeling confused, lonely, and forsaken. Despite their contrasting approaches, neither caregiver provides genuine support for their patient in his dying days. Instead, each creates a profound sense of abandonment, highlighting a lack of true loving care.

While the caregivers in both cases intended to act for their patient's good, neither the tuberculosis patient nor Mr. Watanabe left their doctors' offices with an experience of love. Both experienced a sense of loss, loneliness, and medical abandonment due to the thoughtless presentation of the gift of communication. In one case, it was wrapped in brutal honesty; in the other, blatant dishonesty. In both scenarios, the caregivers are too quick to assume they can determine what is best for their patients, without truly attending to their deeper needs and unique circumstances. This lack of loving attention resulted in care that was ultimately paternalistic (see Chapter 3 for a definition of paternalistic care as care that neglects the recipient's perspective and overflows with assumptions about what is best for them).

In the first example, the terminal tuberculosis patient, instead of feeling empowered by the blunt revelation of absolute truth, experiences loss, despair, and silencing by an arrogant doctor who fails to see his unique needs. The doctor's approach disregards the patient's need to understand his condition and participate in decisions about his remaining days. Insensitive honesty—truth conveyed without loving attention and with thoughtless full disclosure—can be as damaging and hurtful as outright dishonesty.

Truthfulness should not be equated with callous candor. Instead, truthfulness, as a requirement of love, calls for honesty tempered by discretion. Only then can the giver of the communication be counted as trustworthy. Put another way, trust is the result of the gift of communication of truth with love. And

---

[2] Nakayama, "Professionalism in Kurosawa's Medical Dramas," p. 397.
[3] Ibid.

this gift is a gift of self: giving oneself through one's communication to the other. The self-gift of communication is how community begins and how communion is sustained (explored in Chapters 5 and 4, respectively). This is the core argument presented in this last chapter, which offers a critical lesson for GHG, considering the crisis of trust that plagues global health institutions and their leaders.

Distrust in global and public health expert authorities is widespread, particularly during public health emergencies of international concern.[4] These authorities include global leaders like the director of the WHO, national health ministers, and local healthcare professionals such as hospital directors, clinicians, and researchers. All are entrusted as stewards of global and public health, with expert knowledge as one of their most vital resources. It would seem obvious that good stewardship of information and dishonest communication must be incompatible. Yet, the general distrust that plagues global and public health is mainly (though not exclusively) related to instances of non-honest public health communications.[5] One explanation for this dishonesty lies in the conventional wisdom that leaders must appear decisive and infallible, with no room for doubt or limitations. This mindset promotes a duty to project confidence while concealing vulnerabilities, to inspire trust and maintain a sense of peace, stability, and security. However, this traditional leadership approach fosters a paternalistic view—that leaders know what is best for the public and patients—ultimately legitimizing dishonesty as a form of responsible care. I will argue against this conventional notion of leadership.

In too readily making assumptions about what is good for those under their leadership and care, conventional authority often creates a dissonance between the care provided and the care truly needed. Chapter 5 addressed this dissonance through the principle of subsidiarity; in this chapter, I expand on the solution by complementing and operationalizing subsidiarity with the principle of stewardship—specifically stewardship through communication.

This chapter proposes a stewardship model of effective communication for global and public health authorities, building on the tripartite framework of love-based GHG and leadership. Alongside the principles of solidarity (introduced in Chapter 4) and subsidiarity (introduced in Chapter 5), I present stewardship as the third principle of agapic love. Grounded in a philosophical interpretation of truthfulness, stewardship emphasizes honest communication that is tempered with discretion and a reasonable degree of vulnerability. Chapter 6 explores what agape demands of health authorities when communicating laws, policies,

---

[4] See fn. 5.
[5] See, i.e., Brown and de Barra, "A Taxonomy of Non-honesty in Public Health Communication," pp. 86–101.

and their impact on communities experiencing medical suffering. In an era rife with doubt and distrust, trustworthy communication is crucial for global and public health leadership.

Agapic love calls for stewardship, where leaders steward well their expert knowledge for the good of those under their care. This requires good communication. Love does not necessitate leaders to be infallible experts. Instead, I argue that love requires leaders to be humble—communicating their expertise and competence as well as their limitations in knowledge with honesty tempered by discretion. So, love allows—and in some cases even requires—a reasonable degree of disclosed vulnerability regarding the leader's limitations. Applying this stewardship model to GHG underscores the need for health leaders at all levels to prioritize truthful, evidence-based, consistent, and timely communication during public health emergencies. This is the leadership lesson of stewardship, which I identify as the third practical principle of agapic love. Expanding on themes introduced in Chapters 4 and 5, this chapter demonstrates how stewardship operationalizes subsidiarity and reinforces solidarity, creating a comprehensive framework for GHG infused with love.

The chapter is structured into three sections. Section 1 introduces the principle of stewardship and the problem of non-honesty in health communications. Section 2 critiques the commonly proposed ethical solution of full disclosure, where more openness and transparency are assumed to increase accountability—a "Pneumothorax approach" to communication. In revealing the limitations of reckless openness and perfunctory transparency in health contexts, Section 3 then presents my stewardship model of good communication, offering a practical alternative to the issue of non-honesty in global and public health communication.

Section 1. The Principle of Stewardship and the Problem of Deception in Public Health

1.1. Stewardship in the Context of Public Health

The WHO has long employed the concept of stewardship, formally introducing it in the *World Health Report 2000*.[6] The report emphasized stewardship as a guiding principle for governmental actors, particularly health ministries and public health agencies, to manage health systems efficiently and effectively.[7] The WHO defines stewardship as "the careful and responsible

---

[6] WHO, *World Health Report 2000*.
[7] Saltman and Ferroussier, "The Concept of Stewardship in Health Policy," pp. 732–39.

management of the well-being of the population,"[8] equating it with good governance.[9] However, within the global and public health literature, stewardship has a more specific focus on government functions such as oversight, regulatory policy, and accountability in health system management and population health outcomes.[10]

For the WHO, stewardship implies that governments act as "careful and responsible managers"[11] and "effective trustees of national health."[12] As stewards, states serve as agents for their citizens and residents, making decisions on their behalf in a trustworthy manner.[13] Consequently, sound decision-making and trust are fundamental to stewardship. This chapter, therefore, examines how global and public health leaders, as stewards, should communicate laws and policies with sensible (not reckless or perfunctory) transparency and reasonable accountability. Trustworthy communication is vital for maintaining public trust in the decisions, authority, and competence of health leaders.

Building on the WHO's framework, the Nuffield Council on Bioethics proposed that stewardship in public health should be theoretically grounded on John Stuart Mill's liberal "no-harm" principle, which justifies interventions only when an individual's actions may harm others. The Nuffield Council report recommended that public health programs should aim to reduce health risks individuals impose on one another, regulate environmental conditions to sustain health, and avoid coercing adults into healthy behaviors.[14]

Nevertheless, recognizing the limitations of strictly individualistic liberal approaches, the Nuffield Council expands the stewardship model to justify additional interventions. These interventions, though not solely grounded in the no-harm principle, draw on procedural justice and the moral value of community. Such goals include minimizing interventions lacking procedural justice (e.g., democratic decision-making or individual consent), supporting programs that help people overcome addictions and unhealthy behaviors, and ensuring accessible opportunities for a healthy lifestyle, such as safe and convenient spaces for exercise.[15]

---

[8] WHO, *World Health Report 2000*, p. viii.
[9] Barbazza and Tello, "A Review of Health Governance," pp. 1–11.
[10] See: Brinkerhoff, Cross, Sharma, and Williamson, "Stewardship and Health Systems Strengthening," pp. 4–10; WHO, *Health Systems Governance for Universal Health Coverage*, p. 10.
[11] WHO, *World Health Report 2000*, p. viii.
[12] Saltman and Ferroussier, "The Concept of Stewardship in Health Policy," p. 733. See also: WHO, *World Health Report 2000*, p. 45.
[13] Kass, "Stewardship as a Fundamental Element," p. 5.
[14] Nuffield Council on Bioethics, *Public Health: Ethical Issues*, pp. 17–18, para. 2.20. See also: Baldwin, Brownsword, and Schmidt, "Stewardship, Paternalism and Public Health," p. 114.
[15] Nuffield Council on Bioethics, *Public Health: Ethical Issues*, p. 26, para. 2.44.

1.2. Stewardship vs. Paternalism

The Nuffield Council distinguishes stewardship from paternalism—following philosopher Gerald Dworkin's definition of paternalism as "the interference of a state or an individual with another person, against their will, justified by a claim that the person interfered with will be better off or protected from harm"—by defining the limits of reasonable intervention.[16] Unlike paternalism, stewardship avoids highly coercive universal measures, instead prioritizing "respect for individuality by seeking the least intrusive means to achieve policy goals."[17] It seeks a middle ground between excessive individualism and overreaching "nanny-statism."[18] However, the Council argues, libertarian paternalism—a term coined by legal scholar Cass Sunstein and behavioral economist Richard Thaler—which nudges individuals toward better choices while preserving freedom,[19] does not go far enough in addressing health inequalities.[20] The Council endorses, therefore, a "qualified paternalism,"[21] justifying some paternalistic interventions.[22]

The Nuffield Council's stance on paternalism spurred a debate. Public health ethicists Angus Dawson and Marcel Verweij argued that paternalism, conceptually, simply means "wanting to do good for another person," equating it with beneficence.[23] The Council countered that it would be a mistake to reduce paternalism to the intention to do good.[24] I concur. paternalistic actions are not truly beneficent; while paternalistic agents might have good intentions (in willing the good), they do not do true good, because that authentic beneficence requires a loving attention to the uniqueness of the other, recognizing their agency and expertise in determining their own good (as discussed in Chapter 3).

Hence, I propose a modified definition of paternalism within the context of stewardship as a practical principle of love. While Dworkin's definition focuses on interference for another's supposed good, I hold that authentic beneficence, as I defined it in Chapter 3, necessitates instead presence, contemplation, and respect for the other's agency and consent. Thus, paternalism is interference motivated by good intentions but not by the true good of the other, as it lacks the necessary loving attention and recognition of their agency. Of course, in cases where individuals cannot exercise agency (e.g., infants or severely ill patients),

---

[16] Ibid., p.23, para. 2.35. See also: G. Dworkin, "Paternalism."
[17] Nuffield Council on Bioethics, *Public Health: Ethical Issues*, p. 26, para. 2.43.
[18] Coggon, "What Help Is a Steward?" p. 601.
[19] Sunstein and Thaler, "Libertarian Paternalism Is Not an Oxymoron," pp. 1159–1202.
[20] Nuffield Council on Bioethics, *Public Health: Ethical Issues*, p.24, fn. 43; 26, para. 2.40.
[21] Baldwin et al., "Stewardship, Paternalism and Public Health," p. 115.
[22] For a critical view, see Coggon, "What Help Is a Steward?" pp. 599–616.
[23] Dawson and Verweij, "The Steward of the Millian State," p. 194.
[24] Baldwin et al., "Stewardship, Paternalism and Public Health," p. 115.

stewardship requires respecting the agency of proxies who act on their behalf (see Chapter 3).

1.3. The Leader as Steward

This working definition of paternalism also serves the purpose of fleshing out my interpretation of the principle of stewardship, which is not compatible with paternalism.[25] The steward, as I conceive, is a good, loving leader, who is fully present and attentive to the needs of those under their care. The existing concepts of stewardship in the policy space and in the global and public health literatures explored above do not really capture this idea of the steward as a servant who loves those whom they serve. It is an idea reminiscent of the concept's Christian origins, and, in order to tie in the idea of love to stewardship, I will go back to these origins, in Christian moral theology.

As originally articulated by Christian ethics, the principle of stewardship presents the idea that humanity is steward of the earth and therefore we should all be responsible stewards of God's creations.[26] Each human being was given the gifts of time, treasure, and talents, and each has therefore the responsibility to steward them well.[27] More recently, Catholic moral theology literature on the principle of stewardship has focused on the treasures of the natural environment, emphasizing our duty to care for God's creatures and our common home.[28] Nevertheless, the principle of stewardship goes beyond the duty to care for the earth. Among the various treasures we have each received are the people who have been entrusted to our care. For example, our children, our parents (especially in their old age), our closest neighbors, and friends (especially when they fall ill or are facing times of greater need and vulnerability).

The classic example of stewardship in the Bible is the shepherd, who, as a servant of the owner of the sheep, shares with the owner the responsibility to care for those treasured creatures. The shepherd guides, nurtures, protects, and accompanies the sheep through their journey toward green pastures, the destination where they can flourish individually and together. Importantly, for this journey to be successful, the shepherd has to learn how to communicate well with their flock: the shepherd needs to learn the name (the uniqueness) of each

---

[25] For a different perspective, see Wilson, *Public Health and Public Policy*, Ch. 5.
[26] Genesis 1:28.
[27] For a critical analysis of the theological concept of stewardship applied to the context of healthcare, see: Lysaught, "Imagination of Catholic Healthcare," pp. 31–55. For a critical analysis of the Christian principle of stewardship in general, see: Kelly Johnson, *Fear of Beggars: Stewardship and Poverty in Christian Ethics*.
[28] See, e.g., Pope Francis, *Laudato Si*.

of their sheep, and their sheep must trust the good shepherd's voice as they direct them toward green pastures.[29]

Like the good shepherd, we also have a responsibility to care for others. To be more specific, as my interpretation of the principle of solidarity (Chapter 4) requires, in belonging to one another, we share a mutual responsibility to love one another well, and we have a duty to care for one another. In caring for one another, as my reading of the principle of subsidiarity (Chapter 5) further specifies, our care should be orderly, starting by being good, responsible stewards of and for those in need who have been more directly entrusted to our care, and who should therefore have *prima facie* and *ceteris paribus* priority over others in need who are less closely connected neighbors (on *ordo amoris*, see Chapter 4). In this sense, the principle of stewardship, as I conceptualize it, guides our conducts of care, in our unique contribution to good, orderly cooperation with other members of our community.

One important way in which the steward loves well those who have been entrusted to their care is by communicating well with them. Through good communication, we recognize each other's names and voices (meaning the other's agency and unique needs), by which we can build a community of mutual trust, where mutual care fosters belonging in communion and community. This initial iteration of my conception of stewardship points to how the principle of stewardship operationalizes the principle of subsidiarity, which in turn operationalizes the principle of solidarity, forming together a tripartite account of agapic love, wherein communication, community, and communion are central elements.

While the steward is not the owner of the treasures entrusted to them (in this case the people and community under their care), they are accountable to the owner of those treasures (i.e., those same people and community under their care). By accountability here, I mean a responsibility to answer to: that is, a reason-giving relationship (and communication) to the owner and to others in the community.[30] The steward is accountable (or answerable) to the owner primarily on how they nurture the growth of those under their care, and enable their maturity throughout their life journey. This is a key difference between my conception of stewardship and the WHO's, which focuses on the idea of managing the good of public health. The key difference between managing a public good and nurturing growth and maturity is this: the manager focuses on efficiently administering the treasures at hand, whereas the steward focuses on cultivating the unique talents of the treasure and on their development. If successful, the steward should no longer be needed by those whom they guided toward their final destination and full maturity. The steward thus aims ultimately

---

[29] John 10:3–5.
[30] See, e.g., Evans and Rickabaugh, "Living Accountability," pp. 45–64.

to become dispensable and replaceable. This requires self-sacrifice and humility. The steward should leave their self-importance aside, and see themselves as a mere servant of the good of those under their care and the common good of all. In this sense, stewards are more leader than manager (think here of Dante's Beatrice, as discussed in Chapter 5).

By saying this I am not diminishing the value of management; wise management is necessary (though not alone sufficient) for good stewardship. Nevertheless, management and leadership are not synonymous (this difference was introduced in Chapter 5). The manager focuses on administering our limited resources wisely, effectively, and efficiently—among other things by trying to minimize waste and maximize the returns of our industriousness. This is crucial, especially in cases where scarce resources need to be allocated, as in global public health (on the problem of an exclusive focus on efficiency, though, see Chapter 2). There is no functional healthcare system without cost-effective management of resources. In contrast, the leader should focus on attaining a common vision by selflessly serving those under their leadership and care, guiding each of them to grow and achieve their unique purpose in life, caring for others and upholding the common good of their community.[31] In short, the good leader is a steward of a flourishing community.

To be a steward of a flourishing community does not mean all authority for decisions lies with the steward. The steward can, and often does, delegate the tasks of management to others who are as capable, so that they can free themselves to focus on being a better, more present, more attentive leader and guide (on delegation as the characteristic of a humble, wise leader, see Chapter 5). The steward therefore shares the responsibility and decision-making authority to care for those under their leadership with others—including with those being cared for—leading to a collaborative work, and building a sense of belonging and shared life in community (on how co-creation and shared authority for decision-making are key to this, see Chapters 1 and 3).[32]

A key element of the principle of stewardship, as a practical principle of love, is shared authority in decision-making between the leader and those whom they lead and empower. For shared authority in decision-making to work, truthful communication is paramount. More specifically, the steward (e.g., WHO, the ministry of health or public health agency of a nation-state, or local medical authorities) has the duty to care for those under their jurisdiction and who have been entrusted to their care, by providing the structural conditions that allow for truthful communication to happen, so that shared decision-making authority

---

[31] On a love-based leadership, see, e.g., Lee, "Love as a Foundational Principle."
[32] On shared power as central for agapic leadership, see, e.g., Sherman, *Kingdom Calling*, pp. 136–40; Cochran, "Jesus, Agape, and Law."

can be established. In this way, the public health authority as a steward enables each community member to flourish while upholding the common good of all. Stewardship therefore is not primarily about managing people's health (or worse, micro-managing people's behaviors, as the nanny-state does).[33] Instead, stewardship requires the leader to foster an environment of truthful communication conducive to individual flourishing and the common good. This is how I conceive of the principle of stewardship.

Truthful communication is neither blatant dishonesty nor brutal honesty, and instances of paternalism, as I have defined it, can manifest in both cases. This is because in both scenarios the giver of the communication (the leader, authority, or expert) is too quick to assume what is good for those under his jurisdiction and care. Think of the doctors in "Pneumothorax" and *Ikiru*—both lacked loving attention to the deeper needs and unique life circumstances of the recipients of their communication, and both were abounding in assumptions of what would be good for the recipient. This kind of paternalistic communication and conduct is incompatible with my interpretation of the principle of stewardship. In what follows I will discuss how paternalism unfolds within both extremes of blatant dishonesty (Section 1) and brutal honesty (Section 2). Then, in Section 3, I will propose a stewardship model of good communication for expert authorities.

1.4. The Problem of Deception in Public Health Communication

1.4.1. Concealment vs. Deception

By and large, most people agree that honest communication is preferable to dishonest communication.[34] Dishonesty in public health communication undermines the unity and social fabric of communities.[35] But while lies are considered "always and everywhere wrong" (as I will explain below), certain forms of truth concealment can be morally justified for the good of the community.[36] As a process of practical reasoning grounded in prudence, discretion calls

---

[33] For a different perspective, see: Wilson, *Public Health and Public Policy*, Ch. 6.
[34] Brown and de Barra, "A Taxonomy of Non-honesty in Public Health Communication," p. 87. On dishonest communication and moral distress in public health professionals, see: Bow, Schöder-Bäck, Norcliffe-Brown et al., "Telling Them 'That's What It Says in the Guidance.'"
[35] For a different view, justifying lying and deception in the context of medical care and public health, see, e.g., MacKenzie, "Caring by Lying," pp. 877–83; Director, "Public Health Officials Should Almost Always Tell the Truth," pp. 951–66. See also the argument in favor of epistemic paternalism, according to which communicative obligations of expert authorities, such as scientists, allow for the use of lying or the lack of openness and transparency as a means of sustaining public trust in scientific authorities. See, e.g., John, "Epistemic Trust and the Ethics of Science Communication," pp. 75–87; and Ahlstrom-Vij, "Epistemic Paternalism: A Defense."
[36] Tollefsen, *Lying and Christian Ethics*, p. 165.

for such concealment (see Chapter 1). As Aquinas suggests, it is permissible to prudently hide the truth when necessary.[37]

For clarity, I will define *concealment* as the morally permissible withholding of truth and *deception* as the morally impermissible forms of non-honesty. Concealment can take four primary forms[38]:

1. Silence (or evasion): withholding information entirely.
2. Selective truth-telling: providing incomplete information by focusing on certain truths.
3. Filtering information: simplifying truth to make it more accessible and intelligible,[39] akin to "speaking in a language your audience can understand."[40]
4. Equivocation: using ambiguous yet truthful expressions to avoid harm to oneself or others.[41]

Although an erroneous conclusion might be inferred, these four types of concealment of the truth are morally permissible, because the primary intention is to maintain truthful statements rather than to deceive.

Deception, by contrast, is the opposite of truthfulness. It involves morally impermissible speech or conduct where (i) the communicator intends to mislead the recipient, even with good motives, and (ii) the recipient has a right to the truth. This right correlates with a duty to communicate truthfully. The right to receive truth is neither universal nor absolute (think, for example, of professional confidentiality or privacy obligations that may justify withholding certain truths). Yet, global and public health expert authorities have unique communicative responsibilities because of their position of public trust.[42] Their audiences have a legitimate expectation of truthfulness, which is foundational in healthcare messages and public communications.

This expectation does not permit the violation of duties such as patient confidentiality or privacy. Certain forms of concealment—like silence, selective communication, filtering, and specific uses of equivocation—may remain morally permissible and justified in particular contexts, as I will further elaborate in Section 3. However, because of global and public health experts' special

---

[37] Aquinas, *ST*, II-II, q.110, a.3, ad.4.
[38] Tollefsen, *Lying and Christian Ethics*, Ch. 7.
[39] See: Newman, *Apologia Pro Vita Sua*, p. 239.
[40] Pruss, "Lying and Speaking Your Interlocutor's Language," pp. 439–53.
[41] Mental reservation (the practice of using "mixed" sentences, part in speech, and part reserved in the mind) would fall under this forth category of concealment. See: Tollefsen, *Lying and Christian Ethics*, p. 160.
[42] Kelsall, "The Trust-Based Communicative Obligations of Expert Authorities," pp. 288–305.

communicative responsibilities and the public's right to truthfulness, deception by these authorities cannot be morally excused.

1.4.2. Types of Deception in Global and Public Health Communications

Despite being morally unacceptable, non-honest communication persists in global and public health contexts, ranging from silent omission of information (potentially falling under concealment if no intent to deceive exists) to outright lies about the benefits of healthcare interventions or the risks associated with certain behaviors.[43]

The following are the main types of deceptive—or potentially deceptive—practices commonly used by global and public health expert authorities[44]:

1. Lies: directly false statements made with the intent to mislead.
2. Paltering: the use of true statements with the intention to create a misleading impression.
3. Manipulation: the use of emotional or psychological tactics to control others' understanding or choices.
4. Expertise assertion: overstating or falsely claiming authority to persuade others, regardless of the communicator's actual competence or credibility.

Given that deception depends on the communicator's intent to mislead, it is challenging to conclusively classify these practices as deceptive without confirmation of intent. However, for the purposes of this discussion, identifying examples that suggest potential deception is sufficient. Communicating the truth with love is a challenging task, and none of us can achieve perfection in this regard. Yet, by understanding the various forms of deceptive communication, their implications, and their boundaries, we can better examine our consciences and strive to communicate the truth lovingly.

(i) Lies

Lies, as a subset of deception,[45] are defined by philosophers Sissela Bok and Christopher Tollefsen as intentionally deceptive statements.[46] Lies are "always and everywhere wrong" because they harm both personal integrity and the social fabric. Personal integrity is compromised when there is a disconnect between one's internal beliefs and external speech, preventing the liar from being fully

---

[43] Brown and de Barra, "A Taxonomy of Non-honesty in Public Health Communication," pp. 86–101.

[44] The four categories that I propose build on the work by philosopher Rebecca C. H. Brown and psychologist Micheál de Barra: ibid.

[45] Some use lies and deception as synonymous. See, e.g., Fallis, "Lying and Deception," pp. 1–22; Director, "Public Health Officials Should Almost Always Tell the Truth," pp. 951–66.

[46] Bok, *Lying*, p. 13; Tollefsen, *Lying and Christian Ethics*, p. 165.

present to—and therefore from being able to love[47]—the receiver. Furthermore, lies erode trust, the foundation of communal unity.

A striking example of how lies corrode trust can be found in the marketing of infant formula. Despite the WHO's 1981 *International Code of Marketing of Breastmilk Substitutes*, which prohibits promoting formula as comparable to breastmilk,[48] the industry has persistently employed intentionally deceptive claims.[49] Advertisements describing formula as "closest to" or "inspired by" human milk has mislead parents into believing it is nearly equivalent to breastfeeding.[50] These marketing tactics have been widely condemned as unethical, because they exploit parental concerns and contribute to misinformation about infant health and breastfeeding.

While corporate dishonesty in advertising is broadly viewed as scandalous, a more socially accepted yet equally corrosive form of deception is found in white and noble lies, particularly among global and public health authorities. These lies, though often justified as serving a greater good, can equally undermine personal integrity and communal trust in insidious ways. White lies are frequently dismissed as harmless, but their cumulative effect weakens both authenticity and unity. Often told with an ulterior motive—such as an attempt to control reality rather than to conform ourselves to it[51]—white lies create subtle fractures in trust that, over time, can erode relationships and institutions.

Noble lies, also referred to as paternalistic lies, are more explicitly framed as morally justified falsehoods intended to preserve harmony, social stability, or public trust. However, they may also conceal self-interested motives: maintaining appearances, avoiding conflict, protecting reputations, or softening the blow of bad news.[52] Beneath the surface, noble lies often stem from a deeper fear—not just of upsetting others but of losing control over them. Like all forms of lies, they ultimately distort reality rather than align with it, leading to unintended consequences.

The COVID-19 pandemic provided a clear illustration of the dangers of noble lies, particularly in public health messaging. Dr. Anthony Fauci, a leading immunologist, admitted to modifying his public statements to influence public behavior. Initially, he downplayed the benefits of masks to prevent shortages[53]; later, he adjusted herd immunity estimates to encourage vaccination.[54] Though his intentions were arguably benevolent, these shifting narratives led to public

---

[47] On the definition of love as presence, see the Concluding Remarks of Part I of this book.
[48] WHO, *International Code of Marketing Breastmilk Substitutes*.
[49] Rollins, Nigel et al., "Marketing of Commercial Milk Formula."
[50] Arthur Neslen, "Nestle Under Fire for Marketing Claims on Baby Milk Formulas."
[51] I thank Fr Toby Lees OP for making this point clearer.
[52] Bok, *Lying*, p. 222.
[53] Tufekci, "Why Telling People They Don't Need Masks Backfired."
[54] McNeil, "How Much Herd Immunity Is Enough?"

backlash, deepened societal divisions, and contributed to widespread distrust in health authorities.[55] This case demonstrates how even well-meaning deception can undermine credibility and foster suspicion.

White and noble lies can blur the line between deception and manipulation; they often aim to control behavior rather than uphold truth. The erosion of public trust during the pandemic underscores the need for truthfulness in communication, especially from those in positions of authority. As discussed further in the section on manipulation, even seemingly justified lies can have lasting consequences for societal cohesion and trust.

(ii) Paltering
The second type of deceptive communication observed among global and public health expert authorities is paltering, which involves using true statements to intentionally create a misleading impression.[56] Unlike selective truth-telling, which can sometimes be morally permissible (see Section 3), paltering is designed to deceive by oversimplifying or exaggerating information. This approach often minimizes perceived harms while inflating potential benefits, steering people's behavior in a desired direction.

One common method of paltering is through the asymmetric presentation of risks and benefits. Terms like "risk" are used to emphasize the probabilistic nature of harms, while deterministic language is applied to benefits, creating a misleading contrast.[57] Another approach involves the deliberate omission or dilution of uncertainty about the causal relationship between certain exposures, behaviors, and health outcomes. For example, the WHO stated in 2021 that "breastfeeding improves IQ, school attendance, and is associated with higher income in adult life."[58] Given there is no robust evidence of a causal link between breastfeeding and these outcomes—at best, only correlations—the statement conveys a misleading impression. The WHO's phrasing arguably reflects an intention to promote breastfeeding by presenting selective, oversimplified information, while omitting uncertainties related to confounding factors like socioeconomic status and parental intelligence.[59]

This kind of paltering represents a paternalistic oversimplification aimed at guiding people toward what authorities consider best, without providing a careful explanation or thorough justification. Such practices exclude people from meaningful dialogue and informed decision-making. While uncertainty is an inherent aspect of scientific communication (as explored further in Section

---

[55] Prasad, "Op-Ed: Why Did Fauci Move the Herd Immunity Goal Posts?"
[56] Rogers, Zeckhauser, Gino, and Norton, "Artful Paltering," p. 456.
[57] Brown and de Barra, "A Taxonomy of Non-honesty in Public Health Communication," p. 90.
[58] WHO, "Infant and Young Child Feeding."
[59] Brown and de Barra, "A Taxonomy of Non-honesty in Public Health Communication," p. 94.

3),⁶⁰ the deliberate withholding of uncertainty to manipulate public behavior is unjustifiable. As I explain next, this paternalistic oversimplification and manipulation rob people of their agency and ultimately damage public trust in expert authorities.

(iii) Manipulation
Manipulation is another type of deceptive communication used in global and public health, often through morally questionable nudges and interventions. While not all public health nudges are manipulative or unethical—such as campaigns to discourage drunk driving or promote seatbelt use—the degree of influence varies from gentle persuasion to explicit manipulation. Manipulative campaigns try to control people by instilling fear, shame, or guilt to steer people toward desirable behaviors, sometimes by including dishonest, exaggerated, distorted, or untrue information.⁶¹ The key to ethically judge the degree of manipulation and unethical influence of public health nudges and interventions lies in the accuracy of these messages relative to actual risks.⁶²

Manipulative nudges, often employed by paternalistic "nanny states,"⁶³ can undermine individual agency, as people may not fully understand the techniques used to shape their behavior.⁶⁴ This calls for greater democratic scrutiny, particularly during crises when governments adopt more forceful measures.⁶⁵ A prominent example occurred during the early stages of the COVID-19 pandemic. Some countries deliberately employed fear-inducing messages to promote compliance.⁶⁶ While these tactics aimed to foster public safety, they ultimately eroded trust in authorities and highlighted the ethical pitfalls of manipulative public health strategies.⁶⁷

(iv) Expertise Assertion
The fourth type of deceptive communication commonly used by global and public health authorities is what I call "expertise assertion."⁶⁸ This occurs when experts, relying on their authority, deceptively project confidence in their competence. Expertise assertion misrepresents an expert's epistemic status: they present as an infallible and decisive authority, deliberately concealing limitations in their knowledge and uncertainties in their findings,⁶⁹ and thus conveying

---

[60] Ibid., p. 96.
[61] Yowell, "Nudge, Nudge."
[62] Ibid.
[63] On the nanny-state debate, see: Coggon, *The Nanny State Debate*; Wilson, *Public Health and Public Policy*, Ch. 6; Coggon and Tahzib, "The Science of Social Justice," e629.
[64] Yowell, "Nudge, Nudge."
[65] Ibid.
[66] Dodsworth, *A State of Fear*.
[67] See, e.g., Fletcher, Kalageropoulos, and Nielsen, "Trust in UK Government."
[68] I am grateful to Jordan Rudinsky for suggesting this term.
[69] Brown and de Barra, "A Taxonomy of Non-honesty in Public Health Communication," p. 93.

greater confidence and precision than is warranted.[70] Although much epidemiological information is uncertain, global and public health experts rarely acknowledge these uncertainties.[71] I believe this reflects their fear that revealing the limitations of their knowledge could undermine their trust and credibility as authorities (in Section 3, I will challenge this fear with love). This fear leads to a distorted message about the effectiveness of health interventions. While this concealment of uncertainties and inflation of benefits may resemble paltering, expertise assertion differs in that (i) it may or may not involve true statements, and (ii) its main goal is to misrepresent the expert's epistemic status. Some call this "bullshitting."[72]

In his book *On Bullshit*, philosopher Henry Frankfurt argues that "bullshitters" misrepresent themselves by being indifferent to the truth or falsity of their claims.[73] Their goal is not necessarily to lie, but to convey an impression of competence and authority, often by resorting to empty or nonsensical communication. In this sense, the global and public health expert who prioritizes appearances over substance is a bullshitter, obscuring limitations in their knowledge and avoiding accountability.

Global health nonsense (or bullshit) takes many forms—technocratic jargon, meaningless buzzwords, hyperbole, and excessive use of technical abbreviations.[74] All have become increasingly common in global health discourse in an attempt to obfuscate reality.[75] A prime example is the Access to Covid-19 Tools Accelerator (ACT-A), which aimed to speed up the development and equitable distribution of COVID-19 diagnostics, therapeutics, and vaccines. The ACT-A is described using different terms like "accelerator," "framework," "collaboration," "partnership," "initiative," and "platform," with an array of confusing structures such as "facilitation council," "executive hub," "workstreams," "shareholders council," "engagement group," "investors group," and "consensus group."[76] The result of so many different terms, empty of meaning, is obfuscation about what the ACT-A actually is and what are its members' interests, mandates, degrees of legitimacy, and lines of accountability.[77]

---

[70] Ibid., p. 96.
[71] Ibid.
[72] Ibid.
[73] Frankfurt, *On Bullshit*, abstract.
[74] Stuart West and Lindsay Turnbull call this "science speak": West and Turnbull, "Scientific Writing as a Research Skill." See also: Stein Tagmatarchi Storeng, and de Bengy Puyvallée, "Global Health Nonsense."
[75] Stein et al., "Global Health Nonsense."
[76] Ibid. See also: Dalberg, *ACT-Accelerator Strategic Review*.
[77] Stein et al., "Global Health Nonsense." See also: Storeng, de Bengy Puyvallée, and Stein, "COVAX and the Rise of the 'Super Public Private Partnership' for Global Health"; Stein, "Risky Business: COVAX and the Financialization of Global Vaccine Equity."

Often, nonsense (or bullshit) in the form of information deluge aims to show sophistication and knowledge, but the result is confusion, misinformation, and disinformation (I will come back to this in Section 2). This suggests a fear that making information more accessible would render it more assessable—and, therefore, more open to scrutiny and challenge. Again, fear seems to lead to the desire to paternalistically control the other, to dictate how the other will react, respond, and behave.

To be clear, it is not wrong for an expert authority to communicate with conviction in their knowledge, helping the receivers of the communication to infer that the speaker is competent.[78] What is morally wrong is to overcomplicate communications to deliberately obscure limitations. Such behavior violates the public's right to the truth about the uncertainties in scientific knowledge and erodes trust in scientific discourse. Expert authorities, as stewards, have a special responsibility to communicate with truthfulness due to their unique position of public trust.[79] Their duty to communicate well involves an obligation to disclose information with openness and transparency, thoroughly justifying with reason their conclusions and suggested course of action. Deceptive communication, whether through overcomplication or manipulation, is never ethically justifiable. Yet, does the solution lie in absolute honesty and full disclosure? In Section 2, I will explore the pitfalls of the "Pneumothorax approach" to expert communication, which, while aiming for honesty, leads to reckless openness and perfunctory transparency and inclusion.

Section 2. Brutal Honesty and Its Shortcomings

Section 1 presents four different types of non-honest expert communication frequently employed by global and public health authorities. We can discern paternalism behind all four; more often than not, authorities are motivated by good intentions, but they do not act for the true good of the public, because the true good of another necessitates being fully present to that person, beholding them in an act of contemplation and loving attention that respects their agency and acknowledges their will and consent (see my working definition of paternalism in Section 1.1; on my definition of love as presence and a discussion of its contemplative element, see Chapter 3, and the Conclusion to Part 1). However, good the motivations of global and public health authorities, the result of deceptive communications is never good. Deception in the form of lies, paltering, manipulation, and expertise assertion may, as feminist social theorist bell hooks puts it,

---

[78] Tollefsen, *Lying and Christian Ethics*, p. 169.
[79] Kelsall, "The Trust-Based Communicative Obligations of Expert Authorities," pp. 288–305.

"make people feel better, but [it does] not help them to know love,"[80] because "to know love we have to tell the truth to ourselves and to others."[81] Truth and love therefore cannot be divorced.

Acknowledging that truth and love go hand in hand, many would defend brutal honesty as the right and loving way to respond to the problem of non-honesty in global and public health communications. For them, the ethical solution to the problem of deception is the full disclosure of the truth about interventions, where more openness and transparency lead to increased regulation of communications from expert authorities, and improved accountability to the public. I call this the "Pneumothorax approach" to expert communication.

In defending full disclosure, openness, and transparency coupled with more regulation and accountability, the Pneumothorax approach begins with the basic (and mostly uncontroversial) premise that honesty is a good to be pursued and dishonesty a harm to be avoided at all costs. Most could appreciate why honesty is good and necessary for science and medicine, in particular; reporting uncertainties is intrinsic to science.[82] This is how scientific progress happens: through disagreement, through challenging findings, through debate. Likewise, honesty is central for communications in the clinical setting; candidly pondering the tradeoffs between different medical options is intrinsic to medicine. This is how a decision about the best medical choice, for each particular patient, in their unique circumstances, can be reached.[83]

Honesty is vital not only in science and medicine but also for the common good of communities, for at least two reasons. First, honesty is integral to the principle of equal respect for persons[84]: it upholds people's equal dignity (see Chapter 4 for definitions of equality of respect and human dignity). Dishonesty, even when well-intentioned, undermines dignity. By assuming paternalistically what is best for another and attempting to control their responses, and behaviors, dishonesty robs individuals of agency. In contrast, honesty respects their agency and honors their dignity. Second, honesty is an essential component of trust,[85] which is crucial for fostering union and communion within a community. Deceptions, as examined in Section 1, breed distrust, fracturing the fabric that holds communities together.

---

[80] bell hooks, *All About Love*, p. 49.
[81] Ibid., p. 48.
[82] Keohane, Lane, and Oppenheimer, "The Ethics of Scientific Communication under Uncertainty," pp. 358, 362.
[83] On the duty of candor, see: Quick, "Duties of Candor in Healthcare," pp. 324–47.
[84] See, e.g., Keohane et al., "The Ethics of Scientific Communication under Uncertainty," p. 362.
[85] For both philosophers Onora O'Neill and Elizabeth Anderson, honesty is a crucial component of trust. For O'Neill, the three components of trust are honesty, competence, and reliability: O'Neill "Linking Trust to Trustworthiness," pp. 293–300. For Anderson, the three components are honesty, expertise, and epistemic responsibility: Anderson, "Democracy, Public Policy, and Lay Assessments of Scientific Testimony," pp. 145–46.

Honesty is best conceptualized as a virtue,[86] residing in the golden mean between the two extremes of deficient and excessive honesty. Section 1 discusses the problems of deficient honesty, or non-honesty. This section discusses the problems of excessive, brutal honesty (the Pneumothorax approach). As revealed in Section 1, the paternalistic motivation behind deficient honesty renders the communication unloving, robbing its recipients of agency and eroding public trust in expert authorities. Similarly, the core problem of excessive honesty is that it, too, is unloving: here the expert assumes too quickly that the whole truth and nothing but the truth is best for the receiver of their message, and that bluntness is the best way to uphold the agency of the receiver, without attending to how well the receiver of the message is actually able to take in, process, and act on it. Again, then, the excessively honest mode of communication robs recipients of their agency and erodes trust in the giver of the message.

This may seem contradictory. If honesty, as we saw above, upholds the agency and honors the dignity of the recipient of the communication, how can excessive honesty take away the agency of the receiver? And if honesty is an essential component of trust, then how can excessive honesty erode trust in the giver of the message?

2.1. Excessive Honesty and Violation of Agency

Excessive honesty removes rather than upholds the agency of the receiver of the message because reckless transparency typically overwhelms and paralyzes. Crushed by the thoughtless information deluge, the recipient becomes unable to properly reason and choose a course of action in response to the message. Even though the giver of the communication might have intended to uphold the recipient's agency, excessively honest and unfiltered communication can weaken or incapacitate its receiver. In "Pneumothorax," the doctor's thoughtless way of communicating the truth about the terminal stage of the illness leaves the patient feeling disoriented, isolated, and abandoned, rather than empowered and free to choose how to live his last days. Though probably unintentionally so, the doctor's honest communication was ultimately reckless: he failed to attentively see the patient in front of him and his unique needs. As a result, the dying tuberculosis patient leaves feeling utterly lost, crushed, and silenced by an arrogant and condescending doctor who was too quick to assume that the whole truth and nothing but the truth was best.

When the disclosure of truth happens in a such a careless manner—without loving attention to the unique needs of each audience—it lands badly and is

---

[86] White, "Honesty and Discretion."

likely to be rejected. Hence, excessive honesty is better defined as an act of self-expression, rather than an act of communication—communication involves a reciprocal act of giving and receiving; more specifically, of giving oneself through a message that can be received as a gift by the other (as I will further explain in Section 3). Communication, philosopher Onora O'Neill holds, "unlike mere self-expression, is ethically acceptable only when it aims to be accessible and assessable by its audience."[87] So, the absence of loving attention causes a message to fail in accessibility (i.e., intelligibility) and assessability (i.e., examinability).

The brutal, excessive honesty of the Pneumothorax approach, therefore, cannot be ethically acceptable because the giver of the message, in his self-centeredness and patronizing presuppositions, does not go to the trouble of beholding and paying attention to the receivers of his message (on this contemplative element of love as presence, see Chapter 3, and the Concluding Remarks of Part I). His self-absorption, coupled with his paternalistic assumptions, prevents him from being fully present with his audience. In his commitment to full disclosure above all else, the excessively honest communicator hastily and unilaterally decides how to communicate the whole truth, without careful, thoughtful, prudent consideration of how accessible and assessable his message is. In his paternalistic view, he needs to tell, rather than to communicate, the truth; his verdict is final and not open to question or debate. He is what philosopher Elizabeth Anderson would call "epistemically irresponsible": he is not really responsive to the demands of justification[88]; and, therefore, not really committed, I would add, to the loving act of communication.

Though the excessively honest communicator may not be open to questions and debate, this does not necessarily mean that he does not comply with regulations regarding accountability, transparency, and inclusion. In fact, expert authorities who dump all possible data and information on the public, with reckless openness, for the sake of honesty at all costs, and without filtering according to what is audience-relevant (see Section 3 on filtering), often do so in a context of hyper-regulation and excessive preoccupation with following the norms and indicators of accountability.[89] But rooted as they are in paternalistic control, such hyper-regulation and obsessive rule-following lead to a merely perfunctory transparency. Here, accountability becomes a mechanical exercise where the public is invited to formally, though not genuinely, sit at the decision-making table. Rather than being an act of communication where truthful reasons are given with the desire to nurture a communicative exchange with the meaningful

---

[87] O'Neill, *Autonomy and Trust in Bioethics*, p. 186; O'Neill, "Ethics of Communication?" pp. 167–80.
[88] Anderson, "Democracy, Public Policy, and Lay Assessments of Scientific Testimony," pp. 146–47.
[89] O'Neill, *A Question of Trust*.

inclusion of the public, leading to an increased trust in the giver of the communication, the accountability born from brutal honesty does not lead to greater trust in the giver of the communication.

2.2. Excessive Transparency and Erosion of Trust

Given that honesty is an essential component of trust, one would think that more honesty, through increased regulations demanding accountability, transparency, and inclusion, would also lead to more trust in expert authorities.[90] Why would the excessive honesty of expert authorities erode rather than nurture the public's trust in them? A closer look at the consequences of perfunctory transparency, bred in the context of hyper-regulation and excessive preoccupation with the norms and indicators of accountability helps explain why.

The idea of perfunctory transparency can be better appreciated when transparency is conceptualized as a virtue, like honesty. Transparency is providing evidence by putting material into the public domain.[91] As a virtue, like honesty, it is understood as the golden mean: too little transparency leads to secrecy and suspicion; too much is synonymous with reckless openness, and leads to data deluge and confusion.[92] Merely providing loads of evidence in a perfunctory way, putting infinite data out in the public domain for the sake of making information public, is not helpful, because in and of itself it does not serve the true purpose of accountability as an act of communication whereby the authority gives reasons that meet the public's right to receive truthful justification. Transparency alone is sufficient neither for creating an environment of accountability, nor for nurturing a culture of trust. Indeed, excessive and perfunctory transparency decreases trust in expert authorities by breeding confusion, misinformation, and disinformation, and, therefore, suspicion about the truth of the message.[93]

Clearly, then, both dishonest and excessively honest messages in their paternalistic unlovingness cannot be fully received (as accessible and assessable) by the public. They cannot be reciprocated in a fruitful, meaningfully inclusive dialogue where the giver and the receiver share authority to make decisions on how to proceed with a global and public health intervention. In what follows, I present an alternative: a way of viewing communication as a reciprocal act of love. That is to say, one gives of oneself through the gift of good communication, and the

---

[90] O'Neill "Linking Trust to Trustworthiness," pp. 293–300; Anderson, "Democracy, Public Policy, and Lay Assessments of Scientific Testimony," pp. 145–46.
[91] O'Neill, "Ethics of Communication?" p. 173.
[92] O'Neill, *A Question of Trust*; O'Neill, "Ethics of Communication?" p. 178.
[93] O'Neill, *A Question of Trust*.

other responds by reciprocating with an equally vulnerable gift of himself. It is in each other's reasonably vulnerable presence that agape happens. When communication is viewed through the lens of agapic love, which has shared deliberate reasoning at its core (see my definition of agape at the Concluding Remarks of Part I), then agency is respected and trust is able to grow.

Section 3. The Stewardship Model of Good Communication

In this section, I present my stewardship model of good communication for expert authorities and its application to GHG. It responds to the question: what does agape, as a shared journey of presence, require of leaders when they communicate public health decisions? I define communication as an act of love—a gift of self that the communicator offers to those she engages.[94] Through communication, community begins and communion is sustained. The model's ultimate purpose then is to build both community and communion—key upshots of subsidiarity and solidarity, as discussed in Chapters 5 and 4, respectively. In this way, the principle of stewardship operationalizes those two foundational principles.

Communication, understood as a reciprocal act of love, is an ongoing process of shared practical reasoning that unfolds in stages. First, the communicator must craft her message and deliver her gift in an *accessible* way. Then, upon delivery, the audience will decide whether to accept or reject the gift by *assessing* its content. If they decide to accept the gift and receive the message, they will then seek to understand it more fully. Through a back-and-forth exchange, communication then becomes *answerable*, by nurturing a reason-giving relationship between the communicator and the audience.[95]

Communication is *good* when it is accessible (intelligible to the audience), assessable (verifiable and open to examination), and answerable (accountable or responsive).[96] Accessibility, assessability, and answerability are therefore the communicational outcomes that the stewardship model strives to attain—— each corresponding to successive stages in the communication process.

I designed this model primarily for two kinds of authorities: (i) scientific experts in global public health who hold public office, and (ii) policy-makers who, while not scientific experts themselves, hold public roles and make decisions impacting health policy. While the model is focused on public health

---

[94] On the definition of communication as a gift of self, see also: Tollefsen, *Lying and Christian Ethics*, Ch. 5; *Communio et Progression: On the Means of Social Communication*, para. 11.

[95] See, e.g., Evans and Rickabaugh, "Living Accountability," pp. 45–64.

[96] O'Neill, *Autonomy and Trust in Bioethics*, p. 186; O'Neill, "Ethics of Communication?" pp. 167–80; Evans and Rickabaugh, "Living Accountability," pp. 45–64.

communications, it also applies broadly to all leaders—anyone who bears responsibility for others and must communicate truth with love.

Before delving into the detail of my model, I should clarify the premises upon which it is built. These were discussed in previous chapters, but they are essential for understanding what follows.

3.1. The Premises of the Model

The stewardship model of good communication rests on three core premises: equality of dignity, co-responsibility to communicate with truthfulness, and shared decision-making authority.

Because public health communication often involved asymmetry of power, the model begins by affirming equality between the giver and the receiver of communication. They are equal in dignity.[97] As equals, they owe each other mutual respect and loving attention (see Chapter 4 for my definition of dignity as equality of respectful consideration and loving regard). This shared status invites both parties into a reciprocal relationship grounded in truthfulness, requiring them to honor each other's agency and shared decision-making authority.[98]

The second premise —co-responsibility to communicate with truthfulness— follows directly from the first. Truthful communication is neither blatantly dishonest nor brutally honest. It is also incompatible with paternalistic behavior, because truthfulness necessitates an attentiveness rooted in love. I define truthfulness as the communication of truth with love—integrating honesty and discretion. Both the giver and the receiver of communication share a duty to engage in truthful dialogue, respecting each other's dignity, agency, and role in decision-making. Honesty, as defined in Section 2, is the virtue of telling the truth and avoiding deception, including deliberate lies.[99] Discretion, in this context, refers to the justified withholding of truth for prudential reasons (see Chapter 1 for a broader definition of discretion).[100] It is in the integration of honesty and discretion that truth can be communicated with love.

When a communicator discloses a reasonable degree of vulnerability— tempered by discretion—she expresses *agapic love*. As defined in the Concluding Remarks of Part I, *agape* is a process of practical reasoning grounded in prudence and oriented toward the good of the Other. It is not merely an emotional

---

[97] See: Lee, "Love as a Foundational Principle for Humanistic Management."
[98] On the principle of mutual respect as reflected in the practice of reciprocity, see also: Keohane et al., "The Ethics of Scientific Communication under Uncertainty," p. 350.
[99] White, "Honesty and Discretion."
[100] Aquinas, *ST*, II-II, q.110, a.3, ad.4; Tollefsen, *Lying and Christian Ethics*, Ch. 7; White, "Honesty and Discretion."

impulse but a *thinking process*—a constant effort to understand the other in their otherness. Honesty reflects agape by making one vulnerable to the other (though not unreasonably so). Discretion reflects agape by enabling the communicator to: (i) reason carefully when crafting the message as a gift tailored to a particular audience, and (ii) engage in an ongoing, reciprocal deliberation with that audience—establishing a reason-giving relationship.

The third premise is shared decision-making authority, introduced in Chapter 1 and expanded in Chapter 3. While shared decision-making is often invoked in health contexts, it is rarely implemented in public policy. Health policies remain largely top-down, reinforcing the power imbalance between experts and the lay public. But as I argue in Chapter 3, love requires shared authority—that is, it requires a continued process of co-deliberation about the best path forward.

This shared authority can only function if both parties communicate with truthfulness, since both parties bring indispensable forms of expertise that must be communicated clearly to discern the best course of action. To speak of shared authority is thus to acknowledge an "epistemic division of labor"[101] and a "mutual engagement in deliberation."[102] In other words, the complementarity of expertise—where each party brings different but necessary knowledge— grounds their shared authority.

I should clarify, though, that by "complementarity of expertise" I do not mean epistemic equality between the giver and receiver of communication, but rather, the recognition that people hold different kinds of expertise. We are all experts in distinct domains, and our knowledge is complementary—we are both givers and receivers in the process of communication. In the patient–doctor relationship, for example, the doctor has technical expertise in medicine, while the patient has phenomenological expertise—the lived experience of their condition within their specific life circumstances. Both forms of knowledge are necessary, and neither is sufficient on its own.[103] Patient and doctor must work together as a team to determine the best course of treatment for that specific case.

The same rationale applies in global and public health. Scientists offer indispensable knowledge in epidemiology and other health disciplines. Policymakers contribute political, economic, and social insight. The public—including civil society organizations and NGOs—contribute cultural knowledge and local values. All of these forms of expertise are necessary, though none are sufficient in

---

[101] Kitcher, *Science in a Democratic Society*, p. 51.
[102] Ibid. See also: Keohane et al., "The Ethics of Scientific Communication under Uncertainty," p. 348.
[103] For a critical take on the idea of patient expertise, see, e.g., Watson, "Patient Expertise and Medical Authority," pp. 58–71.

isolation. Only together can they shape sound public health decisions that serve the common good of the population.

3.2. The Ingredients of the Model

For good communication, particularly in leadership and caregiving roles, the stewardship model requires three essential ingredients—each arising from the integration of character and reasoning (on agape as both a virtue and a practical reason, see the Introduction).

First, loving attention ensures that communication is accessible by prioritizing the audience's need for understanding. Second, honesty, tempered with discretion and a reasonable degree of vulnerability, makes the message assessable by acknowledging its limitations and inviting shared judgment. Third, empathetic listening makes communication answerable by fostering a two-way dialogue rooted in mutual recognition and responsive accountability.

Loving attention, reasonably vulnerable honesty, and empathetic listening are the core of my proposed model of good communication; each is nurtured and exercised through the "thinking" process of agape.

3.2.1. Loving Attention

Communication begins when the giver prepares a message for her intended audience. For communication to succeed, the message must first be accessible. If it is not intelligible to its audience, communication cannot even begin. Loving attention is what enables accessibility, and is therefore the very foundation of good communication. It initiates the movement toward both community and communion and shapes the entire communication process.

Love is vision perfected: the capacity to see the other person as they truly are, with their virtues and flaws, strengths and limitations, particularities and idiosyncrasies.[104] Loving attention is the practice of presence: by offering my full, attentive presence to the other, I resist paternalism and assumption. Instead of projecting what I think you need, I attune myself to what you need. This is what makes communication audience-relevant, and thus loving.

Here, the virtue of clarity is key: it requires navigating between two extremes—an overly general message so diluted that it loses significance, or a message so excessively detailed that it becomes incomprehensible.[105] Only the reasonable, prudential person can discern the golden mean of clarity, and this is why experts

---

[104] Murdoch, *The Sovereignty of Good*, p. 34. And see the discussion in Chs. 1–3.
[105] On the virtue of clarity applied to the context of the Rule of Law, see, e.g., Yowell, "Legislación, Common Law, y la Virtud de la Claridad," pp. 481–512.

should cultivate virtue of character—not just expertise—if they are to communicate effectively and lovingly.[106] While communication always depends on both the giver and the receiver—and the internal state of the receiver cannot be controlled[107]—the giver remains responsible for cultivating the virtue of clarity by remaining attuned to the audience's state of mind, knowledge, and capacity to engage. Achieving this kind of clarity requires careful filtering of information (as defined in Section 1). Here is where the communicator exercises practical reasoning: discerning with prudence what information is audience-relevant and what may be distracting or misleading. We trusts scientists, researchers, and experts to perform this task—to distill the best available knowledge, while omitting what is outdated, irrelevant, or poor in quality.[108] This filtering must be audience-specific and always aimed at making truth more, not less, accessible. A scientist presenting to peers will filter and frame information differently than when addressing the general public. But these variations must remain internally coherent and, in the case of health authorities, aligned with the underlying science. Adapting a message is not distorting it. Rather, it is an act of intellectual generosity that helps the truth to be received, fostering understanding, rather than confusion or mistrust.

The discerning, audience-specific clarity is a labor of love. As discussed in Chapters 1–3, love is an intellectual process, grounded in prudence and exercised through practical reasoning. It requires the ongoing effort to understand the other in their uniqueness. Loving attention is therefore not passive: it involves judgment and discernment. By offering her full presence, the communicator attunes herself to her audience's needs for intelligibility, and—through reason—how best to craft and deliver the message. In doing so, she meets her addressees where they are, speaks their language, and vulnerably offers herself—through her carefully crafted message—as a gift. This labor of love is what makes communication accessible in the first place. It is what enacts Accessibility through Presence.

3.2.2. Reasonably Vulnerable Honesty

I turn now to the second stage of communication, where the communicator offers herself vulnerably through her communication. Once a message has been crafted and delivered, the audience must then assess it, accepting—or rejecting—it. Essential here is the communicator's reasonably vulnerable honesty—the second ingredient of the stewardship model. Only when the communicator discloses the truth with love, by integrating honesty about the limitations of her

---

[106] I thank Veronica Rodriguez-Blanco for making this point clearer.

[107] As Aquinas puts it, *Quidquid recipitur ad modum recipientis recipitur* (whatever is received is received according to the mode of the receiver). See: *Summa Theologiae*, 1a, q.75, a.5; 3a, q.5.

[108] Grasswick, "Understanding Epistemic Trust, Injustice, and Their Harm," p. 78.

knowledge with discretion, can the message be properly examined. To put it differently, the addressees' ability to assess the message depends on its truthfulness. As a requirement of love, truthfulness calls the communicator to discern with prudence how to reveal her limitations with a vulnerability that is reasonable rather than reckless. Reasonably vulnerable honesty invites further reasoning and understanding, nurturing the communicator's trustworthiness. Reckless vulnerability, by contrast, produces an overwhelming deluge of information that can erodes the self-respect and fosters confusion and mistrust in the audience.

As defined in the Concluding Remarks of Part I, agape—as both a virtue and a practical reason—holds in tension two responsibilities: responsibility to the self (love of self that enables self-constitution, as further discussed in Chapter 2) and responsibility for others (love of neighbor). Love requires a reasonable degree of self-sacrifice for the good of the other. And it is precisely in this tension that the degree of vulnerability called for by truthful communication is discerned.

The act of communicating the truth with reasonably vulnerable honesty is thus a self-sacrificial act of love by the communicator. It allows the audience to assess the message, while gradually fostering their meaningful inclusion in communication process (see Chapter 1 for the concept of meaningful inclusiveness, recapitulated in Section 2 above). Reasonably vulnerable honesty is the condition that makes the shared responsibility for truthfulness—borne by both the giver and the receiver of communication—possible. While the audience's meaningful inclusion is more explicit in the third stage of communication (to be discussed next), it nonetheless depends on a sufficient degree of transparency at this second stage, when the message is being delivered by the communicator and assessed by the audience.

Again, the appropriate level of transparency, attaining the Aristotelian golden mean between excess and insufficiency, will vary; different audiences require different degrees of disclosure for their meaningful inclusion. That is to say, the labor of love the communicator began when she first turned toward her audience, attuned herself to them, and made fully present in crafting an accessible message with loving attention, continues throughout the whole communication process. The full presence that underpins loving attention informs every stages of a communication grounded in love—a "thinking" process about both the content of the message and the responsive actions required of the communicator and the audience alike. As an ongoing effort to reason with and understand the other, agape calls for transparency to be tailored to each specific audience, according to their particular needs for understanding.

For example, when a scientific expert addresses an audience of scientifically trained individuals, reasonably vulnerable honesty may require her to disclose the processes of inference and peer review with enough clarity and detail to allow the audience to verify the limitations of her knowledge and the legitimacy of her conclusions.[109] But when a scientific expert addresses a lay audience—policy-makers or the general public—reasonably vulnerable honesty requires something different. Because the "pluralistic, revisable, and fallible"[110] nature of science is not always intuitive to non-scientists, a more detailed disclosure of the reality of scientific uncertainty is typically helpful—explaining, for instance, that even among equally qualified experts, differing interpretations of uncertainties can lead to divergent conclusions and, consequently, different messages to the public.[111]

If, however, the communicator is a policy-maker rather than a scientist, reasonably vulnerable honesty might involve offering context about the challenges of weighing scientific and non-scientific considerations in decision-making. Global public health policies involve difficult trade-offs among competing priorities, many of which cannot be easily measured or quantified. For instance, during the COVID-19 pandemic, while scientific evidence supported the use of masks, non-scientific considerations—such as concerns about supply shortages for frontline workers—also influenced early policy decisions. Communicating such trade-offs with reasonable vulnerability acknowledges the inherent uncertainties of decision-making in global public health and fosters a more informed and engaged public.

To be sure, openly acknowledging the limitations of one's knowledge and the uncertainties in one's conclusions is difficult. It exposes scientists and policy-makers to scrutiny and requires courage. While reasonably vulnerable honesty demands a loving and reasonable self-sacrifice on the part of the communicator, the audience, in turn, must honor this gift by responding with respectful consideration and loving regard (see Chapter 4). This means actively receiving the message, holding expert authorities accountable with critical discernment, and always respecting the dignity of the communicator. Fostering an environment in which participants feel at ease being reasonably vulnerable in each other's presence enable truthful exchange, avoids dehumanizing communication, and upholds the equal dignity of all. Such an environment is, at its core, grounded in love.

3.2.3. Empathetic Listening

In the first stage, the communicator crafts her message and offers it as a gift, shaped by loving attention and rendered accessible. In the second stage, the audience receives this gift and evaluates its content, deciding whether to accept or reject it. The third stage, however, invites a deeper form of engagement. Once

---

[109] Keohane et al., "The Ethics of Scientific Communication under Uncertainty," p. 352.
[110] Massimi, "Public Trust in Model-based Science."
[111] Keohane et al., "The Ethics of Scientific Communication under Uncertainty," p. 358.

the message is received and the gift accepted, the audience seeks to understand it more fully through a process of digestion and exchange. This stage is not passive, but dialogical; it depends on the capacity to appreciate the giver's reasoning. Such capacity, in turn, rests on the virtue of empathetic listening—an integration of one's character and practical reasoning.

The third stage requires two-way responsiveness: the listener's engagement deepens the giver's capacity to clarify, recalibrate, and respond. Empathetic listening thus fosters mutual answerability and sustains the reason-giving relationship at the heart of good communication. It is particularly vital for expert authorities, whose communication must be not only scientifically sound but also ethically accountable to the concerns of the addressees.

As a reciprocal practice, empathetic listening is a virtue to be cultivated by both the communicator and the recipient. After all, communication is not the transmission of data but the exchange of selves. Mutual understanding requires more than comprehension; it requires a posture of generosity, intellectual humility, and reasonably vulnerable honesty from both parties. Empathetic listening—alongside loving attention and truthful speech—is the third essential ingredient in my stewardship model of good communication. It is especially urgent in today's climate of pervasive distrust, where dismissiveness or suspicion often replaces genuine consideration. Cultivating a character predisposed to listen with empathy makes it possible for truth to be heard, reason to be received, and understanding to unfold. Reason, truth and integrity of character alone cannot break through when the field of communication is clouded by mistrust.[112] Empathetic listening is the virtue that clears the ground.

To frame empathetic listening as part of a mutual exchange is to highlight the kind of reasoning that *agapic love* demands. As discussed in Chapter 2, empathy—drawing on Edith Stein's phenomenological account—is not merely emotional resonance but an intellectual process that begins in encounter. The communicator invites the recipient into an act of ideation and discernment, offering a vulnerable self-revelation through the message.[113] The listener, in turn, must respond through active reflection, grasping not only what is said but why it matters. This interpretive act is itself a gift—a return offering grounded in gratitude for the moral labor of communication (see Chapter 1 on the concept of gratitude).

One might ask why, then, is empathetic listening so relevant for authorities tasked with delivering a public health message. The answer lies in the idea of "responsive accountability." This form of accountability hinges on the virtue of responsiveness—a willingness to be questioned and an openness to correction,

---

[112] I thank Veronica Rodriguez-Blanco for helping me to make this point clearer.
[113] Stein, *On the Problem of Empathy*, pp. 95–96.

regardless of whether one ultimately changes one's view—followed by a timely and reasoned answer. As Anderson explains, "the mark of epistemic responsibility is responsive accountability to the community of inquiries."[114] For experts to be truly responsible, they must respond to demands for justification from their audience. When expert authorities receive queries and commentaries from their audience, they need to listen empathetically if they want to respond well. As stewards, expert authorities hold a position of public trust,[115] and therefore bear a special duty of accountability—not as a perfunctory exercise in transparency, but as a genuine reason-giving dialogue[116]—correlated to the public's right to receive truthful justification.

When responsive accountability is rooted in empathetic listening, and practiced alongside loving attention and reasonably vulnerable honesty, it creates a more horizontal dynamic of communication. This nurtures meaningful inclusiveness, by giving every participant a voice that can correct power imbalances and challenge control. When responsive accountability is paired with meaningful inclusiveness, the result is a reciprocal, two-way exchange: both parties contribute to disambiguating, assessing, and constructing a shared understanding, checking facts and each other's blind spots, and exercising their shared authority for decision-making. This creates an environment where trust grows and community is built—a community marked by belonging and communion in friendship and solidarity. These are the fruits of the shared authority for decision-making that my stewardship model of good communication for leaders enables (see Chapter 3 for the definition of shared authority). Ultimately, communication is the first step toward building community and sustaining communion.

3.3. Applying the Stewardship Model of Good Communication to GHG

My stewardship model of good communication for leaders both rests on and is infused by agapic love, expressed in its three intrinsic ingredients: loving attention, reasonably vulnerable honesty, and empathetic listening. The steward seeks to communicate well, to promote the well-being and development of those they lead, and so the model can guide public health authorities as they communicate health policy decisions.

---

[114] Anderson, "Democracy, Public Policy, and Lay Assessments of Scientific Testimony," p. 146.
[115] Kelsall, "The Trust-Based Communicative Obligations of Expert Authorities," pp. 288–305.
[116] See, e.g., Evans and Rickabaugh, "Living Accountability," pp. 45–64.

In moments of crisis—such as during a declared public health emergency of international concern—people are desperate for definitive answers that restore stability and security. In such contexts, numbers, quantifiable indicators, and scientific evidence help ease social anxiety by offering pragmatic, exact responses to complex ethical dilemmas. Typically, the language of numbers, efficiency, and mathematical trade-offs is the language of experts. In Chapter 5, I have called this "the language of commensurability."

In public health emergencies, we are often exposed to a vast gamut of data about the threat we are under. During the COVID-19 pandemic, for example, a deluge of empirical data emerged, as experts, funding agencies, scientific journals, and journalists shifted their activities to urgent COVID-19 research.[117] This overwhelming focus distorted perceptions of the pandemic's impact and increased the probability of scientific errors.[118] Moreover, as discussed in Section 1, many expert and policy-maker communications were not entirely truthful. Had global public health experts and policy-makers shared their knowledge about SARS-CoV-2 with honesty tempered by discretion and a reasonable degree of vulnerability about their knowledge, the shifting scientific evidence and fluctuating public policies might not have seemed so erratic and arbitrary.[119] Instead, the abundance of COVID-19 data—including misinformation and lies—led to an "infodemic" that fueled confusion, polarization, and generalized distrust in expert authorities,[120] while promoting an overly simplistic "follow the science" slogan.

This one-dimensional view of science implies that empirical data and scientific evidence alone automatically lead to good decisions in global public health. True, empirical evidence provides a sense of certainty amid a pandemic characterized by uncertainty, like COVID-19. Also true, good decision-making in public policy does depend on the availability of reliable data and rigorous analysis. But complex situations, such as global health crises, cannot be resolved solely through mathematical trade-offs. Good decision-making in public policy depends most fundamentally on sound ethical reasoning that ascribes value and normative judgment to empirical facts.[121] Loving attention to the lay public requires ongoing explanations of how this reality constrains decision-making.

---

[117] Pai, "Covidization of Research: What Are the Risks?" p. 1159.
[118] Bramstedt, "The Carnage of Substandard Research during the COVID-19 Pandemic," pp. 803–7; Rzymski, Nowicki, Mullin et al., "Quantity Does Not Equal Quality," 106711.
[119] De Campos-Rudinsky and Undurraga, "Public Health Decisions in the COVID-19 Pandemic Require More than 'Follow the Science,'" pp. 296–99.
[120] Fetzer, Witte, and Hensel, "Global Behaviors and Perceptions at the Onset of the COVID-19 Pandemic," 27082; Scheirer, "A Pandemic of Bad Science," pp. 175–84; Islam, Sarkar, and Khan, "COVID-19-Related Infodemic and Its Impact on Public Health," pp. 1621–29.
[121] De Campos-Rudinsky and Undurraga, "Public Health Decisions in the COVID-19 Pandemic Require More than 'Follow the Science,'" pp. 296–99.

Health policies always involve multiple levels of risks, layers of complexity, and difficult trade-offs among competing policy goals, relative utilities, objective values, and principled reasons. Policy-makers have to make ethical decisions on how various policy components relate to the common good—that is, to the good of each and every member of the community, whose lives are all equally worthy. This is rarely a straightforward, pragmatic process of weighing easily quantifiable components against each other.[122] Objective values and principled reasons, which are policy components, are not easily quantifiable. The most worthwhile things in life are not easily calculable: health, work, education, leisure, family, friendships are all irreducibly basic human goods. That is to say, they are all equally fundamental for the good life of each person and the common good of all. Therefore, they cannot be reduced as mere means to any of the others; nor can they be easily measured against or trump the others. In Chapter 5, I refer to the language of moral values, principled reasons, and basic human goods as "the language of incommensurability," typically spoken by ethicists, theorists, and those who have firsthand experience with these irreducible values.

A long-standing policy issue is reconciling empirical evidence (the language of commensurability) with ethical reasoning (the language of incommensurability). Good leaders recognize that each language is insufficient on its own. They understand that (i) empirical facts alone are inadequate to address ethical questions thoroughly, and (ii) moral principles applied to scarce data do not yield straightforward answers. By appreciating this complementarity, good global public health leaders can guide those under their stewardship toward better decision-making.

Communicating this message of complementarity is challenging. It requires policy-makers to display a certain degree of vulnerability and self-sacrifice. For example, they must explain with reasonably vulnerable honesty that urgent policy decisions—despite their urgency—cannot be rushed because they depend on a careful integration of both empirical evidence and ethical reasoning. Hence, they may risk harsh criticism from empirical scientists, who may favor quantitative data, as well as from the lay public, who might view such caution as slow or inefficient. Although both empirical scientists and the lay public should receive information with an empathetic disposition to truly listen, this has not been the reality experienced by policy-makers when they communicate.

While my stewardship model emphasizes the centrality of responsive accountability—truthful communication paired with timely responses—it also insists on discretion in conveying the inherent difficulties of such decision-making. Communicating this message entails a reasonable degree of self-sacrifice in that policy-makers would need to choose to be vulnerably exposed to

---

[122] Ibid.

such potential criticisms. However, it is precisely this vulnerability that holds the potential to rebuild public trust in global and public health authorities; policy-makers serve as translators bridging the gap between the language of commensurability (spoken by the scientific community) and that of incommensurability (spoken by civil society and NGOs).

The model further requires a similar degree of self-sacrifice and vulnerability from both the scientific community and the lay public in their dialogues with public health policy-makers. From scientists, it demands (i) a reasonably vulnerable and reasonably transparent disclosure of the limitations of their knowledge and the uncertainties in their conclusions, and (ii) a willingness to be questioned and corrected—a core aspect of responsive accountability. In return, the lay public is expected to demonstrate (i) patience with authorities when meaningful inclusiveness and accountability fall short, (ii) a willingness to give the benefit of the doubt to those striving for the common good, and (iii) active participation in ensuring that policy-makers address those incommensurable aspects of life that may otherwise be overlooked.

Here, we see how the idea of expertise complementarity introduced above would play out, in particular in a public health emergency of international concern, but also in contexts of normalcy when the stakes are not as high. The shared decision-making authority that expertise complementarity promotes can help rebuild mutual trust by inviting democratic scrutiny of the statements of all of the stakeholders involved. Furthermore, the horizontal dynamic established by these processes may facilitate a cooperative endeavor where all parties move through three stages of good communication with loving attention, reasonable vulnerability, and empathetic listening to clarify, accurately assess, and construct together an understanding of the issue, building up a community and a sense of communion in friendship and solidarity.

Conclusion

Chapter 6 tackles the question of what agape requires of global and public health authorities when they communicate policy decisions. More precisely, what does agape as a shared journey of presence require of leaders when they communicate public health measures? To answer this question, I have presented my stewardship model for good communication, premised on what agapic love calls for, and discussed how the application of my model could change GHG and leadership for the better.

While love does not necessitate that leaders be infallible experts, I argue that it requires humility of them—to communicate their strengths and vulnerabilities with honesty tempered by discretion. This communication of truth with love will engender enhanced trust and social cohesion (themes introduced in Chapter 1), and therefore greater communion within community (themes introduced in Chapters 4 and 5, respectively). So, love allows—and in some cases even requires—a reasonable degree of disclosed vulnerability regarding the leader's limitations in knowledge. Applying my stewardship model of good communication for expert authorities to the reality of GHG demonstrates the need for health leaders—at the international, national, and local levels alike—to focus on ensuring truthful, evidence-based, consistent, and timely shared communications regarding public health emergencies of international concern among global health stakeholders (including, e.g., WHO member states, international organizations, local medical associations, health research institutions, and local hospitals). This is key if global public health authorities desire to be good leaders, whose expertise the international community respects and whose guidance people trust. This is the leadership lesson of stewardship, which I identified as the third practical principle of agapic love.

The theme of truthful, evidence-based, consistent, and timely shared communications regarding public health emergencies of international concern was introduced in Chapter 4 and further discussed in Chapter 5, as the core purpose of the WHO (the chief coordination authority for GHG). Chapter 6 has gone on to show how the principle of stewardship further operationalizes the principle of subsidiarity (Chapter 5) and therefore the principle of solidarity (Chapter 4), paving the way for understanding how these principles together provide a tripartite framework for a governance in global health that is infused with love.

Concluding Remarks—On Agape and Governance

If you want to go quickly, go alone. If you want to go far, go together.
~ African proverb

Through a shared journey of presence, agape fosters unity in global health institutions. Unity is essential for life in community and must serve as a measure of success in the design of institutions. However, the unity that a shared journey of presence seeks is not the rigid "unity of the atom." It is not a unity of sameness but rather, as theologian Joseph Ratzinger describes, a "multi-unity that grows in love"[1]—a unity that celebrates diversity.

This Part II presented a Principled Tripartite Framework for GHG: an agapic vision for leaders, grounded in the conceptual exploration of agapic love offered in Chapters 1–3. Agapic love, defined as a shared journey of presence, fosters communion and community through communication. Part II explored this central question: *If the primary agapic mission for global health institutions is nurturing spaces of presence with those who suffer, what should GHG look like to reflect this mission as its chief measure of institutional success?*

The answer revealed an agapic vision of institutional success grounded in three practical principles of love—solidarity (Chapter 4), subsidiarity (Chapter 5), and stewardship (Chapter 6). Together, these principles address three complex and enduring challenges in global health: the scarcity of healthcare resources, the reform of GHG, and the erosion of trust in global and public health authorities. Each chapter also distilled a leadership lesson for GHG rooted in agapic love.

Chapter 4 analyzed the perennial issue of scarce healthcare resources and the need for equitable global allocation to contain public health emergencies. It introduced the principle of solidarity, understood in its complementarity with subsidiarity. Together, these principles show that agape allows—indeed, sometimes requires—a reasonable degree of partiality toward and prioritization

---

[1] "[t]he highest unity is not the unity of inflexible monotony. The model of unity or oneness toward which one should strive. Is consequently not the indivisibility of the atom, the smallest unity, which cannot be divided up any further; the authentic acme of unity is the unity created by love. The multi-unity that grows in love is a more radical, truer unity than the unity of the 'atom.'" Ratzinger, *Introduction to Christianity*, p. 179.

of certain individuals and communities. Prioritization is based on varying vulnerabilities, degrees of closeness, and distinct responsibilities of care. This agapic interpretation of solidarity debunks the myth that love requires caring for all equally or homogeneously. Instead, solidarity honors the unity of communion through respect for difference, diversity, and distinctness. This is the leadership lesson of solidarity: agape invites leaders to foster a shared journey of presence while accounting for specific needs and unique contexts.

Chapter 5 examined the recurring question of reforming GHG, with a specific focus on the WHO. It further discussed the second practical principle of love, subsidiarity, in its complementarity with stewardship. Together, these two principles reinforce agape's unwavering commitment to never abandon those in need. Yet, when one is "overcommitted and overextended"[2] like the WHO, these two principles require not only the humble recognition of our limitations as caregivers but also a reasonable delegation of responsibilities to those better positioned to provide care. The agapic interpretation of subsidiarity debunks the myth that love requires doing everything—and hence maintaining control over—all care. To love and care well is not about continually doing more, but about critically discerning what is best for the cared for—acknowledging their uniqueness and respecting their agency—while also recognizing and honoring one's own limitations. Without such critical judgment and humble setting of necessary boundaries, no community of generous, mutual care can be sustained. This, then, is the leadership lesson of subsidiarity.

Finally, Chapter 6 addressed the persistent problem of distrust in global and public health expert authorities, by exploring the third practical principle of love: stewardship. As introduced in Chapter 5, stewardship explains why agape—committed to freedom and respect for the other's agency—requires honest communication with a reasonable degree of vulnerability. Specifically, agape requires that global and public health expert authorities communicate the truth about public health threats while exercising discretion in revealing the limits of their knowledge. This agapic interpretation stewardship debunks the myth that love necessitates the naked truth at all costs, disregarding the need for prudence. Instead, agape grounds good communication in three basic ingredients: loving attention to discern what is audience-relevant, reasonably vulnerable honesty to attain accuracy, and empathetic listening to enable meaningful inclusion of the audience and to foster responsive accountability. These ingredients, together, establish shared authority in decision-making about the best course of action. Without them, genuine communion and strong community cannot endure. This is the leadership lesson of stewardship.

---

[2] WHO, *Draft Twelfth General Programme of Work*.

These three practical principles form my tripartite framework that apply across the macro, meso, and micro levels of GHG—spanning the global, local, and personal dimensions. In Chapter 4, I discuss the agapic principle of solidarity at the global level, illustrating how nations can embark on a shared journey of presence with neighboring countries in need, thereby fostering union and communion. Chapter 5 shifts the focus to the local level by examining the agapic principle of subsidiarity. Here, global health institutions—most notably the WHO and global health donors—are challenged to decentralize power and delegate decision-making authority to local communities. This delegation not only allows local actors to participate meaningfully in global health decision-making but also supports the co-deliberation and co-creation of a shared vision for life and a new governance structure, which are essential for a genuinely shared journey of presence. Finally, Chapter 6 emphasizes the personal dimension through the agapic principle of stewardship. This principle challenges expert global and public health leaders to communicate truthfully and vulnerably, thereby sharing their decision-making authority with those in their care. Good communication, rooted in stewardship, is the foundation upon which strong communities are built and communion is sustained.

This is the agapic vision for the future of GHG. This is what agape and a shared journey of presence require of global health institutions and their leaders. My principled tripartite framework provided the reasons for actions that leaders must take to create and sustainably nurture spaces of encounter and presence, where communities of mutual, multidirectional care can thrive.

Conclusion

> To be great, be whole: don't exaggerate
> Or exclude any part of you.
> Be all in each thing. Put all
> Into the smallest of your acts.
> So too in each lake,
> The whole moon
> Shines because it lives on high.
> Ricardo Reis (1933),
> In Fernando Pessoa, *Poesia*.
> (Translated freely by de Campos-Rudinsky)

The central argument of this book is that love—though often overlooked—must be at the heart of global affairs, for it holds the transformative power to reshape not only the way we engage with one another but also the very structures that govern global institutions. Love is not mere sentimentality; it is a way of reasoning and deliberation about the good of the other—offering my full presence as a gift of self to those who suffer. As Brazilian novelist Clarice Lispector puts it, the process of love unfolds in "attentively gazing at each other."[1] It is there, in "the profound silence of the encounter between two souls"[2] who communicate deeply with one another, that communion happens and community is sustained.

Two convictions guide *The Rule of Love*. First, love, properly understood, matters as much as justice in responding to suffering—if not more. Second, this kind of love—which I call agape—shapes a radically different approach to alleviating suffering, whether at the interpersonal level or through the institutional allocation of responsibilities of care. As a directive for both individual and institutional deliberations, agape grounds a universal yet deeply personal responsibility to care for and about[3] others in their unique needs. If embraced,

---

[1] In the essay *Ao Correr da Maquina*, Lispector writes: "How can we translate the profound silence of the encounter between two souls? It's very difficult to tell: we were attentively gazing at each other, and we stayed that way for a few moments. We were one being. These moments are my secret. There was what is called perfect communion. I call it: deep state of happiness." Lispector, "Ao Correr da Maquina," in Lispector, *A Descoberta do Mundo*.

[2] Ibid.

[3] On the distinction between care for and care about, see: Herring, *Law and the Relational Self*, p. 51; Tronto, *Moral Boundaries*, pp. 127–34.

this reasonably self-sacrificial love—at times silent, yet always "great" and always "whole," as Fernando Pessoa puts it—has the potential to transform how we approach both individual care and GHG.

The Rule of Love had three aims: to define the neglected moral value of love, to establish our shared responsibility to care for the vulnerable, and to challenge the way global health institutions address suffering that falls outside the bounds of justice. By complementing justice with love, this book sought to fill the gap in how we conceptualize and respond to medical suffering caused not only by injustices but also by misfortune or poor choices—conditions that may not easily qualify as unjust.

This work is inherently interdisciplinary, bringing philosophers, theologians, and novelists into conversation with medical anthropologists, organizational psychologists, physicians, nurses, epidemiologists, and global health scholars. This dialogue yielded, in Part I, a rich conceptual analysis of agape in its different expressions—merciful, compassionate, and beneficent love. In Part II, I applied this understanding normatively, culminating in a principled tripartite framework for GHG, built on the principles of solidarity, subsidiarity, and stewardship, explored in Chapters 4–6, respectively.

Through mercy, compassion, and beneficence—and guided by solidarity, subsidiarity, and stewardship—agape provides a holistic response to both individual suffering and the institutional structures that exacerbate it. Agape, as I have defined it, is both universal and personal. It is universal in that it extends to all: we belong to one another, and to belong is to co-create in community. But to say that agapic love is universal does not mean it is homogeneous. There are no one-size-fits-all agapic prescriptions, because agape is also deeply personal. Love must be crafted attentively—with care for the unique person before me, her needs, her wounds.

At the end of Part I, I offered a vision of the three types of agapic love. Caravaggio's *Seven Works of Mercy* (1607) illustrates the merciful, compassionate, and beneficent expressions of agapic presence, understood as a gift of self, and embodying both its active and contemplative dimensions. Now, if you were to ask me for a vision of how agapic love guides actions through its three practical principles, I would point you to *Gran Silencio [Great Silence]* (2008), a sculpture by Chilean artist Mario Irarrázabal. I encountered Don Mario and his work in April 2024, as I was contemplating how to conclude this book. *Gran Silencio*'s evocative portrayal of human figures gathered around an empty well speaks to the principles of solidarity, subsidiarity, and stewardship. It reminds us that love is, ultimately, a journey of shared presence—in which I give myself, through my presence, to accompany you in your suffering.

I interpret the empty well as the immense emptiness that one feels when suffering. There is a hole when one grieves, and to expose this hole is a vulnerable act—sharing an intimate, wounded part of oneself. Yet, this giving of self is also an invitation for others to come closer, to encounter the sufferer at their empty well. In *Gran Silencio,* we see clusters of people who have accepted that invitation. They draw near, honoring the sufferer's gift of vulnerability. And between the clusters, there are spaces. To me, these spaces signify the open invitation for others—for you and me—to join in solidarity and express our shared involvement in the human condition of need.[4]

Those who accepted this invitation do so with great reverence. *Gran Silencio* conveys a moral gravitas –a quiet, respectful attention. Here, I see the agapic principle of subsidiarity at play: the figures do not overstep the boundaries of the well. They seem to respect the agency and the wound of the sufferer. Their silent presence is not overpowering, but gentle, kind, patient; they behold humbly and reverently the sufferer in his uniqueness. Those who receive the sufferer's gift of self also give themselves—wholly and silently—in return. This is, for me, a portrait of agape: the mutual gift of self through a shared, full, deep, respectful, silent presence.

Those who join the sufferer "put all they are," as Pessoa says, into being wholly present. They offer undivided attention, without rushing to heroically fix the problem. They do not try to anxiously fill the hole with empty words of false hope to the sufferer. This would only invalidate the pain, leading to loneliness and despair—as discussed in the Introduction to Chapter 6. Instead, by truthfully communicating their presence through silent loving attention—without deception, and with a reasonable degree of vulnerability, those gathered around the well enact the agapic vision of stewardship. They show up through their solidarity, subsidiarity, and stewardship, and build communion in community through their quiet yet attentive presence.

Agape, the measure by which we should judge ourselves and our institutions is this: to show up and be present, communicating—perhaps without words—that the sufferer is not alone, and that he is seen in his pain. There may be no solution for the suffering, no cure for the illness, no way to fill the well. But agapic solidarity, subsidiarity, and stewardship communicate my presence to the sufferer, assuring him that he has not been abandoned.

Throughout this book, I have sought to show how our relations—whether personal or institutional—should be guided by the moral value of love. I have set out to reclaim the moral authority of love, ultimately suggesting that love is the basis of all ethics—including the ethics that guides global affairs. This is the broader implication of the typology of love and the principled tripartite framework *The Rule of Love* offers: a work in progress, shaped by the particularities of medical suffering, but with implications far beyond the domain of health.

---

[4] See: Botturi, "The Trial of Desire."

Having reclaimed the moral force of love, I hope the book leaves you with this message: love has a stronger moral weight than you might have assumed.

The Rule of Love, in its expressions of mercy, compassion, and beneficence, and in its calls to solidarity, subsidiarity, and stewardship, is ultimately concerned with who we are coming to be through the choices we make in caring for one another. What kind of people are we becoming? What kind of community are we building?

The power of love is the power of presence—whole and shared. We should not suffer alone, and we should not accompany the sufferer alone. As *Gran Silencio* shows, consistently showing up and being present matter. In this journey of shared presence—in which I give myself—my whole self, in accompanying you through your suffering—I grow in love and in humanity, while helping to form a community of mutual care. This is who we are becoming, and the kind of community we are building, when we place agape at the center of our moral reasoning and deliberations. We fill each other's emptiness with the gift of our presence—shared, full, deep, respectful, silent. In this quiet communion, we become more fully human.

This is agape: it makes us human and our institutions humane.

Bibliography

Abimbola, Seye. "The Uses of Knowledge in Global Health." *BMJ Global Health* 6 (2021): e005802. http://dx.doi.org/10.1136/bmjgh-2021-005802.

Abimbola, Seye and Madhukar Pai. "Will Global Health Survive its Decolonization?" *The Lancet* 396, no. 10263 (2021): pp. 1627–28.

Addiss, David G. and Joseph J. Amon. "Apology and Unintended Harm in Global Health." *Health and Human Rights* 10, no. 1 (June 2019): pp. 19–32.

Affun-Adegbulu, C. and O. Adegbulu. "Decolonising Global (Public) Health: From Western Universalism to Global Pluriversalities." *BMJ Global Health* 5 (2020): e002947.

Agreement on Trade-Related Aspects of Intellectual Property Rights (TRIPs), Marrakesh, April 15, 1994, Arts. 30 and 31.

Ahlstrom-Vij, K. *Epistemic Paternalism: A Defense* (London: Palgrave Macmillan, 2013).

Ahmad, Ayesha, Ryoa Chung, Lisa Eckenwiller et al. "What Does It Mean to be Made Vulnerable in the Era of COVID-19?" *The Lancet* 395, no. 10235 (May 2020): p. 1482.

Allo, Awol Kassim. *Law and Resistance: Towards a Performative Epistemology of Law*. PhD thesis (University of Glasgow, 2013), Ch. 3.

Anderson, Carl and Jose Granados. *Called to Love: Approaching John Paul II's Theology of the Body* (New York: Doubleday, 2009).

Anderson, Elizabeth. "Democracy, Public Policy, and Lay Assessments of Scientific Testimony." *Episteme* 8, no. 2 (2011): pp. 144–64.

Anderson, Elizabeth. "Epistemic Justice as a Virtue of Social Institutions." *Social Epistemology* 26, no. 2 (2012): pp. 163–73.

Andolsen, Barbara Hilkert. "Agape in Feminist Ethics." *The Journal of Religious Ethics* 9, no. 1 (1981): pp. 69–83.

Aquinas, Thomas. *Summa Theologica* i-ii, ii-ii (London: Burns Oates & Washbourne, 1912).

Arendt, Hannah. *On Revolution* (London: Faber, 1963).

Arguedas-Ramírez, Gabriela. "Build That Wall! Vaccine Certificates, Passes and Passports, the Distribution of Harms and Decolonial Global Health Justice." *Journal of Global Ethics* 17, no. 3 (2021): pp. 375–87.

Arguedas, Gabriela. "Te Hundo para Luego Tratar de Salvarte." *Revista Paquidermo*, September 7, 2015. https://www.uned.ac.cr/docencia/images/ceced/docs/Te_hundo_para_luego_tratar_de_salvarte.pdf.

Atuire, Caesar Alimsinya. "A Decolonial Framework for Thinking about Sustainable AI: High Level Considerations," *Sustainable AI Conference 2023: Sustainable AI Across Borders*, Institute for Science and Ethics, IWE, Boon, June 21, 2023. Available at: https://www.youtube.com/watch?v=X34QXiALUyw (at 21:15).

Atuire, Caesar Alimsinya. "Some Barriers to Knowledge from the Global South: commentary to Pratt and de Vries." *Journal of Medical Ethics* 49, no. 5 (2023): pp. 335–336.

Atuire, Cesar Alimsinya, Camilla Kong, and Michael Dunn. "Articulating the Sources for an African Normative Framework of Healthcare: Ghana as a Case Study." *Development World Bioethics* 20, Suppl. 4 (2020): pp. 216–27. doi: 10.1111/dewb.12265.

Atuire, Caesar Alimsinya, Lisa Eckenwiler, and Nicole Hassoun. "Just Allocation of COVID-19 Vaccines." *BMJ Global Health* 6 (2021): e004812.

Atuire, Cesar Alimsinya and Nicole Hassoun. "Rethinking Solidarity Towards Equity in Global Health: African Views." *International Journal of Equity Health* 22, no. 1 (March 24, 2023): p. 52. doi: 10.1186/s12939-023-01830-9.

Atuire, Cesar Alimsinya and Olivia U. Rutazibwa. "An African Reading of the COVID-19 Pandemic and the Stakes of Decolonization," July 29, 2021. https://law.yale.edu/yls-today/news/african-reading-covid-19-pandemic-and-stakes-decolonization.
Augustine. *On Christian Teaching*. Trans. R. P. H. Green (Oxford: OUP, 1997), I.28.29. Cited by Eric Gregory, *Politics and Order of Love: An Augustinian Ethic of Democratic Citizenship* (Chicago: University of Chicago Press, 2008), p. 294.
Baha'i prophet. Bahá'u'lláh. "Tablet to Napoleon III." In *The Summons of the Lord of Hosts* (Haifa: Bahá'í World Centre, 2002), pp. 46–56.
Baldwin, Tom, Roger Brownsword, and Harald Schimdt. "Stewardship, Paternalism and Public Health: Further Thoughts." *Public Health Ethics* 2, no. 1 (2009): pp. 113–16.
Bandeira, Manuel. "Pneumothorax." *AllPoetry*, n.d. Accessed November 16, 2025. https://allpoetry.com/Pneumothorax.
Barbazza, E. and J. E. Tello. "A Review of Health Governance: Definitions, Dimensions and Tools to Govern." *Health Policy* 116, no. 1 (2014): pp. 1–11. doi: org/10.1016/j.healthpol.2014.01.007.
Barber, Nicholas and Richard Eckins. "Situating Subsidiarity." *American Journal of Jurisprudence* 61, no. 5 (2016): pp. 5–12.
Barber, Nicholas. *Principles of Constitutionalism* (Oxford: Oxford University Press, 2018).
Barsade, Sigal G. and Olivia A. O'Neill. "What's Love Got to Do with It? A Longitudinal Study of the Culture of Companionate Love and Employee and Client Outcomes in Long-Term Care Setting." *Administrative Science Quarterly* 59, no. 4 (2014): pp. 551–98.
Bauman, Zygmunt. *Postmodern Ethics* (Oxford: Blackwell, 1993).
Baviera, Tomas, William English, and Manuel Guillen. "The 'Logic of Gift': Inspiring Behaviour in Organizations Beyond the Limits of Duty and Exchange." *Business Ethics Quarterly* 26, no. 2 (April 2016): pp. 159–80.
Bazelon, Emily. "People Are Dying. Whom Do We Save First with the Vaccine?" *New York Times Magazine*, December 24, 2020. Accessed May 21, 2021. https://www.nytimes.com/2020/12/24/magazine/who-should-get-the-covid-vaccine-next.html.
Beauchamp, T. L. and J. F. Childress. *Principles of Biomedical Ethics* (Oxford: Oxford University Press, 2001).
Benner, Patricia. *From Novice to Expert* (Menlo Park: Addison-Wesley, 1984).
Berlinger, Nancy. *After Harm: Medical Error and the Ethics of Forgiveness* (Baltimore: Johns Hopkins University Press, 2005).
Besson, Emilie S. Koum. "How to Identify Epistemic Injustice in Global Health Research Funding Practices: A Decolonial Guide." *BMJ Global Health* 7, no. 4 (2022): e008950.
Besson, Samantha. "Subsidiarity in International Human Rights Law—What Is Subsidiary about Human Rights?" *American Journal of Jurisprudence* 61, no. 1 (2016): p. 69.
Bhakuni, Himani and Seye Abimbola. "Epistemic Injustice in Academic Global Health." *The Lancet Global Health* 9 (2021): e1465–70.
Biehl, Andres and Patricio Velasco (eds.). *Pedro Morande: Textos Sociologicos Escogidos* (Santiago: Ediciones UC, 2017).
Biehl, João and Adriana Petryna. "A Critical Global Health." In João Biehl and Adriana Petryna (eds.), *When People Come First: Critical Studies in Global Health* (Princeton: Princeton University Press, 2012).
Biehl, João. "Theorizing Global Health." *Medicine and Anthropology Theory* 3, no. 2 (2003): pp. 127–42.
Block, Jennie Weiss OP, M. Therese Lysaught, and Alexandre A. Martins. "A Prophet to the Peoples: Paul Farmer's Witness and Theological Ethics (Complete Book)." *Journal of Moral Theology* 4 (CTEWC Book Series 4): i–373, Part 3, Ch. 9–11 (2023).
Blumental-Barby, J. "Can Health Care Providers Love Their Patients?" *Bioethics.net* (blog), January 18, 2016. Accessed February 6, 2024. https://bioethicstoday.org/blog/can-health-care-providers-love-their-patients-2/.

Boeck, Patty R. "Presence: A Concept Analysis." *Sage Open* 4, no. 1 (2014). https://doi.org/10.1177/2158244014527990.
Bok, Sissela. *Lying: Moral Choice in Public and Private Life* (Hassocks: The Harvester Press, 1978).
Botturi, Francesco. "The Trial of Desire." In *Traces*, April 2024.
Bow, S. M. A., P. Schöder-Bäck, D. Norcliffe-Brown, J. Wilson, and F. Tahzib. "Telling Them "that's what it says in the guidance" Didn't Feel Good Enough": Moral Distress During the Pandemic in UK Public Health Professionals." *Journal of Public Health* 46, no. 1 (2024): pp. 194–201.
Bow, S. M. A., P. Schöder-Bäck, D. Norcliffe-Brown, J. Wilson, and F. Tahzib. "Moral Distress and Injury in the Public Health Professional Workforce During the COVID-19 Pandemic." *Journal of Public Health* 45, no. 3 (2023): pp. 697–705.
Bramstedt, K. A. "The Carnage of Substandard Research During the COVID-19 Pandemic: A Call for Quality." *Journal of Medical Ethics* 46, no. 12 (2020): pp. 803–7.
Brandt, A. M. "How AIDS Invented Global Health." *New England Journal of Medicine* 368 (2013): pp. 2149–52.
Brandt, Allan M. "How AIDS Invented Global Health." *New England Journal of Medicine* 368, no. 23 (June 6, 2013): pp. 2149–52. doi: 10.1056/NEJMp1305297.
Breithaupt, Fritz. *The Dark Sides of Empathy* (Ithaca: Cornell University Press, 2019).
Brinkerhoff, Derick W., Harry E. Cross, Sanjeev Sharma, and Tim Williamson. "Stewardship and Health Systems Strengthening: An Overview." *Public Administration and Development* 39 (2019): pp. 4–10.
Brito-Pons, Gonzalo and Silvia Librada-Flores. "Compassion in Palliative Care: A Review." *Current Opinion in Supportive and Palliative Care* 12 (2018): pp. 472–79.
Brooks, S., T. Chalder, and C. Gerada. "Doctors Vulnerable to Psychological Distress and Addictions: Treatment from the Practitioner Health Programme." *Journal of Mental Health* 20 (2011): pp. 157–64.
Brown, Rebecca C. H. and Micheal de Barra. "A Taxonomy of Non-honesty in Public Health Communication." *Public Health Ethics* 16, no. 1 (2023): pp. 86–101.
Brown, S. "Compassion and Efficiency Not Mutually Exclusive in Healthcare." *CMAJ: Canadian Medical Association Journal* 191, no. 27 (2019): E775–76. doi: 10.1503/cmaj.109-5773.
Buchanan, Allen. "Preparing for the Next Pandemic." *Social Philosophy and Policy* 40, no. 2 (2023): pp. 283–305. doi: 10.1017/S0265052524000074.
Bulger, Roger J. "The Quest for Mercy: The Forgotten Ingredient in Health Care Reform." *West Journal of Medicine* 167 (1997): pp. 362–73.
Bull, Malcolm. *On Mercy* (Princeton: Princeton University Press, 2019).
Burci, Gian Luca. "The Outbreak of COVID-19 Coronavirus: Are the International Health Regulations Fit for Purpose?" *EJIL: TALK!* (February 27, 2020). www.ejiltalk.org/the-outbreak-of-covid-19-coronavirus-are-the-international-health-regulations-fit-for-purpose/.
Butler, Judith. "Performative Acts and Gender Constitutions: An Essay in Phenomenology and Feminist Theory." *Theater Journal* 50, no. 5 (December 1988): pp. 519–31.
Byanyima, Winnie, Karl Lauterbach, and Margaret M. Kavanagh. "Community Pandemic Response: The Importance of Action Led by Communities and the Public Sector." *The Lancet* 40, no. 10373 (January 28, 2023): pp. 253–55.
Cahill, Maria. "Theorizing Subsidiarity: Towards an Ontology—Sensitive Approach." *International Journal of Constitutional Law* 15 (2017): pp. 201–13.
Caldwell, Cam and Sylvia Atwijuka. "'I See You!'—The Zulu Insight to Caring Leadership." *Journal of Values-Based Leadership* 11, no. 1 (2018): Art. 13.
Camosy, Charles C. *Peter Singer and Christian Ethics: Beyond Polarization* (Cambridge: Cambridge University Press, 2012).
Campagna, Giordana. "The Miracle of Mercy." *Oxford Journal of Legal Studies* 41, no. 4 (2021): pp. 1096–1118.

Campbell, Fiona Kumari. *Contours of Ableism: The Production of Disability and Abledness* (New York: Palgrave Macmillan, 2009).
Carney, P. "The UK Government's COVID-19 Policy: What Does 'Guided by the Science' Mean in Practice?" *Frontiers of Political Science* 3 (2021): 624068.
Carozza, Paolo G. "Subsidiarity as a Structural Principle of International Human Rights Law." *American Journal of International Law* 97 (2003): pp. 38–78.
Carozza, Paolo G. and Luigi Crema. "On Solidarity in International Law." Caritas in Veritate Foundation, 2014, p. 8.
Carozza, Paolo G. "The Problematic Applicability of Subsidiarity to International Law and Institutions." *American Journal of Jurisprudence* 61 (2016): p. 51.
Caston, Ruth R. and Robert A. Kaster (eds.). *Hope, Joy, and Affection in the Classical World* (Oxford: Oxford University Press, 2016).
Catechism of the Catholic Church, 2nd ed. (Vatican City: Libreria Editrice Vaticana, 1997), §2447.
Center for Compassion and Global Health. "The Value of Apology: Communication, Restitution, and Relationship; A Conversation with Chris King." July 7, 2017. http://ccagh.org/conversations/personal-stories/chris-king/.
Chaplin, Jonathan. "Subsidiarity: The Concept and the Connections." *Ethical Perspective* 4 (1997): pp. 117–30.
Chung, Ryoa. "Structural Health Vulnerability: Health Inequalities, Structural and Epistemic Injustice." *Journal of Social Philosophy* 52 (2021): pp. 201–16.
Cicero. *Tusculan Disputations*. J. E. King, tr. (Cambridge: Harvard University Press, 1927).
Clinton, Chelsea and Sridhar, Devi. *Governing Global Health: Who Runs the World and Why* (Oxford: Oxford University Press, 2017).
Cochran Jr., Robert F. "Jesus, Agape, and Law." In Robert F. Cochran Jr. and Zachary R. Calo (eds.), *Agape, Justice, and the Law: How might the Christian Love Shape the Law?* (Cambridge: Cambridge University Press, 2017), pp. 13–37.
Coggon, John. *The Nanny State Debate: A Place Where Words Don't Do Justice*. Faculty of Public Health. 2018. https://www.fph.org.uk/media/1972/fph-nannystatedebate-report-final.pdf.
Coggon, John and Tahzib, Farhang. "The Science of Social Justice: Assuring the Conditions for Ethics and Equity at the Heart of Public Health." *Journal of Public Health* 43, no. 4 (2021): e629–31.
Coggon, John. "What Helps Us a Steward? Stewardship, Political Theory, and Public Health Law and Ethics." *Northern Ireland Legal Quarterly* 62, no. 4 (2011): pp. 599–616.
Collins, Stephanie. *The Core of Care Ethics* (New York: Palgrave Macmillan, 2015).
Compassion Integrity Training (CIT). "About the Program." https://www.compassionaintegrity.org/about-the-program/.
Confucius. *The Analects*.
Coplan, Amy. "Understanding Empathy: Its Features and Effects." In A. Coplan and P. Goldie (eds.), *Empathy: Philosophical and Psychological Perspectives* (Oxford: Oxford University Press, 2011), pp. 2–18.
Cordelli, Chiara. "Prospective Duties and the Demands of Beneficence." *Ethics* 128 (2018): pp. 373–401.
Cousiño, Carlos and Eduardo Valenzuela. *Politización y Monetarización en América Latina* (Santiago: Instituto de Estudios de la Sociedad, 2012).
Criss, Doug and Leah Asmelash. "The Problem with Always Asking Black People to Forgive," October 4, 2019, *CNN*, https://edition.cnn.com/2019/10/03/us/black-americans-forgiveness-trnd/index.html.
Cushing, P. and T. Lewis. "Negotiating Mutuality and Agency in Care-Giving Relationships with Women with Intellectual Disabilities." *Hypatia* 17 (2002): p. 173.
da Silva, M. "Subsidiarity and the Allocation of Governmental Powers." *The Canadian Journal of Law and Jurisprudence* 36, no. 1 (November 8, 2022): pp. 83–111. doi: 10.1017/cjlj.2022.26.

Dalai Lama XIV and Thubten Chodron. *Buddhism: One Teacher, Many Traditions* (Somerville: Wisdom Publications, 2014).
Dalai Lama. "Dialogues." In *Visions of Compassion: Western Scientists and Tibetan Buddhists Examine Human Nature*, edited by R. J. Davidson and A. Harrington (New York: Oxford University Press, 2002), p. 225.
Dalberg. *ACT-Accelerator Strategic Review*. World Health Organization, 2021. www.who.int/publications/m/item/act-accelerator-strategic-review.
Dante. *Inferno*, Canto 34.
Darwall, Stephen. "Empathy, Sympathy, Care." *Philosophical Studies: An International Journal for Philosophy in the Analytic Tradition* 89, no. 2/3 (1998): pp. 261–82.
Darwall, Stephen. *Welfare and Rational Care* (Princeton: Princeton University Press, 2002), p. 15.
Darwall, Stephen. "Reply to Griffin, Raz, and Wolff." *Utilitas* 18 (2006): pp. 441–42.
Darwall, Stephen. "Being With." *The Southern Journal of Philosophy* 49 (2011): pp. 4–24.
Darwall, Stephen. "Being With." *The Southern Journal of Philosophy* 49 (2011): pp. 4–24.
Darwall, Stephen. *Morality, Authority, and Law: Essays in Second-Personal Ethics I* (Oxford: OUP, 2013).
Darwall, Stephen. "Love's Second Personal Character: Reciprocal Holding, Beholding, and Upholding." In E. E. Kroeker and K. Schauroech (eds.), *Love, Reason, and Morality* (New York: Routledge, 2018), pp. 93–109.
Daugirdas, Kristina and Gian Luca Burci. "Financing the World Health Organization: What Lessons for Multilateralism?" *International Organizations Law Review* 16 (2019): pp. 299–338.
Davidson, Kief and Pedro Kos, *Bending the Arc*, Documentary, 2017. https://bendingthearcfilm.com/.
Davies, Ben and Julian Savulescu. "Solidarity and Responsibility in Health Care." *Public Health Ethics* 12 (2019): pp. 133–44.
Dawson, Angus and Marcel Verweij. "The Steward of the Millian State." *Public Health Ethics* 1, no. 3 (2008): pp. 193–95.
Dawson, Angus and Marcel Verweij. "Solidarity: A Moral Concept in Need of Clarification." *Public Health Ethics* 5 (2012): pp. 1–5.
de Campos, Thana C. *The Global Health Crisis: Ethical Responsibilities* (Cambridge: Cambridge University Press, 2017).
de Campos, Thana C. "Guiding Principles of Global Health Governance in Times of Pandemics: Solidarity, Subsidiarity, and Stewardship." *American Journal of Bioethics* 20, no. 7 (2020): pp. 212–14.
de Campos, Thana C. "A European Take on Global Public Health: Applying the Catholic Principle of Subsidiarity to Global Health Governance." *Journal of Moral Theology* 1 (CTEWC Book Series 1) (2021): pp. 141–51.
de Campos-Rudinsky, Thana C. "Intellectual Property and Essential Medicines in the COVID-19 Pandemic." *International Affairs* 97, no. 2 (2021): pp. 523–37.
de Campos-Rudinsky, Thana C. "Solidarity and Global Allocation of COVID-19 Vaccines: A Question of Equality?" In Tom Angier, Iain T. Benson, and Mark D. Retter (eds.), *The Cambridge Handbook on Natural Law and Human Rights* (Cambridge: Cambridge University Press, 2022), pp. 465–82.
de Campos-Rudinsky, Thana C. "Flourishing Through Suffering: The Limits of Sentience and the Ethics of Communal Meaning-Making." In *Cambridge Quarterly of Healthcare Ethics* (forthcoming).
de Campos-Rudinsky, Thana C. and Mariana Canales. "Global Health Governance and The Principle of Subsidiarity: In Defense of a Robust Decentralization Approach." *International Journal of Constitutional Law* 20, no. 1 (2022): pp. 177–203.

de Campos-Rudinsky, Thana C. and E. Undurraga. "Public Health Decisions in the COVID-19 Pandemic Require More Than 'Follow the Science.'" *Journal of Medical Ethics* 47 (2021): pp. 296–9.

de Campos-Rudinsky, Thana C., Sarah L. Bosha, Daniel Wainstock et al. "Decolonising Global Health: Why the New Pandemic Agreement Should Have Included the Principle of Subsidiarity." *The Lancet Global Health*, 12, no. 7 (2024): e1200–3. doi: 10.1016/S2214-109X(24)00186-4.

de Zulueta, P. C. "Developing Compassionate Leadership in Health Care: An Integrative Review." *Journal of Healthcare Leadership* 8, no. 1 (2016): pp. 1–10.

Debeulin, Severine and Clemens Sedmak (eds.). *Integral Human Development—Catholic Social Teaching and the Capability Approach* (Notra Dame: Notre Dame Press, 2023).

Decety, Jean (ed.) *Empathy: From Bench to Bedside* (Cambridge: MIT Press, 2011).

Derrida, Jacques. *Donner le temps: 1—La fausse monnaie* (Paris: Galilee, 1991).

Dewar, Belinda, Elizabeth Adamson, Stephen Smith, Joyce Surfleet, and Linda King. "Clarifying Misconceptions about Compassionate Care." *Journal of Advanced Nursing* 70, no. 8 (2015): pp. 1738–47.

Director, Samuel. "Public Health Officials Should Almost Always Tell the Truth." *Journal of Applied Ethics* 40, no. 5 (2023): pp. 951–66.

Dodds, Michael. *Thomas Aquinas, Human Suffering, and the Unchanging God of Love* (Oxford: Oxford University Press, 2008).

Dodsworth, Laura. *A State of Fear: How the UK Government Weaponized Fear During the COVID-19 Pandemic* (London: Pinter & Martin Ltd., 2021).

Domingo-Osle, Monica and Rafael Domingo. "Redefining Nursing Solidarity." *Nursing Ethics* 29 (2022): pp. 651–59.

Dostoyevsky, Fyodor. *The Brothers Karamazov*, Richard Pevear and Larissa Volokhonsky (trans.) (New York: Farrar, Straus and Giroux, 1990).

Douglas, Benedict. "Love and Human Rights." *Oxford Journal of Legal Studies* 43, no. 2 (Summer 2023): pp. 273–97.

Dugdale, L. "Dying, a Lost Art." In L. Dugdale (ed.), *Dying in the Twenty-First Century: Toward a New Ethical Framework for the Art of Dying Well* (Cambridge: MIT Press, 2015), pp. 3–18.

Dugdale, Lydia. "Patient as Gift." *Hastings Center Report—In Practice* (July–August 2019): pp. 4–5.

Duxbury, Neil. "Golden Rule Reasoning, Moral Judgment, and Law." *Notre Dame L. Rev.* 84 (2009): pp. 1529–1605.

Dworkin, Gerald. "Paternalism." In Edward N. Zalta (ed.), The Stanford Encyclopedia of Philosophy (Fall 2020). https://plato.stanford.edu/archives/fall2020/entries/paternalism/.

Dworkin, Ronald. *Justice for Hedgehogs* (Cambridge: Harvard University Press, 2011).

Dworkin, Ronald. *Sovereign Virtue: The Theory and Practice of Equality* (Cambridge: Harvard University Press, 2000).

Dworkin, Ronald. *Taking Rights Seriously* (Cambridge: Harvard University Press, 1977).

Ebels-Duggan, Kyla. "Against Beneficence: A Normative Account of Love." *Ethics* 119 (2008): p. 142.

Eccleston-Turner, M. "COVID-19 Symposium: The Declaration of a Public Health Emergency of International Concern in International Law." *Opinio Juris* (2020). Available at: http://opiniojuris.org/2020/03/31/covid-19-symposium-the-declaration-of-a-public-health-emergency-of-international-concern-in-international-law/.

Eckenwiler, Lisa, Christine Straehle, and Ryoa Chung. "Global Solidarity, Migration and Global Health Inequity." *Bioethics* 26 (2012): pp. 382–90.

Ekeocha, Obianuju. *Target Africa: Ideological Neocolonialism in the Twenty-First Century* (San Francisco: Ignatius Press, 2018).

Eliot, T. S. *The Elder Statesman* (London: Faber and Faber, 1959).

Emanuel, Ezekiel J. et al. "Ethical Framework for Global Vaccine Allocation." *Science* 369, no. 6509 (2020): pp. 1309–12.

Emanuel, Ezekiel J., Allen Buchanan, Shuk Ying Chan et al. "On the Ethics of Vaccine Nationalism: The Case for the Fair Priority for Residents Framework." *Ethics and International Affairs* 35, no. 4 (2021): pp. 543–62.

Emanuel, Ezekiel J., Govind Persad, Adam Kern et al. "On the Ethics of Vaccine Nationalism." *Science* 369, no. 6511 (2020): pp. 1035–36.

Emilie Koum, Besson. "Confronting Whiteness and Decolonizing Global Health Institutions." *The Lancet* 397, no. 10929 (June 19, 2021): pp. 2328–29.

Emmons, Robert. "Pay It Forward." In *Greater Good Magazine: Science-Based Insights for a Meaningful Life*, June 1, 2007. https://greatergood.berkeley.edu/article/item/pay_it_forward.

Engster, D. *The Heart of Justice: Care Ethics and Political Theory* (Oxford: Oxford University Press, 2007).

Enright, Robert D. *Forgiveness is a Choice: A Step-by-Step Process for Resolving Anger and Restoring Hope* (Washington, DC: American Psychological Association, 2001).

Enright, Robert D. and Richard P. Fitzgibbons. *Helping Clients Forgive: An Empirical Guide for Resolving Anger and Restoring Hope* (Washington, DC: American Psychological Association, 2000).

Evans, C. Stephen and Brandon Rickabaugh. "Living Accountability: Accountability as a Virtue." *International Philosophical Quarterly* 62, no. 1 (2022): pp. 45–64.

Evans, Michelle and Augusto Zimmermann. "The Global Relevance of Subsidiarity: An Overview." In Michelle Evans and Augusto Zimmermann (eds.), *Global Perspective on Subsidiarity* 1, 2 (Newcastle upon Tyne: Cambridge Scholars Publishing, 2014), pp. 1–7.

Fabre, Cecile. *Whose Body Is It Anyway? Justice and Integrity of the Person* (Oxford: Oxford University Press, 2006).

Faden, Ruth and Tom Beauchamp. *A History and Theory of Informed Consent* (Oxford: Oxford University Press, 1986).

Fallis, Don. "Lying and Deception." *Philosophers' Imprint* 10, no. 11 (2010): pp. 1–22.

Farmer, Paul. *Fevers, Feuds, and Diamonds: Ebola and the Ravages of History* (New York: Farrar, Straus and Giroux, 2020).

Fassin, Didier. *Humanitarian Reason—A Moral History of the Present* (Oakland: University of California Press, 2011).

Feinberg, Joel. *Harm to Others—The Moral Limits of the Criminal Law* (Oxford: Oxford University Press, 1987), Ch. 4, pp. 126–85.

Feinberg, Joel. "Supererogation and Rules." *Ethics* 71, no. 4 (1961): pp. 276–88.

Ferguson, Kyle and Arthur Caplan. "Love Thy Neighbor? Allocating Vaccines in a World of Competing Obligations." *Journal of Medical Ethics* 47, no. 12 (2021): e20. Accessed June 22, 2021. https://jme.bmj.com/content/47/12/e20.

Fetzer, T. R., M. Witte, and L. Hensel. "Global Behaviors and Perceptions at the Onset of the COVID-19 Pandemic." NBER Working Paper No. 27082, 2020.

Fineman, Martha. *The Autonomy Myth* (New York: New Press, 2004).

Fineman, Martha. "The Vulnerable Subject: Anchoring Equality in the Human Condition." In M. Fineman (ed.). *Transcending the Boundaries of Law: Generations of Feminism and Legal Theory* (Abingdon: Routledge, 2011), p. 168.

Finnis, John. *Aquinas—Moral, Political, and Legal Theory* (Oxford: Oxford University Press, 1998).

Finnis, John. "Equality and Differences." *American Journal of Jurisprudence* 56 (2011): p. 17.

Finnis, John. "Judicial Law-Making and the 'Living' Instrumentalisation of the ECHR." In Richard Ekins, Paul Yowell, and Nick Barber (eds.), *Lord Sumption and the Limits of the Law* (Hart Publishing, 2016), pp. 73–120.

Finnis, John. *Natural Law and Natural Rights* (Oxford: Clarendon Press, 1980).

Finnis, John. "Subsidiarity's Roots and History: Some Observations." *American Journal of Jurisprudence* 61, no. 1 (2016): p. 134.

Fletcher, Richard, Antonis Kalageropoulos, and Rasmus Kleis Nielsen. "Trust in UK Government and News Media COVID-19 Information Down, Concerns Over Misinformation from Government and Politicians Up." June 1, 2020. Doi: 10.60625/risj-2mev-7795.
Francis, Pope. *Laudato Si—On Care for Our Common Home*, Encyclical Letter (Vatican City: Vatican Press, 2015).
Frankfurt, Harry G. *Reasons to Love* (Princeton: Princeton University Press, 2004).
Frankl, Viktor E. *Man's Searching for Meaning—An Introduction to Logotherapy* (Boston: Beacon Press, 1992).
Frost, Robert. *The Road Not Taken*, 1916.
Gewirth, Alan. "Private Philanthropy and Positive Rights." In Paul Ellen Frankel, Fred D. Miller Jr., Jeffry Paul, and John Aherns (eds.), *Beneficence, Philanthropy and Public Good* (Oxford: Blackwell, 1987), pp. 56–78.
Gilbert, Paul. "The Evolution and Social Dynamics of Compassion." *Social and Personality Psychology Compass* 9 (2015): pp. 239–54.
Gilligan, Carol. *In a Different Voice* (Cambridge: Harvard University Press, 1982).
Goetz, Jennifer L., Dacher Keltner, and Emiliana Simon-Thomas. "Compassion: An Evolutionary Analysis and Empirical Review." *Psychological Bulletin* 136, no. 3 (2010): pp. 351–74.
Goodin, Robert. *Protecting the Vulnerable* (Chicago: University of Chicago Press, 1985).
Gosepath, Stefan. "The Principle of Subsidiarity." In Andreas Follesdal and Thomas Pogge (eds.), *Real World Justice: Grounds, Principles, Human Rights, and Social Institutions* (Dordrecht: Springer Netherlands, 2005), pp. 157–70.
Gostin, Lawrence O. "Ebola: Towards an International Health Systems Fund." *The Lancet* 384 (2014): e49.
Gostin, Lawrence O. "COVID-19 Reveals Urgent Need to Strengthen the World Health Organization." *JAMA Forum* 323, no. 23 (April 30, 2020): pp. 2361–2. doi:10.1001/jama.2020.8486
Gostin, Lawrence O. "9 Steps to End COVID-19 and Prevent the Next Pandemic: Essential Outcomes from the World Health Assembly." 2 *JAMA Health Forum* 6 (2021).
Gostin, Lawrence O. and Emily A. Mok. "Innovative Solutions to Closing the Health Gap between Rich and Poor: A Special Symposium on Global Health Governance." *Journal of Law, Medicine and Ethics* 38, no. 3 (2010): pp. 451–58.
Gostin, Lawrence O. and Eric A. Friedman. "Ebola: A Crisis in Global Health Leadership." *The Lancet* 384 (2014): p. 1323.
Gostin, Lawrence O. and Sarah Wetter. "Using COVID-19 to Strengthen the WHO: Promoting Health and Science above Politics." *The Milbank Quarterly* (May 6, 2020).
Gostin, Lawrence O., D. M. Chirwa, H. Clark et al. "The WHO's 75th Anniversary: WHO at a Pivotal Moment in History." *BMJ Global Health* 8 (2023): e012344. doi: 10.1136/bmjgh-2023-012344.
Gostin, Lawrence O., Devi Sridhar, and Daniel Hougendobler. "The Normative Authority of the WHO." *Public Health* 121 (2015): pp. 857–67.
Gostin, Lawrence O., K. A. Klock, H. Clark et al. "Financing the Future of WHO." *The Lancet* 399 (2022): pp. 1445–7.
Gould, Carol C. "Solidarity and the Problem of Structural Injustice in Healthcare." *Bioethics* 32 (2018): pp. 541–52.
Grant, Adam. *Give and Take—Why Helping Others Drives Our Success* (London: Penguin, 2013).
Grant, Liz, Corinne Reid, Heather Buesseler, and David Addiss "A Compassion Narrative for the Sustainable Development Goals: Conscious and Connected Action." *The Lancet* 400, no. 10345 (July 2, 2022): pp. 7–8. doi: 0.1016/S0140-6736(22)01061-3.
Grasswick, Heidi. "Understanding Epistemic Trust, Injustice, and Their Harm." *Royal Institute of Philosophy Supplement* 84 (2018): p. 78.

Gregory, Eric. "Agape and Special Relations in a Global Economy: Theological Sources." In Douglas A. Hicks and Mark Valeri (eds.), *Global Neighbors: Christian Faith and Moral Obligation in Today's Economy* (Grand Rapids: William B. Eerdmans Publishing Company, 2008), pp. 16–42.

Gregory, Eric. *Politics and Order of Love: An Augustinian Ethic of Democratic Citizenship* (Chicago: University of Chicago Press, 2008).

Grisez, Germain, Joseph Boyle, and John Finnis. "Practical Principles, Moral Truth, and Ultimate Ends." *American Journal of Jurisprudence* 32 (1987): pp. 99–151.

Griswold, Charles. *Forgiveness: A Philosophical Exploration* (Cambridge: Cambridge University Press, 2007).

Gruen, Lori. *Entangled Empathy: An Alternative for Our Relationships with Animals*, Brooklin: Lantern, 2015.

Gyekye, K. *Tradition and Modernity* (New York: Oxford University Press, 1997).

Halpen, Jodi. *From Detached Concern to Empathy: Humanizing Medical Practice* (Oxford: Oxford University Press, 2001).

Halpern, Jodi. "Clinical Empathy in Medical Care." In Jean Decety (ed.), *Empathy: From Bench to Bedside* (Cambridge: MIT Press, 2011), Ch. 13, pp. 229–44.

Harman, Sophie. *Global Health Governance* (London: Routledge, 2012).

Harrel, E., L. Berland, J. Jacobson, and D. G. Addiss. "Compassionate Leadership: Essential for the Future of Tropical Medicine and Global Health." *American Journal of Tropical Medicine and Hygiene* 105 (2021): pp. 1450–52.

Harry, Frankfurt. "Autonomy, Necessity, and Love." In his *Necessity, Volition, and Love* (New York: Cambridge University Press, 1999), pp. 129–41.

Harry, Frankfurt. "On Caring." In his *Necessity, Volition, and Love* (New York: Cambridge University Press, 1999), pp. 155–80.

Hart, H. L. A. "Discretion." *Harvard Law Review* 127 (2013): pp. 652–65.

Heidland, Miriam James. *Loved as I Am: An Invitation to Conversion, Healing, and Freedom Through Jesus* (Notre Dame: Ave Maria Press, 2014).

Held, Virginia. "Care and Human Rights." In S. Rowan Cruft, Matthew Liao, and Massimo Renzo (eds.), *Philosophical Foundations of Human Rights* (Oxford: Oxford University Press, 2015), Ch. 35, pp. 624–52.

Held, Virginia. *The Ethics of Care: Personal, Political, and Global* (Oxford: Oxford University Press, 2006).

Henry D. Kass. "Stewardship as a Fundamental Element in Images of Public Administration." *Dialogue* 10, no. 2 (1988): pp. 2–48.

Henry G. Frankfurt, *On Bullshit* (Princeton: Princeton University Press, 2005).

Herlitz, Anders, Zohar Lederman, Jennifer Miller, Marc Fleurbaey, and Sridhar Venkatapuram. "Just Allocation of COVID-19 Vaccines." *BMJ Global Health* 6 (2021): e004812. doi: 10.1136/bmjgh-2020-004812.

Herring, Jonathan. *Caring and the Law* (Oxford: Hart, 2013).

Herring, Jonathan. *Vulnerable Adults and the Law* (Oxford: Oxford University Press, 2016).

Herring, Jonathan. "Compassion, Ethics of Care and Legal Rights." *International Journal of Law in Context* 13, no. 2 (2017): pp. 158–71.

Herring, Jonathan. *Law and the Relational Self* (Cambridge: Cambridge University Press, 2019).

Herring, Jonathan. "Sharing Vulnerabilities in the Woman Patient/Doctor Encounter." *The New Bioethics* 28, no. 3 (2022): pp. 223–37.

Höffe, Otfried. "Subsidiarity as a Principle in the Philosophy of Government." *Regional & Federal Studies* 6 (1996): pp. 56–73.

Hojat, Mohammadreza, Joseph S. Gonnella, Thomas J. Nasca et al. "Physician Empathy: Definition, Components, Measurement, and Relationship to Gender and Specialty." *American Journal of Psychiatry* 159, no. 9 (2002): pp. 1563–69.

Holmgren, Margaret R. "Forgiveness and the Intrinsic Value of Persons." *American Philosophical Quarterly* 30 (1993): pp. 341–52.

hooks, bell. *All about Love* (New York: Harper Collins, 2001).

Hordern, Joshua. *Compassion in Healthcare—Pilgrimage, Practice, and Civic Life* (Oxford: Oxford University Press, 2020).

Howick, Jeremy, Andrew Moscrop, Alexander Mebius et al. "Effects of Empathy and Positive Communication in Healthcare Consultations: A Systematic Review and Meta-Analysis." *Journal of the Royal Society of Medicine* 111, no. 7 (2018): pp. 240–52.

Howick, Jeremy, Satvinder Mittoo, Linda Abel, Joel Halpern, and Stewart W. Mercer. "A Price Tag on Clinical Empathy? Factors Influencing Its Cost-Effectiveness." *Journal of the Royal Society of Medicine* 113, no. 10 (2020): pp. 389–93.

Howick, Jeremy, Valeria Bizzari, and Hajira Dambha-Miller. "Therapeutic Empathy: What It Is and What It Isn't." *Journal of the Royal Society of Medicine* 111, no. 1 (2018): pp. 233–36.

Hume, David. "An Enquiry Concerning the Principles of Morals." In L. A. Selby-Bigge (ed.) and revised by P. H. Nidditch, *Enquiries Concerning Human Understanding and Concerning the Principles of Morals*, 3rd ed. (Oxford: Clarendon Press, 1975), p. 220.

Hume, David. *A Treatise of Human Nature*, edited by L. A. Selby-Bigge and revised by P. H. Nidditch, 2nd ed. (Oxford: Clarendon Press, 1978).

Hurst Hannum. *Rescuing Human Rights: A Radically Moderate Approach* (Cambridge: Cambridge University Press, 2019).

Islam, Md Saiful, Tonmooy Sakar, Sazzad Hossain Khan et al. "COVID-19-Related Infodemic and Its Impact on Public Health: A Global Social Media Analysis." *American Journal of Tropical Medicine and Hygiene* 103, no. 4 (2020): pp. 1621–29.

Jackson, Timothy P. *The Priority of Love: Christian Charity and Social Justice* (Princeton: Princeton University Press, 2003).

Jazaieri, Hooria, K. McGonigal, T. Jinpa, J. Doty, J. Gross, and P. Goldin. "A Randomized Controlled Trial of Compassion Cultivation Training: Effects on Mindfulness, Affect, and Emotion Regulation." *Motivation and Emotion* 38, no. 1 (2014): pp. 23–35.

Jecker, Nancy S., Caleb Atuire, and Susan J. Bull. "Towards a New Model of Global Health Justice: The Case of COVID-19 Vaccines." *Journal of Medical Ethics* (April 29, 2022). doi: 10.1136/medethics-2022-108165.

Jecker, Nancy S., Aaron G. Wightman, Douglas S. Diekema et al. "Vaccine Ethics: An Ethical Framework for Global Distribution of COVID 19 Vaccines." *Journal of Medical Ethics* 47, no. 5 (2021): p. 308.

Jeffrey, David. "Clarifying Empathy: The First Step to More Humane Clinical Care." *British Journal of General Practice* 66 (2016): e143–45.

Jennings, Bruce and Angus Dawson. "Solidarity in the Moral Imagination of Bioethics." *Hastings Center Report* 45, no. 5 (2015): pp. 31–38.

Jennings, Bruce. "Relational Ethics for Public Health: Interpreting Solidarity and Care." *Health Care Analysis: HCA: Journal of Health Philosophy and Policy* 27 (2019): pp. 4–12.

Jesse, M. T. et al. "Professional Interpersonal Dynamics and Burnout in European Transplant Surgeons." *Clinical Transplantation* 31, no. 4 (2017): doi: 10.1111/ctr.12928.

Jha, Ashish K. "A Race to Restore Confidence in The World Health Organization." *Health Affairs* (April 6, 2017). https://www.healthaffairs.org/do/10.1377/hblog20170406.059519/full/.

Jinpa, Thupten. *A Fearless Heart: How the Courage to be Compassionate Can Transform Our Lives* (New York: Avery Publishing Group, 2015).

John Paul II. *Centesimus Annus*, n. 48 (May 31, 1991), para. 5. www.vatican.va/content/john-paul-ii/en/encyclicals/documents/hf_jp-ii_enc_01051991_centesimus-annus.html.

John Paul II. *Man and Woman He Created Them: A Theology of the Body*. #18:4 (Vatican Holy See: Pauline Press, 2006).

Johnson, Kelly. *Fear of Beggars: Stewardship and Poverty in Christian Ethics* (Grand Rapids: William B Eerdmans Publishers, 2007).

Kant, Immanuel. *Metaphysics of Morals*. II, 1.1. 25–30 (450).
Kass, Henry D. "Stewardship as a Fundamental Element in Images of Public Administration." *Dialogue* 10, no. 2 (1988): pp. 2–48.
Kaster, Robert A. *Hope, Joy, and Affection in the Classical World* (Oxford: Oxford University Press, 2016).
Kaunda, C. J. "Sawubonda: A Theo-Ethic for Everyday Decolonial Gestures." *Acta Theologica* 43, no. 1 (2023): pp. 41–59.
Kelly, Christine. "Making 'Care' Accessible: Personal Assistance for Disabled People and the Politics of Language." *Critical Social Policy* 31 (2011): pp. 562–64.
Kelsall, Joshua. "The Trust-Based Communicative Obligations of Expert Authorities." *Journal of Applied Philosophy* 38, no. 2 (2020): pp. 288–305.
Kemper, Kathi J. and Mubashir Khirallah. "Acute Effects of Online Mind-Body Skills Training on Resilience, Mindfulness, and Empathy." *Journal of Evidence-Based Complementary & Alternative Medicine* 20, no. 4 (2015): pp. 247–53.
Keohane, Robert, Melissa Lane, and Michael Oppenheimer. "The Ethics of Scientific Communication Under Uncertainty." *Politics, Philosophy, and Economics* 13, no. 4 (2014): pp. 343–68.
Kerasidou, Angeliki and Ruth Horn. "Making Space for Empathy: Supporting Doctors in the Emotional Labour of Clinical Care." *BMC Medical Ethics* 17, no. 1 (2016): p. 8.
Kerasidou, Angeliki, Kristine Bærøe, Zackary Berger, and Amy E. Caruso Brown. "The Need for Empathetic Healthcare Systems." *Journal of Medical Ethics* (July 24, 2020): medethics-2019-105921. doi: 10.1136/medethics-2019-105921. Epub ahead of print. PMID: 32709754.
Kerasidou, Angeliki. "Empathy and Efficiency in Healthcare at Times of Austerity." *Health Care Analysis* 27, no. 3 (2019): pp. 171–84.
Khan, Mishal et al. "Decolonising Global Health in 2021: A Roadmap to Move from Rhetoric to Reform." *BMJ Global Health* 6, no. 3 (2021): e005604.
Khoza, Reuel J. *Let Africa Lead* (Sunninghill: Vezubuntu, 2005).
Kickbusch, Ilona and Krishna S. Reddy. "Global Health Governance—The Next Political Revolution." *Public Health* 129 (2015): pp. 838–42.
King Jr., Martin Luther. *A Gift of Love—Sermons from Strength to Love and Other Preachings* (Boston: Beacon, 2012).
King, Martin Luther, Jr. "The Strength to Love." In *A Testament of Hope—The Essential Writings and Speeches* (San Francisco: Harper One, 1986), pp. 491–517.
King, Martin Luther Jr. "An Experiment in Love." In *A Testament of Hope* (San Francisco: Harper Collins, 1991), pp. 16–20.
King, Martin Luther, Jr. "Loving Your Enemies." In *A Gift of Love—Sermons From Strength to Love and Other Preachings* (Boston: Beacon, 2012), pp. 45–55.
King, Martin Luther, Jr. "Draft of Chapter IV "Love in Action." The Papers of Martin Luther King Jr., Vol. VI: Advocate of the Social Gospel, September 1948–March 1963. https://kinginstitute.stanford.edu/king-papers/documents/draft-chapter-iv-love-action.
Kitcher, Philip. *Science in a Democratic Society* (Amherst and New York: Prometheus Books, 2011).
Kittay, Eva Feder. *Learning from My Daughter: The Value and Care of Disabled Minds* (Oxford: Oxford University Press, 2019).
Kittay, Eva Feder and Diana T. Meyers (eds.). *Women and Moral Theory* (Lanham: Rowman and Littlefield, 1987).
Kizito, O. and F. Juma. "Catholic Social Justice Principles: An African Philosophical Response." *Arts and Social Science Journal* 6, no. 2 (2015): p. 107. doi: 10.4172/2151-6200.1000107.
Kolers, A. "What Does Solidarity Do for Bioethics?" *Journal of Medical Ethics* 47 (2021): pp. 122–28.
Konrath, Sara. "The Empathy Paradox: Increasing Disconnection in the Age of Increasing Connection." In *Handbook of Research on Technoself: Identity in a Technological Society*, edited by Rocci Luppicini (Hearshey: IGI Global, 2012), pp. 204–28.

Koum Besson, E. "Confronting Whiteness and Decolonizing Global Health Institutions." *The Lancet* 397, 10929 (June 19, 2021): pp. 2328–29.
Krishek, S. "How Faith Secures the Morality of Love." In *The Routledge Handbook of Love in Philosophy*, edited by A. M. Martin (New York: Routledge, 2019), pp. 252–63.
Kurosawa, Akira (dir.). 生きる - *Ikiru*, produced by Tōhō, 1952.
Lamb, Christina, Daniel Wainstock, and Thana C. de Campos-Rudinsky. "Ethics of Love for End-of-Life Care: Beyond Autonomy and Efficiency." *American Journal of Bioethics* 23, no. 11 (2023): pp. 76–78.
Lederach, John Paul and Angela Jill Lederach. *When Blood and Bones Cry Out: Journeys through the Soundscape of Healing and Reconciliation* (New York: Oxford University Press, 2010).
Lee, Kelley and Tikki Pang (Pangestu). "WHO: Retirement or Reinvention." *Public Health* 128, no. 2 (2014): 119–23.
Lee, Matthew T. "Love as a Foundational Principle for Humanistic Management." In Michael Pirson (ed.), *Love and Organization: Lessons of Love for Human Dignity, Leadership, and Motivation* (Abingdon: Routledge, 2022), pp. 5–38.
Lévínas, Emmanuel. *Totality and Infinity: An Essay on Exteriority*. Translated by Alphonso Lingis (Pittsburgh: Duquesne University Press, 1969).
Lewis, C. S. *The Four Loves* (London: William Collins, 2012).
Liden, Jon. "The WHO and Global Health Governance: Post 1990." *Public Health* 128 (2014): p. 141.
Lie, Reider K. and Franklin G. Miller. "Allocating a COVID-19 Vaccine: Balancing National and International Responsibilities." *Milbank Quarterly* 99, no. 2 (2021): p. 450.
Lispector, Clarice "Ao Correr da Maquina." In Clarice Lispector, *A Descoberta do Mundo* (Rio de Janeiro: Rocco, 1999), p. 228.
List, Christian and Philip Pettit. *Group Agency* (Oxford: Oxford University Press, 2022).
Lynch, Kathleen. "Love Labour as Dstinct and Non-commodifiable Form of Care Labour." *The Sociological Review* 55, no. 3 (2007): pp. 550–70.
Lysaught, Therese M. *Caritas in Communion—Theological Foundations of Catholic Health Care* (Washington, DC: The Catholic Health Association of the United States, 2014).
Lysaught, Therese M. "Ritual and Practice." In L. Dugdale (ed.), *Dying in the Twenty-First Century: Toward a New Ethical Framework for the Art of Dying Well* (Cambridge: MIT Press, 2015), pp. 67–86.
Lysaught, Therese M. "Imagination of Catholic Healthcare." *Christian Bioethics* 26, no. 1 (2020): pp. 31–55.
Lysaught, Therese M., Beth Reece, Marcia A. Grand Ortega et al. "Building Caregiver Resiliency in Global Health: Embodying the Catholic Social Tradition in the Face of COVID-19." *The Linacre Quarterly* 89, no. 2 (2022): pp. 184–205.
MacAskill, W. "Effective Altruism: Introduction." *Essays in Philosophy* 18, no. 1 (2017): p. 1.
MacIntyre, Alasdair. *Dependent Rational Animals: Why Human Beings Need the Virtues* (Chicago: Open Court, 1999).
MacIntyre, Alasdair. *Edith Stein: A Philosophical Prologue 1913–1922* (Lanham: Rowman and Littlefield, 2006), Ch. 9.
Mack, Eric. "Bad Samaritanism and the Causation of Harm." *Philosophy and Public Affairs* 9 (1980): pp. 230–59.
MacKenzie, Jordan. "Caring by Lying." *Bioethics* 35 (2021): pp. 877–83.
Mackey, Tim K. "The Ebola Outbreak: Catalyzing a 'Shift' in Global Health Governance?" *BMC Infectious Disease* 16 (2016): p. 699.
Mackey, Tim K. and Bryan A. Liang. "A United Nations Global Panel for GHG." *Social Science & Medicine* 76 (2013): pp. 12–13.
Malm, Heidi M. "Liberalism, Bad Samaritan Law, and Legal Paternalism." *Ethics* 106, no. 1 (1995): pp. 4–31.

Malm, Heidi M. "Bad Samaritan Laws: Harm, Help, or Hype?" *Law and Philosophy* 19, no. 6 (2000): pp. 707–50.
Margalit, Avishai. *The Decent Society* (Caimbridge: Harvard University Press, 1996).
Martins, Alexandre A. *The Cry of the Poor, Liberation Ethics and Justice in Health Care* (Lanham: Lexington Books, 2020).
Martins, Alexandre A. "'The Preferential Option for the Poor as an Existential Commitment.'" In Alexandre A. Martins (ed.), *The Cry for the Poor: Liberation Ethics and Justice in Healthcare* (Lanham: Lexington Books, 2020), pp. 59–75.
Martins, Alexandre A. "Bioética e Saúde Global a Partir de Baixo: O Global a Partir da Realidade Local." *ATeo* 25, no. 67 (January/June 2021): pp. 100–18.
Martins, Alexandre A. "Ethics and Equity in Global Health: The Preferential Option for the Poor." *Journal of Moral Theology*, 1 (CTEWC Book Series 1) (2021): pp. 96–105.
Martins, Alexandre A. "Theological Bioethics and Public Health from the Margins: Epistemology and Latin American Liberation Theology in Bioethics." *The National Catholic Bioethics Quarterly* (Summer 2022): pp. 239–55.
Massimi, Michela. "Public Trust in Model-based Science: Moving Beyond the 'View from Nowhere,'" In *OUP Blog* (July 29, 2022). https://blog.oup.com/2022/07/public-trust-in-model-based-science-moving-beyond-the-view-from-nowhere/.
Martins, Alexander A. A escuta como método e os pobres/oprimidos como sujeitos: por uma bioética global plural. *Revista Pistis & Praxis, Teologia e Pastoral*, PUCPRESS 15, no. 2 (02 maio/ago 2023): pp. 270–91.
Mauss, Marcel. *Essai sur le don: Forme et raison de l'échange dans les sociétés archaïques*. L'année sociologique 1 (1924): pp. 30–186.
Mbiti, J. S. *African Religions and Philosophy* (London: Heinemann, 1970).
McCormick, Neil. *H.L.A. Hart* (Redwood City: Stanford University Press, 2008).
McDaniel, Kris. *Edith Stein: On the Problem of Empathy*. In Eric Schliesser (ed.), *Ten Neglected Classics of Philosophy* (Oxford: Oxford University, 2016), p. 198.
McIntyre, Alison. "Guilty Bystanders? On the Legitimacy of Duty to Rescue Statues." *Philosophy and Public Affairs* 23, no. 2 (1994): pp. 157–91.
McNeil, Donald G. Jr. "How Much Herd Immunity is Enough." *The New York Times* (December 24, 2020). Retrieved March 25, 2024. https://www.nytimes.com/2020/12/24/world/how-much-herd-immunity-is-enough.html.
Mealer, M., R. Hodapp, D. Conrad et al. "Designing a Resilience Program for Critical Care Nurses." *AACN Advanced Critical Care* 28, no. 4 (2017): pp. 359–65.
Meier, Benjamin Mason, Allyn Taylor, Mark Eccleston-Turner, Roojin Habibi, Sharifah Sekalala, and Lawrence O. Gostin. "The World Health Organization in Global Health Law." *Journal of Law, Medicine, and Ethics* 48 (2020): pp. 796–99.
Menkiti, I. A. Person and Community in African Traditional Thought. In R. A. Wright (ed.), *African Philosophy: An Introduction* (Lanham: University Press of America, 1984), pp. 171–81.
Mercer, S. W. and W. J. Reynolds. "Empathy and Quality of Care." *British Journal of General Practice* 52 suppl. (2002): S9–12.
Michael, Griffin and Jennie Weiss Block (eds.). *In the Company of the Poor—Conversations with Dr Paul Farmer and Fr Gustavo Gutierrez* (Maryknoll, New York: Orbis Books), 2013.
Miller, Sarah Clark. "A Kantian Ethic of Care." In Barbara S. Andrew, Jean Clare Keller, and Lisa H. Schwartzman (eds.), *Feminist Interventions in Ethics and Politics: Feminist Ethics and Social Theory* (Lanham: Rowman & Littlefield Publishers, 2005), pp. 111–30.
Miller, Sarah Clark. "Need, Care, and Obligation." In *The Philosophy of Need* (Cambridge: Cambridge University Press, 2006), pp. 137–60.
Milo, Caterina. *Informed Consent to Abortion: Building Bridges of Dialogue in the Medical Encounter* (Oxford: Oxford University Press, 2025).
Miner, Robert. "The Difficulties of Mercy: Reading Thomas Aquinas on 'Misericordia.'" *Studies in Christian Ethics* 28, no. 1 (2015): pp. 70–85.

Minow, Martha. *When Should Law Forgive* (New York: W. W. Norton & Company, 2019).
Moon, S., J. Leigh, L. Woskie, F. Checchi, V. Dzau, M. Fallah et al. "Post Ebola Reforms: Ample Analysis, Inadequate Action." *British Medical Journal* 356 (2017): j280.
Mormina, Maru. "Knowledge, Expertise and Science Advice During COVID-19: In Search of Epistemic Justice for the 'Wicked' Problem of Post-Normal Times." *Social Epistemology* 36, no. 6 (2022): pp. 671–85.
Morris, Jenny. "Care or Empowerment: A Disability Rights Perspective." *Social Policy and Administration* 31 (1997): p. 54.
Murdoch, Iris. *The Sovereignty of Good* (London: Routledge & Kegan, 1970).
Murphy, Jeffrey G. "Mercy and Legal Justice." *Social Philosophy and Policy* 4 (1986): pp. 1–14.
Murphy, Liam B. "The Demands of Beneficence." *Philosophy and Public Affairs* 22, no. 4 (1993): pp. 267–92.
Murray, Christopher J. L. "The Global Burden of Disease Study at 30 Years." *Nature Medicine* 28 (2022): pp. 2019–26. https://doi.org/10.1038/s41591-022-01990-1.
Nakayama, Don K. "Professionalism in Kurosawa's Medical Dramas." *Journal of Surgical Education* 66, no. 6 (2009): pp. 395–98.
Neslen, Arthur. "Nestle Under Fire for Marketing Claims on Baby Milk Formulas." *The Guardian* (February 1, 2018). https://www.theguardian.com/business/2018/feb/01/nestle-under-fire-for-marketing-claims-on-baby-milk-formulas.
Newman, John Henry. *Apologia, Apologia Pro Vita Sua* (New York: Penguin Books, 1994).
Newman, Louis E. "The Quality of Mercy: on the Duty to Forgive in the Judaic Tradition." *The Journal of Religious Ethics* 15, no. 2 (Fall 1987): pp. 155–72.
Noddings, Nel. *Caring: A Feminine Approach to Ethics and Moral Education* (Berkeley: University of California Press, 1984).
Nouwen, Henri. *Bread for the Journey* (New York: Haper One, 2006).
Nuffield Council on Bioethics. *Public Health: Ethical Issues* (Cambridge: Cambridge Publishers, 2007).
Nussbaum, Martha C. "Equity and Mercy." *Philosophy and Public Affairs* 22, no. 2 (Spring 1993): pp. 83–125.
Nussbaum, Martha C. "Compassion: The Basic Social Emotion." *Social Policy and Philosophy* 13 (1996): pp. 27–41.
Nussbaum, Martha. *Upheavals of Thought: The Intelligence of Emotions* (Cambridge: Cambridge University Press, 2011).
Nussbaum, Martha. *Political Emotions—Why Love Matters for Justice* (Cambridge: Harvard University Press, 2013).
Nussbaum, Martha C. "If You Could See This Heart—Mozart's Mercy." In Ruth R. Caston and Robert A. Kaster (eds.), *Hope, Joy, and Affection in the Classical World* (Oxford: Oxford University Press, 2016), pp. 226–40.
O'Neill, Onora. *Faces of Hunger* (Crows Nest: Allen & Unwin, 1986).
O'Neil, Onora. *Autonomy and Trust in Bioethics* (Cambridge: Cambridge: Cambridge University Press, 2002).
O'Neill, Onora. "Public Health or Clinical Ethics: thinking beyond borders." *Ethics and International Affairs* 16, no. 2 (2002): pp. 35–45. doi: 10.1111/j.1747-7093.2002.tb00395.x.
O'Neill, Onora. "Ethics of Communication?" *European Journal of Philosophy* 17, no. 2 (2009): pp. 167–80.
O'Neill, Onora. "Linking Trust to Trustworthiness." *International Journal of Philosophical Studies* 26, no. 92 (2018): pp. 293–300.
O'Neill, Onora. *Reith Lectures 2002: A Question of Trust*. BBC Radio, 2002. https://www.immagic.com/eLibrary/ARCHIVES/GENERAL/BBC_UK/B020000O.pdf.
Ortúzar, Pablo. "Prólogo." In Pablo Ortúzar (ed.), Subsidariedad: Más allá del estado y del mercado (Santiago: Instituto de Estudios de la Sociedad, 2015).
Outka, Gene. *Agape: An Ethical Analysis* (New Haven: Yale University Press, 1972).

Oxhandler, Holly K. "Namaste Theory: A Quantitative Grounded Theory on Religion and Spirituality in Mental Health Treatment." *Religions* 8, no. 9 (2017): p. 168.
Oxhandler, Holly K. *The Soul of the Helper—Seven Stages to Seeing the Sacred Within Yourself So You Can See It in Others* (West Conshohocken: Templeton Press, 2022).
Pai, M. "Covidization of Research: What Are the Risks?" *Nature Medicine* 26, no. 8 (2020): p. 1159.
Paul II, John. *Man and Woman He Created Them: A Theology of the Body* (London: Pauline Press, 2006).
Pellegrino, E. D. "The Internal Morality of Clinical Medicine—A Paradigm for the Ethics of the Helping and Healing Professions." In H. Tristram Engelhardt Jr. and Fabrice Jotterand (eds.), *The Philosophy of Medicine Reborn—A Pellegrino Reader* (Notre Dame: Notre Dame University Press, 2011), p. 72.
Pellegrino, Edmund. "The Four Principles and the Doctor-Patient Relationship: The Need for a Better Linkage." In R. Gillon (ed.), *Principles of Health Care Ethics*, 1st ed. (London: John Wiley & Sons, 1994).
Pellegrino, Edmund D. and David C. Thomasma. "The Conflict Between Autonomy and Beneficence in Medical Ethics: Proposal for a Resolution." *Journal of Contemporary Health Law & Policy* 3 (1987): pp. 23–46.
Pellegrino, Edmund D. and David C. Thomasma. *For the Patient's Good: The Restoration of Beneficence in Health Care* (New York: Oxford University Press, 1988).
Perillo, Davide. *Your Names Are Written in Heaven: The World of Rose Busingye* (Seattle: Slant Books, 2024).
Perry, Adam. "Mercy." *Philosophy and Public Affairs* 46, no. 1 (2018): pp. 60–89. https://doi.org/10.1111/papa.12006.
Philip, Jacques. *Interior Freedom*, trans. Helena Scott (New York: Scepter, 2002).
Philpott, Daniel. "An Ethic of Political Reconciliation." *Ethics and International Affairs* 23, no. 4 (2009): pp. 389–407.
Piper, Josef. *Happiness and Contemplation* (South Bend: St. Augustine Press, 1958).
Pope Francis. *Fratelli Tutti—On Fraternity and Social Friendship* (Vatican City: Vatican Press, 2020).
Pope Francis. *Laudato Si: On Care for Our Common Home* (Vatican: Holy See, 2015).
Post, S. G., L. E. Ng, J. E. Fischel et al. "Routine, Empathic and Compassionate Patient Care, Definitions, Development, Obstacles, Education and Beneficiaries." *Journal Evaluation in Clinical Practice* 20 (2014): pp. 872–90.
Potter, Nancy (ed.). *Trauma, Truth and Reconciliation: Healing Damaged Relationships* (Oxford: Oxford University Press, 2006).
Prainsack, B. and A. Buyx. *Solidarity in Biomedicine and Beyond* (Cambridge and New York: Cambridge University Press, 2017).
Prasad, V. "Op-Ed: Why Did Fauci Move the Herd Immunity Goal Posts?" *MedPage Today* (December 29, 2020). https://www.medpagetoday.com/opinion/vinay-prasad/90445.
Pruss, Alexander. "Lying and Speaking Your Interlocutor's Language." *The Thomist* 63 (1999): pp. 439–53.
Quick, Oliver. "Duties of Candor in Healthcare: The Truth, the Whole Truth, and Nothing but the Truth?" *Medical Law Review* 30, no. 2 (2022): pp. 324–34.
Ramose, M. B. "The Philosophy of Ubuntu and Ubuntu as a Philosophy." In P. H. Coetzee and A. P. J. Roux (eds.), *Philosophy from Africa*, 2nd ed. (Cape Town: Oxford University Press, 2002), pp. 230–38.
Ramphele, M. "Citizenship Challenges for South Africa's Young Democracy." *Journal of American Academy of Arts and Sciences, Daedalus* 130 (2001): pp. 1–17.
Ratzinger, Joseph. *Introduction to Christianity* (San Francisco: Ignatius press, 2004).
Raz, Joseph. "Legal Principles and Limits of Law." *Yale Law Journal* 81 (1972): pp. 823–54.
Raz, Joseph. "Permissions and Supererogation." *American Philosophical Quarterly* 12, no. 2 (1975): pp. 161–68.

Raz, Joseph. *The Morality of Freedom* (Oxford: Oxford University Press, 1986).
Rejman, Ewa. *International Law as a Tool to Protect Mother's Rights*, JSD dissertation (The University of Notre Dame, 2025).
Reuters Institute for the Study of Journalism. *Trust in UK Government and News Media Covid-19 Information Down, Concerns over Misinformation.* Reuters Institute for the Study of Journalism. 2020. https://reutersinstitute.politics.ox.ac.uk/trust-uk-government-and-news-media-covid-19-information-down-concerns-over-misinformation.
Reynolds, Joel Michael. "Infinite Responsibility in the Bedpan: Response Ethics, Care Ethics, and the Phenomenology of Dependency Work." *Hypatia* 31, no. 4 (2016): pp. 779–94.
Reynolds, Joel Michael. *The Life Worth Living: Disability, Pain, and Morality* (Minneapolis: University of Minnesota Press, 2022).
Richardson, E. T. *Epidemic Illusions: And the Coloniality of Global Public Health* (Cambridge: MIT Press, 2020).
Ricœur, Paul. "Love and Justice." *Philosophy and Social Criticism* 21, no. 5/6 (1995): pp. 23–39.
Ripstein, Arthur. "Three Duties to Rescue: Moral, Civil, and Criminal." *Law and Philosophy* 19, no. 6 (2000): pp. 751–79.
Ritzki, Rudi Muhammad. "Report of the Independent Expert on Human Rights and International Solidarity, Rudi Muhammad Rizki." UNHCR, July 5, 2010, UN Doc No. A/HRC/15/32, para. 58.
Robinson, Fiona. "After Liberalism in World Politics? Toward an International Political Theory." *Ethics and Social Welfare* 4, no. 2 (July 2010): pp. 130–44.
Rollins, Nigel, Ellen Piwoz, Phillip Baker et al. "Marketing of Commercial Milk Formula: A System to Caputure Parents, Communities, Science, and Policy." *The Lancet* 401, no. 10375 (2023): pp. 486–502.
Rogers, T., R. Zeckhauser, F. Gino, and M. I. Norton. "Artful Paltering: The Risks and Rewards of Using Truthful Statements to Mislead Others." *Journal of Personality and Social Psychology* 112, no. 3 (2016): pp. 456–73.
Ruger, Jennifer Prah. "Global Health Governance as a Shared Health Governance." *Journal of Epidemiology and Community Health* 66, no. 7 (2012): 653–61.
Ruger, Jennifer Prah. "Global Health Justice and Government." *American Journal of Bioethics* 12, no. 12 (2012): pp. 35–54.
Ruger, Jennifer Prah. "Positive Public Health Ethics: Toward Flourishing and Resilient Communities and Individuals." *American Journal of Bioethics* 20, no. 7 (2020): pp. 44–54.
Ruger, Jennifer Prah. "The Future of Global Health Governance," *Penn on the World After Covid-19*, August 20, 2020. https://global.upenn.edu/perryworldhouse/news/future-global-health-governance.
Rutschman, Ana Santos and Julia Barnes-Waise. "The COVID-19 Vaccine Patent Waiver: The Wrong Tool for the Right Goal." *Harvard Law Petrie Flom Center, Bill of Rights Blog* (May 5, 2021). Accessed May 22, 2021. https://blog.petrieflom.law.harvard.edu/2021/05/05/covid-vaccine-patent-waiver/.
Rzymski, P., M. Nowicki, G. E. Mullin et al. "Quantity Does Not Equal Quality: Scientific Principles Cannot Be Sacrificed." *International Immunopharmacology* 86 (2020): p. 106711.
Saltman, R. B. and O. Ferroussier Davis. "The Concept of Stewardship in Health Policy." *Bulletin of the World Health Organization* 78, no. 6 (2000): pp. 732–39.
Sam, P. "Redefining Vulnerability in the Era of COVID-19." *The Lancet* 395, no. 10230 (2020): p. 1089.
Samra, Rajvinder. "Empathy and Burnout in Medicine—Acknowledging Risks and Opportunities." *Journal of General Internal Medicine* 33 (2018): pp. 991–93.
Sandel, Michael J. "The Procedural Republic and the Unencumbered Self." *Political Theory* 12 (1984): pp. 81–96.
Sandel, Michael J. *Public Philosophy: Essays on Morality in Politics* (Cambridge: Harvard University Press, 2005).

Savulescu, Julian, Ingmar Persson, Dominic Wilkinson et al. "Utilitarianism and Pandemic." *Bioethics* 34, no. 6 (2020): p. 620.
Scanlon, T. M. *Why Does Inequality Matter?* (Oxford: Oxford University Press, 2018).
Scheirer, W. "A Pandemic of Bad Science." *Bulletin of the Atomic Scientists* 76, no. 4 (2020): pp. 175–84.
Second Vatican Council. "*Communio Et Progression—On the Means of Social Communication*. Vatican, May 23, 1971, para. 11. Available at: https://www.vatican.va/roman_curia/pontific al_councils/pccs/documents/rc_pc_pccs_doc_23051971_communio_en.html.
Sedmak, Clemens. *Enacting Integral Human Development* (Maryknoll: Orbis Books, 2023).
Sekalala, Sharifah, Lisa Forman, Timothy Hodgson et al. "Decolonising Human Rights: How Intellectual Property Laws Result in Unequal Access to the COVID-19 Vaccine." *BMJ Global Health* 6 (2021): e006169.
Seneca, *Dialogues and Essays*, trans. John Davie, 3rd ed. (Oxford: Oxford University Press, 2007).
Seneca. *De Beneficiis*, iv.
Seneca. *De Clementia*. Seneca M 2.7.3.
Shakespeare, William. *The Complete Works of William Shakespeare*, Stanley Wells and Gary Taylor (eds.) (Oxford: Oxford University Press, 1986).
Shamasunder, S., S. M. Holmes, T. Goronga et al. "COVID-19 Reveals Weak Health Systems by Design: Why We Must Re-make Global Health in this Historic Moment." *Global Public Health* 15 (2020): pp. 1083–89.
Shanafelt, Tait D., Omar Hasan, Lotte N. Dyrbye et al. "Changes in Burnout and Satisfaction with Work-Life Balance in Physicians and the General U.S. Working Population Between 2011 and 2014." *Mayo Clinic Proceedings* 90, no. 12 (2015): pp. 1600–13.
Shapiro, Shauna, Ronald Siegel, and Kristin D. Neff. "Paradoxes of Mindfulness." *Mindfulness* (June 2, 2018). https://doi.org/10.1007/s12671-018-0957-5.
Sherman, Amy. *Kingdom Calling: Vocational Stewardship for the Common Good* (Downers Grove: InterVarsity Press, 2011).
Shue, Henry. *Basic Rights: Subsistence, Affluence, and US Foreign Policy* (Princeton: Princeton University Press, 1980).
Sinclair, S., J. M. Norris, S. J. McConnell et al. "Compassion: A Scoping Review of the Healthcare Literature." *BMC Palliative Care BioMed Central* 15 (2016): p. 6.
Sinclair, S., S. McClement, S. Raffin-Bouchal et al. "Compassion in Healthcare: An Empirical Model." *Journal of Pain Symptom Manage* 5 (2016): pp. 193–203.
Sinclair, Shane, Karla Beamer, Thomas F. Hack et al. "Sympathy, Empathy, and Compassion: A Grounded Theory Study of Palliative Care Patients' Understandings, Experiences, and Preferences." *Palliative Medicine* 31, no. 5 (2017): pp. 437–47. doi: 10.1177/0269216316663499.
Sinclair, S., T. F. Hack, S. Raffin-Bouchal et al. "What Are Healthcare Providers' Understandings and Experiences of Compassion? The Healthcare Compassion Model: A Grounded Theory Study of Healthcare Providers in Canada." *BMJ Open* 8 (2018): e019701.
Sinclair, Shane., Karla Beamer, Thomas F. Hack, S. McClement, S. Raffin Bouchal, H. Chochinov, and N. Hagen. "Sympathy, Empathy and Compassion: Palliative Care Patients' Understandings, Experiences and Preferences." *Palliative Medicine* 31, no. 5 (2016): pp. 437–47. doi.org/10.1177/0269216316663499.
Sindane, J. *Ubuntu and nation building* (Pretoria: Ubuntu School of Philosophy, 1994).
Singer, Peter. "Famine, Affluence, and Morality." *Philosophy and Public Affairs* 1, no. 3 (1972): pp. 229–43.
Singer, Peter. "The Logic of Effective Altruism." *Boston Review—A Political and Literary Forum*, July 1, 2015. Accessed May 2021. http://bostonreview.net/forum/peter-singer-logic-effect ive-altruism.

Singer, Peter. "The Ethics of Prioritizing COVID-19 Vaccination." *Project Syndicate*, January 19, 2021. Accessed May 21, 2021. https://www.project-syndicate.org/commentary/ethics-of-covid19-vaccine-priorities-by-peter-singer-2021-01?barrier=accesspaylog.

Singer, Peter. "The Why and How of Effective Altruism." *Effective Altruism*. https://www.effectivealtruism.org/peter-singer-ted.

Sirleaf, Matiangai. "White Health as Global Health." *AJIL Unbound* 117, no. 88 (2023): pp. 88–93.

Smith, Adam. *The Theory of Moral Sentiments*, Knud Haakonssen, ed. (Cambridge: Cambridge University Press, 2012).

Smith, Angela M. "Institutional Apologies and Forgiveness." In Brandon Warmke, Dana Kay Nelkin, and Michael McKenna (eds.), *Forgiveness and Its Moral Dimensions* (New York: Oxford University Press, 2021), pp. 146–71.

Snead, O. Carter. *What It Means to Be Human—The Case for the Body in Public Bioethics* (Cambridge: Harvard University Press, 2020).

Spezio, M., G. Peterson, and R. Roberts. "Humility as Openness to Others: Interactive Humility in the Context of L'Arche." *Journal of Moral Education* 48 (2019): p. 27.

St. Teresa of Avila. "Interior Castle." In *The Collected Works of St Teresa of Avila*, Vol II, trans. Kieran Kavanaugh, OCD, and Otilio Rodriguez, OCD (Washington, DC: ICS Publications, 1980).

Stein, Edith. *On the Problem of Empathy* (Washington, DC: ICS, 1989).

Stein, F. "Risky Business: COVAX and the Financialization of Global Vaccine Equity." *Global Health* 17 (2021). doi: 10.1186/s12992-021-00763-8.

Stein, Felix, Katerini Tagmatarchi Storeng, and Antonine de Bengy Puyvallée. "Global Health Nonsense." *BMJ* 379 (December 19, 2022): p. o2932. http://dx.doi.org/10.1136/bmj.o2932.

Stephen, John. "Epistemic Trust and the Ethics of Science Communication: Against Transparency, Openness, Transparency, and Honesty." *Social Epistemology* 32, no. 2 (2018): pp. 75–87.

Storeng, K. T., A. de Bengy Puyvallée, and F. Stein "COVAX and the Rise of the 'Super Public Private Partnership' for Global Health." *Global Public Health* 18, no. 1 (January 2023). doi: 10.1080/17441692.2021.1987502.

Stump, Elenor. *Wandering in Darkness—Narrative and the Problem of Suffering* (Oxford: Oxford University Press, 2010).

Stump, Eleonore. "Love, by All Accounts." *Proceedings and Addresses of the American Philosophical Association* 80 (2006): pp. 25–43.

Stump, Eleonore. "The Sunflower: Guilt, Forgiveness, and Reconciliation." In Brandon Warmke, Dana Kay Nelkin, and Michael McKenna (eds.), *Forgiveness and Its Moral Dimensions* (New York: Oxford University Press, 2021), pp. 172–96.

Sunstein, Cass R. and Richard H. Thaler. "Libertarian Paternalism Is Not an Oxymoron." *The University of Chicago Law Review* 70, no. 4 (Autumn 2003): pp. 1159–1202.

Sunstein, Cass R. and Richard H. Thaler. "Libertarian Paternalism." *American Economic Review* 93 (2003): pp. 175–79.

Suzuki, T. and P. Carus (trans.). T'ai-Shang Kan-Ying P'ien (*Treatise of the Exalted One on Response and Retribution*) (La Salle: Open Court, 1906). https://terebess.hu/english/taishang.html.

Syed, Shams. "Unit Head of Quality of Care for the World Health Organizations on Compassion: An Engine for Quality Primary Care," October 20, 2022. https://www.youtube.com/watch?v=B1iNIpvhT88.

Tahzib, Farhang. "Building Bridges Between Public Health and Law." *European Journal of Public Health* 29, Suppl. 4 (November 2019): ckz185.720.

Tasioulas, John. "Mercy." *Proceedings of the Aristotelian Society, New Series* 103 (2003): pp. 101–32.

Tate, Tyler. "Objective Suffering: What is it? What Could it be?" *Cambridge Quarterly of Healthcare Ethics*, Published online (2005): pp. 1–9.

Tate, Tyler and Joseph Clair. "Love Your Patient as Yourself—On Reviving the Broken Heart of American Medical Ethics." *Hasting Center Report* 53, no. 2 (2023): 12–25.
Tate, Tyler and Robert Pearlman. "What We Mean When We Talk About Suffering—and Why Eric Cassell Should Not Have the Last Word." *Perspectives in Biology and Medicine* 62, no. 1 (2019): pp. 95–110.
Taylor, Charles. *Malaise of Modernity* (Toronto: House of Anansi, 1991).
Taylor, Charles. *Sources of the Self: The Making of Modern Identity* (Cambridge: Harvard University Press, 1989).
Taylor, Charles. *The Ethics of Authenticity* (Cambridge: Harvard University Press, 1991).
ter Meulen, R. *Solidarity and Justice in Health and Social Care* (Cambridge: Cambridge University Press, 2017).
Thirioux, Berangere, Francois Birault, and Nematollah Jaafari. "Empathy Is a Protective Factor of Burnout in Physicians: New Neuro-Phenomenological Hypotheses Regarding Empathy and Sympathy in Care Relationships." *Frontiers in Psychology* 7 (2016): p. 763.
Thompson, Marjorie J. *Forgiveness—A Lenten Study* (Louisville: Westminster John Knox Press, 2014).
Tollefsen, Christopher. *Lying and Christian Ethics* (Cambridge: Cambridge University Press, 2015).
Toussaint, Loren L., Everett L. Worthington, and David R. Williams (eds.). *Forgiveness and Health: Scientific Evidence and Theories Relating Forgiveness to Better Health* (Dordrecht: Springer, 2015).
Treaty of Lisbon Amending the Treaty on European Union and the Treaty establishing the European Community, December 13, 2007, O.J. (C 306) 1, art. 3b.
Tronto, Joan C. *Moral Boundaries: A Political Argument for an Ethic of Care* (London: Routledge, 1993).
Tronto, Joan C. "Creating Caring Institutions: Politics, Plurality, and Purpose." *Ethics and Social Welfare* 4, no. 2 (2010): pp. 158–71.
Trzeciak, S. "How 40 Seconds of Compassion Could Save a Life" (2019). Accessed May 9, 2024. https://www.youtube.com/watch?v=elW69hyPUuI.
Trzeciak, S. and A. Mazzarelli. *Compassionomics: The Revolutionary Scientific Evidence That Caring Makes a Difference* (Pensacola: Studer Group, 2019).
Tuckness, Alex and John M. Parrish. *The Decline of Mercy in Public Life* (Cambridge: Cambridge University Press, 2014).
Tufekci, Z. (2020). "Why Telling People They Don't Need Masks Backfired." *The New York Times*. Published March 17, 2020. Retrieved March 25, 2024. https://www.nytimes.com/2020/03/17/opinion/coronavirus-face-masks.html.
Twambley, John Paul. "Mercy and Forgiveness." *Analysis*, 36 (1976): pp. 84–7.
United Nations Human Rights. "Independent Expert on Human Rights and International Solidarity." https://www.ohchr.org/en/special-procedures/ie-international-solidarity.
United Nations Human Rights. A/HRC/12/27, *Promotion and Protection of All Human Rights, Civil, Political, Economic, Social, and Cultural Rights, Including the Right to Development*, July 22, 2009, para. 19.
United Nations Human Rights. A/HRC/35/35, *Report of the Independent Expert on Human Rights and International Solidarity*, April 25, 2017, Annex, Art. 1, p. 17. https://documents-dds-ny.un.org/doc/UNDOC/GEN/G17/099/39/PDF/G1709939.pdf?OpenElement.
United Nations Human Rights. A/HRC/53/32, *Revised Draft Declaration on Human Rights and International Solidarity*, May 2, 2023, Annex, Art. 1, p. 14. https://www.uio.no/for-ansatte/enhetssider/jus/ior/aktuelle-saker/2023/revised-draft-declaration.pdf.
Urbina, F. J. *A Critique of Proportionality and Balancing* (Cambridge: Cambridge University Press, 2017).
Vachon, Dominic O. *How Doctors Care—The Science of Compassion and Balanced Caring in Medicine* (San Diego: Cognella, Incorporated, 2018).

Van Ness, Daniel W. *Abolitionism: A Revolutionary Movement* (Lanham: Lexington Books, 2010).
VanderWeele, Tyler J. "Is Forgiveness a Public Health Issue?" *American Journal of Public Health* 108, no. 2 (2018): pp. 189–90.
Vanier, Jean. *Becoming Human* (New York: Paulist Press, 1998).
Venkatapuram, Sridhar and Anna C. Zielinska. "Covid Vaccine Patent Waivers are for Health Sovereignty." *The Hastings Center—Bioethics Forum Essay*, June 1, 2021. https://www.thehastingscenter.org/covid-vaccine-patent-waivers-are-for-health-sovereignty/.
Verghese, Abraham. "The Importance of Being." *Health Affairs (Millwood)* 35, no. 10 (2016): pp. 1924–27.
Villarreal, Pedro A. "The Law of the WHO and the COVID-19 Pandemic Reformism." *German Yearbook of International Law* 64 (2021): pp. 11–40.
Vischer, Robert K. "Subsidiarity as a Principle of Governance: Beyond Devolution." *Indiana Law Review* 35 (2001): pp. 103–42.
von Balthasar, Hans Urs. *Love Alone Is Credible* (San Francisco: Ignatius Press, 2004).
Wainstock, D. and A. Katz. "Advancing Rare Disease Policy in Latin America: A Call to Action." *The Lancet Regional Health—Americas* 18 (2023): 100434. doi: 10.1016/j.lana.2023.100434.
Waldron, Jeremy. "Welfare and the Images of Charity." *The Philosophical Quarterly* 36, no. 145 (1986): pp. 463–82.
Waldron, Jeremy. *One Another's Equal* (Oxford: Oxford University Press, 2017).
Waldstein, Michael. "Introduction," John Paul II, in *Man and Woman He Created Them—A Theology of the Body* (Boston: Pauline, 2006), pp. 665–735.
Ward, Terence. *The Guardian of Mercy* (New York: Arcade Publishing, 2017).
Warmke, Brandon, Dana Kay Nelkin, and Michael McKenna (eds.). *Forgiveness and Its Moral Dimensions* (New York: Oxford University Press, 2021).
Watson, Jamie Carlin. "Patient Expertise and Medical Authority: Epistemic Implications for the Provider-Patient Relationship." *The Journal of Medicine and Philosophy* 49 (2024): pp. 58–71.
Weil, Simone. *Waiting for God* (New York: Harper and Row, 1951).
Weinrib, Ernest J. "The Case for a Duty to Rescue." *Yale Law Journal* 90 (1980): pp. 247–93.
West-Oram, P. G. and A. Buyx. "Global Health Solidarity." *Public Health Ethics* 10 (2017): pp. 212–24.
West, S. and L. Turnbull. "Scientific Writing as a Research Skill" (Oxford University Press Blog, February 2, 2024). https://blog.oup.com/2024/02/scientific-writing-as-a-research-skill/.
White, P. Quinn. "Honesty and Discretion." *Philosophy and Public Affairs* 50, no. 1 (2021): pp. 6–49.
White, P. Quinn. "Love First." *Philosophical and Phenomenological Research* 110, no. 3 (2025): pp. 854–86.
Whitebrook, Maureen. "Compassion as a Political Virtue." *Political Studies* 50 (2002): pp. 529–44.
WHO. *Constitution of the World Health Organization* (Geneva, WHO, 1948).
WHO. *International Code of Marketing Breastmilk Substitutes* (Geneva: WHO, 1981).
WHO. *World Health Report 2000* (Geneva: WHO, 2000).
WHO. *Task Force on Resource Mobilization and Management Strategies. Situation and Diagnosis.* 2013a. https://www.who.int/about/who_reform/TFRMMS-report-annex-2013.pdf?ua=1.
WHO. *Draft Twelfth General Programme of Work.* A66/6, para. 50. 2013b. https://apps.who.int/gb/ebwha/pdf_files/WHA66/A66_6-en.pdf.
WHO. *Health Systems Governance for Universal Health Coverage: Action Plan* (Geneva: WHO, Department of Health Systems Governance and Financing, 2014).
WHO. "Infant and Young Child Feeding." 2021. https://www.who.int/news-room/fact-sheets/detail/infant-and-young-child-feeding.

WHO. "Emergencies: International Health Regulations and Emergency Committees." Accessed June 22, 2024. https://www.who.int/health-topics/international-health-regulations.
WHO. "Compassion and Primary Healthcare." 2025. https://www.who.int/publications/i/item/9789240105249.
WHO. "The Concept of Stewardship in Health Policy." *Bulletin of the World Health Organization* 78, no. 6, (2000): pp. 732–39.
WHO. *Noncommunicable Diseases* (Geneva: WHO). https://www.who.int/health-topics/noncommunicable-diseases#tab=tab_1.
Wildemann Kane, Laura. "Childhood, Growth, and Dependency in Liberal Political Philosophy." *Hypatia* 36 (2016): pp. 156–70.
Wilson, James. *Public Health and Public Policy* (Oxford: Oxford University Press, 2021).
Wiredu, K. "The Moral Foundations of an African Culture." In K. Wiredu and K. Gyekye (eds.), *Person and Community: Ghanaian Philosophical Studies I* (Washington, DC: Council for Research in Values and Philosophy, 1992), pp. 193–206.
Wojtyla, Karol. *Love and Responsibility* (San Francisco: Ignatius Press, 1981).
Wojtyla, Karol. *The Acting Person*, trans. Andrzej Potocki (New York: Springer, 1979).
Wojtyla, Karol. *Person and Community—Selected Essays* (New York: Peter Lang, 1993).
Worline, Monica and Jane Dutton. *Awakening Compassion in the Workplace: The Quiet Power That Elevates People and Organizations* (Oakland: Berrett-Koehler Publishers, 2017).
Worthington, Everett L. *Forgiveness and Reconciliation: Theory and Application* (New York: Taylor & Francis, 2006).
Wolterstorff, Nicholas. "Love, Justice, and the Law." In Robert F. Cochran Jr. and Zachary R. Calo (eds.), *Agape, Justice, and the Law: How might the Christian Love Shape the Law?* (Cambridge: Cambridge University Press, 2017), pp. 101–24.
Wright, Randall. *Summer in The Forest*. Documentary, 2018. http://www.summerintheforest.com/.
Wu Howard, Angela. "Religious Exceptions to General Laws: Toward an Evaluative Framework, with Special Reference to the American Constitutional Context." DPhil thesis, The University of Oxford, 2022.
Yeh, Ming-Jui. "Confucian Welfarism: Intellectual Origins of Solidarity for Health and Welfare Systems." *Public Health Ethics* (2023): phad021.
Youde, Jeremy. *Global Health Governance in International Society* (Oxford: Oxford University Press, 2018).
Yowell, Paul. "Legislación, Common Law, y la Virtud de la Claridad." *Revista Chilena de Derecho* 39, no. 2 (2012): pp. 481–512. doi.org/10.4067/S0718-34372012000200010.
Yowell, Paul. "Nudge, Nudge." *First Things*, November 16, 2021. https://www.firstthings.com/web-exclusives/2021/11/nudge-nudge.
Zulman, D. M., M. C. Haverfield, J. G. Shaw et al. "Practices to Foster Physician Presence and Connection with Patients in the Clinical Encounter." *JAMA* 323, no. 1 (2020): pp. 70–81.
Zyblock, D. M. "Nursing Presence in Contemporary Nursing Practice." *Nursing Forum* 45 (2010): pp. 120–24.

Index

For the benefit of digital users, indexed terms that span two pages (e.g., 52–53) may, on occasion, appear on only one of those pages.

A

accessibility, 233–34, 239–41. See also communication; loving attention
accompaniment
  as shared presence in compassion, 182–83
  shared presence in L'Arche and Partners in Health, 119–20
  as shared presence in solidarity, 184–85
  See also presence; friendship; solidarity; empathy
active participation
  core to freedom and development, 204–5
  part of empathy and presence, 76
  patients as co-experts, 113–14
  as requirement of meaningful inclusion, 177, 191–92, 200–1
  for shared authority, 200–1
  in shared responsibilities, 205–6
  See also responsibility; participation; subsidiarity
agape
  agape as a foundation of governance, 177, 178, 216–18, 249–51, 252–55
  definition and nature of, 121–22, 175, 201–2, 237–38, 252–53
  relationship to justice, 177, 195, 252–53
  as shared journey of presence, 102–4, 116–18, 177, 236
  universal yet personal responsibility, 93, 110, 178, 201–2
  See also beneficence; compassion; justice; love; mercy; presence; solidarity; subsidiarity; stewardship
agency
  colonial subtraction of, 45–47, 148, 187, 205
  relational and moral dimensions of, 38–40, 91–92, 111, 208
  authentic vs. imposed autonomy, 98–100, 177, 203–5, 222
  restoration through mercy, 21, 24, 39–40, 47–48
  See also autonomy; paternalism; subsidiarity

alterity
  basis of ethical encounter, 116–17
  coloniality suppressing alterity, 187
  Levinasian ethics, 77–78
  presence as encountering otherness, 116–17, 118
  See also Other; presence; relationality
answerability,
  of communication, 236–37
  through empathetic listening, 242–44
  responsive accountability, 243–44, 247
apology
  institutional apology, 23–24
  Papua New Guinea example, 22–23
  role in mercy and forgiveness, 23
  See also forgiveness; mercy
Aquinas, Thomas
  on benevolence vs beneficence, 91–92
  on compassion, 104–5
  on concealment, 224–25
  on discretion and truth, 224–25
  on supererogation, 104–5
Aristotle/Aristotelian
  friendship and the good life, 178
  on the golden mean and subsidiarity, 155, 177, 203–5
  on the golden mean in clarity, 239–40
  on the golden mean in honesty, 233–34, 239–40
  on the golden mean in transparency, 235, 239–41
  on the golden mean of care, 73–74, 193–94
  on the golden mean of the virtue of beneficence, 95–98, 100–3
  on the golden mean of the virtue of compassion, 81–82, 84
  prudence and patience in leadership, 201–2
  virtue ethics, 99–100, 177
assessability, 236–37, 240–41
  See also communication; honesty

INDEX

Augustine, St. *See* ordo amoris
autonomy
  limits of individualistic approach, 103–5, 107–9, 204–5
  relational and moral dimensions of, 38–39, 111, 203–5, 238–39
  relationship to paternalism, 98–99, 217, 220–21
  respecting freedom of the Other, 91–92
  See also agency; paternalism; responsibility

B

Beauchamp, Tom, 92–93, 94
beneficence, 90, 91–94, 95–98, 100–3
  beneficence as principle in bioethics, 92
  beneficence in relation to love and justice, 93–94, 177, 203, 249–51, 253
  contemplative vs. active conduct, 90–91, 116–18, 201–2, 239–41
  presence as core feature, 111–14, 116–18
  limits and distortions in global health, 96–97, 182, 184, 217–18, 224
  See also benevolence; compassion; love; mercy
benevolence,
  degrees of benevolence and paternalism, 95–97, 220–21
  intellectual step preceding beneficence, 91–92, 93
  virtue of willing the good of the other, 94–95, 99–100
  See also beneficence; paternalism
Bok, Sissela, 226–27
boundaries
  ethical and relational limits, 205–6
  in leadership presence, 176
  for self-care and resilience, 63–64, 73–74, 84–87
  See also leadership; self-care
burnout
  causes and mechanisms, 62–64
  prevention and mitigation, 64–66, 70, 212–13
  See also self-care; resilience

C

Caravaggio's Seven Works of Mercy, 91–92, 99–100
Childress, James, 91–92, 99–100
clarity,
  excessive transparency, 235–36
  virtue of clarity and intellectual humility, 234, 239–40
  See also communication, loving attention,

coloniality
  colonial origins of global health, 143–45, 148
  decolonial response, 119–20, 184–85, 187, 191–92, 205
  epistemic injustice and coloniality, 39–41, 148, 187, 205, 227–31, 247
  as subtraction of agency, 45–47, 148, 187, 205, 220–21
  See also agency; autonomy; decoloniality; epistemic injustice; paternalism
common good, 219, 221–24, 245–46
  See also justice; stewardship
communication
  accessibility, 233–34, 239–41
  answerability, 236–37, 243–44
  assessability, 236–37, 240–41
  dishonest communication, 224–31
  as gift-of-self, 216–17, 236
  Stewardship Model of Communication, 236–39, 244–47
  truthful communication, 216–17, 218, 223–25, 236–39
  See also honesty; presence; stewardship; truth; agape
communion
  mutual care and reciprocity, 140, 144, 249
  relationship to community, 140, 216–17, 236, 244–47, 249–51
  unity in diversity, 168, 249, 252–53
  See also community; presence
community
  belonging in community, 144, 208, 252–53
  building through communication, 216–17, 236, 245, 252
  of mutual care, 140, 144, 167–68, 176, 184–85, 252–53
  relationship to communion, 116–17, 140, 141–42, 168, 249–50, 252–53
  unity in diversity, 144, 168, 184–85, 249–50
  See also communion; solidarity
companionship
  companionship as presence in suffering, 252–55
  relation to reconciliation, 116–18, 167–68
  restoration of companionship, 21, 24, 25–26, 250
compassion
  Compassion Cultivation Training (CCT), 119–21
  compassionate care, 106–10, 216
  distinction from pity, 101–3, 104–5
  as relational attentiveness, 106–9, 115–18, 216, 239–41, 243
  See also empathy; justice; mercy

concealment, 224–26
contemplation, 239–41, 252–53
co-responsibility. *See* responsibility
COVID-19 pandemic
    communication failures and example of masks, 227–29
    data deluge/ infodemic, 231, 245
    lessons for agape-based governance, 245–47
    misinformation and erosion of trust, 217–18, 227–29, 231, 245–47
    vaccine allocation, 245

D

Darwall, Stephen, 99–101, 103–4, 105, 111
deception
    distinguished from concealment, 225–26
    effects of deception, 216, 225, 226–28
    ethical analysis, 226–27
    examples in global and public health, 227–31
    paternalistic deception, 220–21, 227–29
    types of deception, 226–31
    See also concealment; lies; manipulation; noble lies, paltering; truthfulness
decolonization
    decolonial approaches to global health, 177, 186–87, 193–94, 205
    meaningful inclusion in, 213–14
    mercy-based decoloniality, 47–48
    restoring agency in decoloniality, 8, 10, 134, 205
    See also agency; coloniality; justice; mercy
dependence, 106–11. *See also* agency; autonomy; vulnerability
Derrida, Jacques, 41–43
dignity
    dignity and moral agency, 38–40
    dignity and respect in communication, 237, 242–43
    equality of dignity, 144–45, 237
    human dignity, 139, 144–45, 146–47
    relational dignity, 144–45
    See also agency; justice; presence
discernment
    discernment in beneficence and paternalism, 97–99, 100–3
    discernment in mercy and forgiveness, 33–34, 47–48
    discernment in stewardship and communication, 239–43
    discernment in subsidiarity and shared authority, 199–203, 205
    moral and communal discernment, 239–40, 241, 253–54
    prudential reasoning, 239–41
    See also prudence; responsibility

discretion
    honesty tempered with discretion, 216–17, 237–39, 241–43
    morally permissible concealment, 225
    in mercy, 33–34, 47–48
    relationship to prudence, 33–34, 239–41
    in truthful communication, 216–17, 218, 223–25, 237–39
    See also honesty; prudence
dishonesty, 216–18, 224–26
    See also deception; lies; noble lies; paltering
duty of care
    moral duty in crises, 220–24, 237, 252–53
    professional and civic obligations, 217–18, 244–47
    reciprocal and community responsibility, 176, 178, 191–92, 207–9, 237–39
    See also responsibility; subsidiarity
dying to self, 69–70, 72, 73, 74, 75–76, 78
    See also empathy; presence; self-sacrifice

E

effective altruism, 146–47, 149
Eliot, T.S., 81
empathetic listening
    in clinical and institutional empathy, 72–73
    as ingredient of Stewardship Model, 210, 239, 242–44, 247
    role in good leadership, 191–92
    See also communication; compassion; empathy; leadership; presence; shared authority
empathy
    definition and stages, 66–70, 243
    limits of projection, 61–63, 183–84
    relationship to compassion, 182–84
    role in leadership and inclusion, 184–85, 191–92, 201–2
    See also compassion; presence; vulnerability
epistemic democracy, 52, 187, 205, 247
    See also participation; shared authority; subsidiarity
epistemic humility, 68–70, 176, 186–87, 191–92, 216–17, 237–39
    See also empathy; leadership; stewardship
epistemic injustice
    colonial roots, 45–47, 186–87
    marginalization in global health, 182–85
    restoration through mercy and subsidiarity, 47–48, 205
    See also coloniality; justice; mercy; subsidiarity

INDEX

equality
  equality of care and concern, 143–44, 160
  equality of dignity and respect, 60, 99–100, 142–43, 148, 166–67, 237, 252–53
  equality of treatment and resources, 149, 151–52, 166–67
equity
  equity in global health, 57–58, 143, 148, 186–87, 245–47
  relational fairness, 88, 166–67, 205–6
expertise assertion, 226, 229–32
expertise complementarity, 238–47

F
Farmer, Paul, 183–85
Fassin, Didier, 36
filtering information, 225, 234–35, 239–40
Finnis, John, 149, 160–69, 203–4
forgiveness
  forgiveness and transformation, 39–41, 253–55
  models of forgiveness (Enright; Worthington), 34–35
  process of forgiveness, 27–28
  relationship to mercy and reconciliation, 11, 21, 23–26, 31, 34–35, 40, 41, 49, 51–53, 129, 204
  See also mercy; reconciliation
Frankfurt, Henry G., 94–95, 230
friendship
  accompaniment and community in friendship, 110, 119–21
  friendship in solidarity and subsidiarity, 182–83, 191–92, 199
  friendship in suffering and presence, 82–83, 253–54
  mutual self-giving in friendship, 178
  See also accompaniment; solidarity

G
generosity
  corrupted vs virtuous generosity, 29, 212–13
  generous accompaniment, 119–21
  generous presence, 119–21, 252–55
  gratuitous generosity, 20, 29, 201–2
  self-giving generosity in leadership, 201–2
gift
  gift in communication, 236, 239–41
  gift-giving beyond equivalence, 29–31
  gift-of-self, 31, 201–2, 212–13, 216–17
  logic of gift, 29–31, 236
  reciprocal gift-of-self, 31–32, 69–70, 242–44
  unconditional gift, 25–26, 29, 41–42, 101, 107, 110, 124, 126–28
  See also generosity; mercy

gift-giving, 29–31, 119–21, 236. *See also* generosity; reciprocity
giver, 27–31, 32–33, 239–42. *See also* gift: gift-of-self; self-sacrifice
global health governance (GHG)
  definition, 20, 22, 139
  relation to coloniality, 45–47
  and the WHO, 150–54, 160, 244–47
Global North, 46–47, 183–85, 186, 193–94, 227–29
Global South, 45–46, 47–48, 183–85, 187, 205, 228–29
gratitude, 32–33, 243–44, 253–54. *See also* gift; mercy

H
honesty
  brutal honesty, 232–35
  excessive vs deficient honesty, 232–35
  honesty in stewardship communication, 182, 200–1, 210
  relation to discretion, 216–17, 237, 245–46
  relationship to trust, 216–18, 245–47
  virtue of honesty, 232–33, 239–42
  See also communication; lies; truth; truthfulness
hooks, bell, 48–49, 99, 124, 231–32
human flourishing, 92, 94–95, 110
humility, 37–38, 40–41. *See also* leadership; vulnerability

I
injustice *see* epistemic injustice
interdependence
  embodied interdependence, 13–14, 82–84, 107, 110, 114, 128, 131, 142, 143, 144, 166, 173–74, 178, 191–92, 253–54
  as expression of solidarity and shared life, 178, 205
  interdependence in crises, 247
  See also solidarity; subsidiarity

J
justice
  epistemic justice, 148, 187
  relationship to love, 92, 253
  relationship to mercy, 142, 145–46, 253
  restorative justice, 253
  structural justice in global health, 139–40
  See also epistemic justice, love; mercy

K
King, Martin Luther Jr. 25, 28, 47, 124, 168
knowledge
  knowing the Other, 91–94, 100–1, 184–86

local and contextual knowledge, 183, 184, 186, 205, 207–8
self-knowledge, 110, 117
See also epistemic humility; expertise complementarity

L

leadership
agapic leadership, 175–76, 178, 191–92, 201–2, 212–13
characteristics of good leadership, 176, 191–92, 201–2, 212–13, 214
See also agency; communication; humility; stewardship; subsidiarity

Lévinas, Emmanuel,
on communication, 243, 244
on encounter, 77–78, 116–17, 118
on "Infinity in the Other," 77–78
on the Other, 77–78, 116–17, 118, 243
on presence, 77–78, 116–17, 118
on responsibility, 77–78, 79, 118, 252–53
See also Other

lies
distinguished from concealment, 224–25
examples and moral definition, 215–16, 226–28, 232
noble lies, 227–28
white lies, 227
See also deception; truth; truthfulness; white lies

logic of equivalence, 29–31, 41–44
logic of superabundance, 29–31, 39–41

love
as the core argument of the book, 252–53
definition as agape, 90–91, 94–95
love and agency, 99–101
love as foundation of solidarity, subsidiarity, stewardship, 249–51
love as presence, 116–18
love as universal yet personal responsibility, 93, 252–53
relationship of love to justice, 253
See also agape; benevolence; beneficence; compassion; mercy; presence; solidarity; subsidiarity; stewardship

loving attention
as attentiveness, 2–3, 22–23, 72–73, 81–82
ingredient of Stewardship Model of Good Communication, 239–41
non-paternalistic communication, 224–25
See also compassion; compassionate care; communication; empathy

M

MacIntyre, Alasdair, 30, 107, 109
manipulation, 226, 228–29, 231–32
See also, deception; noble lies; white lies
Mauss, Marcel, 41–43
meaningful inclusion, 71–72, 76–77, 146
meekness, 37–38
mercy
definition and aspects of, 91, 93, 95, 100–3, 212–13
gratuitous generosity, 24, 39–40, 95
in leadership and judgment, 193–94, 220–21
mutual vulnerability, 26–27, 118
restoration of agency, 24, 39–40, 47–48, 187
See also forgiveness; justice; love
mercy-based decoloniality, 47–48
Mill, John Stuart, 219
mindfulness, 58–59, 67–68. *See also* empathy; presence; compassion
Murdoch, Iris,
on loving attention, 76, 77–78
on the loving gaze, 77–78
on loving regard, 147
on vision perfected, 239
See also loving attention, presence
mutual vulnerability, 77–78, 82–83, 178, 193–94
See also reciprocity; solidarity

O

O'Neill, Onora, 233–34, 243–44
Openness to the other
in compassion and empathy, 67–68, 78
in governance and leadership, 191–92, 200–1
to the Other, 38–39, 77–78, 184–85, 191–92
reckless openness, 234–35
in shared authority, 238
See also communication; transparency
ordo amoris, 155, 157–59, 195, 207. *See also* love; prudence; solidarity
Other
agency of the Other, 99–101
benevolence toward the Other, 91–94
encounter with the Other, 36, 38–39, 77–78, 116–18, 252–53
ethical responsibility to the Other, 237–38, 241, 243, 245, 255
manipulation of the Other, 229
seeing the Other as they are, 239
See also alterity; responsibility
Outka, Gene, 63–64, 162, 166

P

paltering, 228–30. *See also* deception; lies
participation
    meaningful vs. perfunctory participation, 191–92, 234–35
    participation through shared authority, 217, 223, 237–39, 243–44
    See also active participation; subsidiarity
paternalism
    definition and forms, 91–92, 95–96, 99, 184–86, 203–4, 220–21, 228–31
    overriding agency, 98–99, 177, 182–86, 203–4
    paternalism in communication, 216, 217–18, 224, 229, 231–32, 233, 234–35
    relation to stewardship, 192, 201–2
    See also autonomy; benevolence; stewardship
pay-it-forward, 30. *See also* logic of superabundance
Pellegrino, Edmund, 92
Pity (distinction from compassion) 26–27, 55–58. *See also* compassion; mercy
power
    asymmetries in global health, 36, 45–47, 180, 187, 237–38, 244
    centralization of power, 177, 190–91
    manipulative uses of power, 229
    power dynamics in mercy, 35–41
    power vs. love-based leadership, 191–92
    See also coloniality; justice; leadership
presence
    being fully present, 116–18, 167
    in beneficence, 111–22
    in community and communion, 140, 141–42, 216–17, 236, 252–53
    in compassion, 143–44
    as gift-of-self, 116–18, 167, 201–2, 239–41
    in mercy, 144
    shared journey of presence, 140, 167, 252–53
    vulnerable presence, 166
    See also accompaniment; empathy; love
prudence
    prudence in mercy, 143
    prudence in stewardship and communication, 244–45
    prudential reasoning in ordering loves, 116, 153–54, 158
    relational wisdom in prioritization, 157–58
    See also discernment; leadership; virtue
public health emergencies of international concern, 176–77, 182, 210, 212, 217, 245, 247, 248
    See also stewardship; trust; public trust

public trust
    erosion of trust, 182, 227–28, 229, 234, 235
    trust and honest communication, 192, 229–30
    trust in authorities and institutions, 217, 245, 248
    See also communication; honesty; transparency

R

reasonably vulnerable honesty
    ingredient of Stewardship Model, 239, 240–42
    reasonable degree of vulnerability, 190–91, 192, 200–1, 254
    See also honesty, vulnerability
reciprocal gift-of-self
    in communication as gift, 236
    in empathy, 69–70
    in the formation of community, 82–83
    in mercy, 20–21, 31–32
    in mutual exchange and presence, 243–44, 254
reciprocity
    bi-directional reciprocity, 41–42, 199, 212–13
    multi-directional reciprocity, 41, 212–13
    reciprocity in community and relationships, 64–65, 82–83, 102–3, 109–10, 121
    reciprocal silent presence, 254
    reciprocity in solidarity and subsidiarity, 177, 178, 199
    See also gift; mutuality; solidarity
reconciliation
    distinguished from mercy, 24, 167–68
    healing communion, 252–53
    moral and social restoration, 118, 167–68
    restoration of companionship, 116–17, 167–68
    See also forgiveness; justice
relationality
    relational community through compassion, 82–83
    relational ethics and subsidiarity, 177, 191–92
    relational moral obligations, 237
    vs. individualism, 182–85
    See also community; compassion; presence
repentance 23–24, 31–32. *See also* forgiveness; mercy
resilience
    moral resilience in leadership, 201–2
    resilience through agency restored, 39–41
    resilience through participation and boundaries, 64–65, 73–74, 76
    See also forgiveness; mercy

responsibility
co-responsibility, 155, 172
moral responsibility in leadership, 216, 220–21
reciprocal responsibility, 156, 167–68
responsibility and agency, 38–39, 111
responsibility in communication, 216–17, 218, 245
responsibility in love, 20–21, 93–94
responsibility to neighbors / differentiated responsibility, 156–57
shared responsibility in subsidiarity, 155, 177
universal responsibility, 20, 90
See also agency, empathy; epistemic responsibility; stewardship
responsive accountability, 239, 243–44, 246–47
See also empathetic listening; Stewardship Model of Good Communication
Ricœur, Paul, 29–31, 42–43

S

self-care, 11–12, 63–65, *70*, 73–74, 84–87, 176
See also boundaries; resilience
self-emptying, 37–38. *See also* self-sacrifice
self-sacrifice, 93, 114, 118. *See also* agape; beneficence; self-sacrifice
Seneca, 32–33, 41–42
shared authority
co-creating institutional governance, 77
shared authority and stewardship, 223–24
shared authority in decision-making, 112–14, 238
shared authority in global health, 75–76, 113, 244
See also participation; subsidiarity
shared ends, 112–13, 114–16. *See also* agency; community
Singer, Peter, 146–47, 148–51, 158–59
solidarity
definition and core meaning, 20–21, 139, 140, 146
equal dignity in solidarity, 145, 166
mutual care, 144, 167–68
solidarity and community life, 167–68
solidarity and subsidiarity, 155–56
solidarity as friendship, 143, 167–68
solidarity vs nationalism, 146
solidarity in pandemics, 139–40, 145–47
See also accompaniment; interdependence; subsidiarity
Stein, Edith, 67–69, 70, 243

stewardship
communication as stewardship, 236–39
concept of stewardship, 215, 216–18
leader as steward, 245
management of resources / prudential stewardship, 139
stewardship in global governance, 244–47
See also leadership; subsidiarity; truthfulness
Stewardship Model of Good Communication, 216–17, 223–24, 236–47
See also communication; stewardship
subsidiarity
concept and definition, 155
relationship to justice, 139
scale of moral responsibility, 153–54
subsidiarity in governance, 244–47
See also agency; participation; solidarity
suffering, 23, 38, 237–38, 245, 253–54, 255
See also compassion; presence
Sunstein, Cass R., 220
See also paternalism
supererogation, 24
sympathy
contrast with empathy, 143–44
self-centered compassion, 143–44

T

transparency
degrees of transparency, 235, 245
openness in governance, 245
as virtue, 245
See also communication; trust; truthfulness
trust
erosion of trust, 24, 217, 227–28, 229, 234, 235, 245
foundation of cooperation, 51–52, 199, 250–51
relationship to communication, 192, 200–1, 216–17, 248
trust-building, 51–52, 192, 200–1, 216–17, 248
See also communication; honesty; transparency
truth
excesses and deficits of honesty, 233–34, 245
relation to deception, 224–31
responsible truth-telling in uncertainty, 239–41, 245
See also communication; honesty; truthfulness

truthfulness
 communication of truth with love, 200–1, 210, 216–17, 236–38
 honesty tempered with discretion, 192, 201–2, 216–17, 224–25, 237–38
 truthfulness as virtue in governance, 210, 248
 truthfulness vs brutal honesty, 232–35
 See also honesty; stewardship

U

Ubuntu (African philosophy of personhood), 164
 See also community

unconditional love
 conceptual notion of unconditional gift, 29
 See also forgiveness; love; mercy

unity
 unity in diversity, 249, 252–53
 unity through communication and cooperation, 216–17, 245–46, 254
 unity through mercy, 31–32, 52–53
 See also community; communion

universal love, 5, 123, 139, 163. *See also* **agape**

V

Vanier, Jean, 109, 119–21

victim. *See* agency (restoration through mercy)

virtue
 virtue ethics (Aristotelian) 59–60, 84, 177, 203
 virtue in communication and clarity, 239–40
 virtue in leadership (prudence, humility, justice), 176, 201–2, 213–14, 250, 255
 virtue in moral formation, 29
 See also leadership; prudence

vulnerability
 as moral condition and humility, 38–39, 176
 mutual vulnerability, 20–21, 38–39, 69–70, 82–83, 184–85, 193–94, 245–47, 255
 reasonable vulnerability 201–2, 216–17, 218, 237–42
 vulnerability in relationships of care, 73, 105–9
 vulnerability in suffering and presence, 253–54
 See also dependence; empathy; presence

vulnerable presence, 38–39, 81–82, 201–2, 254, 255
 See also presence; vulnerability

W

white lies, 227–28
 See also deception

white savior/ white supremacy, 177, 178, 186–87
 See also coloniality; power

WHO (World Health Organization)
 challenges of subsidiarity, 192, 193–97, 250
 leadership in global governance, 176–82, 218–20, 245–48
 stewardship of information, 210, 217
 See also communication, leadership; global health governance; stewardship

wisdom
 integration of knowledge and love, 177, 201–2, 255
 prudential discernment, 68–69, 176, 201–2, 239
 wisdom in maturity and self-knowledge, 101, 110
 See also prudence; virtue

witness
 embodied testimony to love, 201–2
 moral and institutional example, 201–2, 212–13
 See also leadership; love